TRINITY IN AQUINAS

TRINITY IN AQUINAS

Gilles Emery, OP

Professor of Dogmatic Theology
University of Fribourg

Sapientia Press
of Ave Maria University

Sapientia Press
of Ave Maria University
24 Frank Lloyd Wright Drive
Ann Arbor, MI 48106
888-343-8607

Printed in the United States of America.

Library of Congress Control Number: 2006900966

ISBN-10: 0-9706106-2-9

ISBN-13: 978-0-9706106-2-1

Cover:
The Pierpont Morgan Library, New York. M. 791, f.4v.
Photography: David A. Loggie

Table of Contents

Preface

THE SEVEN studies gathered in this volume need no other recommendation than themselves to awaken interest, but it will not be useless to present their author and to underline the originality of his works. Professor of dogmatic theology at the University of Fribourg (Switzerland) for nearly ten years, Father Gilles Emery came to the attention of the theological public through a thesis on Trinity and creation in St. Thomas and his contemporaries.[1] This book, hailed immediately as one of the most convincing signs of the current Thomist renewal, witnesses not only to the scientific qualities that are equally manifest in the studies in the present volume. It also demonstrates, by the evidence of the texts, that for Aquinas and the other medievals, the creative and saving work common to the whole Trinity is also that of each divine person, and that each one brings to it his proper mark. In opposition to the doctrine, as widespread as it is simplistic, that neo-Thomism attributes to Aquinas by seeing in the creation only the prolonging of the *De Deo uno,* Thomas Aquinas teaches on the contrary that the Father creates through the Son and in the Spirit in such a manner that the processions internal to the Trinity are

---

[1] Gilles Emery, *La Trinité créatrice: Trinité et Création dans les commentaires aux Sentences de Thomas d'Aquin et de ses précurseurs Albert le Grand et Bonaventure* (Paris: Vrin, 1995).

the cause, the reason, and the exemplar of the creation of the world with its creatures, and of their return to God.

Since this first monumental work, Father Emery has published numerous studies, which are impossible to enumerate here, although one ought to reserve a special mention to his volume that provides a French translation and commentary on two Opuscules of St. Thomas.[2] This book is not simply marked by the accuracy of its translation; it is the rare quality of its annotation that must be praised: abundant and precise at the same time, it is exemplary of the work that must be done today by the disciples of Aquinas if they want to make the thought of Aquinas accessible for our times. Parallel to these diverse works, Gilles Emery has never ceased to pursue his research in medieval Trinitarian theology and in particular that of St. Thomas. But his activity of teaching has kept him from being enclosed in his specialty; he has therefore also given intelligent and sustained attention to contemporary theological production and he publishes regularly in the *Revue Thomiste*: a Chronicle in which he reviews works of Trinitarian theology that have appeared in diverse languages. Precious for the enormous quantity of information that they communicate, these chronicles are also precious for the method employed: The content of the book is always here exposed with amplitude and precision; and when criticism is necessary, it is always constructive and courteous. These contributions are models of what one ought to aim for in this genre, however difficult it may be.

If we now turn to the works collected here, a simple glance at the table of contents suffices to assure us of their homogeneity. In direct extension of his first book, the author has pursued his research on the theology of the Trinity in St. Thomas, his predecessors, and his contemporaries, but also in modern theology. More generally, the first study may be read as a historical introduction; the others follow the chronological order of the works of Aquinas: the *Sentences,* the

---

2 St. Thomas Aquinas, *Traités: Les raisons de la foi, Les articles de la foi et les sacre-ments de l'Eglise,* Introduction, translation from the Latin, and annotation by Gilles Emery (Paris: Cerf, 1999).

Summa contra Gentiles, the *Summa theologiae.* Because of its importance, the *Summa theologiae* gives rise to two other studies. The first, essentialism or personalism, explains St. Thomas's purpose in dialogue with his modern readers; as for the second, the *Filioque,* it extends these reflections on the personalism of St. Thomas. The study of the *Commentary on St. John* completes the ensemble through the examination of what becomes of Trinitarian doctrine when Thomas exposes it in the framework of a biblical commentary. Without directly entering into the content of each of these studies, and still less into the detail of the analyses whose nuances defy summary, we would like simply to signal what seems to us to be most characteristic in the method employed by Thomas as well as by his commentator.

The study which opens the collection is placed under the sign of the history of the treatise of the Trinity in the medieval period. Trinitarian theology certainly did not begin with the scholastics, who made appeal to the works of the Fathers of the Church in order to assure their own reflections; but Gilles Emery here attempts to retrace the evolution that leads from Roscellinus (teacher of Abelard) and Anselm of Canterbury, at the beginning of the twelfth century, to Thomas Aquinas and his contemporaries, as regards how to think of unity and plurality in God; Father Emery underlines, at the same time, the characteristics of each author. Thus one is struck to see that the divergences among these thinkers—often quite remarkable—are not reduced to simple nuances; there is indeed between them a difference of attitude in the approach to the mystery. The most notable difference concerns the role that they accord to reason in the domain of the truths of faith. All are distinguished by their confidence in the capacities of reason for the investigation of the mystery, but certain authors are more intrepid than others and do not fear to employ *rationes necessariae* that they consider to be demonstrative. This not only characterizes the first attempts of Abelard, Anselm, or Richard of Saint-Victor, but also, in an unexpected manner, those of St. Bonaventure and the Franciscans. Thus one is surprised to see that Thomas Aquinas appears much less "rationalistic" than most. The reason is simple: Bonaventure, for example, does not make a clear distinction between the order of the faith and the order of reason and this is why he can claim to prove the plurality of persons in God by necessary reasons. For Thomas, on the contrary, if it is necessary without any doubt to affirm the existence of a plurality of persons in God, it is not necessary by depending on reasons that in the realm of faith have no constraining force, but uniquely by reason of faith. On the other hand, *Trinitate supposita,* he can make use of theological arguments, but he knows and says that these Trinitarian analogies are only probable arguments, not necessary ones, and are indications that allow the clarification of the mystery for those who contemplate it without ever being able to appropriate it. Behold here the theologian recalled to the modesty of his purpose. This can seem self-evident, but one cannot underline it too strongly, since it is always presupposed not only in all his reflection on the Trinity, but in the entire work of St. Thomas.

In relationship to the preceding one, the second study reveals at once that the purpose is specified according to three different points. First, the consideration is focused on two immediate predecessors of Thomas: on the one side, his own teacher, Albert the Great; on the other, Bonaventure; these are two authors to whom he owes much. Thus, it is no longer (as with the first study) about a series of diverse works examined as part of a development process carried out at length, but a single work, the *Book of the Sentences* of Peter Lombard, commented on by three different authors. Finally, as regards the subject itself, the analysis no longer bears on the manner of reconciling unity and plurality in God, but rather on the way in which each of the three divine persons is implicated in the going out of creatures from God and in their return to him *(exitus–reditus)*. Each of these three points is rich in teachings. As regards the last, the content, I have already given a glimpse of it by summarizing in the first lines of this Preface the purpose of the great dissertation of the author; this second study makes it more exact and its concise form allows an easier understanding of what is essential.[3] As regards the second point, the way in which the author has centered his analysis on the *Commentary of the Sentences* is a very sensible path. Certainly, no author writing about Thomas can allow himself to ignore this writing from Thomas's youth, but one rarely considers it for itself. By taking it as an object of a monograph of this amplitude, Gilles Emery created an innovative work, but by placing it in relation to other authors he took yet another step further, and this step deserves to be strongly underlined. Too often, Thomas Aquinas has been considered as an author in himself, as if he had no antecedents—a Melchizedek of theology, as Fr. Congar liked to say—but if one makes the effort to read him in the light of history one quickly sees that nothing is more false. The examination of Thomas's relationship to his predecessors, on the contrary, allows one to specify the way in which he took his place in the history of thought. Without question, Thomas inherited from Albert and Bonaventure most of the elements that he uses, but while in their writings they are dispersed or mentioned in passing, without receiving the value that they call for, Thomas takes them into his own commentary, organizes them in a systematic manner, and makes them bearers of a rigorous synthetic construction. This example takes on emblematic value because what is thus set in relief as regards the *Commentary of the Sentences* holds generally for Thomas's entire work. Thomas certainly is a profoundly innovative thinker, but before being the founder of a school he is first an heir. One can only understand him correctly in this perspective.

The purpose of the third study also offers its singularities, and we regret to have to leave the major part to the side. Here it is no longer about situating Thomas in relation to other authors, but about discovering what is without doubt his most personal work, about treating it with a deeper understanding and seeing its place by relation to his other works in an internal comparative perspective. It

---

[3] Compare another earlier article by the same author: "Le Père et l'oeuvre trinitaire de création selon le Commentaire des Sentences de S. Thomas d'Aquin," in *Ordo sapientiae et amoris: Hommage au Professeur Jean-Pierre Torrell,* ed. Carlos-Josaphat Pinto de Oliveira (Fribourg: Éditions universitaires, 1993), pp. 85–117.

is even more interesting that the literary genre of *Summa contra Gentiles* has been and continues to be passionately discussed: some want to see here a *Summa* of philosophy; others only recognize an imperfect rough draft of what the *Summa theologiae* will realize in a mature manner. On the contrary, the attentive examination to which we are invited shows, on the one hand, the theological character of the work: The simple presence of the treatise on the Trinity (and its 462 biblical references) suffices to support this claim—and that of the treatise on the incarnation reinforces it. On the other hand, the very structure of the chapters on the Trinity shows, in addition, the wise construction of the whole of the work. All readers have certainly remarked its division between the truths of faith accessible in a certain manner to reason (Books I–III) and those that are entirely inaccessible (Book IV), but this study is the first, to my knowledge, that displays the more subtle structure that forms the unity of the ensemble of theological material. To Book I (God in himself) corresponds chapters 2 to 26 in Book IV (what is believed about God beyond reason: the Trinity), while to Book II (procession of creatures *a Deo*) corresponds chapters 27 to 78 of Book IV (what God does above reason: the Incarnation and what follows from it), and to Book III (the ordination of creatures to God as their end) corresponds chapters 79 to 97 of Book IV, which set forth and thoroughly investigate what Christians hope from God as the ultimate end of man (resurrection of the body and beatitude of souls). The finesse of this construction, whose detail one will see later, does not exclude, however, the fundamental theological structure of the *exitus–reditus* of creatures with regard to God (a constant structure in all the works of St. Thomas); but it suggests in a very explicit way that Trinitarian reflection is not limited to the contemplation of the Trinity in itself and that such reflection is extended in the consideration of the presence and of the creative and salvific work of the three persons in the world. This is a theme that we will find again, since it constitutes a veritable "red line" in the work of St. Thomas.

Of the works of Thomas Aquinas, many authors seem only to know the *Summa theologiae;* this is certainly not without reason, but it would be unfortunate to remain there. This is so because—it is a surprising observation and naturally arouses curiosity—if Thomas spoke of the Trinity in most of his great works, he did so in a different manner each time. This does not mean that he would have judged his first essays unsatisfactory and that he would have perfected them little by little, but rather that he constructed his works in accord with the goal that he proposed. Thus in the *Summa contra Gentiles,* whose specific purpose is to manifest the truth of the catholic faith, he emphasizes first the givens of Scripture and the refutation of heresies before coming to the speculative explication. In the *Summa theologiae* on the other hand—which benefits from the research done in the *De potentia*—the faith being presupposed, Thomas turns immediately to the theological notions necessary for rendering account of faith in the Trinity with regard to the believing intelligence. It is necessary to read attentively these luminous pages consecrated to the plan of the Trinitarian treatise in the *Summa.* As everywhere in Thomas's writings, but more here than elsewhere, the method clarifies the content and brings out the profound structural unity of the treatise: The immanent Trinity is never opposed to the economic Trinity; the persons are never seen separately from the essence; furthermore the notions used (procession, relation, person) never appear as a superstructure exteriorly imposed by man to God; they are rather, in their order of succession, the most precise expression of what the divine reality itself imposes on the faith that receives it.

Since I cannot include everything in this Preface, I will underline only a few of the most illuminating points for us, and first of all the progress of Thomas's work in relationship to the Sentences. It is not only the change in structure of the exposition that reveals an author in his maturity and henceforth master of his options; many other points allow one to perceive how he developed little by little his doctrine of the Word (the generation of the Son is no longer conceived as a procession by way of nature, but rather in the manner of an intellectual procession) and his doctrine of the Holy Spirit as love (he no longer understands by that the act of loving, but the fruit of the act of love of the Father and the Son).

The manner in which Thomas uses his sources and the way in which he corrects them in comparison with each other is also one of these points that must not be left unseen. We have already said that in the *Sentences* Thomas retained much of Albert and Bonaventure and, naturally, Aristotle. We find Aristotle again in the *Summa* and Thomas notably borrows his distinction between the immanent action (that is accomplished in the interior of the agent itself: to feel, to know, to will) and the transitive action (that is exerted on the exterior object: to cut, to construct, to warm). Against Sabellianism and Arianism, this doctrine has been decisive for understanding that the divine persons do not emerge from a transitive action and are not constituted as such by their action in the world. This, however, was not sufficient; it was necessary at the same time to correct and extend Aristotle's anthropology and to show that immanent actions, too, produce a fruit. This is what Thomas does when he reinterprets Aristotle in the light of Augustine by underlining the internal fecundity of the acts of the intellect and of the will: These immanent acts have in God a term that subsists, the Word and Love, who therefore are divine persons equal to the Father.

The two preceding points have immense interest in showing a genius at work, but the third is no less revealing. Thomas ends his Trinitarian research by examining its extension in the life of grace: The presence of the whole Trinity in one's soul "in the manner in which the known is found in the knower and the loved in the lover." This doctrine of the indwelling of God in the saints that has delighted generations of mystics has an integral part in the Trinitarian reflection of Thomas. Only those theologians who have failed to read Thomas to the end dare claim that he considered the Trinity in a splendid isolation. This doctrine of the Word and Love here manifests its fecundity and shows the mutual clarification that anthropology and Trinitarian doctrine supply for each other. But this does not say enough; here and elsewhere, Gilles Emery rightly underscores that Trinitarian doctrine is found at the center of theology in all its amplitude. This is accomplished first in a general way by the reattachment to the eternal processions of the entire creative and salvific work. More particularly, it holds also for the teaching on Christ since the doctrine of the Word allows one to demonstrate the fittingness of the incarnation of the Son and constitutes the privileged articulation between Trinitarian theology and Christology. This reflects equally upon anthropology, with the doctrine of the image of God that is found at the center of reflections on the habitation of the Trinity in the soul; this doctrine has, in its turn, its repercussion on moral theology, notably as regards the theological virtues, and on eschatology, with the teaching on the vision and fruition of God. We can add that this doctrine responds to the difficulty evoked on the first page of this essay. Trinitarian theology should not be instrumentalized at the service of other interests, but, without their being in any way subordinated, it illumines all theological reflection worthy of the name.

After having read under the guidance of Fr. Emery these three great Trinitarian expositions of Thomas Aquinas, the moment has come to make in his company a halt for reflection. It is all the more necessary to recognize that the whole twentieth century has been a tributary of the artificial opposition—established in 1892 by Théodore de Régnon—between a "Greek" conception, for which the point of departure for Trinitarian theology is found in the consideration of the persons, and a "Latin" conception, which, on the contrary, begins with a consideration of the divine essence before coming to the plurality of the persons. This opposition between a "personalist" conception of the Trinity and an "essentialist" conception had become an undisputed commonplace; so that when Karl Rahner (followed by numerous disciples) took up the relay toward the middle of the century, it was easy for him to denounce the division between the treatise *De Deo Uno* and the treatise *De Deo Trino* which then plagued the teaching of theology, and to deplore that speculative reflection on the "immanent Trinity" remains foreign to the consideration of the action of God in the world, regrettably separated from the "economic Trinity" at work in the history of salvation.

Rahner certainly had reason to stigmatize this harmful separation, but he was wrong to attribute to Thomas Aquinas the responsibility for this state of affairs, as if he were the first to introduce
this division. Gilles Emery has no difficulty in showing first that
there are not two sections (the essence and the persons) in the
treatise of St. Thomas, but rather three, because the procession of
creatures is there included. There is, therefore, no gap in the continuity between God and his work of creation and salvation and,
by the same token, neither is there any separation between the
immanent Trinity and the economic Trinity. The famous Rahnerian
axiom—"The Trinity of the economy of salvation is the immanent Trinity and vice versa"—is nowhere better verified than in
St. Thomas. He has no treatise "of the one God" separated from
the treatise of the Trinity, but simply two approaches to the same
God depending on whether one considers in him what is common to the three persons or what is proper to each of them. Far
from inventing this structure himself and thus opposing the
Greek Fathers, Thomas is on the contrary their direct heir, since
he received it from the Cappodocian Fathers through the intermediary of Augustine and John Damascene. As regards the
alleged priority given to the essence over the persons, it suffices
to read the titles of the Questions of the treatise of the Trinity in
the *Summa* in order to perceive that fifteen of the seventeen
Questions are placed under the title, "the persons." If the exposition itself opens with two Questions on the notion of procession
and on that of relation, they have no other goal than to introduce to the intelligence what the person is. It is moreover only
by reason of the pedagogical option proper to the *Summa;* elsewhere, on the contrary, Thomas can very well use a different
order: person—distinction—relation. Gilles Emery, without
doubt, is right when he writes that the plan followed by Thomas
"manifests a resolute option in favor of a doctrine governed by
the notion of person."

But this is only the most exterior aspect of this study, its "apologetic" side in the best sense of the word: It renders justice to

Thomas to whom these deviations, as grave as they are unfounded, have been attributed. If it was first necessary to re-establish the pure and simple truth, the essential remains still to be discovered; therefore it is necessary to read this superb work in its entirety and follow its author in his careful analysis of Thomas's doctrine in order to experience the intense intellectual jubilation felt at discovering the beauty and splendor of truth. The author demands much from his readers and his essay requires sustained attention, but he knew how to make comprehensible and share the contemplative finality of the Trinitarian theology of Thomas without ceasing to underscore its practical repercussion in the Christian life. The creative and salvific work of the Trinity is accomplished in the extension of the processions of the divine persons: The Spirit giver of grace leads back to the Word creator and both lead back to the Father, the first origin of the creation; their common objective being finally to bring humanity into the beatitude of Trinitarian communion.

Since this Preface is centered preferentially on the method employed by St. Thomas and, following him, by his commentator, we must not fail to draw attention to the connection between the third study, discussed above, and the sixth study which we will now address. In speaking of the Trinity in the *Summa contra Gentiles,* Gilles Emery had touched in passing upon the question of *Filioque,* but only from the point of view of St. Thomas's method of work. This was one of the signs of the importance of this aspect for a correct approach to the question; thus it is not surprising that Fr. Emery now returns to it in more ample manner. Actually, in a subject as sensitive as that of the procession of the Holy Spirit *ab utroque,* Thomas could only be particularly attentive to assure the rigor of his approach. For him, undoubtedly, the procession of the Spirit *a Filio* is a truth that belongs to the faith; therefore it is not a question of attempting to establish it by a strict demonstration. But he also knows that the Greek theologians think differently from the Latins on this subject and therefore, while recognizing the legitimacy of other ways of expressing it, he strives to make manifest to believers exercising reason the necessity of this procession of the Spirit from the Father and the

Son in order rationally to render account of faith in the Trinity. Beyond the Greeks, whose faith he does not deny despite his incomprehension of their position, it is a necessary truth of salvation that he defends against Arianism and especially Sabellianism.

For no other subject, without doubt, did Thomas put into practice in such an ample and coherent manner the principles that he recommends employing in any theological debate: It is necessary before all else to use the authorities acknowledged by the other party. In this case, since for Christians the authority of the Scripture and the Fathers is undisputed, he therefore gives priority to these two sources. From this point of view, the change of method between the *Commentary on the Sentences* and the later works is astonishing: While in the youthful work the argumentation is almost exclusively rational and borrowed (from Albert the Great) and is only accompanied by rare biblical or patristic references, it is entirely otherwise in the later works: references to Scripture— always placed at the first level—do not cease multiplying, and similarly patristic and conciliar authorities are always growing. Thomas notably takes great care to promote in the Greek sources that which agrees with the teaching of the Latin doctors. If he has difficulty understanding the exact position of the Cappadocians, he shows himself to be very close to the Alexandrians; one is even confounded by his insight in understanding the issue at stake in difficult texts and by his lucidity as regards the impossibility of attributing to Cyril of Alexandria the position that Theodoret of Cyrus credited to him. He does not renounce the use of rational arguments and he deploys an impressive series of them, but they only come in the third place. He is conscious of their strength and does not hesitate to speak of "evident reasons" that demonstrate the procession of the Holy Spirit *ab utroque*. This does not mean that he appealed to the *rationes necessariae* that he had rejected, because his demonstration presupposed faith in the Trinity. But the latter being possessed, the demonstration concludes necessarily.

The doctrinal content in play in this study is evidently of primary importance (we highlight, among others, the Christological realism of the life of grace linked to the doctrine of the procession of the Holy Spirit *a Filio*). If we have chosen to draw attention to the quality of the approach it is by reason of its pertinence and, here again, its exemplary range. It reveals a methodological attitude constant in Thomas Aquinas in his hearing of the Word of God in Holy Scripture: He thinks in symbiosis with all of the Tradition, dogmatic and theological. At the same time, this study also teaches us the necessity for the reader today of conducting a rigorous analysis if he wants to understand with exactitude the teaching of the Master.

The final pages that remain for us to discuss confirm our choice to highlight the problems of method in order to underscore the interest of this volume. Indeed, the author mentions them clearly among the objectives of his study of the *Commentary on St. John*. It is necessary, nevertheless, to say something about the first part (the most extended), rich in teachings. The careful comparison of this *Commentary* with the *Summa theologiae* allows one to notice that, with the exception of purely technical discussions, the essential part of Trinitarian doctrine is found in the *Commentary* as well as in the *Summa*. Certain points, however, are more developed in the former: for example the unity of knowledge and love between the Father and the Son or the action of the divine persons in the world (in particular that of the Holy Spirit, much more generously treated). Above all, one cannot fail to note the enhancement of the soteriological argument. One knows well the Fathers' reasoning in the Christological debate in favor of the integrity of the humanity assumed by the Word: "What has not been assumed has not been saved." But it is much more rare, to my knowledge, to find this type of argumentation within Trinitarian doctrine. Thomas makes use of this argument against the Arians in both senses: In the *Summa theologiae,* he says for example that it is by reason of their divinity that the persons of the Son and the Spirit are capable of saving us; but in the *Commentary,* he uses an inverse reasoning: He begins with the reality of our salvation in order to infer the divinity of the Son and the Spirit, since it is through them that we are saved. He proceeds similarly as regards another great divine work: One can be certain that the Word is God, because everything was created by him. One sees without difficulty that this intervention of soteriology at the heart of Trinitarian doctrine bears in advance the ultimate response to the false problem of the relationship between the immanent Trinity and the economical Trinity that one seemed to discover in Thomas. This suspicion was founded upon a misunderstanding.

The difference between the *Commentary* and the *Summa* is above all in the organization of the material. While the *Summa* is ordered by the *ordo disciplinae* (order of rigorous pedagogical exposition), the *Commentary*, by definition, follows the text step by step and gives, in accord with its purpose, the necessary explications. It has therefore all the characteristics of an exegesis; but Thomas's exegesis differs greatly from ours, because it integrates speculative theology into the very explication of the text, in such a way that the doctrinal content arises from the biblical text itself without being superimposed on it. One also discovers that Trinitarian theology contains three steps: The mystery is first received in the faith taught by the Scriptures; there follows then the reflection on the being and the properties of the divine persons (theology of the immanent Trinity); finally comes the reflection on the creative and salvific action of the divine persons in the light of the properties and the relations of the persons (theology of the economic Trinity). As the author says so well: "The doctrine of the economic Trinity (third step) is achieved when a speculative reflection on the divine persons (second step) is applied to the agency of the persons discovered in the reading of Scripture (first step). In this way, Trinitarian theology moves from Scripture to Scripture."

The *Commentary* has therefore the enormous advantage of best underscoring the continued presence of Scripture in the theological reflection of Thomas. It helps therefore to identify the biblical context of many themes better than the more concise text of the *Summa*. But Fr. Emery shows equally—this is no longer new to us—the other roots of this exegesis by explicitly naming the patristic authorities who are hidden beneath the argumentation of the *Summa*. In both cases, the immense effort of documentation undertaken for the

Catena aurea shows through, the veritable gold mine from which Thomas constantly draws. Another aspect of the method, namely the treatment of Trinitarian heresies, is especially prominent in the *Commentary*. Thomas is convinced and often repeats that the manifestation of the truth is inseparable from the rejection of the error that is there opposed. But make no mistake, it is not polemic; Thomas wants to "understand" the error and he is persuaded that its interest comes from its depth more than from its diffusion; it is in this way that the refutation of heresy enters into the purpose of his speculative theology, which is to lead to the contemplation of the truth. From this point of view the proximity between the *Commentary* and the *Summa contra Gentiles,* which witnesses the same preoccupation, is greater than with the *Summa theologiae.*

Depending on whether one wishes to be initiated to a certain work or to a precise problem, each study of this collection can be read for itself, independently of the others. It would be more beneficial to read them as we have taken them, in the chronological order of the presented works. One cannot miss noting the progress of Thomas himself by passing from one work to the other and by being taken in by his doctrine and its profundity; this speaks for itself. But one will be equally impressed, we believe, by the work that Gilles Emery has developed in less than ten years. We spoke at the outset of the coherence and continuity of his research, its openness and amplitude. From study to study, one discovers an author with clear and concise style, with flawless erudition, in possession of a tested method, a scholar who cleaves to the texts and examines them in their singularity without assimilating them to each other too quickly, who knows how to underscore the constants of Thomas's work and to bring out his perspicacity without fearing the occasion of pointing out his weaknesses. Unlike others, Gilles Emery is not content with paraphrasing what has already been said on the theme that he treats; he belongs to the rare category of authors who explore the depths of their subject and this is why he profoundly renews all that he touches. After having reread these texts, as I just finished doing in order to write this Preface, I believe

I can say that the secret of his success resides in what comprised the strength of Thomas Aquinas himself: attention to the sources and their rigorous investigation with a perfect honesty that does not exclude the cordial adhesion to the theses of the Master.

Jean-Pierre Torrell, OP
University of Fribourg
Switzerland

Foreword

THE TRINITY is not a simple object of study among others: When the Church confesses her faith, it is the Trinity that she proclaims.[1] When Christians announce the Gospel, they confess their faith in the Father almighty, in the incarnated Son, and in the Spirit who gives life. The Trinity constitutes the heart of all Christian teaching. One therefore rejoices to be able to state that for several decades Trinitarian theology has experienced a real renewal. Studies of Trinitarian theology flourish today in great number: biblical studies, patristic studies, historical studies, systematic essays. The repercussions of Trinitarian faith are equally abundantly explored, in order to renew our understanding of creation and salvation, in all their dimensions. Researches are multiplied in order to better perceive and discover the fruitfulness of Trinitarian faith.

In this vast movement of rediscovery, the contribution of St. Thomas also merits to be received with a new attention. The Trinity occupies the central place in his theology: "The Christian faith consists principally in the confession of the Holy Trinity" (St. Thomas, *On the Reasons of the Faith,* chapter 1). But, too often, clichés work to obscure the reading of St. Thomas: For certain authors, at the mercy of hasty interpretations, the Trinitarian doctrine proposed by

---

[1] Teresa Bede, with the assistance of Matthew Levering, translated the Foreword and the Preface.

St. Thomas is detached from the economy of creation and salvation, or too little rooted in Holy Scripture, or not respectful enough of the mystery that surpasses human reason. Such clichés, too widespread even today, cannot withstand an attentive reading of the works of St. Thomas. It is necessary then, as a beginning, to take up the reading of Aquinas again, in order to discover there the riches of his teaching.

In order to be well understood, the teaching of St. Thomas on the Trinity requires a historical approach and a speculative approach. On the one hand, St. Thomas's purpose cannot be correctly understood if one does not place it in the context of scholastic theology, and more precisely in the theological movement of the twelfth and thirteenth centuries (the golden age of Trinitarian reflection in the West). It is necessary to read St. Thomas by paying attention to his sources, to the debates that animated the Trinitarian reflection of his time, as well as to the progress of his own thought in the works that he wrote. On the other hand, St. Thomas wished to give a profound understanding of the doctrine of the Church on the Trinity, a theological contemplation by means of the resources of human intelligence enlightened by the faith. A purely historical study is therefore insufficient. The reading of St. Thomas demands understanding of the stakes of his reflection, his theological method, and the intellectual means that he deploys, without forgetting the connections with the other domains of theological reflection. St. Thomas wanted to achieve a synthesis: Only a speculative approach can help us to perceive this synthesis.

The speculative approach to St. Thomas's thought is not opposed to a historical approach. The reading of St. Thomas actually demands that these two approaches be properly reunited. The speculative undertanding of the thought of St. Thomas—this is our profound conviction—must benefit from the contribution of a historical reading and, reciprocally, it is by paying attention to the doctrinal contents that a historical approach bears fruit.

The studies collected in this volume do not pretend to supply a complete exposé of the Trinitarian doctrine of St. Thomas; this remains an area in which there is still much to do. These studies simply seek to present certain aspects of St. Thomas's teaching, while also proposing a method of reading. Thus, we have sought to expose the thought of St. Thomas by considering certain of his works in a distinct manner, in order to follow the progress of his reflection: his commentary on *Sentences,* the *Summa contra Gentiles,* the *Summa theologiae,* and the *Commentary on St. John.* The first study rather modestly seeks to present the theological movement in which the reflection of St. Thomas is inscribed. This historical approach shows itself particularly fruitful in exposing the connection of Trinitarian faith and faith in the creation, which the second study presents. The doctrine of the procession of the Holy Spirit for its part manifests the close link that connects biblical theology and speculative theology in St. Thomas. This profoundly biblical inspiration of St. Thomas's Trinitarian theology appears in full light in his commentary on St. John.

With the exception of the presentation of the Trinitarian doctrine of the *Summa theologiae,* which was written especially for the present volume, these studies were carried out independently from one another. Their collection in this book, however, is not arbitrary: Each of them constitutes a stage in the reading of St. Thomas's Trinitarian theology; together they attempt to provide the foundations which permit one, we hope, to understand better the synthesis of Trinitarian theology that St. Thomas offers us.

It is an agreeable duty to thank my friend Matthew Levering, without whom this book would not have seen the day. He conceived of the project to translate and gather these studies, and he also presided over the practical aspects of the realization of this work under the auspices of Sapientia Press. If this book can be of some use to its readers, the merit belongs in large part to him. My continuing gratitude is addressed equally to Father Jean-Pierre Torrell, OP, who led me to the study of St. Thomas's Trinitarian theology, thereby enabling me to discover and make known an inspiring field of research.

Gilles Emery, OP
Washington, DC
September 2002

The Threeness and Oneness of God in Twelfth- to Fourteenth-Century Scholasticism

"THERE IS no subject where error is more dangerous, research more laborious, and discovery more fruitful than the oneness of the Trinity *(unitas Trinitatis)* of the Father, the Son, and the Holy Spirit."[1] This warning of Augustine, which Peter Lombard puts at the beginning of his inquiry on the Trinity in his *Sentences*[2] and which commentators have often repeated, sets the tone for Trinitarian research during the golden age of scholasticism: The theological explanation of faith in the Trinitarian oneness of God, as Albert the Great makes explicit, is made with the conviction that here lies the goal of human existence, but that a mistake in this area would entail the destruction of the whole edifice of the faith.[3] There

---

[1] Translation by Robert Williams of "Trinité et unité de Dieu dans la scolastique. XIIe–XIVe siècle," in *Le christianisme est-il un monothéisme? Actes du 3e cycle de théologie systématique des Facultés de théologie de Suisse romande,* ed. Pierre Gisel and Gilles Emery (Geneva: Labor et Fides, 2001), pp. 195–220. English translation published in *Nova et Vetera* (English): 1 (2003): 43–74.

[2] Peter Lombard, *Sententiae,* Book I, d. 2, ch. 1: *Sententiae in IV Libris distinctae,* ed. I. Brady (Grottaferrata/Rome: Collegii S. Bonaventurae ad Claras Aquas, [tom. I/2] 1971), p. 62; Augustine, *De Trinitate* I,III,5.

[3] In his commentary on the *Sentences,* Albert the Great devotes two articles to the discussion of Augustine's warning quoted by Lombard: Albert the Great, I Sent., d. 2, a. 6–7 *(Opera omnia,* ed. Auguste Borgnet, vol. 25 [Paris: Louis Vivès, 1893], p. 60); see also Thomas Aquinas, I Sent., d. 2, expositio textus *(Scriptum super Libros Sententiarum,* ed. Pierre Mandonnet, vol. 1 [Paris: Lethielleux, 1929], p. 77).

is more to these observations than mere convention. For the history of Trinitarian doctrine during the scholastic period demonstrates the often laborious search for balance, punctuated by ecclesiastical sanctions and giving rise to hardheaded divergences among theologians. Without writing a history of Trinitarian doctrine, this study will attempt to outline some of the salient aspects of the relationship between the oneness and the threeness of God in scholastic thought by pointing out the decisive stages in this thought from the twelfth century until the beginning of the fourteenth century in order to highlight the *loci* of the question and the main ways of answering it.

Threeness and Oneness in the Beginning of Scholasticism, Ecclesiastical Reactions, and Interventions

The Trinitarian question constitutes the great theme of twelfth-century theology.[4] Two tensions may be cited as characteristic of this blossoming of Trinitarian theology. The first has to do with the method of investigation. The initiators of the scholastic method, considering the content of the faith by means of the rational resources of language and philosophy, ran into opposition from those who held to a traditional theology in the patristic and contemplative vein. The second tension concerns the stress put either upon the divine oneness or upon the plurality of persons in the difficult search for balance. These difficulties are illustrated in Abelard's writings and the reactions they aroused.

Roscellinus, Anselm, and Abelard

One of Abelard's first masters, Roscellinus of Compiègne (ca. 1050–ca. 1120), created a lively controversy by his refusal to agree that the three divine persons were a single reality *(una res)*. For Roscellinus, affirming the single reality of the three divine persons

---

[4] Antonio Terracciano, "Dibattito sulla Trinità e orientamenti teologici nel XII secolo," *Asprenas* 34 (1987): 284–303.

would no longer allow us to safeguard the deposit of faith since (according to the Catholic faith) of these persons only the Son became flesh. Consequently, for fear of Patripassianism, Roscellinus held that the three divine persons are three realities *(tres res)* that have, however, one same will and one same power. He compared them to three angels or three souls, which are likewise *tres res*. Here we are at the beginnings of the scholastic problem to which the masters of the thirteenth century still bear witness: "Can the three persons be called 'three realities' *(tres res)*?"[5] In his *Epistola de incarnatione Verbi,* Anselm of Canterbury addressed a sharp reply to Roscellinus's thesis. Seeing Roscellinus as a nominalist dialectician, Anselm criticizes him for his tritheism: "Either he intends to profess three gods, or he does not understand what he is saying."[6] In Anselm's opinion, the reason for such an error lies in a poor grasp of the relationship between individuals and universals: "For in what way can those who do not yet understand how several specifically human beings are one human being understand in the most hidden and highest nature how several persons, each of whom is complete God, are one God?"[7] According to Anselm, Roscellinus's thesis introduces a breach in the one substance of God.[8] Thus Anselm attacks "those contemporary dialecticians *(dialectici)* or, rather, the heretics of dialectics who consider universal essences to be merely vocal

---

[5] Peter Lombard, who highlights the Augustinian sources, will bring the question into the twelfth century (Peter Lombard, *Sententiae,* Book I, d. 25, ch. 2, n. 4–5, pp. 193–94); Lombard uses the expression *"tres res,"* and likewise affirms *"una summa res"* in the Trinity by distinguishing between the Essence *(una res)* and the persons *(tres res)*; his commentators will echo this; see in particular Bonaventure, I *Sent.,* d. 25, dub. 3 (*Opera omnia,* vol. 1 [Quaracchi: Editiones PP. Collegii S. Bonaventurae, 1882], 446); Thomas Aquinas, I *Sent.,* d. 25, q. 1, a. 4, pp. 611–13.

[6] Anselm, *Epistola de incarnatione Verbi,* ch. 2 (Anselm of Canterbury, *The Major Works,* ed. Brian Davies and Gillian R. Evans [Oxford/New York: Oxford University Press, 1998], 238).

[7] Ibid., ch. 1, p. 237.

[8] Roscellinus will vigorously deny affirming a substantial plurality in God and distances himself from the tritheism charge in a letter he sent to Abelard on this subject (PL 178, 357–72). For an overview of Roscellinus's Trinitarian thought: Johann Hofmeier, *Die Trinitätslehre des Hugo von St. Viktor* (Munich: Max Hueber Verlag, 1963), pp. 9–26.

emanations."[9] The Abbot of Bec answers Roscellinus theologically with the distinction between what is common and one in God (the divine Essence) and what is distinct (the properties, the persons). The three divine persons are a single *res* (substance, essence); if we wish to speak of *tres res,* we must include under the word *res* the relations rather than the substance.[10] Anselm retraces the main elements of his answer in a letter addressed to Foulques, Bishop of Beauvais, to be read before the assembly of the Council of Soissons (about 1092), which rejected Roscellinus's Trinitarian error.[11] Thus the eleventh century ends with a clear affirmation of the divine oneness *(una res)*, with the intention of avoiding the danger of tritheism created by the new dialectics.

In the wake of Anselm, Abelard (1079–1142) likewise reacted against Roscellinus's thesis. In a letter that he addressed to the Bishop of Paris toward 1120, the Master of Le Pallet explains that the main purpose of his writings on the Trinity was to refute Roscellinus's tritheistic heresy condemned at the Council of Soissons.[12] The aim of *Theologia Summi Boni* and its succeeding elaborations *(Theologia Christiana, Theologia Scholarium)* is to furnish a defense of the traditional Trinitarian doctrine against the new "dialecticians." However Abelard organizes this defense on the very grounds of dialectics.[13] For our purpose (which is not to consider the whole of Trinitarian theology but only the threeness–oneness relationship), Abelard's central thesis consists in focusing on the

---

[9] Anselm, *Epistola de incarnatione Verbi,* ch. 1, p. 237. This nominalism or "vocalism" of Roscellinus (only words or vocal sounds and individual things exist; nothing is made up of parts) is considered the historical starting point of the dispute over universals: cf. Alain de Libera, *La querelle des universaux de Platon à la fin du Moyen Âge* (Paris: Seuil, 1996), pp. 142–46.

[10] Anselm, *Epistola de incarnatione Verbi,* ch. 2 (pp. 239–40).

[11] See Michel Corbin, *L'oeuvre de S. Anselme de Cantorbéry,* vol. 1 (Paris: Cerf, 1988), pp. 262–65.

[12] Constant J. Mews, "Introduction" to *Petri Abaelardi Theologia "Summi Boni"* (Turnhout: Brepols, 1987), 39; cf. PL 178, pp. 355–58.

[13] We should understand by dialectics the logical method of language analysis and rational study applied to the pronouncements of faith and the maxims of the Fathers; cf. Franz Courth, *Trinität in der Scholastik* (Freiburg i.B.: Herder, 1985), pp. 30–50; Jean Jolivet, *La théologie d'Abélard* (Paris: Cerf, 1997).

three divine persons starting with the triad of divine attributes: power, wisdom, kindness *(potentia, sapientia, benignitas)*. The Father "is called Father by reason of this unique power of his majesty"; the Son is called Son "because we find in him a particular wisdom"; as for the Holy Spirit, he is so called "in accordance with the grace of his goodness." Thus "the name Father designates power; the name Son, wisdom; and the name Holy Spirit, the sentiment that is favorable to creatures." In a word: "To say then that God is three persons is the same as saying that the divine substance is mighty, wise, and good." This is the way Abelard envisions the Trinity, from a rational perspective starting with the notion of the highest good *(summum bonum, tota boni perfectio)*, which consists in the three characteristics of power, wisdom, and goodness.[14]

Abelard has a clear-cut view of God's oneness (one single and singular substance) as well as of the properties that distinguish the persons.[15] If he accurately grasps the threeness in the oneness by means of the relative properties and processions (generation and procession), nevertheless he does not give up explaining these properties in the threefold manner described above. The properties of the Father, the Son, and Holy Spirit are distinct "for the Father is called Father only by the fact that he is mighty *(potens)*, the Son by the fact that he can know *(discretus, potens discernere)*, and the Holy Spirit by the fact that he is good *(benignus)*."[16] The problem raised by such

---

[14] Abelard, *Theologia Summi Boni*, Book I, ch. II (ed. Constant J. Mews [Turnhout: Brepols, 1987], pp. 86–88). This is the thesis that opens Abelard's Trinitarian reflection in his first *Theology*; the later *Theologies* develop and complete this starting point but they do not substantially modify this initial position.

[15] "What is proper to the Father is to exist through Himself, not through another, and to beget from all eternity a Son who is co-eternal with Him; what is proper to the Son is to be begotten, and to have been begotten by the Father only, to be neither created nor made nor proceeding but only begotten. As for the Holy Spirit, what is proper to Him is to proceed from the Father and the Son both, to be neither created nor made nor begotten but only to proceed" (ibid., Book II, ch. I, pp. 124–25). We recognize here the doctrine of the "four properties" formalized by the subsequent tradition of the Schools.

[16] Ibid., Book II, ch. IV, n. 103 (pp. 150–51). The end of the chapter takes up this thesis again: "For God the Father, who is a person according to the very meaning of the name, must be defined in an exact way as divine Power, i.e., mighty God; God the Son, as divine Wisdom; the Spirit of God as divine

reasoning, which Abelard was well aware of, is the following: How
do we distinguish the persons by attributes that also designate what
is one in God (common power, wisdom, and goodness)?

Abelard's answer has recourse to the language and grammatical structure of our statements: "Words taken in themselves have
exactly the same value, or are equivalent as to what they signify,
but even so they do not keep this value if they enter into a construction."[17] Thus, in the statements we form about God as Trinity, we must distinguish those that concern the identity of essence
(power common to the three persons) from those that concern the
identity of the property (the Father is mighty, and so on; power,
wisdom, kindness as personal properties). Elsewhere, Abelard will
explain the threesome of wisdom–power–goodness by the famous
"similitude" of the bronze seal: the bronze material, the seal made
of this bronze, and this seal at the moment of actually sealing
(identity of substance, diversity of properties).[18] This construct
allows Abelard to shed light on the Trinitarian dimension of creation and salvation history: He attributes to the Father that which
has to do with power (creation *ex nihilo,* sending his Son), to the
Son he assigns whatever has to do with wisdom (to judge, perceive), and he attributes to the Holy Spirit what pertains to the
actions of divine grace.[19]

Clearly Abelard had no intention of attributing to the Father an
essential power superior to the Son's, and we may well believe that
he himself understood the usage of the power attribute in accordance with the connection that associates essential power with
what would later be called notional power (power to beget, power

Goodness. Thus the Father differs from the Son through His property or definition *(proprietate siue diffinitione),* i.e., He is other than Him; in the same
way, the one and the other differ from the Holy Spirit" (p. 152; also see further
on, pp. 152–53).

[17] Ibid., Book III, ch. XI [38] (p. 173).

[18] See for example Abelard, *Theologia Scholarium* II, 112 (Turnhout: Brepols,
1987), pp. 462–63; cf. Sergio Paolo Bonanni, *Parlare della Trinità: Lettura
della Theologia Scholarium di Abelardo* (Rome: Ed. Pontifica Università Gregoriana, 1996), pp. 185–221.

[19] Abelard, *Theologia Summi Boni,* Book III, ch. I, n. 48–50 (pp. 177–79).

to breathe forth).[20] Abelard recognizes that the reasons he puts forth
are adaptations drawn from what we know from creatures, which in
no way allow us to "understand," but he finds these reasons as sufficient in disproving the sophisms of the dialecticians.[21] The fact
remains that in his doctrine, Abelard, determined in particular by his
polemic against the tritheism with which he reproaches Roscellinus,
lays the stress clearly on the oneness of the divine substance. Thus,
he does not accept without qualification the use of the words "three"
or "several" *(multa)* in reference to God; God is "several persons,"
but He is not "several," and there is not in God "three in and of
itself" *(tria per se)*. Adding the word "three" to the word "persons" in
the expression "three persons" is only accidental *(accidentaliter)*. Here
Abelard provides the historical source of the scholastic question on
"numerical terms" in the discourse on God.[22] He is clear that we
cannot properly apply number to God. Since he only considers
number insofar as it comes under quantity, Abelard rejects numerical
plurality in God, thereby also excluding the possibility that plurality
of persons is plurality "per se." There is a multiplicity of properties
but there is no numerical diversity or plurality in God.[23]

Furthermore, the use of the power–wisdom–goodness ternary
leads Abelard to affirm that the philosophers, and above all Plato—
"the greatest of philosophers"—bore witness to the Trinity (the Platonic doctrine of God the Father of the world, of the *Nous,* and of
the world soul). Plato even "taught what is essential concerning the
Trinity."[24] This enthusiastic Christian Platonism, which will flower
again in the "school" of Chartres, is expressed in flag-waving fashion
at the end of the *Theologia Summi Boni:* All men (Christians, Jews,
pagans) can have access to the Trinitarian faith through their natural
reason, for "as we have said, the fact that God is Father, Son, and
Holy Spirit is equivalent to the fact that God is Power, Wisdom, and

20 S. P. Bonanni, *Parlare della Trinità,* pp. 86–102, 184.
21 Abelard, *Theologia Summi Boni,* Book II, ch. III (p. 138–39).
22 See for example St. Thomas Aquinas, *Summa theologiae,* I, q. 30, a. 3.
23 Abelard, *Theologia Summi Boni,* Book III, ch. I, n. 5–6 (pp. 159–60).
24 "Plato . . . totius trinitatis summam post prophetas patenter edocuit" (ibid.,
Book I, ch. V, n. 36, pp. 98–99).

Goodness; since no man with common sense, be he Jew or gentile, doubts this, it seems that no one lacks this faith."[25] Such an affirmation, taken out of the proper context of Abelard's thought, could only reinforce the suspicion of modalism (the primacy of the divine One) that would be brought against him. Abelard provides the terms of the famous scholastic question, repeated by so many bachelors and masters: Can the Trinity be known by natural reason?[26]

Very early on Abelard became the object of a twofold criticism: rationalism (he wants to make the Trinity understood, Gautier of Mortagne will say of him) and modalism (disappearance of the Trinity in the divine oneness).[27] Bernard of Clairvaux, less cognizant of Abelard's original theses, will add an accusation of Arianism or subordinationism.[28] Abelard underwent a first censure (condemnation of his *Theologia*) at the provincial Council of Soissons in 1121, most certainly under the heading of Sabellianism. Then, consequent to the intervention of William of Saint-Thierry and Bernard of Clairvaux, his teaching suffered a second condemnation at the Council of Sens in 1140. The first error in the lists of "heretical chapters" imputed to him concerns the Trinitarian use of the wisdom–power–goodness ternary, and targets the subordinationism that, in the judgment of the censors, this usage implies.[29] In spite of these *calamitates* (Abelard wrote an account of them), it is to his credit that in a sharp reaction to any tritheism he laid the foundations of the scholastic treatment of the problem: the use of logic in dealing with the Trinity; the connection between the essential attributes of God and the properties of the persons; the reflection on the Trinity starting with the idea of the Good; the rough draft of a reflection on "number" in

---

[25] Ibid., Book III, ch. V (pp. 200–1).

[26] See for example Thomas Aquinas, *ST* I, q. 32, a. 1.

[27] See the letter of Roscellinus, which criticizes Abelard of a certain Sabellianism (PL 178, pp. 368–69).

[28] For these accusations of heresy directed at Abelard, see J. Hofmeier, *Die Trinitätslehre des Hugo von St. Viktor,* pp. 9–26.

[29] "Quod Pater sit plena potentia, Filius quaedam potentia, Spiritus Sanctus nulla potentia" (Capitula haeresum XIX, n. 1); see Constant J. Mews, "The Lists of Heresies Imputed to Peter Abelard," *Revue Bénédictine* 95 (1985): pp. 73–110 (here p. 108).

God; the question of the Trinity in the face of natural reason; and so on. We must note in particular that Abelard's theses will lead to the elaboration of the doctrine of "appropriations," that is, the assignment of a common attribute (power, wisdom, goodness) to a particular divine person on account of a real affinity of this attribute with the property of the person (for example, the affinity between the common attribute of power and the property of the Father who is without principle). This however does not reserve an essential attribute to a particular person in an exclusive way.[30]

Gilbert de la Porrée

Gilbert de la Porrée (†1154) was Chancelor of Chartres, then professor at Paris before becoming Bishop of Poitiers in 1142. An eminent figure in twelfth-century theology and initiator of a movement in the Schools (the "Porretans"), he brings to the reflection on the threeness and oneness of God tools furnished by Boethius, on whose *opuscula sacra* he wrote a commentary. Like Abelard, he was attacked on several occasions for his teaching on the Trinity. Preoccupied with showing how the Trinity is reconcilable with the oneness of God, he excited a huge debate on the divine simplicity.[31]

With Gilbert the problem shifts from the analysis of language to the theory of sciences and crystallizes around the doctrine of relation in God. To his inquiry on God, Gilbert applies the *rationes*

---

[30] For this elaboration (12th–13th centuries) see Jean Châtillon, "*Unitas, aequalitas, concordia vel connexio.* Recherches sur les Origines de la Théorie Thomiste des Appropriations (*Sum. Theol.,* I, q. 39, art. 7–8)," in *St. Thomas Aquinas 1274–1974: Commemorative Studies,* ed. Armand A. Maurer, vol. 1 (Toronto: Pontifical Institute of Medieval Studies, 1974), pp. 337–79.

[31] Martin A. Schmidt, *Gottheit und Trinität nach dem Kommentar des Gilbert Porreta zu Boethius De Trinitate* (Basel: Verlag für Recht und Gesellschaft, 1956); Michael F. Williams, *The Teaching of Gilbert Porreta on the Trinity as Found in his Commentaries on Boethius* (Rome: Ed. Pontificia Università Gregoriana, 1951); Michael Stickelbroeck, *Mysterium Venerandum: Der trinitarische Gedanke im Werk des Bernhard von Clairvaux* (Münster: Aschendorff, 1994), pp. 39–63; Marcia L. Colish, "Gilbert, The Early Porretans, and Peter Lombard: Semantics and Theology," in *Gilbert de Poitiers et ses contemporains aux origines de la "Logica modernorum,"* ed. Jean Jolivet and Alain de Libera (Naples: Bibliopolis, 1987), pp. 229–50.

theologicae (study of the principles of created reality, the realm of abstraction, centered on the oneness and simplicity of God) and the *rationes naturales* (study of physical realities, the realm of the concrete created reality, analogies to which theology appeals to show the distinction of persons). In the realm of natural things, Gilbert highlights Boethius's distinction between abstract forms *(quo est)* and the concrete object *(quod est)*; so, on this basis, he affirms an analogous distinction in God. Without introducing a veritable real difference in God, Gilbert tends to attribute a certain objective value to our modes of knowledge (grasping of the object, then knowledge of the form), or, rather, he fails to distinguish the divine reality from what comes under our knowledge of God (starting from created realities).

Such a "realism of knowledge," as one could call it and which closely associated the logical and ontological orders, provoked a vigorous reaction from numerous theologians, particularly St. Bernard of Clairvaux, although St. Bernard did not really do justice to Gilbert's thought when he accused him of dividing God, that is, of placing a difference between *God* and *the divine essence (Deus et divinitas)*, and of introducing a similar difference between the divine person and the property (for example, the person of the Father and his relational property of Fatherhood). Such is the first error imputed to Gilbert and condemned by his adversaries at the Council of Reims (or at its end) in 1148. As a matter of fact, this censure concerns Gilbert's disciples more than the Master's own thought.[32] Without condemning Gilbert, Pope Eugenius III nevertheless made

---

[32] André Hayen, "Le concile de Reims et l'erreur théologique de Gilbert de la Porrée," *Archives d'Histoire Doctrinale et Littéraire du Moyen Âge* 10–11 (1936): pp. 29–102; cf. the profession of faith opposed by St. Bernard (ibid., p. 44): "Credimus simplicem naturam diuinitatis *esse* Deum, nec aliquo sensu catholico posse negari, quin diuinitas sit Deus, et Deus diuinitas . . . Credimus solum Deum Patrem, Filium et Spiritum Sanctum eternum *esse*, nec aliquas omnino *res* siue relationes, siue proprietates, siue singularitates uel unitates dicantur, et huiusmodi alia, in Deo, et *esse* ab eterno, que non sint Deus." So Bernard affirms that whatever is in God is God Himself. See also Heinrich Denzinger, *Enchiridion symbolorum definitionum et declarationum de rebus fidei et morum*, n. 745.

a doctrinal decision: "As regards the first [chapter] only, the Roman Pontiff defined that no reasoning should make a division between nature and person in theology, and that God *(Deus)* should be called divine essence *(divina essentia)* not only according to the sense of the ablative but also according to the sense of the nominative."[33] Henceforth, the divine simplicity is imperative for all scholastic theologians: absolute identity of God and the divine essence; identity of the person and the essence; identity of the person (the Father) and the relational property of this person (Fatherhood).

As regards relation, Gilbert continues the heritage of Boethius for whom in God "substance preserves the [unity], relation introduces a multiple element in the Trinity *(substantia continent unitatem, relatio multiplicat trinitatem)*. Hence only terms belonging to relation may be applied singly to each."[34] In order to preserve the oneness of the divine essence, which is absolutely identical in each person, Gilbert explains that relation is not attributed *secundum rem*: It does not modify the essence, it is not something *(aliquid)* but a relationship with something *(ad aliquid)*. We do not contrast the divine persons by reason of their essence, rather they are distinguished by relation, which Gilbert declares is "extrinsic" or "affixed from the outside" *(extrinsecus affixa)*.[35] Here, the term "extrinsic" means that relation is not a matter of the essential nature—that is, oneness—but of the nature of the distinction among the persons, which does not affect the essential oneness. This extrinsic character rests upon a comparison with the makeup of a natural individual *(rationes naturales)*. Here again Gilbert is reproached for introducing a division in God by making a distinction between the divine

---

33 A. Hayen, "Le concile de Reims," pp. 40–41; H. Denzinger, *Enchiridion symbolorum,* n. 746.

34 Boethius, *De Trinitate,* ch. 5 6 (English translation: Boethius, *The Theological Tractates,* trans. Hugh F. Stewart and E. K. Rand [Cambridge, MA: Harvard University Press, 1973]).

35 Gilbert de la Porrée, *Expositio in Boecii de Trinitate* I. 5, n. 43 (*The Commentaries on Boethius by Gilbert of Poitiers,* ed. Nikolaus M. Häring [Toronto: Pontifical Institute of Medieval Studies, 1966], p. 148); cf., ibid., II, 1, n. 37 (pp. 170–71). For a general survey and a commentary on the texts, see M. E. Williams, *The Teaching of Gilbert Porreta,* pp. 64–72.

essence and the personal relations, to the detriment of the person's simplicity. Whatever its historical relevance, this reproach sets up the scholastic form of "Porretanism" as the classic example of the Trinitarian theology that Peter Lombard characterizes as heretical in his *Sentences*.[36] It runs through the whole of theological literature on the Trinity from the twelfth to the fourteenth centuries and, consequently, determines almost without exception theological reflection on the relationship between essence and personal properties, that is, on oneness and threeness in God.

Peter Lombard and Joachim of Fiore

Another misunderstanding helped to clarify the relationship between the Trinity and the oneness of God. It was the controversy around Joachim of Fiore (†1202) regarding the relationship of the three persons with the substance of God, the divine *res*. The debate has to do with the accusations Joachim directed at Peter Lombard on this point. In his *Sententiae,* the definitive version of which dates from the years 1155–58, Peter Lombard adopted a position drastically different from Roscellinus's, which was explained above. Peter Lombard affirms, no doubt against Gilbert de la Porrée, the absolute prerogatives of God's oneness: God the Trinity is "a single and unique supreme reality" *(una summa res).*[37] Since the divine essence is this *una et summa res,* Peter Lombard refuses to accept formulas like: "the Father begets the divine essence," "the divine essence begets the Son." Since the divine essence or substance is the very reality of God the Trinity, Peter Lombard thinks that we cannot speak of this essence as generating or being generated or proceeding: That would mean that the essence begets itself, that is, that God the Trinity begets himself. It does not belong to the essence or substance but to the person to be the object of generation or proceeding.[38]

---

[36] Peter Lombard, *Sententiae* I, d. 33, ch. 1 (t. I/2, pp. 242–43). Peter Lombard seems to have taken part in a consistory that Eugenius III convoked at Paris in 1247 to examine Gilbert's teaching; in a harsh judgment, he took the side of St. Bernard (cf. the *"Prolegomena,"* vol. I/1, pp. 28*–30*).

[37] *Sententiae* I, d. 25, ch. 2, n. 5 (t. I/2, p. 194, with the note on this n. 5).

[38] Ibid., d. 5, ch. 1 (pp. 80–87).

This understanding of the three persons as *una res* that does not beget and is not begotten aroused the profound incomprehension and opposition of Joachim of Fiore. Attached to other traditional formulas that use the word "substance" or "essence" to mean person or hypostasis, Joachim rejects the terminology that is the rule with Peter Lombard. Since Joachim does not grasp Lombard's analysis, which distinguishes the *modi loquendi* (generation is not attributed to the substance but to the person of this substance), he cannot accept a "*summa res* that does not beget, is not begotten, and does not proceed." In his eyes such a *summa res* would constitute a fourth reality next to the *res generans,* the *res genita,* and the *res procedens* (Father, Son, and Holy Spirit). For Joachim, Peter Lombard thus expounds a "quaternity" in God, in a synthesis of Sabellianism and Arianism together.[39] Witness to a monastic wisdom opposed to the new learning of the doctors, attached to traditional formulas, and not grasping the analysis of language that Peter Lombard made use of, Joachim did not understand Lombard. The Fourth Lateran Council vigorously challenged his interpretation of Peter Lombard: The Council condemned the opuscule in which Joachim formulated his accusation of heresy against Peter Lombard, and accuses Joachim— not without another misunderstanding—of conceiving the divine oneness as a collective unity *("unitatem . . . quasi collectivam"),* in the way several men are a single people.[40]

---

[39] Joachim's *libellus* or *tractatus (De unitate seu essentia trinitatis),* which the Fourth Lateran Council called into question, is lost or, rather, has never been found. A text certainly by Joachim explicitly mentions this accusation of "quaternity" directed at Peter Lombard; this occurs in the work *De vita Sancti Benedicti et de officio divino secundum eius doctrinam;* see the edition of Cipriano Baraut, *Analecta Sacra Tarraconensia,* vol. 24 (Barcelona: Biblioteca Balmes, 1951), pp. 76–77: "Abolita primo impietate Sabelii, qui personas negavit, secundo pravitate Arii, qui unitatem scidit, tertio blasphemia Petri, qui unitatem a Trinitate divi dens, quaternitatem inducit." We find the whole case history, with numerous texts and the aim of clarifying Joachim's thought through use of the opuscule *Confessio trinitatis,* in Axel Mehlmann, *De unitate trinitatis: Forschungen und Dokumente zur Trinitätstheologie Joachims von Fiore im Zusammenhang mit senem verschollenen Traktat gegen Petrus Lombardus* (Diss. Freiburg im Breisgau, 1991).

[40] *Decrees of the Ecumenical Councils,* 2 vols., ed. Norman P. Tanner (Washington, DC: Georgetown University Press, 1990), vol. 1, pp. 231–33.

As a consequence, the Council proclaims a profession of faith
cum Petro (i.e., with Peter Lombard) in the unique divine *res* that
does not beget, is not begotten, and does not proceed since each of
the persons is this divine reality. The intervention of Lateran IV
bears witness to the acceptance of a very vivid expression of the
divine oneness in which the three persons are seen as a unique *res* to
which we cannot attribute any distinct notional act since this *res* is
the Trinity. In the wake of Lateran IV, most thirteenth-century theologians would adopt this conception of the oneness of the divine
res,[41] firmly putting aside the attempt to conceive of Trinitarian
oneness through a social or collective representation.

The Rejection of Trinitarian Monotheism by the Cathars

We know of medieval Christianity's missionary debate with Islam,
starting with Peter the Venerable. Faced with the accusation of
"tritheism," Christian theologians in this debate were led to present
the Trinitarian faith in the framework of a strict monotheism (the
three persons are not three gods but a single God), as, for example,
Thomas Aquinas bears witness.[42] The affirmation of the Trinitarian
oneness is also at work within Christendom, with the Cathars' rejection of this doctrine in the background. As a rule, twelfth- and thirteenth-century Catharism diluted monotheism with dualism and
rejected the consubstantiality or equality of the Father, Son, and
Holy Spirit. The Trinitarian thought of the Catharist movement was

---

[41] As an exception, we find some authors who reject the position of Lateran IV:
see Fiona Robb, "A Late Thirteenth Century Attack on the Fourth Lateran
Council: The *Liber contra Lombardum* and Contemporary Debates on the
Trinity," *Recherches de Théologie Ancienne et Médiévale* 62 (1995): pp. 110–44.
For thirteenth-century scholastic reactions regarding Joachim, see Giovanni
Di Napoli, "Gioachino da Fiore e Pietro Lombardo," *Rivista di Filosofia Neo-
scolastica* 71 (1979): pp. 621–85, especially pp. 661–74.

[42] Thomas wrote a treatise addressed to a missionary confronted with Islam in
Syria, who asked him for arguments for preaching: Saint Thomas d'Aquin, *Les
raisons de la foi,* Introduction, traduction et notes par Gilles Emery (Paris:
Cerf, 1999). See also Joseph Kenny, "Saint Thomas Aquinas: Reasons for the
Faith Against Muslim Objections (and one objection of the Greeks and Arme-
nians) to the Cantor of Antioch," *Islamochristiana* 22 (1996): pp. 31–52.

complicated and diverse. The Dominican Moneta of Cremona distinguishes in his monumental *Summa against the Cathars and Waldensians,* written around 1241, two main doctrinal groups among the Cathars: the radical dualists, who thought of the Son and Holy Spirit as creatures; and the mitigated dualists, who held to the divinity of the Father, Son, and Holy Spirit, but in a subordinating manner (the Son being inferior to the Father, and the Holy Spirit inferior to the Son).[43] The Catharist texts seem to reveal still other currents: denial of the Trinity and modalism (the Trinity begins with the birth of Jesus, the Son and the Holy Spirit will be reabsorbed into the divine oneness at the end of time). In any case, the oneness of essence of the three persons appears unthinkable for Catharism.[44]

In this context, Catholic authors strive in particular to showcase the consubstantiality of the Father and of the Son, as well as the full divinity of the person of the Holy Spirit. If we take into account the impact of the Catharist question on the mission of the Church and on the theology related to it, reflection in light of dualism and the denial of the Trinity (neo-Arianism or subordinationism) will lead to putting divine oneness at the forefront of Catholic doctrine, the perfect consubstantiality of the three persons who are a single God, *bona Trinitas.* We have a good example of this in the profession of faith, *Firmiter credimus,* of Lateran IV, which, reacting to Catharism, puts the accent clearly on the oneness of God the Creator ("the one principle of all things"), as well as on the oneness and consubstantiality of the Trinity ("three persons but one absolutely simple essence, substance or nature").[45]

---

[43] Moneta Cremonensis, *Adversus Catharos et Valdenses libri quinque,* ed. Thomas Augustinus Ricchinius (Rome: Ex typographia Palladis, 1743 [Reprint Ridgewood, Greg Riss, 1966]), lib. I, c. I, p. 4 and 6; lib. III, c. III, pars I, pp. 234 and 237–38; lib. III, c. V, pp. 265 and 268. For the worth of Moneta's oral and written documentation, see Gerhard Rottenwöhrer, *Der Katharismus,* vol. 1/1 (Bad Honnef: Bock und Herchen, 1982), pp 59–63. See also the *Summa de Catharis* of the convert, Raynerius Sacconi, who, around 1250, recounts the history of the Cathars: Francis Sanjek, "Raynerius Sacconi, O.P., *Summa de Catharis,*" *Archivum Fratrum Praedicatorum* 44 (1974): pp. 31–60, especially p. 51.

[44] Georg Schmitz-Valckenberg, *Grundlehren katharischer Sekten des 13. Jahrhunderts* (Munich: Schöningh, 1971), pp. 136–43 and 152–57.

[45] *Decrees of the Ecumenical Councils,* vol. 1, p. 230.

Threeness and Oneness: Paths of Knowledge

In twelfth- and thirteenth-century scholastic thinking, the relationship between threeness and oneness crystallizes around two main questions: first, our knowledge of the Trinity; and, second, the articulation of person and of divine essence around the notion of relation. Concerning the first question, we can distinguish three kinds of responses in scholastic theology.

From Oneness to the Trinity: The "Necessary Reasons"

An important theological current that ran through twelfth- and thirteenth-century thinking sought to demonstrate the faith in the Trinity by means of arguments imposed by reason, starting from the divine oneness or from the attributes connected to the oneness of God. In his *Monologion* (1076), St. Anselm inaugurates the way of such "necessary reasons." As we know, Anselm first establishes the necessary existence of God the Creator. However, his reflection does not stop at this theistic perspective. Beginning with chapters 9 to 12 of the *Monologion,* Anselm perceives an exemplary form *(forma)* of the things to be created, an archetypical form existing in the mind of the Creator: a word *(locutio)* in God's mind. In this way, Anselm is led to detect the person of the Word in a dialectical discovery within the *unum aliquid* of chapters 1 to 4. Reflection on the unique Creator thus leads to the elucidation of a *locutio rerum,* the eternal Word, in which God the Creator speaks himself and knows himself, and through which He speaks creatures (chapters 32 to 35). At a later stage, Anselm extends his reflection to include the Holy Spirit: In the supreme Spirit, where he notes the mutual relationship of Father and Son, he detects the love of self that, as reason rightly holds, this Spirit must have for himself and which appears as the mutual love of the Father and the Son (chapters 49 to 58).

Starting with a monotheistic affirmation in this fashion, Anselm elaborates an explanation of the Trinity on the basis of the properties of God-Spirit (Word and Love). This reflection, in conformity with the request that Anselm had received and which he recalls in his *Prologue,* intends "nothing whatsoever to be argued on the basis of the authority of Scripture, but the constraints of reason concisely to prove, and the clarity of truth clearly to show, in the plain style, with everyday arguments, and down-to-earth dialectic, the conclusions of distinct investigations."[46] Anselm's thinking works from within the faith, a thinking he views as a "meditation on the meaning of the faith" rather than as a philosophical elaboration on the Trinity.[47] Nevertheless, he gives an explanation of Trinitarian faith starting with a consideration of the divine oneness with reasons that "reach their conclusion necessarily, as it were *(quasi necessarium)."*[48] Thus Anselm transmits to the scholastics a theological plan of rational reflection that discovers the threeness in the oneness.

Above were mentioned Abelard's theses, which, in another kind of reflection, attributes a discovery of the Trinity to philosophers, more precisely to the Platonists; Abelard recognizes in natural reason a capacity to raise itself toward the Trinitarian mystery. Before getting to the grand syntheses of the thirteenth century, we must highlight an important step in the history of doctrine: Richard of St. Victor. In his *De Trinitate* (about 1170), whose major theme is the Trinity–oneness relationship, the Master of St. Victor takes a methodological approach that is comparable to Anselm's. Within a knowledge derived from faith, Richard aims at presenting "not only plausible but necessary reasons *(necessarias rationes)"* in order to show the truth of the faith. His plan, which proceeds from faith to knowledge *(de fide ad cognitionem),* is summed up in the Prologue: "Let us try . . . to understand by reason what we believe *(comprehendere*

---

46 Anselm of Canterbury, *The Major Works,* ed. Brian Davies and Gillian R. Evans (Oxford/New York: Oxford University Press, 1998), p. 5.

47 In the *Prooemium of the Proslogion,* Anselm describes the plan of the *Monologion* in this way: "Exemplum meditandi de ratione fidei"; correlatively, the *Proslogion* follows the proposition of "faith seeking understanding *(fides quaerens intellectum)"* (ibid., pp. 82–83).

48 *Monologion* 1, ibid., p. 11. See Renato Perino, *La dottrina di S. Anselmo nel quadro nel suo metodo teologico e del suo concetto di Dio* (Rome: Herder, 1952); Olegario González, *Misterio Trinitario y existencia humana: Estudio histórico teológico en torno a San Buenaventura* (Madrid: Rialp, 1966), pp. 260–94; Paul Vignaux, "Nécessité des raisons dans le Monologion," *Revue des Sciences Philosophiques et Théologiques* 64 (1980): pp. 3–25.

ratione quod tenemus ex fide).[49] The reasons brought forth are not detached from the mystery of faith (Richard escapes the accusation of rationalism); these reasons, however, do not merely constitute motives of "convenience": They are rationally necessary because the truth they deal with is itself necessary.

In a search that joins the learning of the Schools with the contemplative wisdom of the cloister, Richard of St. Victor is convinced of the validity of this theological approach concerning the Trinity: "Since we are dealing with the exposition of necessary realities, I am absolutely persuaded that there are not only plausible but also necessary arguments *(necessaria argumenta)*."[50] The starting point of Richard's thinking lies in the concept of God as perfect sovereign Good: eternal Being who is the unique primordial substance. The movement from oneness to the Trinity is made by means of the notion of the good and, more precisely, by that of charity. Such are the grand theses of Book III of the *De Trinitate*: The fullness of bliss and the fullness of the divine glory likewise postulate a plurality of persons, just as does the fullness of charity. It is in this construct that Richard lays out his conception of *condignus* and *condilectus*. With the same rigor, he strives to establish the necessary equality of the three persons in oneness, and so shows that there can be but three persons in the one divine nature (Book V). This plan of articulating the oneness and the threeness in a logical, metaphysical, contemplative, and esthetic exercise of reason informed by faith will constitute a lasting fascination in scholastic thought, as St. Bonaventure magnificently illustrates.

Bonaventure of Bagnoregio (†1274) offers the first great synthesis of the elucidation of the oneness–threeness relationship in the tra-

---

[49] Richard of Saint Victor, *De Trinitate,* ed. Gaston Salet (Paris: Cerf, 1999), p. 55.

[50] Ibid., I, IV (pp. 70–71). For the exposition of the Trinitarian faith by means of the resources of reason in Richard (necessary reasons), see O. González, *Misterio trinitario y existencia humana,* pp. 263–95; Nico Den Bok, *Communicating the Most High: A Systematic Study of Person and Trinity in the Theology of Richard of St. Victor* (Paris/Turnhout: Brepols, 1996), pp. 151–201. On the central place of charity in this Trinitarian elaboration, see Pierluigi Cacciapuoti, *"Deus existentia amoris": Teologia della carità e teologia della Trinità negli scritti di Riccardo di San Vittore* (Paris/Turnhout: Brepols, 1998).

dition of Augustine, Anselm, and Richard, to which from now on the Dionysian heritage will be joined. Bonaventure's Franciscan masters had already put forward the notion of the Good to account for threeness in oneness. In the *Summa fratris Alexandri,* which Bonaventure draws on, sovereign goodness provides the reason for "number" in God: God's goodness is the motive for the plurality of persons insofar as it belongs to goodness to communicate itself (following the axiom developed in the *Divine Names* of Pseudo-Dionysius). Since God's goodness is perfect, its communication will be perfect, and this perfection consists in transmitting the whole of the divine substance by way of nature (the generation of the Son) and will (the spiration of the Holy Spirit).[51] In his commentary on the *Sentences* (about 1250), Bonaventure combines the Dionysian medieval tradition with the legacy of Anselm and Richard by developing "necessary reasons" around the following themes.[52]

First, there is the motif of beatitude, goodness, charity, and joy (themes stemming from Richard of St. Victor). Each of these divine attributes leads us to suppose a plurality of persons since their perfection or fullness cannot be realized in a solitary mode; the perfection of beatitude, et cetera, entails a communication and a plurality in God. The theme of goodness in particular runs through this work of Bonaventure, who explains in his homilies on the *Hexaemeron,* for example, that if the Father did not pour himself out fully by begetting a Son equal to himself, he would not be perfect for his goodness would not communicate itself in the highest mode of intrinsic diffusion (we could then conceive of something better and greater than the Father, which is an Anselmian argument).[53] If there were no Trinity

---

[51] *Summa fratris Alexandri,* Book I, p. 1, inq. 2, tract. un., q. 3, c. 5 (Alexander of Hales, *Summa Theologica,* vol. 1 [Quaracchi: Editiones Collegii S. Bonaventurae ad Claras Aquas, 1924], #317).

[52] Bonaventure, I *Sent.,* d. 2, a. un., q. 2, fund. 1–4 (*Opera omnia,* vol. 1 [Quaracchi: Ed. Collegii S. Bonaventurae, 1882], 53). On these necessary reasons in Bonaventure's Trinitarian theology, see O. González, *Misterio trinitario y existencia humana,* pp. 99–505; for the Trinitarian theme of goodness and primacy, see G. Emery, *La Trinité créatrice,* pp. 173–84.

[53] Bonaventure, *Hexaemeron* XI, 11 (*Opera omnia,* vol. 5 [Quaracchi: Ed. Collegii S. Bonaventurae, 1891], pp. 381–82).

of persons, "God would not be the highest Good because he would not pour himself out completely."[54]

Second, there is the theme of perfection. The highest perfection consists in producing a being of the same nature; this "multiplication" cannot take place through an otherness of essence in God since the divine essence is necessarily unique. Therefore it takes place through an otherness of consubstantial persons.

The third theme is that of simplicity. It comes down to simplicity, observes Bonaventure, that one nature exists in several supposits (the case with the universal), but it is through a fault in simplicity that nature multiplies these supposits; therefore the perfection of the divine simplicity leads us to recognize in it a plurality of consubstantial supposits.

Finally, there is the theme of primacy. For Bonaventure, who develops here a central insight of his metaphysics, primacy *(primitas)* designates the fullness of the source; if a reality is primary, it is because of this primacy that it is the source of other realities *(quia primum, ideo principium)*.[55] Primacy designates the fecundity and the "well-springness" *(fontalitas)* of primordial reality. For the Franciscan Master, it is in virtue of this principle that the unbegetability of the Father (the Father is "without principle") designates in positive fashion his "fullness as source" *(plenitudo fontalis)*. In the background of this principle, we recognize the Platonic theme of the universal exemplarity of the One, as well as Aristotle's reflection on the cause of truth.[56] Bonaventure's axiom of primacy gives rise to a two-stage reflection. First of all, this axiom concerns the essential oneness of God (being absolutely first, God is the Creator); Bonaventure then applies it to the personal plurality around the person of the Father: "The divine essence, which is primary, is the principle of the other

[54] Bonaventure, *Itinerarium mentis in Deum,* ch. VI, 1–2 (*Opera omnia,* vol. 5, pp. 310–11. English translation: *St. Bonaventure's Itinerarium mentis in Deum,* trans. Philotheus Boehner (St. Bonaventure, NY: Franciscan Institute, 1956, reprinted 1998), pp. 89–91.

[55] Bonaventure, I *Sent.,* d. 7, a. un., q. 2, concl.; d. 27, p. 1, a. un., q. 2, ad 3 (*Opera omnia,* vol. 1, pp. 139 and 470).

[56] Aristotle, *Metaphysics* II (a), 993b24–994a1; cf. Bonaventure, II *Sent.,* d. 3, p. 1, a. 1, q. 2, fund. 2 (*Opera omnia,* vol. 2, 94).

essences; thus, in the same way, the person of the Father, since it is primary (the Father does not come forth from any other) is the principle and possesses fecundity toward the persons." Here Bonaventure's thought introduces the idea of God's supreme actuality *(summa actualitas)*. In God there is nothing in a state of potency; what is in God exists in a perfect state of act; there is no potentiality in God but a supereminent actualization of every perfection.[57] This allows him to conclude: "In God, this fecundity relative to God can only exist in act; it is therefore necessary *(necese est)* to posit a plurality of persons."[58]

The primacy theme, whose importance cannot be underestimated, runs through Bonaventure's whole work. Together with goodness, primacy constitutes in Bonaventure the pivot of the oneness–threeness articulation. This characteristic trait of Bonaventuran metaphysics shows goodness, in the words of Théodore de Régnon, as the expansibility by virtue of which the supreme oneness is a primacy. He likewise grounds God's actions (creation and salvation) in the transcendent communication of the divine life: the intra-Trinitarian wellspringness *(fontalitas)* is the source of God's *fontalitas* toward his creatures.[59]

So, for Bonaventure, the primacy of the supreme Principle (God) includes the Trinity *(primitas . . . includit trinitatem)*: God is threeness from the very fact that He is first. Bonaventure's theological plan is not limited to establishing the noncontradiction or the harmony between oneness and threeness, but it aims at showing that a right consideration of the divine oneness necessarily entails the Trinitarian affirmation: The affirmation of the Trinity is "included" in the affirmation of the oneness, and it is theology's task to do a kind of "disenvelopment" to bring out the richness of this Trinitarian oneness using

---

[57] On this theme, see Klaus Obenauer, *Summa Actualitas: Zum Verhältnis von Einheit und Verschiedenheit in der Dreieinigkeitslehre des heiligen Bonaventura* (Frankfurt am Main: Lang, 1996).

[58] Bonaventure, I *Sent.,* d. 2, a. un., q. 2, fund. 4 *(Opera omnia,* vol. 1, p. 53).

[59] Bonaventure, *Disputed Questions on the Mystery of the Trinity,* q. 8, ad 7 *(Opera omnia,* vol. 5, p. 115). This question 8 is entirely devoted to the Primacy–Trinity articulation. For the notion of *primitas,* see O. González, *Misterio trinitario y existencia humana,* pp. 143–62; Luc Mathieu, *La Trinité créatrice d'après S. Bonaventure* (Paris: Ed. Franciscaines, 1992), pp. 41–56 and 125–28.

the resources of reason. Such is the fundamental aim of his eight *Disputed Questions on the Mystery of the Trinity*. Thus, Bonaventure can explain: "We have to posit in God a plurality of persons, as the Faith teaches and *as the reasons put forth show.*" Having evoked the simplicity and primacy of God, he concludes: "With these conditions in mind, it is necessary to posit a plurality of persons."[60] To be sure, Bonaventure excludes the possibility that philosophers could have known the Trinity through the resources of natural reason alone. He also acknowledges that for non-Christians the affirmation of a Trinitarian oneness presents a contradiction.[61] An understanding that discovers and posits the Trinity on the basis of unity is "an understanding elevated by faith."[62] It is therefore not a question of a philosophical demonstration of the Trinity, but rather of what we might call "reasons for the faith." We should add that Bonaventure does not make the clear distinction between the order of faith and that of reason such as we see, for example, in Thomas Aquinas. Doubtless, we can characterize this approach, which initiated a whole school of thought, as a kind of rational knowledge at the heart of a mystical experience. Bonaventure bears witness to the persistence of a theology that puts forward a contemplative elevation of the mind, with its rational resources (necessity), toward the object of faith.

This search for necessary reasons postulating the Trinity in the name of a certain understanding of the divine oneness does not end with Bonaventure. Other authors will pursue it at the end of the thirteenth century and into the fourteenth century. Here we can take by way of example the thought of Henry of Ghent ([†]1293). His Trinitarian theology, founded on the Thomistic doctrine of the Word and of Love, follows in the footsteps of Thomas Aquinas rather than in those of Bonaventure. Nonetheless, he succeeds in adapting Bonventure's thesis. For Henry, it is through faith that we affirm the generation of

[60] Bonaventure, I *Sent.*, d. 2, a. un., q. 2, sol. (*Opera omnia*, vol. 1, p. 54).

[61] Bonaventure, *Disputed Questions on the Mystery of the Trinity*, q. 2, a. 2, sol. (*Opera omnia*, vol. 5, p. 65).

[62] Bonaventure, *Hexaëmeron* XI, 5 (*Opera omnia*, vol. 5, p. 381); cf. *Disputed Questions on the Mystery of the Trinity*, q. 2, a. 2, sol.: "anima aliquatenus per fidem purgata et elevata" (*Opera omnia*, vol. 5, p. 65).

the Word and the procession of Love in God. Nevertheless, after faith has made the Trinity known to us, we can *prove its necessity* by rational arguments.[63] Indeed, Henry holds that the perfection of intellectual activity in God necessarily demands the fruitful "production" of a Word; likewise, the perfection of the willing and loving activity in God demands the spiration of the Holy Spirit. The perfection of God's spiritual activity necessarily entails the personal distinction of the Father, his Word, and his Love; this reason can establish.[64]

Quite logically, Henry draws the following extraordinary conclusion: If there had only been the essential intelligence and will of the one God (i.e., oneness without threeness), God could not have created the world with wisdom and freedom. The person of the Word, conceived as the manifestation and expression of the Father's knowledge, is required in order to grasp the creative act. In the same way, the person of the Spirit, conceived as the fruit of a surge of fruitful love, is required in order to perceive the creative activity of the divine will. The procession of the Son and the Spirit must *necessarily* be presupposed before creative activity.[65] This argument is not new, but the concrete form of its elaboration is original: It combines the Trinitarian doctrine of Thomas (doctrine of the Word and Love, creative causality of the Trinitarian processions) with Bonaventure's articulation of the oneness and threeness (necessity). Here we perceive that necessity affects just as much the oneness–Trinity relationship as the Trinity–creation relationship.

Threeness and Oneness:
Two Distinct Orders of Knowledge
Faced with this flow of "necessary reasons," other theologians make a clearer distinction between what is of faith and what constitutes

---

[63] Henry of Ghent, *Quodlibet* VI, q. 2 (*Opera omnia,* vol. 10, ed. Gordon A. Wilson [Louvain/Leiden: Leuven University Press/Brill, 1987], 36): "Postquam tamen ex fide tenemus istas emanationes in Deo, ipsarum necessitatem in se manuductione rationis possumus probare."

[64] Ibid., VI, q. 1 (pp. 2–31); cf. ibid., VI, q. 2 (p. 36).

[65] Ibid., VI, q. 2 (pp. 33–40). In conclusion, Henry states: "Dicimus quod productio divinarum personarum necessario praecedit productionem creaturarum tamquam causa eorum" (p. 37).

the realm of rational research. It is to their credit that they devised
the thesis that most often won acceptance in subsequent theology.
The most characteristic example is without a doubt Thomas
Aquinas (†1274). For Aquinas, as for Bonaventure, philosophical
reason ("natural reason") is incapable of reaching a knowledge of
the Trinity. Philosophical (metaphysical) reasoning succeeds in
knowing God as the first cause of creatures; now, the creative
action is common to the three persons who act here in virtue of
their common essence; consequently, philosophical reason can only
attain to the attributes that belong to God by reason of his oneness
of essence.[66] Correlatively, it is only through faith that the believer
can perceive the way in which the divine persons, in virtue of their
properties, are distinctly involved in creative and salvific action.[67]
Pursuing his reflection, Thomas Aquinas does away with the "necessary reasons" that Bonaventure invoked to go from oneness to
the affirmation of the Trinity: "We must state without ambiguity
that there is in God a plurality of supposits or persons in the oneness of the essence, *not because of reasons put forward that do not
reach a conclusion with necessity,* but because of the truth of the
faith."[68] Bonaventure's reasoning seems to him to be a pious
rationalism that endangers the faith by wanting to prove too much,
for it takes away from the dignity of the faith. For Thomas, it is
only on the basis of revelation in salvation history that we can recognize a Trinity in oneness.[69] Theological arguments (the famous
Trinitarian analogies) only constitute probable arguments, indications, or adaptations that allow believers exercising reason to show
what we hold on faith but without any compelling necessity.[70]
These analogies, however, make manifest that what is proposed to
our faith is not impossible, and they show that arguments against
the faith can be refuted (such arguments against the Trinity are not

---

[66] Thomas Aquinas, *Summa theologiae* I, q. 32, a. 1 (Rome: Ed. Paulinae 1988),
pp. 162–64.

[67] This, according to Thomas Aquinas, is the "motive" of the revelation of the
Trinity: To understand that creation is a Trinitarian work and that the action
and gift of the divine persons accomplish our salvation (*ST* I, q. 32, a. 1, ad 3).

[68] Thomas Aquinas, I *Sent.,* d. 2, q. 1, a. 4, sol., p. 74.

[69] Thomas Aquinas, *ST* I, q. 32, a. 1.

[70] Thomas Aquinas, I *Sent.,* d. 3, q. 1, a. 4, ad 3 *(adaptationes quaedam)*; *ST*
II–II, q. 1, a. 5, ad 2 *(persuasiones quaedam).*

compelling). For this reason, Aquinas makes a fundamental methodological distinction in the consideration of oneness and threeness. Effectively, Trinitarian epistemology involves two distinct orders of knowledge: that which concerns the divine essence (oneness), which natural reason can reach to a certain extent, and that which concerns the distinction of persons (Trinity), to which only faith gives access.[71] The articulation of the two orders is assured by analogies in a reflection of which faith is the principle (Word, Love, relation, person).

Threeness and Oneness:
Two Separate Orders of Knowledge

Directly opposed to Bonaventure's theses, a third current breaks the connection between threeness and oneness in the order of knowledge. This extreme position is well illustrated by Durandus of Saint-Pourçain (†1334), the "Modern Doctor" who was Lector of the Papal Court in Avignon. Durandus bears witness to a new stage of thinking that dissociates two ways of knowing: On the one hand, science, and on the other, authority. Faith and theology fall under authority and not science. For Durandus, an article of faith is defined precisely by its non-demonstrability and its unscientific nature. Reacting against the epistemology of Thomas Aquinas, he brushes aside the validity of analogies to illustrate the Trinitarian mystery (Word and Love). For Thomas, Christian theology cannot prove the faith, but it can show that the rational arguments put forward against the faith are not strictly imperative. For Durandus, there is no way to establish rationally that belief in the Trinity does not contain anything impossible. Reason is incapable of strictly disproving that the doctrine of the Trinity does not contain contradictions. Also, when he confronts objections against the existence of a Trinity in oneness, Durandus simply offers no response: Such a project would be useless by definition. Durandus of Saint-Pourçain thus bears witness to the shift in perspective

---

[71] Hence the *Summa theologiae*'s treatise *de Deo* has three parts: first, what concerns the oneness of essence; second, what concerns the distinction of persons; and, third, what concerns the procession of creatures *a Deo* (*ST* I, q. 2, prol.).

that is at work in the fourteenth century: A gulf opens between the theological order and the philosophical order, bringing with it an isolation of faith and theology (authority) when confronted with the prerogatives of reason (science).[72]

Thus we are in the presence of three kinds of epistemology concerning the oneness–threeness relationship. They correspond to three different attitudes of discussion on the matter, either on the philosophical level or on the missionary level. First, there is the reasoning that aims at establishing rationally *(rationes necessariae)* the Christian belief in the Trinity (the missionary aspect could be illustrated by Raymond Martin or Raymond Lull). Second, there is a "defensive" apologetic reasoning that does not appeal to necessary reasons to affirm the Trinitarian faith, but which thinks itself capable, on the rational level, of disproving arguments advanced against belief in the Trinity (Thomas Aquinas).[73] Third, we find an attitude that abandons this apologetic intellectual project by separating the order of the divine oneness from the order of the Trinity (Durandus of Saint-Pourçain).

The Divine Essence (Oneness) and the Persons (Threeness)

With the scholastics, the articulation of the divine oneness and of the Trinity takes place in the discussion, at the speculative level, on the relationship between the divine essence and the persons. The common position, whose precision resulted from the debate on the theses of Gilbert de la Porrée, is well illustrated by Peter Lombard in the middle of the twelfth century: Each person, taken by himself, is absolutely and really identical with the divine essence, and the three persons are one and the same divine essence or substance *(una summa res)*.[74] The threeness of persons is affirmed within a very

---

[72] See Gilles Emery, "Dieu, la foi et la théologie chez Durand de Saint-Pourçain," *Revue thomiste* 99 (1999): pp. 659–99.

[73] Vincent Serverat, "*L'irrisio fidei*. Encore sur Raymond Lulle et Thomas d'Aquin," *RT* 90 (1990): pp. 436–48.

[74] Peter Lombard, *Sententiae,* Book I, d. 34, ch. 1–2 (pp. 246–51).

strict understanding of the divine oneness (monotheism). Afterwards, theologians will try to establish a difference between the reality of God himself and our way of knowing, which entails a diversity of concepts. Person and essence are identical in God's reality, but the *concepts* of person and essence are different. We affirm, then, a "real identity" and a "distinction of reason" between the person and the essence.[75] Against "Porretanism" the scholastic masters of the thirteenth century did not fail, in general, to make clear that the relational property is not added to the essence *(extrinsecus affixa)*; the relational property is "nothing other" than the essence.[76]

The problematic Augustinian and anti-Porretan issues lead to the seeking of the ultimate articulation of the Trinity and oneness in the theory of relation. Thomas Aquinas's thought plays a decisive role here and will determine the subsequent discussion (it will provoke either agreement or critical reservation). Aquinas understands the divine person as a subsisting relation. More precisely, the concept of "divine person" signifies relation insofar as this relation is endowed with the consistency of a reality that subsists (i.e., relation as hypostasis).[77] If the Dominican Master can conceive of the person as a relation, it is because of his analysis of relation. Thomas's thought starts with the categorial conception of relation as an accident existing not "between" things but "in" things. Developing Aristotle's line of thought (*Categories* 7 and *Metaphysics* D, 15), Thomas Aquinas distinguishes two aspects of relation, as in each of the nine genera of Aristotelian accidents: first, the existence of the accident *(esse)*; and, second, the definition or proper nature of this accident *(ratio)*. As far as its *ratio* is concerned, relation presents a unique character among the accidents: It does not directly affect its subject, it is not an intrinsic determination of its subject, but is a pure relationship to another *(ad aliud)*. Relation has here an "ecstatic" character, a sort of metaphysical simplicity that allows its direct attribution to

---

[75] See for example Albert the Great, I *Sent.,* d. 34, a. 1–3 (*Opera omnia,* vol. 26, pp. 162–68).

[76] See for example Bonaventure, I *Sent.,* d. 33, a. 1, q. 2 (*Opera omnia,* vol. 1, pp. 574–76). Duns Scotus' formal distinction does not alter this oneness.

[77] Thomas Aquinas, *ST* I, q. 29, a. 4.

God. Yet as to its existence *(esse)*, relation, as one of the categories, possesses the mode of existence proper to accidents, that is, inherence in a subject (existence in and through another).

The application of this analysis to God is clear: As regards existence, the *esse* of the divine relation is the very being of the unique divine essence; under the aspect of its existence, relation is purely and simply identified with the unique being of God. As regards its definition or proper nature, relation is transposed in God as a pure relationship of "opposition" according to origin (fatherhood, filiation, procession). Under this second aspect, relation does not consist in a determination of the divine essence, but only in an interpersonal reference according to origin.[78]

Thus it is within the theme of relation that Thomas Aquinas arranges the question of the relationship between oneness and threeness. For Aquinas, the unique essence is not on one side and relation on the other. Everything comes together in relation, which comprises the element of personal distinction *(ratio)* and the element of the divine hypostatic subsistence *(esse)*. Here we see quite well that, contrary to what will become the common teaching of the Thomistic school, Thomas Aquinas does not make a division between a treatise "De Deo uno" and De Deo trino." Rather, in the analysis of relation he brings together the aspect of the common essence of the three persons (subsistence of the divine *esse*) and the aspect of the distinction of persons (relationship of origin). These two aspects together constitute the notion of the divine person. That is why priority is given neither to the essence nor to the mutual relationship, but instead to the *person* that unites these two dimensions.[79] For the same reason, the study of God's creative and salvific action in the world will have to take into account a twofold aspect: that of the divine essence (the three persons act in virtue of their one essence), but also of the personal property (each person acts according to his distinct property).[80]

---

[78] Ibid. Cf. *ST* I, q. 28, a. 2.

[79] For this analysis, see chapter 5 below; cf. Hans Christian Schmidbaur, *Personarum Trinitas: Die trinitarische Gotteslehre des heiligen Thomas von Aquin* (St. Ottilien: EOS Verlag, 1995).

[80] See for example Thomas Aquinas, I *Sent.,* d. 32, q. 1, a. 3.

Theological schools will diverge on the place we should give to relation in respect to origin (procession). In the analysis of the oneness–threeness relationship within the notion of "person," the theological movement stemming from Bonaventure will tend to stress the action of generation and procession, while the movement stemming from Thomas Aquinas stresses relation.[81] In like manner, the school of thought linked to Aquinas attributes the constitution of the divine person to relation, understood in its full sense according to the two aspects mentioned above; the followers of Bonaventure will retain the possibility of looking upon the divine person as constituted by an absolute rather than relational element (Duns Scotus).[82] Where the mystical tradition coming from Dionysius is emphasized in pronounced fashion (Eckhart), the One appears to present itself to experience as the core of the mystery, beyond the Trinity of persons; still we must qualify this judgment with Eckhart's own perspective, which looks at the relationship between God's oneness and man's union with God.[83] But the great majority of authors agree in finding in the notion of person the synthesis or convergence of the aspect of oneness and plurality in God.

Unity and Plurality: The Transcendentals

The elucidation of plurality within unity requires a final clarification. Roscellinus and Abelard faced the problem of "number" in God without succeeding in solving it satisfactorily. The solution will not be forthcoming except by recourse to the doctrine of the transcendentals. For the scholastic authors, who are generally quite attached to the divine oneness, there could be no question of a plurality that would prejudice the oneness of God. By this very fact, quantitative

---

[81] For a general survey. Michael Schmaus, *Der Liber propugnatorius des Thomas Anglicus und die Lehrunterschiede zwischen Thomas von Aquin und Duns Scotus,* II/1: *Die trinitarischen Lehrdifferenzen: Systematische Darstellung und historische Würdigung* (Münster: Aschendorff, 1930), pp. 385–589.

[82] Friedrich Wetter, *Die Trinitätslehre des Johannes Duns Scotus* (Münster: Aschendorff, 1967), pp. 283–342.

[83] Cf. Alain de Libera, "L'Un ou la Trinité? Sur un aspect trop connu de la théologie eckhartienne," *Revue des Sciences Religieuses* 70 (1996): pp. 31–47.

plurality has to be excluded (which Abelard had achieved by omitting numerical plurality). In the twelfth century, Peter Lombard attributes a purely negative significance to numbers (*one, two, three* persons): The expression "*one* God" excludes a plurality of gods; the expression "three persons" excludes the solitude of one person (modalism), and so on.[84] On this score, Lombard will be opposed by other masters maintaining, in a more common fashion, the positive function of these "numbers" and not merely their negative significance. But how can we speak of "number" in God without destroying the oneness? In spite of the differences of Schools (affirmation–negation relationship, formal distinction), the scholastic solution that will dominate for a long time resides in the recourse to transcendental oneness,[85] which we can explain here with the thought of Thomas Aquinas.

Using the concepts inherited from Aristotle, Aquinas excludes a material plurality from God to keep a formal plurality in the order of the transcendentals and not in the quantitative order. The transcendental one is the one "convertible with being." The transcendental one signifies being in its undividedness: It adds nothing positive to being; rather it consists in the denial of a division (being is one in so far as it is undivided). The affirmation of the divine oneness thus consists in the denial of a division and in the affirmation of the very reality to which we attribute oneness: "The one that is convertible with being posits affirmatively being itself, but it adds nothing to being unless the denial of a division." "When we say, 'The [divine] essence is one,' the term 'one' signifies the essence in its undividedness; when we say, 'The person is one,' this attribute signifies the person in its undividedness."[86] Correlatively, Aquinas puts forward the new concept of "transcendental multitude" *(multitudo secundum quod est transcendens)* to account for the plurality of

---

[84] Peter Lombard, *Sententiae,* Book I, d. 24 (pp. 187–89).

[85] See for example Albert the Great, I *Sent.,* d. 24, a. 3 (*Opera omnia,* vol. 25, pp. 610–14).

[86] Thomas Aquinas, *Quaestiones disputatae de potentia,* q. 9, a. 7 (*Quaestiones disputatae,* ed. Pio Bazzi, vol. 2 [Turin: Marietti, 1965], 243) and *ST* I, q. 30, a. 3. On this question, see in particular Giovanni Ventimiglia, *Differenza e contraddizione* (Milan: Vita e Pensiero, 1997), pp. 191–245.

persons who are only one God. This transcendental multitude consists in the affirmation of the oneness of each thing within the multiplicity (oneness of each person), while adding that each person is
really distinct from the other persons (one person is not the
other).[87] The wholly original concept of *transcendental multitude* (a
concept that is truly nonsensical for a strict neo-Platonist) expresses,
through Aquinas's pen, a radical Christian novelty in understanding
the relations between the One and the Many. The introduction of
the multitude *(multitudo)* among the transcendentals clearly comes
as the expression of the eminent status of the *plurality* that the
Christian faith recognizes in God. In the sweep of this thesis,
Aquinas can express the eminently positive status of created plurality: Intra-Trinitarian relation (distinction) is the cause, the reason,
and the exemplar of distinction in creatures. The Trinitarian distinction is, for Aquinas, the cause not only of the distinction of creation
(distinction between God and the world), but also of the plurality
of creatures: "Relation in God surpasses in causality what in creatures is the principle of distinction; for it is through the procession
of distinct divine persons that the whole process of creatures as well
as the multiplication of creatures is caused."[88] With Thomas
Aquinas, medieval thought bears witness to an astounding effort to
promote plurality on the metaphysical plain, to wed Trinitarian theology to creation theology: Plurality receives the eminent status of a
transcendental, while Trinitarian relation exercises a creative causality that establishes created plurality and confers on it the value of an
expression of the Trinitarian mystery.

Conclusions

1. If we consider its general sweep, Latin scholasticism fundamentally constitutes a theology of Trinitarian oneness. The

---

[87] Thomas Aquinas, *De potentia,* q. 9, a. 7. Thus the transcendental multitude
consists in the affirmation of each reality as one and in a twofold negation
(undividedness of each person and mutual distinction of the persons).

[88] Thomas Aquinas, I *Sent.,* d. 26, q. 2, a. 2, ad 2; cf. G. Emery, *La Trinité créatrice,* pp. 445–54.

plurality of persons in God falls within a very strict monotheism, which the doctrinal debates and the ecclesiastical
context reinforce. This strict grasp of the divine oneness,
much to the fore in the consideration of the immanent Trinity, is not forsaken when the scholastics showcase the distinct
role of the persons in creation and salvation.

2. The threeness–oneness articulation is marked constantly by
   the apologetic project of "necessary reasons" and by discussion of it in debates. Even at the beginning of the fourteenth
   century, when a certain breach in the faith–reason harmony
   arose, epistemological questions remained at the core of
   scholastic reflection.

3. From its beginnings, scholasticism is characterized by remarkable progress in analyzing language, and by the use of important metaphysical resources to account for the oneness of the
   Trinity. The presence of biblical reflection remains important
   for the great twelfth- and thirteenth-century masters of theology (whose primary task was to expound Sacred Scripture).
   But already the danger of a break between biblical reflection
   and speculative theology is felt when this latter would lose its
   contact with the reading of the Bible.

4. With Thomas Aquinas in particular, the threeness–oneness
   articulation is made through an analysis of relation and within the notion of *person,* which represents the height of theological thinking about God. Correlatively, plurality in the
   Trinity allows us to consider created plurality in a new way
   (transcendental multitude, creative causality of the Trinitarian distinction). This reflection on person, in Thomas
   Aquinas and in other authors, certainly represents the greatest contribution of scholastic theology to the oneness–
   threeness relationship.

CHAPTER TWO

Trinity and Creation:
The Trinitarian Principle of the Creation in the Commentaries of Albert the Great, Bonaventure, and Thomas Aquinas on the *Sentences*

RESEARCH INTO a Trinitarian doctrine of the Creation touches upon a number of overlapping fields of current interest in theology, as much in the domain of Trinitarian theology as in that of a Christian doctrine of Creation.[1] It is particularly concerned with a two-way link,[2] which carries implications defined concisely by Thomas Aquinas:

> The knowledge of the divine persons was necessary to us on two grounds. The first is to enable us to think rightly on the subject of the creation of things. . . . The second reason, and the principal one, is to give us a true notion of the salvation of mankind. . . .[3]

---

[1] Translation by Heather Buttery of "Trinité et création. Le principe trinitaire de la création dans les commentaires d'Albert le Grand, de Bonaventure et de Thomas d'Aquin sur les Sentences," *RSPT* 79 (1995): pp. 405–30. This contribution will reconsider certain aspects developed in my book: *La Trinité créatrice: Trinité et Création dans les commentaires aux Sentences de Thomas d'Aquin et de ses précurseurs Albert le Grand et Bonaventure* (Paris: Vrin, 1995).

[2] See for example the reflections offered by Hans Urs von Balthasar, "Création et Trinité," *Communio* 13 (1988): pp. 9–17; Giuseppe M. Salvati, "Dimensione trinitaria della creazione," in La creazione, *Dio, il cosmo, l'uomo,* ed. R. Gerardi (Roma: Studium, 1990), pp. 65–93; Martin Gelabert, "La creación a la luz del misterio trinitario," *Escritos del Vedat* 22 (1992): pp. 7–45.

[3] Thomas Aquinas, *ST* I, q. 32, a. 1, ad 3: "Cognitio divinarum personarum fuit necessaria nobis dupliciter. Uno modo, ad recte sentiendum de creatione

Faith in the Trinity enlightens our understanding of God's action in the world (creation, providence, incarnation, sanctification), and this action in turn brings in elements which are important in order for us to grasp the mystery of the Trinitarian God. In his commentary on the *Sentences,* his first theological synthesis,[4] Aquinas gives especial prominence to the creative causality of the divine persons, and in a general sense to the Trinitarian dimension of divine action *ad extra.*[5] This emphasis finds expression particularly in the following statement: "The procession of the persons is the cause and the reason (the model, the origin) for the procession of creatures."[6]

The systematic application of this affirmation (in the commentary on the first Book) was a novel feature, as was the underlying doctrinal synthesis: The statement follows on from several doctrinal points developed by Bonaventure and by Albert, revealing what was original in the young Thomas's Trinitarian thought as well as what he had inherited. The aim of this study is to sketch out the basic foundations and significance of the pronouncement, after an initial

---

rerum. . . . Alio modo, et principalius, ad recte sentiendum de salute generis humani. . . ."

[4] Thomas's teachings on the *Sentences* date very probably from the years 1252–54; the writing of the commentary *(Scriptum)* however extends beyond the timespan allotted to Thomas as bachelor of theology appointed to comment on the *Sentences:* see Jean-Pierre Torrell, *Saint Thomas Aquinas,* vol. 1, *The Person and His Work* (Washington, DC: The Catholic University of America Press, 1996), pp. 39–45 and 332.

[5] See especially the texts presented by Francesco Marinelli, *Personalismo trinitario nella storia della salvezza: Rapporti tra la SS.ma Trinità e le opere ad extra nello Scriptum super Sententiis di San Tommaso* (Rome/Paris: Pontificia Università Lateranense/Vrin, 1969); see also Francis Ruello, "Saint Thomas et Pierre Lombard. Les relations trinitaires et la structure du commentaire des Sentences de saint Thomas d'Aquin," *Studi tomistici* 1 (1974): 176–209; Gilfredo Marengo, *Trinità e creazione: Indagine sulla teologia di Tommaso d'Aquino* (Rome: Città Nuova, 1990), pp. 27–59; Idem, "Il principio trinitario della creazione nella teologia di Tommaso d'Aquino," *Studi tomistici* 44 (1991): 183–88.

[6] The same affirmation also appears in Thomas's later teaching, even though its significance and import had by then acquired other nuances of meaning (see especially *De potentia,* q. 10, a. 2, arg. 19, sed contra 2, and ad 19; *ST* I, q. 45, a. 6, sol. and ad 1; a. 7, ad 3).

identification of some of the groundwork which the young Thomas would have found in the writings of Albert and Bonaventure. Their teachings on the subject of the Trinitarian creation[7] will not be discussed in detail here, as this would require close textual reading of very many sources.[8] This study will be limited to an inquiry about the Trinitarian principle of creation in general, within the body of Trinitarian theology (the commentary on the first Book).

Trinity and Creation in the Commentary of Albert

Albert's commentary on the *Sentences*[9] does not devote a special section to the study of the Trinitarian creation. The theme appears to be scattered throughout various questions in the commentary, rather than addressed in a structured way, and we will only look at two of its most significant points: The creative causality of the procession of the divine persons, and then the understanding of this causality within the structure of the origin–return of creatures.

The Thesis of the Creative Causality of the Procession of the Divine Persons

The connection between the Trinity and creation is brought out with greatest significance in Albert's teaching on the subject of *order* and *principle,* evident as early as the general Prologue of his commentary. It is here, within the analysis of power as the principle of

---

7 Close analysis shows that Trinitarian faith has more significant repercussions for Thomas's treatise on creation than it does in the work of Albert or Bonaventure.

8 Such was the aim of the work mentioned above (footnote 1).

9 The exact date of Albert's arrival in Paris, where he was sent to read the *Sentences,* is subject to debate; it can probably be placed around 1243 or a little earlier. Albert became a master of theology in 1245, but the commentary was still being written after this: The fourth Book was not finished before 1249 in Cologne. For chronological information see especially Odon Lottin, "Problèmes concernant la 'Summa de creaturis' et le Commentaire des Sentences de saint Albert le Grand," *RTAM* 17 (1950): 319–28; James A. Weisheipl, "The Life and Works of St. Albert the Great," in *Albertus Magnus and the Sciences: Commemorative Essays 1980* (Toronto: Pontifical Institute of Mediaeval Studies, 1980), pp. 13–51. We will be following the text of the Borgnet edition, vol. 25ss.

action and in the analysis of the very name of *principle,* that Albert
formulates most clearly the causality of the Trinitarian processions
with regard to creation:

> Anselm says that the procession of the persons is the cause
> of the procession of creatures, as appears to be the case in
> this verse: *For he spoke, and it came to be; he commanded,*
> *and it stood firm,* etc. [Psalm 33:9 (32:9) and 148:5]; and
> in this: *By the word of the Lord the heavens were made*
> [Psalm 33:6 (32:6)]. And Augustine explains it thus: *He*
> *engendered the Word by whom all things were to be made.*
> Thus, since the cause is anterior to the effect caused, it
> appears that the power by which the persons proceed is
> anterior to the power of creating and operating. The same
> [teaching] is derived from John 1:3, *All things came into*
> *being through him.* It is therefore necessary to presuppose
> the Word and the power of the procession of the Word
> before all things.[10]

The aim of this argument is to posit the anteriority of "notional
power" (the power of engendering the Son and of spirating the
Holy Spirit) with regard to the power of creating and acting in the
world. Albert has already explained that the power of engendering
may be considered in two ways. As rooted in the essence, the power
is common to the three persons and concerns notional acts as much
as it does creation. If however we consider the acts themselves, the
power will have a proper character in the case of notional acts (only
the Father engenders his Son) and revert to the three divine persons
in common in the case of the creation (creation is an act of the three

---

[10] I *Sent.,* d. 20, a. 3, sed contra: "Anselmus dicit, quod processio personarum est
causa processionis creaturarum: sicut etiam patet in illo versu: *Ipse dixit, et*
facta sunt: ipse mandavit, et creata sunt (Ps 32: 9; Ps 148: 5): et illo, *Verbo*
Domini coeli firmati sunt, and so on. (Ps 32: 6). Quod exponens Augustinus,
dicit: *Verbum genuit in quo erat ut fieret:* cum ergo causa sit ante causatum,
videtur quod potentia qua procedunt personae, sit ante potentiam creandi et
operandi. Idem accipitur, Joan. 1: 3, *Omnia per ipsum facta sunt:* ergo necesse
est Verbum et potentiam processionis Verbi omnibus praesupponere." Albert's
response adopts this thesis as regards the power determined by the act.

persons).[11] Therefore, in addressing the divine acts, we should maintain the anteriority of the "notional" power in comparison with the power of creation. Albert establishes this anteriority by means of the causality of the procession of the persons with regard to the procession of creatures. It is thus the order of reality which allows the relevant concepts to be put into an organized structure: The cause is anterior to the effect caused, and the procession of the Word must be anterior to everything else.

The reader may have noticed, alongside the citation of John 1:3, the reference to the Augustinian exegesis of Psalm 148:5 (Psalm 32:9). This theological material clearly suggests the central position of the Word in Albert's Trinitarian doctrine of the creation. The note is struck right from the general Prologue of the commentary, which presents the subject matter of the *Sentences* arranged around the Son and Wisdom. Making use of the Augustinian theological material which Thomas was also to take up, Albert finds in the generation of the Word, the cause and the reason for the production of creatures, following the teaching of Augustine: "For he spoke, and it came to be (Psalm 148:5; cf. Psalm 32:9); that is to say: he engendered the Word by whom all things were made."[12] In a closer examination of

---

[11] The power of engendering is thus intermediate between the essence (*quid*: that which has its roots in essence) and the person in his personal property (*ad aliquid*: consideration of the notional act): "secundum rationem intelligendi medium est inter pure essentiale et pure personale" (I *Sent.*, d. 7. a. 2, sol.); cf. d. 7, a. 4; d. 20, a. 3, sol. Thomas was to adopt the same approach.

[12] Albert, *Sent.*, prol.: "Sicut enim dicit, Psal. 32, 9: Ipse dixit, et facta sunt. Et dixit Augustinus, id est, Verbum genuit in quo erat ut fieret." Albert was to cite the phrase again in I *Sent.*, d. 20, a. 3, sed contra; d. 27, a. 6, sol.; d. 29, a. 2, sed contra 2; II *Sent.*, d. 13, a. 4, quaest. 1; it was already present in the *Summa de creaturis* (*De IV coaequaevis*, tract. 4, q. 73, a. 3, ad quaest. 9). This formula is a paraphrasing of several expressions by Augustine, *De Genesi ad litteram*, Book II, VI (CSEL 28/1, 39–42, cf. PL 34, 267–68); cf. *De Genesi ad litteram*, Book I, II, 4–1, III, 8 (CSEL 28/1, 5–7; cf. PL 34, 248); Book III, XX, 31–32 (CSEL 28/1, 86–87; cf. PL 34, 292–93). We find it expressed in these terms in William of Auxerre, *Summa aurea*, Book II, tract. 8, c. 2, q. 1, a. 4 (ed. Jean Ribaillier, vol. 2/1 [Grottaferrata: Ed. Collegii S. Bonaventurae, 1982], 182): "*Dixit*, id est Verbum genuit in quo erat ut fieret lux." This exegesis from Augustine had already been summarized by Peter Lombard in his *Glossa on Psalm* 148: 5 (PL 191, 1285) and in the *Sentences*,

the significance of Wisdom *primogenita* and its work in the *exitus* of
creatures *a prima causa,* Albert establishes from the very first pages of
his commentary that the *ordo* of the Word to the creature is that of
the cause toward the thing caused: *ordo causae ad causatum.* In terms
of the relationship involved, we find here an analogy *per prius et posterius* between the nature which the Son receives from the Father
through generation, and that which the creature receives from his
Creator. Albert calls upon the authority of St. Basil at this point, as
Bonaventure and Thomas were also to do: "To receive a nature is
common to the Son and to all creatures."[13] Divine Wisdom (the
Son, by appropriation) is thus "ordered" in two ways: according to
the order of nature in the Trinity (origin), and according to the
causality which it exercises in creation.[14] The quotation from Augustine, in the context of the discussion of power, is moreover accompanied by a reference to St. Anselm, found also later in Albert's *Summa
theologiae.*[15] Excluding this reference to Anselm, Augustine's words

Book II, dist. 13, ch. 6 (vol. I/2, [Quaracchi: Ed. Collegii S. Bonaventurae,
1971], 393); cf. *Summa halensis,* Book I, p. 1, inq. 2, tract. un., q. 1, t. 1, c. 2
(vol. 1 [Quaracchi: Ed. Collegii S. Bonaventurae], #296, p. 419b).

[13] Albert, *Sent.,* prol.: "Accipere naturam Filio cum omni creatura commune est."
Basil, *Homilia* XV, *De fide,* n. 2 (PG 31, 467–68). This quotation from Basil is
also found in the examination of the name *principle* (I *Sent.,* d. 29, a. 1,
quaestiunc., contra 1 and ad 1). The affirmation is extended to the Holy Spirit
in the *De resurrectione,* tract. 4, q. 3, a. 7, ad 2 (Cologne edition, vol. 26, p.
350). See Bonaventure, I *Sent.,* d. 29, a. 1, q. 2, arg. 1 and ad 1; Thomas, I
Sent., d. 29, q. un., a. 2, qla 1, arg. 1; d. 44, q. un., a. 1, arg. 2 and ad 2; III
Sent., d. 4, q. 1, a. 2, qla 2, ad 2.

[14] See especially Albert, I *Sent.,* d. 2, a. 24, ad 2; a. 25.

[15] Albert the Great, *Summa theologiae,* Book I, tract. 3, q. 13, c. 3, arg. 2 and ad
2; q. 18, c. 1 *in fine.* The *Summa theologiae* (Book I, Cologne edition, vol.
34/1) was also to make use of it in the Prologue introducing the treatise on the
processions, to explain the arrangement of the theological material (Book I,
tract. 7, prol.); see also tract. 9, q. 41, c. 1, a. 1, qla 2. An examination of the
concordance of Anselm's works edited by Gillian R. Evans (*Concordance to the
Works of St. Anselm,* 4 vol. [New York: Kraus International Publications,1984])
has not led to the identification of any such statement on Anselm's part, as
attributed by Albert; it is however worth consulting the *De processione Spiritus
sancti,* ch. 9 (ed. Franciscus S. Schmitt [Stuttgart: F. Frommann, 1968], vol. 2,
203, v. 4–6; cf. PL 158, 309B = c. 16); *Monologion,* ch. 9–10; 29 ss., notably
ch. 10 (vol. 1, 24–25; cf. PL 158, 158–59) and ch. 33 (vol. 1,51–53; cf. PL
158, 187–88). In similar contexts, Albert frequently brings in Augustine and

constitute in very precise terms the thesis which Thomas was to place at the heart of his commentary on the first Book.

We find the same affirmation in the discussion of the name "principle" *(principium)*, and in an altogether similar context. Having demonstrated the analogy present in the meaning of this name *principle* when the "principle of the divine person" and the "principle of the creature" are being discussed, Albert raises the question of the anteriority of one signification over the other. In order to establish the priority of the "principle of the person" (personal or "notional" relationship) in our conceptual order, in accordance with the "true reason of the principle which is taken from the act," he brings in the following argument:

> According to Anselm, the procession of the persons is the cause of the procession of the creatures; and this is indicated also by Augustine when he explains these words "God speaks, that this or that may be done:" in other words, *he engendered the Word by whom all things were to be made.*[16]

Once again, Albert is thinking of the order of our concepts in approaching the mystery of God, and therefore he appeals to the causality of Trinitarian processions. As regards the reality referred to by the terms which we use to name God, the "notional" relation of the principle (relation of a divine person to another divine person) is prior to the relation of the principle toward creatures (relation of the three divine persons to creatures), just as the Trinitarian processions are held to pre-exist the creation, since they are its cause.

An in-depth study of many other texts would be helpful in explaining this teaching, but a consideration of the following passage, taken from his *De resurrectione,* will at least enable us to appreciate

---

Anselm in order to define the relationship between the Word and creatures; see especially I *Sent.,* d. 27, a. 6, sed contra 1–2; d. 28, a. 10, quaest. 1, arg. 3–4; d. 36, a. 11; sed contra 2.

[16] I *Sent.,* d. 29, a. 2, sed contra 2: "Item, Anselmus vult, quod processio personarum causa sit processionis creaturarum: et hoc etiam innuit Augustinus, cum illud, *Dixit Deus,* fiat hoc vel illud, sic exponit, *id est, verbum genuit in quo erat ut fieret.*"

Albert's constancy of thought. We should note particularly the idea of *reductio* governing this mode of thinking, and directing the theological reflection toward the Father as the source of Godhead, the principle without principle:

> . . . Being issued from a principle is the case in creatures and divine persons, as Basil says: the Son and the Holy Spirit, in common with all creatures, "receive," but possessing by nature is proper [to them]. This is why the production of the persons by their principle *(principiatio personarum)* precedes the production of creatures *(principiatio creaturarum)* as its cause, and the latter "leads back" *(reducitur)* to the former as the effect ["leads back"] to its cause. The production of the persons by their principle "leads back" moreover to the principle of the divinity which is the innascible Father.[17]

All the principal themes which give rise to the formulation of the causality of the Trinitarian processions are in evidence here. The concept of "principle," firstly, accounts for a link between the divine persons and creation: It is the principal source in Albert's work for a doctrine of Trinitarian creation. Here as in the *Sentences,* this concept is associated with the affirmation of the anteriority of the Trinitarian processions, based upon the causality of these same processions. The idea of *"reductio"* is in fact what characterizes the approach adopted by Albert: reduction of the procession of creatures to its principle, namely the procession of the divine persons,

---

[17] *De resurrectione,* tract. 4, q. 3, a. 7, ad 2 (Cologne edition, vol. 26, 350, in the context of fruition): ". . . Principiatum enim invenitur in creaturis et in personis divinis, sicut dicit Basilius, quod accipere filio et spiritui sancto cum omni creatura commune est, sed habere per naturam proprium. Unde principiatio personarum praecedit principiationem creaturarum ut causa, et ista reducitur in illam sicut effectus in causam. Principiatio autem personarum ulterius reducitur in principium totius divinitatis, et hoc est pater innascibilis." For the reference to Basil, see footnote 13 above. The *De resurrectione,* written during Albert's time in Paris, predates the writing of the commentary on the *Sentences,* cf. Wilhelm Kübel, *Prolegomena* in vol. 26 of the Cologne edition (Münster: Aschendorff, 1958), p. X.

and then reduction of the procession of the persons to the Father himself. Albert's thesis thus leads to the discovery of the source and the ultimate reason for the divine communication (Trinity and creation) in the Father.

The analysis of personal names such as Word, Love, Gift provides a detailed description of this causality of the Trinity in terms of the properties of the persons. Albert explains that the Word who is "spoken" by the Father proceeds as the *ratio* of the "utterance" of creatures, not on the part of the Father who speaks it (the Son possesses no reason of principle with regard to the Father), but on the part of creatures *(ratio dictionis ex parte rei dictae)*.[18] The Father thus knows in the Son everything of which the Son is the "sufficient principle," because he has engendered him as such *(per hoc quod genuit eum in ratione talis principii)*.[19] In a similar way, the Holy Spirit as Love and Gift is the reason for all that God gives to creatures by way of love. The eternal procession of the Holy Spirit thus precedes, as their cause and their reason, all the gifts accorded in his temporal procession.[20] Such analysis is not however given priority in Albert's commentary. Most of the passages aim rather to distinguish between the sense of what is personal or notional, and what is relating to the divine essence in the expressions which describe a relationship between the divine persons and creation,[21] without presenting a real synthesis of the Trinitarian creation.

The causality of the processions of the divine persons is located within the fundamental theological discourse on the Trinity. Theology traces its source back to the knowledge of faith; its development however takes place by means of analogies which allow us to name the Trinitarian God, known through creatures. The commentary on the Divine Names, dating from the period when Albert and Thomas

---

[18] I *Sent..*, d. 32, a. 1, sol. and ad 10; cf. a. 3, sol.

[19] I *Sent..*, d. 32, a. 3, sol.

[20] I *Sent..*, d. 18, a. 1; cf. d. 13, a. 4, arg. 2 and ad 2; d. 14, a. 13, ad 3; d. 18, a. 2, ad 3; a. 3; a. 6, ad 3. Most texts which examine the relation of the Holy Spirit toward creatures are less concerned with creation as such than with the mission of the divine person (grace).

[21] See for example I *Sent.,* d. 10, a. 3; d. 10, a. 6; d. 27, a. 4; a. 6; d. 28, a. 10.

had the closest working relationship,[22] provides useful insights in this respect. Although imperfect, the representation of the Trinity in creatures (vestige, image) permits faith-based understanding to know and to name the creative Trinity:

> The eternal generation of the Son by the Father and the distinction between all the persons is shared in a certain manner by creatures, being represented by the vestige and the image. This is why, aided by faith, we are able to arrive at some degree of knowledge of the persons by means of creatures.[23]

This teaching brings in the doctrine of analogy and of the divine names, based on participation. The reality designated by the names "Father," "Son," and so forth, exists truly and in a proper sense in God, from whom paternity and filiation are "derived" by creatures in a participatory form.[24] Without this, our discourse on the Trinity would be devoid of rational content. All paternity, whether spiritual or material, in other words all communication of being must therefore be traced back (cf. the method of *"reductio"*) to the Father as to its first model *(exemplar primum, primum dans esse)*.[25] If we take into account the entire Trinitarian process by which the divine persons are known and named, we must acknowledge that "it is by this procession (the procession of the persons) that all procession in heaven and on earth is caused and named."[26] The metaphysics of participation, associated here with the causality of the Trinitarian

---

[22] Cf. James A. Weisheipl, *Thomas d'Aquino and Albert His Teacher* (Toronto: Pontifical Institute of Mediaeval Studies, 1980). The commentary on the *Divine Names* should be dated around 1250.

[23] *Super Dion. de div. nom.,* ch. 2, #56 (here ad 2; Cologne edition, vol. 37/1, 81): "Aeterna generatio filii a patre et distinctio omnium personarum participatur aliquo modo a creaturis, repraesentata per vestigium et imaginem. Unde possumus iuvante fide ex creaturis in cognitionem aliquam personarum venire;" cf. arg. 2; cf. *Super Dion. myst. theol.,* ch. 1 (Cologne edition, vol. 37/2, 455).

[24] See especially *Super Dion. de div. nom.,* ch. 2 (#37 and 63–64).

[25] *Super Dion. de div. nom.,* ch. 2 (#64).

[26] *Super Dion. de div. nom.,* ch. 1, #39 (at the end of the analysis of the name "trinitas"): "Est ergo sententia huius partis, quod deus dicitur trinitas propter tres personas, quae distinguuntur secundum processum unius ab altera eminenter.

processions, provides a real basis for our knowledge of the Trinity. Albert reminds us of this once again when, as in the *Sentences,* he establishes the priority of the power of generation over the power of creation: "the act of creation must require the prior procession of the persons."[27]

Let us end this brief survey by noting that Albert saw the divine bounty (the sovereign good) as providing the link between an examination of Trinitarian and creative communication, bringing in as impetus the divine *discretio* (distinction between the persons and distinction between God and all that proceeds outside of him):

> It is fitting that the sovereign good communicates itself not only in the diversity of essence through the production of creatures, but also in the identity [of essence] through the processions of the persons.[28]

This role played by divine bounty suggests the connection between the procession of the persons and the *exitus–reditus* structure, and directed by the dynamics of divine goodness.

The Divine Persons, the Exitus, and the Reditus

The structure of origin–return makes an appearance at various highly significant points during the course of the commentary on the *Sentences.* It is thus featured as part of the analysis of the concept of procession itself, within a Trinitarian context (the procession of the Holy Spirit). Albert makes particular use here of the dynamics of

---

Et ab hoc processu causatur et nominatur omnis processus in caelo et in terra, et sic iterum patet, quod dicitur per eminentiam et per causam." This thesis is derived from Eph 3:15.

[27] *Super Dion. de div. nom.,* ch. 4, #120 (here ad 7–9): "Cum enim omnis creatura procedat per creationem sub vestigio vel imagine repraesentans trinitatem personarum, *oportet, quod actus creationis praesupponat processionem personarum,* et ita potentia [generandi], ut dictum est, praecedit potentiam [creandi] secundum rationem intelligendi."

[28] *Super Dion. de div. nom.,* ch. 2, #27: "Decet enim summum bonum, ut communicet se non solum in diversitate essentiae per productionem creaturarum, sed etiam in identitate secundum processiones personarum." See Francis Ruello, *Les "Noms Divins" et leurs "raisons" selon saint Albert le Grand commentateur du "De divinis nominibus"* (Paris: Vrin, 1963), pp. 118–24.

love, suggesting the image of a "circle" of procession within the Trinity (origin in the Father and return to the Father): He who loves proceeds in some way toward the one who is loved, and the loved one returns to the lover, within a context of reciprocal love *(egressus–regressus)* which gives rise to a *medium* consisting of love.[29] Some degree of reservation, however, is included in the proposition of this idea of circular motion *(motus circularis, circularis exitus, regyratio)*: The image of the circle (origin and return to the principle) may be considered appropriate for the procession of the persons, but only to the extent that the reciprocal love of the Father and the Son implies a "return" of love to the Father (union of the persons), and that the power of spiration is communicated to the Son by the Father, thus referring back to the Father because of his *auctoritas.*[30] Strictly speaking, the *exitus–reditus* motion is not accomplished within the Trinity itself, but in its work in the world.[31] Creatures "exit," "flow out," or "proceed" from God outside of the unity of divine essence,[32] and return to God in whom they have their end, rational creatures being brought back to their principle by the temporal processions of the divine persons.[33] All creatures issue from God, all is sustained and governed by him, and all returns to him.[34] This circular structure finds its chief expression in the Incarnation of the Son, in whom the "conjunction" of the *ultimum* (man) to the *primum* (God) is accomplished, thus bringing about the perfect completion of the circle.[35] We are not thinking here of the "circle" required for the perfect completion of the universe *(exitus a principio* and *ordo ad finem: circulus ordinis),* but of free intervention by God in the world through the union of humanity with divinity: It is, Albert emphasizes, an entirely gratuitous intervention.[36]

---

[29] I *Sent.,* d. 11, a. 1, sol.

[30] Ibid., a. 1, ad 3, ad 4, ad 5 and 9 (with arguments).

[31] Ibid., a. 1, arg. 6 and ad 6.

[32] See for example I *Sent.,* d. 11, a. 1, ad 2; d. 4, div. text.: "flux" of the persons and "flux" of creatures *ab ipsis (personis).*

[33] See for example I *Sent.,* d. 14, a. 3, ad 3; cf. a. 4, ad object.

[34] See especially II *Sent.,* d. 1, a. 12, sol.

[35] III *Sent.,* d. 20, a. 4, sed contra 5; cf. d. 1, a. 1, arg. 3.

[36] III *Sent.,* d. 20, a. 4, ad object. 5.

The application of the origin–return scheme to the work of the three divine persons in the world finds its most striking expression in the explanation of texts from St. Augustine and St. Hilary. Albert explains that the Father is "as much the principle with regard to the Son and the Spirit as he is in his relationship with creatures," since the Son and the Holy Spirit derive their creative activity from him; he is the "author" of the work of creation and also the end, "he to whom all is returned by creatures and equally by the divine persons."[37] The Son and the Holy Spirit, for their part, exercise their influence as much in the *exitus* as in the *reductio* of creatures: All is produced and returned to the Father by the Son and the Holy Spirit. Within this Trinitarian structure of the history of salvation, the Holy Spirit brings back *(convertit)* to himself and to the Son, the Son brings back to himself and to the Father, and here, in the Father without principle, "all relation ceases." In terms of personal relations, this conversion may be summarized by the following formula: "The person who proceeds from another person brings back to that other person, according to the order of nature, what he has received from that other person."[38] The action of the Trinity *ad extra* thus reproduces the order of the divine nature in the Trinity: The Father creates all things through the Son and the Holy Spirit who proceed from him, and all is returned to the Father through the mission of the Holy Spirit and of the Son.

---

[37] I *Sent.*, d. 3, a. 17: "Pater enim consideratur tripliciter, scilicet, ut principium non de principio, tam respectu personarum quam respectu creaturarum. . . . Et Pater accipitur ut finis in quem omnia referuntur, et a creaturis, et a personis: quia Filius in illum refert quod est, a quo habet ut sit. . . . Si vero consideratur ut finis, tunc convenit ei ad quod omnia reducuntur sive revertuntur." Cf. Peter Lombard, *Sententiae, Book I*, dist. 3, ch. 7–8 (vol. 1/2, 70–71); Augustine, *De Trinitate* VI, X, 12 (CCSL 50, 242; cf. PL 42, 932); *De vera religione* LV, 113 (CCSL 32, 259–60; cf. PL 34, 172); on this last passage, see the study by Olivier du Roy, *L'intelligence de la foi en la Trinité selon saint Augustin: Genèse de sa théologie trinitaire jusqu'en 391* (Paris: Etudes Augustiniennes, 1966), pp. 369–79 and 418–19.

[38] I *Sent.*, d. 31, a. 14, ad quaest. 2: "Persona enim quae est ab alia, refert in eam per naturae ordinem quod habet ab ea." Cf. St. Hilary, *De Synodis* 59, XXVI (PL 10, 521); see also *De Synodis* 38, XXVI (*ed. cit.,* 512); *Sententiae*, Book I, dist. 31, ch. 2, n. 8 (vol. I/2, 288).

This teaching taken as a whole brings together very many points of doctrine: the principle and order, the anteriority and the causality of the procession of the persons with regard to the procession of creatures, the procession of the Word and of the Gift as *ratio* of the created effects, participation as the foundation of our discourse on the Trinity, the origin of creatures from the Father and their return to the Father, through the work of the Son and the Holy Spirit. The doctrine of the Trinitarian creation is not presented as a particular point at issue but rather as a fundamental theme the signification of which extends throughout Trinitarian theology as a whole. In a new synthesis, which shows a more systematic use of the relationship of causality existing between the Trinity and creation, and also greater attention to aspects of overall structure, Thomas was to re-examine most of the points brought out by Albert.

Trinity and Creation in the Commentary of Bonaventure

Bonaventure's thinking on the subject of the creative Trinity is intimately linked to the main features of his Trinitarian theology. It is through the systematic application of these elements that this theme assumes such importance in his commentary on the first Book of the *Sentences*. The principal characteristics of Bonaventure's thinking in this domain may be condensed into two fundamental ideas: the diffusion of the sovereign good, coupled with divine fecundity (primacy and plenitude of fecundity in the Father); and then the exemplarity of the Son and of the Holy Spirit. We will extend our brief examination of these with an outline of the theme of the *"reductio"* of creatures to God through the Son and the Holy Spirit.

The Diffusion of the Sovereign Good and Divine Fecundity

In his research into the basic elements of communication in God through the procession of the persons, Bonaventure gives particular and extraordinary prominence to the concepts of good and of primacy.[39] By virtue of his sovereign bounty, God spreads within himself through natural diffusion; causing his bounty to burst out beyond himself, he spreads *ad extra* through volitional diffusion. Following one of the central ideas from the *Summa* of Alexander of Hales,[40] Bonaventure sees in the sovereign and perfect communication of bounty within God one of the chief reasons why faith-based reason is able to grasp the plurality of the persons in God.[41] In the same way, divine bounty is the "reason" (the *ratio*) for divine communication through creation. Bonaventure was to speak of "diffusion of good" in a strict sense in the case of "extrinsic" and "volitional" diffusion (creation). Intrinsic and natural communication *(diffusio intra)* is not motivated strictly by the pure reason of good, but that of good within a hypostasis capable of producing another.[42] The concept of good thus explains, and differentiates between, Trinitarian fecundity and creative fecundity.[43]

The second fundamental concept is that of primacy *(primitas)*. The fecundity of the "first," as in the case of good, concerns creation as much as it concerns the Trinitarian processions. In terms of the persons, the primacy of the Father designates that ultimate perfection which is the conclusion of the Franciscan theologian's quest into the mystery of divine communication: This primacy

---

[39] See especially the general studies of O. González, *Misterio Trinitario y existencia humana*, pp. 117–90 and 506–36; L. Mathieu, *La Trinité créatrice*, pp. 19–58.

[40] *Summa fratris Alexandri,* Book 1, p. 1, inq. 2, tract. un., q. 3, c. 5; vol. 1 (Quaracchi: Ed. Collegii S. Bonaventurae, 1924), #317; cf. #295, *secunda ratio;* #297, ad 23 and ad 24; #319, ad 4. For the communication of good in creation, see for example *Summa fratris Alexandri,* Book 1, p. 1, inq. 1, tract. 3, q. 3, m. 2, c. 3 (*ed. cit.,* #110; cf. #115, 352, 370, and so on). See also Alexander, *Glossa in I Sent.,* d. 1, #36; vol. 1 (Quaracchi: Ed. Collegii S. Bonaventurae, 1951), 23.

[41] Bonaventure, I *Sent.,* d. 2, a. un., q. 2, fund. 1: "cum bonitatis sit summe se communicare;" cf. concl.

[42] Bonaventure, I *Sent.,* d. 19, p. 1, a. un., q. 2, ad 3.

[43] For Bonaventure, good exercises its influence in the order of efficiency as much as in the order of finality (I *Sent.,* d. 45, a. 2, q. 1, concl.; cf. II *Sent.,* d. 1, p. 2, dubium 1); associated with the circular structure of origin and end, good thus features at the heart of the understanding of divine causality, within a perspective which is heavily influenced by the Dionysian tradition (see d. 45, *loc. cit.*).

supplies the fundamental reason for the fecundity of the Father who, as the principle of all divinity (fullness as source), produces other persons.[44] We find here, at the heart of St. Bonaventure's thinking on the Father, a principle which was to be used by Thomas in his commentary in order to explain the connection between the Trinity and creation: Within a given genre, primacy provides the reason for the role of principle assumed by the first "element" in this genre with regard to that which comes afterwards.[45]

The Procession of the Son and of the Holy Spirit: Exemplarity and Causality

Bonaventure develops his theological understanding of the procession of the persons on the basis of the fecundity of the nature of and volition (liberality) in God. By virtue of divine perfection, a nature which is supreme in its fecundity and a will which is supreme in its liberality "cannot not produce a person."[46] From this perspective, it is the use of the twin term nature–volition which leads Bonaventure the theologian toward a more specific description of the relationship which needs to be established between the divine productions (the Trinity and creation). In order to locate the role of volition within generation in God, Bonaventure compares and contrasts the procession of the persons with creation, using the roles of nature and volition in each as criteria.[47] This analysis brings into prominence the

---

[44] I *Sent.*, d. 11, a. un., q. 2, concl.: "ratio primitatis est ratio principiandi, sive fecunditatis." The theme features already among the reasons cited in favour of the existence of a plurality of persons in God (d. 2, a. un., q. 2, fund. 1, concl. and ad 4); cf. d. 7, a. un., q. 2, ad 6; d. 27, p. 1, a. un., q. 2, ad 3, *solutio auctoris;* d. 28, a. un., q. 2, concl. In addition to the studies indicated in footnote 39, see especially Alejandro de Villalmonte, "El Padre plenitud fontal de la Deidad," in *S. Bonaventura 1274–1974, Volumen commemorativum,* vol. 4 (Grottaferrata: Ed. Collegii S. Bonaventurae, 1974), pp. 221–42; Edward J. Butterworth, *The Doctrine of the Trinity in Saint Thomas Aquinas and Saint Bonaventure,* Diss. Fordham University (New York: UMI, 1985), pp. 215–35.

[45] I *Sent.*, d. 27, p. 1, a. un., q. 2, ad 3 *(sol. auctoris)*: "ratio primitatis in aliquo genere est ratio principiandi in illo." Bonaventure applies the argument to the fecundity of the Father who produces other persons, and also to the fecundity of the creative essence; cf. II *Sent.*, d. 1, p. 2, a. 1, q. 1, concl.

[46] I *Sent.*, d. 10, a. un., q. 1, concl.

[47] I *Sent.*, d. 6, q. un., a. 2.

dependency inherent in the relationship linking the production of creatures to the procession of the persons. Bonaventure establishes this dependency by showing that the generation of the Son takes place by reason of exemplarity *(secundum rationem exemplaritatis)*,[48] using the parallel offered by the procession of the Holy Spirit. The Holy Spirit proceeds by way of liberality, within the Trinity, as the reason for liberality *(ratio liberalitatis)*, since he is the Love who is the "Gift in whom all gifts are given." The creature, in turn, proceeds as that which is caused or accomplished through liberality *(quod fit vel datur ex liberalitate)*. In a similar way, creatures proceed from God as an effect produced *(exemplatum)* by their exemplary principle, while the Son proceeds as the exemplary reason or as the "reason for producing according to exemplarity" *(ratio exemplandi)*. The Son thus proceeds as the exemplar himself or the exemplary reason for other realities *(sicut ipsum exemplar vel ratio exemplandi cetera)*,[49] the reason *(ratio artificiandi)* for that which is made by the divine art *(artificiatum)*.[50]

Following the line of argument offered by William of Auxerre, Bonaventure does not restrict himself to placing this exemplarity of the procession of the Son in the context of appropriation, but sees in it a characteristic properly belonging to the Son.[51] Christian Platonism finds its ultimate expression here: The world of ideas *(mundus archetypus)* is properly identified with the second person of the Trinity. The archetype may be considered under the aspect of knowledge: From this viewpoint, all of the Trinity is the archetype of the

---

[48] Ibid., a. 3.

[49] Ibid., concl., ad 3 and ad 4.

[50] I *Sent.,* d. 10, a. 1, q. 1, ad 3. Bonaventure is here incorporating into an examination of nature (the Son), that of the intellect and of art (Word), for this mode of procession according to exemplarity cannot be anything other than "natural" (d. 6, a. un., q. 3, concl.).

[51] I *Sent.,* d. 6, q. un., a. 3, ad 4: ". . . Idea sive mundus archetypus non tantum appropriatum est ipsi Filio, verum etiam proprium." William of Auxerre had already, as Bonaventure was to do, drawn attention to the parallel between the Holy Spirit (he is properly the Gift in whom all gifts are given) and the Son (he is properly the idea, the archetype of creatures); cf. *Summa aurea,* Book II, tract. 1, c. 1, sed contra 2 and sol. (vol. 2/1, ed. Jean Ribaillier [Grottaferrata: Ed. Collegii S. Bonaventurae, 1982], p. 13); c. 2, sol. *(ed. cit.,* p. 16).

created world. But, if we add to this view the aspect of emanation *(ratio emanandi)*, we must acknowledge that the Son is properly the exemplar.[52] If we are to take emanation into account, we have to consider as a whole both the origin of the persons, and the relationship with creatures: The Son proceeds as *ratio exemplandi*. Generally speaking, we must thus recognize that the generation of the Son is the exemplary reason for all emanation. The same principle was to direct Thomas's thinking when he attributed the procession of creatures to the procession of the Son: a perfect Image who possesses the plenitude of divine perfection, archetype, and reason for the production of creatures by way of an imitation of nature.[53]

As regards the Holy Spirit, as Bonaventure pointed out when establishing the exemplarity which belongs to the Son, he is the reason for the production of creatures by the divine liberality *(ratio liberalitatis)*, the reason for desiring and for giving *(ratio volendi, ratio dandi)*, inasmuch as creatures proceed "outside" of God as that which is accomplished, desired, and given through liberality *(liberaliter factum, volitum, donatum)*.[54] Bonaventure shows that the processions of the persons pre-exist the production of creatures, because they are its *ratio*. Their causality is cited in order to establish the mode of the procession of the persons: Before the production of creatures, we must acknowledge the eternal emanation of the Word, in whom the Father disposed all things that were to be made. For the same reason, the emanation of a person in whom the Father desires and gives all things is necessary: such is the Holy Spirit, who proceeds by the mode of liberality.[55] This analysis of the divine attributes constitutes one of Bonaventure's most penetrating examinations of the connection between the Trinitarian mystery and creation.

---

[52] Ibid., ad 4; III *Sent.,* d. 11, a. 1, q. 2, fund. 4.

[53] Thomas, I *Sent.,* d. 10, q. un., a. 1, sol.

[54] Bonaventure, I *Sent.,* d. 10, a. 1, q. 1, ad 1.

[55] Ibid., fund. 4: "Omnes creaturae a Deo procedunt per cognitionem, et voluntatem; sed ante creaturarum productionem ponere fuit in divinis emanationem Verbi ab aeterno, in quo Pater omnia fienda disposuit: ergo pari ratione necesse fuit emanare personam, in qua omnia vellet et donaret; sed talis procedit per modum liberalitatis: ergo, and so on."

These explanations are developed in the study of the properties of the persons, which demonstrates the prominence given by Bonaventure to exemplarism in the understanding of the relations between the divine persons and creatures. Amongst many other texts, the study of the name "Gift" offers a remarkable example of this exemplarist doctrine, and of its application by Bonaventure. Examining the formula "the Holy Spirit is the Gift by whom all gifts are given," Bonaventure attributes to the Holy Spirit (in a proper way and not simply by appropriation) the exemplary causality with regard to created gifts. In this sense, the Holy Spirit proceeds as the first Gift, "in such a way that every right and free act of giving takes place after this [first act of giving] and receives from it the very nature af an act of giving."[56] The affirmation being made should be understood correctly. Bonaventure is not affirming that the created gifts are the effect of the Holy Spirit alone (they are caused by the whole Trinity). This is rather a question of exemplary causality under the aspect of the mode of procession of the divine person, as we saw in the study of the procession of the Son *(ratio exemplandi)*. The theological approach directing this argument is that of *"reductio"* to *"primum,"* already encountered in the study of the Father and wielded here in the domain of exemplarity:

> The Holy Spirit is the first Gift; but all that which is posterior must be led back to that which is anterior. Therefore, every gift is led back to the Gift who is the Holy Spirit. And therefore, in every gift, the reason for giving comes from the Holy Spirit.[57]

In the same way, the procession of the divine persons is prior to the creation and to salvation, as Bonaventure explains in this striking pneumatological adaptation of the Prologue of St. John:

---

56 I *Sent.*, d. 18, a. un., q. 1, concl.: "Ipse enim procedit per modum primi doni, ita quod omnis donatio recta et gratuita post illam est et ab illa accipit rationem donationis;" see also d. 17, p. 1, a. un., q. 1, concl. If the Holy Spirit did not exist (!), this exemplarity of the act of giving as such would no longer be found in God (ibid., ad 4).

57 Ibid., fund. 3: "Spiritus sanctus est primum donum; sed omne posterius ad prius reducitur: ergo omne donum reducitur ad donum, quod est Spiritus sanctus: ergo in omnibus donis ratio donationis est per Spiritum sanctum; ergo and so on."

The notion of Gift relates to the distribution of grace in the
same way that the notion of Word relates to the production
of things. But in the beginning, before the production of
things, was the Word. Thus in the beginning, before the
conferring of grace, was the Gift.[58]

The causality of the processions of the persons is thus enshrined
in the overlap between the two leading themes of Bonaventure's
thought: exemplarity and primacy.

The Reductio of Creatures to God through the Son and the Holy Spirit

With the theme of the Holy Spirit as Gift, we have already entered
into the domain of salvation. Without conducting an exhaustive
exploration of the Trinitarian dimension of the return to God, it
will nonetheless be of interest to point out briefly the permanent
presence of the ideas of "mediation" and of "reduction" which
guide Bonaventure's thinking. We come across them especially in
connection with the passages from Augustine and Hilary already
cited in a similar context in Albert's work.[59] The Son and the Holy
Spirit are named, more so than the Father, by names which bear a
relationship with creatures (Word, Gift). According to our way of
knowing, the Son and the Holy Spirit are a *quasi medium* between
us and God," and by appropriation "it is they who lead us back to
God" *(sunt reducentes ad Deum),* the Father being the "principle" to
whom we are brought back ("reduced").[60] Going one step further,
Bonaventure attributes this *reductio* to the Son, for it is in his
image that we become children of God: All subsequent reality must
be "led back" by the first in the genre.[61] The Holy Spirit himself,

---

[58] Ibid., q. 2, contra 5 (= fund. 5): "Sicut se habet ratio verbi ad rerum productionem, sic se habet ratio doni ad gratiarum distributionem; sed ante rerum
productionem in principio fuit Verbum: ergo ante gratiarum collationem in
principio fuit Donum."

[59] See above, footnotes 37 and 38.

[60] I *Sent.,* d. 27, p. 2, a. un., q. 2, ad 5.

[61] III *Sent.,* d. 1, a. 2, q. 3, concl. On this theme of *"reductio"* by the Son as
"ontological *prius,*" see Alexander Gerken, *La théologie du Verbe: La relation*

since he proceeds from the Son, is "reduced" to the Father by the Son with the creatures whom he leads back *(per Filium cum aliis ad Patrem reducitur),* and this is why the *reductio* is appropriated to the Son. This theological structure shows the Father as being the Source from whom all proceeds and to whom all is "brought back" by the Son: *(fontale principium, a quo omnia et in quem omnia per Filium reducuntur).*[62]

What we are assessing here is the fecundity of the major themes of Bonaventurian thought in the context of the Trinitarian theology of creation and salvation. The close linking of these themes (diffusion of good, primacy, exemplarity, analysis of the mode of procession of the divine persons, mediation, order, and *reductio*) is Bonaventure's original contribution to the field of Trinitarian creation, and gives fundamental coherence to his teaching.

Trinitarian Creation in Thomas's Commentary on the *Sentences*

In a new synthesis, Thomas develops most of the elements encountered in Albert's and in Bonaventure's work. His commentary, however, far more than those of his predecessors, gives extraordinary prominence to the causality of the Trinitarian processions: The procession of the divine persons is the cause, the reason, the origin, or the archetype of the procession of creatures. Thomas sees in this the main foundations for the structure of the *exitus–reditus* which is the inspiration behind his theological examination of all reality and dictates the organizational arrangement of his commentary.[63] He also sees in it a theological instrument rigorously brought into play in various aspects of Trinitarian theology. These may be divided into three groups: the procession of the Holy Spirit as Love and his temporal procession; the doctrine of the Word and of Love; the doctrine of relations and the question of the name "principle," in the

---

entre l'incarnation et la création selon S. Bonaventure (Paris: Editions Franciscaines, 1970), pp. 35–40 and 215–51.

[62] I *Sent.,* d. 31, p. 2, dubium 7, concl.

[63] Thomas, *Sent.,* prol.; I *Sent.,* d. 2, div. text.; cf. III *Sent.,* d. 1, div. text.

context of origin.[64] Without attempting a detailed examination, we
will sketch an outline of the issues and implications involved in this
teaching, distinguishing between those elements which were part of
the inherited tradition and those which reveal the profound originality of the theological thinking of the young Thomas.

The Creative Trinity and the Structure of the Sentences

Two main ideas structure Thomas's commentary, defining the structure of all reality and the organizational approach of theology: the
procession and the *origin–return* scheme. The precise connection
between these two fundamental ideas is provided by the thesis of
the causality of the procession of the persons with regard to the procession of creatures.

The theme first appears as part of the general introduction in
Thomas's Prologue, which is drawn up with the greatest precision
and presents various elements stage by stage, and developed in each
section, like a theological work in miniature.[65] The Prologue sets
out the theological project of the young Thomas, resolutely following the structure of Trinitarian economy, taking Wisdom as its
standpoint, and being dominated by the figure of the Son. The
fundamental notion presented in this little fresco of the works of
Wisdom is that of procession. The theme of procession (derivation,
origin, effusion, process, *exitus,* flux) is illustrated by numerous
images associated with the metaphor of the river (cf. Bonaventure's
general *Prooemium*) and provides a profoundly dynamic overall
framework for the interpretation of all reality. God is characterized
by the flux of the divine persons in the unity of essence, and the
process of creation is derived from the procession of the persons.[66]

---

[64] I *Sent.,* d. 10, q. un., a. 1; d. 14, q. 1, a. 1; d. 14, q. 2, a. 2; d. 26, q. 2, a. 2,
arg. 2 and ad 2; d. 27, q. 2, a. 3, ad 6; d. 29, q. 1, a. 2, qla 2; d. 32, q. 1, a. 3.

[65] A detailed analysis will reveal the highly meticulous literary style of this Prologue,
a feature which generally receives little acknowledgment in the works devoted to
Thomas's commentary; the reader is directed to Henk Schoot, "Theologisch
miniatuur: de proloog op het Scriptum," *Werkgroep Thomas van Aquino, Jaarboek* 5 (1985): 73–84.

[66] The study by F. Ruello on the structure of the commentary ("Saint Thomas et
Pierre Lombard," pp. 176–209) concluded that the notion of "principle" held

In the same way that a stream issues from a river, the temporal procession of creatures [issues] from the eternal procession of the persons. This is why it is said in the Psalm [148:5]: *He commanded and they were created:* "He engendered the Word by whom all things were to be made," says Augustine. That which is first is always the cause of that which comes afterwards, according to the Philosopher: this is why the first procession is the cause and the reason for every procession which follows.[67]

The eternal procession of the Son is the cause and the reason for all later processions. Thomas declares this to be the case when referring to Augustine,[68] using theological material and wording which are very close to the parallel texts found in St. Albert's work. Furthermore, the reference to Aristotle[69] brings out the notion of primacy (Bonaventure), here applied to the procession of the Son. The Trinitarian

---

priority. The notion of principle is less prominent, however, in the Prologue than is that of procession. The term itself is not featured. The two notions are certainly connected, but insufficient emphasis has perhaps been given so far to Thomas's decision to opt for an approach dominated by the idea of procession (flux, derivation, *exitus,* and so on), supported by the thesis of the causality of the divine processions with regard to the procession of creatures, and by the structure of origin–return.

67 Thomas, *Sent.,* prol.: "Sicut trames a fluvio derivatur, ita processus temporalis creaturarum ab aeterno processu personarum: unde in Psalmo dicitur 'Dixit et facta sunt,' idest Verbum genuit in quo erat ut fieret, secundum Augustinum. Semper enim illud quod est primum est causa eorum quae sunt post, secundum Philosophum; unde primus processus est causa et ratio omnis sequentis processionis." The text cited is the one edited by Father Pierre Mandonnet, vol. 1 (Paris: Lethielleux, 1929). Grateful acknowledgment is given to Father Adriano Oliva and Father Louis-Jacques Bataillon of the Leonine Commission, who generously provided additional information.

68 See above, footnote 12.

69 This principle is frequently cited by Thomas, formulated in a variety of different ways which modify its meaning. He refers to two passages in Aristotle's *Metaphysics,* Book II (a): 993 b 24–993 b 30, and 994 a 11–13. For the first, generally mentioned (about ten instances in the commentary on the *Sentences,* although the reference is not always explicit), see Vincent de Couesnongle, "La causalité du maximum," *RSPT* 38 (1954): 433–44 and 658–80. In Thomas's work, see especially, for I *Sent.*; d. 5, q. 1, a. 1, ad 1; d. 18, q. un., a. 3, contra 2; d. 19, q. 5, a. 1; d. 24, q. 1, a. 1; d. 32, q. 1, a. 3; d. 35, q. un., a. 3, contra 2. Cf. Bonaventure, II *Sent.,* d. 3, p. 1, a. 1, q. 2, fund. 2; III *Sent.,* d. 1, a. 2, q. 3.

processions henceforth provide the foundation for all "which follows."
Thomas was to restate this in the Prologue to his *Super Boetium de
Trinitate,* shortly after the commentary on the Sentences: The *De
Trinitate* is about "the Trinity of the persons, from the procession of
whom every other nativity or procession derives."[70] However, the
Trinity of the persons "arises" from the first nativity, that is from the
generation by which the Father engenders his Wisdom[71] for all eter-
nity. The eternal nativity of the Son, because it is the *first,* thus constitutes the origin *(initium)* from which every later procession or nativity
"derives."[72] The affirmation should be understood in its widest sense:
Because of its primacy, the nativity of the Son is not only the *initium*
of the procession of creatures, but *also* of the procession of the Holy
Spirit, since the Spirit proceeds from the Father and from the Son.[73]
Thomas thus sees in the generation of the Son the origin of "every
later procession" (the procession of the Spirit and the procession of
creatures, each evidently at their respective level).

The extended development of this idea of procession fits har-
moniously into the structure of origin–return. The groundwork for
setting this structure was evident in the work of Thomas's predecessors, particularly in Albert's work[74] (though neither Albert nor

---

[70] *Super Boet. de Trin.,* prol.: "Eius namque doctrina in tres partes diuiditur.
Prima namque est *de trinitate personarum, ex quarum processione omnis alia
natiuitas uel processio deriuatur*" (Leonine edition, vol. 50, 76).

[71] Ibid.: "Materia siquidem huius operis est in una diuina essentia trinitas personarum, que consurgit ex prima natiuitate, qua diuina Sapientia a Patre eter-
naliter generatur."

[72] Ibid.: "Que quidem natiuitas initium est cuiuslibet natiuitatis alterius, cum
ipsa sola sit perfecte naturam capiens generantis, alie uero omnes imperfecte
sunt, secundum quas genitum aut partem substantie generantis accipit, aut
substantie similitudinem: unde oportet quod a predicta natiuitate omnis alia
natiuitas per quandam imitationem deriuetur: Eph. III 'Ex quo omnis paterni-
tas in celo et in terra nominatur.' Et propter hoc Filius dicitur 'primogenitus
omnis creature,' Col. I, ut natiuitatis origo et imitatio designetur, non eadem
generationis ratio."

[73] Ibid.: "Nec solum creaturarum est initium predicta natiuitas, set etiam Spiritus
sancti, qui a generante genitoque procedit."

[74] James A. Weisheipl (*Friar Thomas d'Aquino: His Life, Thought, and Works*
[Washington, DC: The Catholic University of America Press, 1983], pp.
70–71) suggested in this context a probable influence of Alexander of Hales's
Glossa on the Sentences. My own research points to the more direct influence of

Bonaventure made such pointed use of it for determining the structure of their commentary). But it is the prominence and altogether original treatment afforded by Thomas to Trinitarian theology, which we should emphasize here. If the creature "comes out" of God, it is because, for all eternity, the Son "comes out" of the Father. If rational creatures (human persons and angels) are in a position to return to the Father, it is because the Son leads them to the Father. In mankind, the whole universe comes back to its source: "Having restored the condition of mankind, in a certain manner he restored all that which had been made for mankind."[75] The incarnation of the Son brings about the return *(reversio)* of natural goods to their principle, and reunites the creature with its principle. Man is considered here as a "microcosm," and in Christ the *ultimum* (man) is united to the *primum* (God). In the Son and through the Son, the entire universe thus "returns to its principle."[76] This synthesis thus presents the Father as the one from whom all comes and to whom all returns, through the eternal procession and the temporal procession (the incarnation and mission) of the Son.[77]

This Trinitarian structure of creation and salvation is expressed by the *exitus–reditus* schema: *Exitus a principio* of the divine persons in the unity of essence (Book I) and *exitus* of creatures in a diversity of essence (Book II); *reditus* from the perspective of the *reducens* (Book III), and in line with that which is required from the creatures

Albert the Great; see, for example, amongst many texts, Albert, *Super Dion. de div. nom.*, ch. 1, #32–33 (Cologne edition, vol. 37/1, pp. 17–18): *exitus a Deo then reditus in ipsum*. The *exitus* has two aspects: the reason for the production *(ratio producendi)*, and then the actual thing which is produced. Regarding the *reditus*, Albert makes a distinction between two main aspects: the return or recall from the perspective of the one who is calling *(ex parte revocantis)*, and from the perspective of the one being recalled *(ex parte revocati)*. In terms of its principal features, this is exactly the structure proposed by Thomas.

75 *Sent.*, prol.: ". . . Reparato hominis statu, quodammodo omnia reparavit quae propter hominem facta sunt;" cf. IV *Sent.*, d. 48, q. 1, a. 1, sol.

76 III *Sent.*, prol.: "Ed ideo quando humana natura per incarnationis mysterium Deo conjuncta est, omnia flumina naturalium bonitatum ad suum principium reflexa redierunt. . . ." The theme was to be taken up again in a highly significant way (the image of the circle), in the question of the reason for the incarnation (III *Sent.*, d. 1, q. 1, a. 3, arg. 1, sol. and ad 1).

77 On this point I agree with F. Ruello, "Saint Thomas et Pierre Lombard," p. 209.

being "led back" (Book IV). The internal connections in the first
Book (Trinity and attributes of God the creator), as well as the connections between the first two Books *(exitus),* are in a very precise
sense dependent upon the creative causality of the processions of
the persons:

> The exitus of the persons in the unity of essence is the cause
> of the exitus of creatures in a diversity of essence *(exitus
> enim personarum in unitate essentiae est causa exitus creatu-
> rarum in essentiae diversitate).*[78]

From this viewpoint, the analysis of the attributes of God the
creator (I *Sent.* d. 35–48) can be seen as a direct extension of Trinitarian theology, since it concerns "the causality in the divine persons with regard to the production of creatures" *(causalitas in
divinis personis respectu productionis creaturarum).*[79] The priority of
the *De Trinitate* treatise is thus not simply a matter of pedagogical
interest, but is concerned with a real priority (causality) which dictates the approach of the theologian. Two main themes make up
the metaphysical context of this structure: the causality of the
"first" (cf. Bonaventure), and the derivation (procession, flux, and
so on, cf. Albert) of that which is created "outside" of God. The
temporal procession of the persons, moreover, provides the cause
and the reason for the return.[80] The structural organization of the
entire body of theological material thus depends upon the procession of the divine persons: their *exitus* allows for the *exitus* of crea-

---

[78] I *Sent.,* d. 2, div. text.; III *Sent.,* d. 1, div. text. The twin term "unity"—"diversity of essence" is present from Thomas's Prologue onward *(ordo and modus creationis)*: It is also found in the works of Albert and Bonaventure, but not in
this context (see however the usage of the notion of "flux" in Albert, I *Sent.,* d.
4, div. text.). The theme is also connected to the diffusion of the sovereign
good in *diversitate essentiae* by the production of creatures, and *in identitate
essentiae* by the production of the persons. See for example Albert, *Super Dion.
de div. nom.,* ch. 2 (#27); cf. ch. 4 (#119 and 120). Bonaventure, I *Sent.,* d. 19,
p. 1, a. un., q. 2, ad 3: *diffusio intra* (processions of the persons *in unitate naturae*) and *diffusio extra* (production of creatures); cf. d. 44, a. 1, q. 2, ad 4; d.
45, a. 2, q. 1, concl.

[79] I *Sent.,* d. 2, div. text.; see also d. 35, div. text.

[80] I *Sent.,* d. 14, q. 2, a. 2; cf. d. 14, q. 1, a. 1; d. 15, q. 4, a. 1.

tures, and their mission ("invisible" and "visible") brings creatures back to their source.

The Generation of the Son and the Procession of the Spirit

Going back to Bonaventure's analysis of nature and volition in God, Thomas compares and contrasts the procession of the persons and that of creatures in the light of the twin term nature–volition *(natura–voluntas)*. These two modes suffice to provide an explanation for all acts in creatures (natural agent and volitional agent) which are "reduced" to their cause and their archetype: the two divine processions.[81] Like Bonaventure, Thomas includes here a consideration of the intellect when considering nature, distinguishing between the created effect produced by the divine attributes *(principiatum)* and the procession of the persons which is the reason for the production of the effects *(ratio principiandi)*. The Holy Spirit, as Love, proceeds as the reason for the production of creatures by the divine will, while the Son is engendered as the Word or the Art by whom God (the Father) creates all things.[82] Carrying on again from Bonaventure, who did not, however, base his argument on this, Thomas then establishes the procession of the Holy Spirit as Love through the *reductio* of the production of creatures to the principle which is the reason for divine liberality *(principium quod sit quasi ratio totius liberalis collationis)*, just as the production of creatures in terms of nature may be "led back" to the procession of the Son which is its principle, archetype, and reason.[83]

---

[81] Thomas, I *Sent.,* d. 10, q. un., a. 5, sol. Albert, when attempting to explain the "number" of persons in God, was more concerned with exploring the possibilities offered by the twin term intellect–volition (d. 10, a. 12; cf. a. 2, ad 6); he also made a distinction between the divine productions *intra essentiam and extra essentiam.*

[82] Thomas, I *Sent.,* d. 6, q. un., a. 2, sol.; d. 13, q. un., a. 3, ad 4; cf. Bonaventure, I *Sent.,* d. 6, a. un., q. 3. Thomas's terminology also echoes that of Albert on the subject of the *principiatio* of creatures by the *principiatio* of the persons (see above, footnote 17).

[83] I *Sent.,* d. 10, q. un., a. 1; cf. Bonaventure, I *Sent.,* d. 10, a. 1, q. 1, arg. 4, contra 1, ad 1 and ad 3.

This argument relies, on one hand, on faith (there can be no "proof" of the Trinity by necessary reasons), and, on the other, on the following principle: "The procession of the persons, which is perfect, must be the reason and the cause for the procession of creatures."[84] Without resorting to the method of appropriation, Thomas makes a direct link between the procession of creatures and that of the persons in a proper way. In the case of nature, exemplarity (exemplary efficiency) occupies a dominant position. In the case of the procession of the Holy Spirit, the causality proper to volition and to love is highlighted: God creates because he loves.[85] The expression *causa et ratio* is thus located at the meeting point of efficient causality, exemplary causality, and finality: It accounts for free divine acts and for their intelligibility. In a more general sense, the Trinitarian processions are considered to be the *first* process (the first procession of nature and first procession of the will), which, being *perfect,* is the reason for the process of creation.[86] This idea of primacy and of perfection, already present in the Prologue and in the study of generation,[87] here again provides the basis for the understanding of the causality of the procession of the persons; it is closely linked with the idea of *reductio,* namely a *reductio* "to the first principle which is the cause of all later processions."

This article devoted to the procession of the Holy Spirit occupies a unique position in Thomas's work: He was never again to make use

---

[84] Thomas, ibid., sol.: "Supposita autem, secundum fidem nostram, processione divinarum personarum in unitate essentiae, ad cujus probationem ratio sufficiens non invenitur, oportet processionem personarum, quae perfecta est, *esse* rationem et causam processionis creaturae."

[85] We are here in the domain of the final causality, cf. *Responsio ad magistrum Ioannem de Vercellis de art. CVIII,* art. 24 (Leonine edition, vol. 42, pp. 283–84).

[86] Thomas, I *Sent.,* d. 10, q. un., a. 1, ad 2.

[87] Generation exists *per prius* in God from whom it "derives" or descends into creatures who imitate it in an imperfect manner (d. 4, a. 1, sol.). The metaphysics of derivation plays a dominant role in the understanding of the relations between God and the world in Thomas's commentary (analogy by reference to a "first"). See Bernard Montagnes, *La doctrine de l'analogie de l'être d'après saint Thomas d'Aquin* (Louvain/Paris: Publications Universitaires de Louvain/Béatrice-Nauwelaerts, 1963), pp. 45–53 and 67–81. The young Thomas's teaching in this domain follows that of Albert very closely (p. 73).

of this line of argument. The value and the role of the thesis of the causality of the Trinitarian processions relies on the analysis of divine attributes, and on the ideas of exemplarity, primacy, and perfection *(reductio)* which dominate Aquinas's first theological synthesis.

Trinity, Creation, and Mission

The causality of the processions of the persons has appeared up to now as a foundation of the structure of the commentary *(exitus–reditus)* and as an instrument of Trinitarian theology (procession of the Son and of Love). In the treatise on the missions, Thomas brings these two aspects together: The causality of the Trinitarian processions provides the general framework for the theological reflection, and supplies a tool which will be invaluable in the examination of several questions.

Thomas makes use of it first of all in order to establish the existence of the temporal procession of the Holy Spirit: Just as the generation of the Son is the reason for the entire production of creatures *(ratio totius productionis creaturae),* the procession of the Holy Spirit as Love of the Father and of the Son is the *ratio* in which God accords to the creature the effects of his love *(ratio in qua Deus omnem effectum amoris largiatur).* The whole exposition is based upon the following principle: "processiones personarum aeternae sunt causa et ratio productionis creaturarum."[88] In this context, Thomas is no longer concerned with the production of creatures by the divine will in a general sense (creation), but is thinking of the effects of divine will in the mission of the person (grace). This initial exposition thus needs to identify in greater detail the nature of the effects of the Holy Spirit in the *exitus* and the *reditus.*

In order to identify the effects attributed to the Holy Spirit in his mission, Thomas again resorts to the same theological method, and his answer takes the form of the most condensed synthesis of the whole commentary. The exposition is based upon the circular

---

[88] I *Sent.,* d. 14, q. 1, a. 1, sol. Thomas points out in addition that the eternal personal relation is included in the temporal relation (the effect of love given to the creature), since it is its *ratio* (a. 2, sol.).

structure *(circulatio)* of the real, which takes place around a unique reality (God as principle and end) by means of the same *media*: The procession from the principle and the return to the end are accomplished *per eadem*. The audacity of this theological insight lies in the identification of these *media* with the processions of the divine persons: Just as they are the *ratio productionis creaturarum a primo principio,* the processions of the Son and of the Holy Spirit are the *ratio redeundi in finem*. The function of "descending" and "ascending" mediation of the "intermediary" realities, emphasized by the Dionysian tradition (Albert), is here overtly applied to the procession of the persons.[89] This affirmation is a rendering of the tenet of the faith: The Father creates through the Son and through the Holy Spirit, and it is through the Son and the Holy Spirit that we are united with the ultimate end. Ever faithful to that view of the end which governs his approach to the *reditus,* Thomas consigns the effects of the mission to the domain of the union with the end (grace and glory), while the causality of the procession of the persons in the *exitus* concerns the effects by which we subsist in our natural being. This causality in the exitus may be compared with Dionysius's teaching on the procession of divine wisdom and goodness in creatures.[90] There is no suggestion here of any sort of natural *reditus,* but only of the return of rational creatures who are capable of receiving the "seal" of the divine persons and of being united with the Trinity by grace and glory.

Thomas bases his explanations upon the two passages of St. Augustine *(De vera religione)* and St. Hilary already cited within different contexts in the works of Albert and Bonaventure: The Father is the "principle" to which we return, the Son is the "form" which

---

[89] The idea is omnipresent in Albert's commentary on the *Celestial Hierarchy*. Our knowledge of God is subject to the same rule: "per eadem media de primo venitur ad ultimum et de ultimo ad primum" (Albert, *Super Dion. myst. theol.,* ch. 2, q. 2, arg. 2; Cologne edition, vol. 37/2, p. 467). Thomas would have been able to see this principle included in William of Moerbeke's later translation of Prolus's *Elementatio theologica* (prop. 38; ed. Helmut Boese [Leuven: University Press, 1987], p. 23). See also Thomas, II *Sent.,* d. 38, q. un., a. 1, sol.

[90] See also I *Sent.,* d. 8, q. 3, a. 1, ad 1; d. 13, q. un., a. 1, sol.

we follow, and the Holy Spirit is the grace by which we are reconciled. "To one single without-principle and principle of all [namely the Father], we bring back all things through the Son."[91] The Father appears once again as the one who creates through the persons proceeding from him, and as the one to whom we are brought back by the mission of the Son and of the Holy Spirit.[92] Christian prayer, when it is addressed to God the Father, expresses this Trinitarian structure through a sort of *reductio* of the persons to the Father, since the Father is the principle without principle to whom the Son and the Holy Spirit bring us back.[93]

The same structure appears again in the article asserting the existence of the invisible mission of the Son. Here Thomas does not point out the relation of love with its object (the mission of the Holy Spirit), but he develops the theme of similitude and exemplary causality which provides an explanation for the mission of the Son. This similitude, in the *exitus,* expresses the bounty of the creator (the theme of Trinitarian vestiges). But, within the order of the return (Thomas speaks here of *reductio rationalis creaturae in Deum*), the Son is sent inasmuch as he is "represented" in the souls of the just by a similitude, the origin and archetype of which are the eternal property of the divine person *(quae est exemplata et originata ab ipsa proprietate relationis aeternae).*[94] The Father appears here once again as the *principium* or the *ultimum* to which we are led by the divine person who is sent. Within this highly dynamic perspective, the Son and the Holy Spirit are given to us so that we may receive them in a new way as "bringing us to the end and uniting us

---

[91] Thomas, I *Sent.,* d. 14, q. 2, a. 2, sol.; see above, footnotes 37, 38, and 59.

[92] I was able to show this in another study: "Le Père et l'œuvre trinitaire de création selon le Commentaire des *Sentences* de S. Thomas d'Aquin," in *Ordo sapientiae et amoris: Hommage au Professeur Jean-Pierre Torrell OP à l'occasion de son 65e anniversaire,* ed. Carlos-Josaphat Pinto de Oliveira (Fribourg: Editions universitaires, 1993), pp. 85–117.

[93] IV *Sent.,* d. 15, q. 4, a. 5, qla 3, ad 1.

[94] I *Sent.,* d. 15, q. 4, a. 1, sol. Here, as in the mission of the Holy Spirit, we are touching upon an area in which Thomas acknowledges a proper relation of creatures with the divine persons (exemplarity and terminatio in a similitude of the eternal property, cf. d. 30, q. un., a. 2, sol.).

to God" *(habentur personae divinae novo modo quasi ductrices in finem vel conjungentes).*[95]

Two principal lines of thought emerge from this teaching. The first concerns the doctrine of the inhabitation of the divine persons, and in this context the influence of Alexander of Hales's *Summa* should be emphasized, rather than that of Albert or Bonaventure.[96] The second concerns the general framework of Thomas's teaching: The *exitus–reditus* on one hand, and the causality of the procession of the persons on the other. Although Thomas's thinking appears to display remarkable originality here, various pointers may be identified in the works of Albert and Bonaventure. The *origin–return* structure had already been used by Bonaventure in order to explain how God is present in all creatures and how he dwells in the just.[97] The idea of *circulatio/regyratio* associated with the processions of the persons appears to be a theme previously analyzed by Albert in his study of the concept of procession, and one which Thomas employs systematically but only in the context of *ad extra* works. The idea of the double procession of divine bounty may also be traced back to St. Albert. The German Dominican distinguished between two processions: firstly, the diffusion of good through creation *(bonum est diffusivum sui et esse,* according to Dionysius), which may be seen in effects such as being, life, sensibility, and intellectual power (Thomas's "natural" gifts); secondly, the temporal procession of the divine person by the gifts of grace which manifest this person.[98] Thomas's explanation goes far beyond the idea of manifestation which seemed to satisfy Albert, but Thomas uses the same structure, extending it through an overall view of the causality of the divine persons in the *exitus* and the *reditus.*

---

[95] I *Sent.,* d. 15, q. 4, a. 1, sol.

[96] Amongst the many works available, see Francis L. B. Cunningham, *The Indwelling of the Trinity: A Historico-Doctrinal Study of the Theory of St. Thomas Aquinas* (Dubuque: The Priory Press, 1955), pp. 253–62 and 273–84 (see table 1, pp. 362–71).

[97] Bonaventure, I *Sent.,* d. 37, p. 1, a. 3, q. 2, concl. (God's mode of existence in things).

[98] Albert, I *Sent.,* d. 14, a. 1, ad 3; cf. arg. 3; cf. d. 3, a. 17; d. 10, a. 6, arg. 3 and ad 3.

The Word and Love

The analysis of the names *Word* and *Love,* carrying on from the explanations already given, addresses once again the causality of the processions of the persons. The theme is brought in here in order to supply the reason for the following: A name proper to a divine person (Word, Gift) can imply a relation with creatures. The divine essence is not the only relevant factor in the relation of God toward his creatures. The rule of the unity of the Trinity in its operation *ad extra* (the divine names which designate a relation with creatures signify the divine essence) thus only constitutes one aspect of the problem, as has already been suggested in the explanations provided by Bonaventure.[99] Every divine name signifying a relation with the creature leads toward an understanding of the divine essence, but, Thomas adds:

> Since not only the divine essence, but also the procession of the persons which is the reason for the production of creatures, implies a relation with the creature, a personal feature may also be signified with a relation to the creature.[100]

The analysis of the formula "the Father and the Son love us through the Holy Spirit" provides further details. (Thomas, in this context, shows more interest than Albert or Bonaventure in the relation between the Trinity and creatures).[101] We find here the principal elements which we encountered earlier, except for the structure of origin–return. The main problem at this point is one of language: When Thomas says that the Father and the Son love us through the

---

[99] Bonaventure, I *Sent.,* d. 27, p. 2, a. un., q. 2, ad 5. The Franciscan master was here referring to the teaching of Augustine concerning the divine persons in the *reditus*: the very teaching which Thomas made use of earlier in order to explain the meaning of the causality of the procession of the persons in the *reditus* (d. 14, q. 2, a. 2).

[100] Thomas, I *Sent.,* d. 27, q. 2, a. 3, ad 6: "Sed quia non tantum essentia habet ordinem ad creaturam, sed etiam processio personalis, quae est ratio processionis creaturarum; ideo potest etiam aliquid personale cum respectu ad creaturam significari."

[101] Thomas, I *Sent.,* d. 32, q. 1, a. 3; see Albert, I *Sent.,* d. 10, a. 6, sol.; d. 32, a. 7, ad 3; Bonaventure, I *Sent.,* d. 10, dubium 3, and d. 32, a. 1, q. 1, ad 4–5.

Holy Spirit *(Pater et Filius diligunt nos Spiritu Sancto)*, the verb *to love* may be taken in the sense of essence or of a notional act. If it is taken in the sense of essence, the dilection takes on an essential meaning (the essential efficiency of the whole Trinity), while the ablative *Spiritu Sancto* designates the reason for the efficiency *(ratio efficientiae)* on the part of the effects, of which the reason and the origin *(ratio et origo)* is the procession of the Holy Spirit, just as the Word is the reason for creatures inasmuch as they issue from God by the mode of the intellect. If the verb "to love" is taken in the sense of a notional act, it signifies principally this personal *ratio efficientiae,* and then leads on to the understanding of the relation of efficiency which belongs to the divine essence.[102]

Such analysis is an expression of the following reality: The Father spirates the Holy Spirit who is Love in person and who is the reason for every liberal gift made by God to his creatures. The general rule governing these explanations is thus formulated as follows: Efficiency is certainly attributed to all the Trinity (the divine essence) but "the procession of the divine persons is also in a sense the origin of the procession of creatures." The attribution of the *ratio efficientiae* to the person (to his procession) is based precisely upon this theological principle. Once again, Thomas defends his explanations by calling upon the argument already produced in the Prologue: "since all that is first within a genre is the cause of that which comes afterwards."[103] The idea of primacy remains constantly linked to the causality of the procession of the persons, allowing the manifestation of the personal aspect (Word, Love) of the relations which the Trinity maintains with its creatures.

The Origin: The "Relation" and the "Principle"

There is one last series of questions which finally brings in the causality of the processions of the persons, in the context of the origin. Firstly, in his doctrine of relation, at the summit of his Trinitarian

---

[102] Thomas, ibid., sol.
[103] Ibid.: "Sciendum tamen ad ejus intellectum, quod processio divinarum personarum est et quaedam origo processionis creaturarum; cum omne quod est primum in aliquo genere sit causa eorum quae sunt post."

theology, Thomas calls upon the causality of the processions of the persons in order to establish the prerogatives of the relation as the proper principle of the distinction between the divine hypostases. In terms of its "quantity," the divine relation is the least substantial being possible: It possesses the smallest consistency of being, as it is only a relation of opposition. But, in terms of dignity and causality, distinction and relation in God is greater than all other distinctions or relations. Thomas shows on one hand that the distinction between the divine hypostases is the *first* distinction by highlighting its causality: The procession of the persons is the *cause* of the procession of creatures.[104] He shows on the other hand that the divine distinction/relation is greater in terms of causality than any other distinction/relation for, as he explains, "the procession of the distinct divine persons is the cause of the procession and multiplication of all creatures" *(ex processione personarum distinctarum causatur omnis creaturarum processio et multiplicatio)*.[105]

The distinction of the persons is thus the cause of that other distinction which is the production of creatures (creation implies a distinction between God and that which proceeds outside of God), and is also the source of the distinctions between creatures (their multiplication). This passage, which is unparalleled in the commentaries of Albert or Bonaventure, is of great importance in Thomas's teaching on the one and the many, and raises highly significant suggestions about the sense of distinction and multiplicity. It is moreover of greatest interest, for the purposes of this present study, that Thomas introduces this theme within the context of the doctrine of relation, the main feature of his Trinitarian theology.

---

[104] I *Sent.,* d. 26, q. 2, a. 2, arg. 2 (cf. ad 2). The theme of *primacy* occupies a central position once again here. But while in previous texts primacy supplied the reason for causality, here it is causality which supplies the reason for primacy. This idea, found constantly in Thomas's work, operates in two directions: that which is first is the cause, and that which is the cause is first.

[105] Ibid., ad 2. Multiplication is thus imbued with an eminently positive connotation. In the theology of creation, the multiplication of creatures is connected with the blessing of the seventh day (Gen 2:3): it is ordered to the participation of the divine being by creatures "as far as they are able" (II *Sent.,* d. 15, q. 3, a. 3, sol.).

The study of the name "principle," finally, takes up the theme of the causality of the processions of the persons again and, more precisely, of their exemplarity. Having recalled the analogy brought in by the notion of principle when considering the principle of the person (personal relation of origin) and the principle of creatures (relation common to the Trinity as a whole), Thomas raises the question of the anteriority of one meaning of *principium* over the other. The article which examines this problem is a restatement of Albert's teaching, even to the extent of the details of the explanation.[106] Thomas bases his response on the causality of the processions of the persons:

> The procession of creatures finds its exemplar in the procession of the divine persons. This is why, speaking in absolute terms, *principle* is referred to firstly in relation to the person, and then in relation to the creature.[107]

Albert produced a similar argument in the same context (the order of our concepts in understanding how God is "principle"), but here Aquinas stresses divine exemplarity.[108] The innovatory element in this response lies in the attribution of exemplarity to the procession of the persons taken as a whole. Previously, Thomas had developed this theme of exemplarity with reference to the processions observed in creatures (created agents), and had also applied it to the creative causality of the procession of the Son, then to the mission of the divine persons. The question of the "principle" provides a general affirmation of the exemplarity of the Trinitarian processions.

---

[106] Thomas, I *Sent.*, d. 29, q. un., q. 2, qla 2; Albert, I *Sent.*, d. 29, a. 2.

[107] Thomas, I *Sent.*, d. 29, q. un., a. 2, qla 2, sol.: "Ad id quod ulterius quaeritur, dicendum quod processio creaturarum exemplatur a processione divinarum personarum; unde, absolute loquendo, per prius dicitur principium respectu personae quam respectu creaturae."

[108] Regarding Albert's argument, see above footnotes 10, 16, and 27. Thomas's response, like that of Albert, is located in the examination of the problem of the power of engendering and of creating: The divine person or his notional act is conceptually "anterior" to the divine essence taken as having a relation with creatures (Thomas, I *Sent.*, d. 7, q. 1, a. 3, ad 4).

Conclusion

We can now summarize the results of our study into Aquinas's first teaching on the creative Trinity and into its sources. The Trinitarian concept of creation is underlined by Albert the Great (the notion of principle, analogy, and divine names) and by Bonaventure (divine fecundity, exemplarity, and mediation) in the very heart of their Trinitarian theology. Continuing the work of his predecessors, but in a more systematic manner, Thomas Aquinas gives a central position to the Trinitarian principle of creation: The procession of the divine persons is the cause of and the reason for the procession of creatures. This causality of the Trinity constitutes the cornerstone of the structure of Thomas's commentary (an origin–return structure), which extends its influence to numerous questions of Trinitarian theology (the generation of the Son, the procession of the Holy Spirit, divine missions, the doctrine of the Word and Love, and the concepts of principle and relation).

The main theological themes associated with the "causality of the procession of the divine persons" in Aquinas are: the derivation of realities created with reference to divine perfection (Albert); the fecundity or causality of the *primum* (Bonaventure); divine exemplarity and the *reductio* to the principle (Bonaventure, and also Albert); and the order of concepts involving a relation of a divine person to creatures (Albert). The incorporation of the *exitus–reditus* scheme into the structure of the commentary and into the doctrine of the missions makes full provision for this teaching, conferring a central position to the causality of the Trinitarian procession in the synthesis of the young Thomas.

Most elements developed by Thomas on the causality of the Trinitarian processions may be seen as having precedents in the works of Albert and Bonaventure. The rigorous and systematic use of this thesis however is proper to St. Thomas's teaching and altogether original. It also reveals, at a deeper level, a theological *mode of thinking* which pays particular attention to the personal dimension of divine actions *ad extra*: The causality of the Trinity throws light on the mystery of the Trinity itself and on the theological approach to all reality.

This conclusion should lead to considerable reinterpretation of the role often attributed to St. Thomas in the history of Trinitarian theology. Theological manuals, on one hand, readily describe his doctrine of the Creator as being dominated exclusively by the figure of the one God. On the other hand, contemporary theology's reassessment of what is called the "economic Trinity" is often presented as being in opposition to a western theological tradition of which Thomas is held to be one of the main representatives. A full examination of the teaching in St. Thomas's later works remains to be undertaken, but it is certain that, in his commentary on the *Sentences,* St. Thomas defies this description by presenting a theology which is profoundly characterized by the Trinitarian dimension of creation and of the history of salvation.

CHAPTER THREE

The Treatise of St. Thomas on the Trinity in the *Summa contra Gentiles*

THE STRUCTURE that Thomas Aquinas imposed upon his major works is of prime importance in understanding the very nature of his thought, since to a very large extent the form he gives to his syntheses is indicative of the doctrine being discussed: *sapientis est ordinare.*[1] The structure and the method of the treatises within a given body of doctrine reveal the same preoccupation, and Trinitarian theology provides one of the earliest examples.

It is immediately obvious from the structure of the Trinitarian treatise in the *Summa theologiae*—with its three pillars consisting of the concepts of procession, relation, and persons—that the theory of relation occupies a pivotal position, as does the personalism of St. Thomas. The doctrine of the persons and of their relationships (including those in the economy: the divine missions) constitute quite clearly for Aquinas the summit to which Trinitarian thinking leads us. The treatise on the Trinity in the *Summa theologiae (Prima pars)* consists of three main parts: the procession or origin (q. 27), the relations of origin (q. 28), and then the divine persons (q. 29–43). The precise aim of the first two discussions is to provide the theologian with all that he needs to grasp the persons and their constitution (which, on another level, is also the case with the treatise devoted to

---

[1] Translation by Heather Buttery of "Le traité de saint Thomas sur la Trinité dans la *Somme contre les Gentils,*" *RT* 96 (1996): 5–40.

the unity of essence in q. 2–26). As regards the rest of this treatise, it is directly and entirely constructed around the divine persons.[2]

In comparison with this *ordo doctrinae* of the *Summa theologiae*, which offers both a pedagogic and scientific examination of the *intellectus fidei*, the Trinitarian section of the *Summa contra Gentiles*, written a few years earlier,[3] displays an original and slightly different approach. The main ideas present in the synthesis of the *Summa theologiae* are already there, but the structure of the treatise, the use of doctrinal sources, and even Thomas's declared purpose reveal different points of emphasis which all point to the fundamental orientations of the Angelic Doctor's Trinitarian doctrine. Studies of St. Thomas's Trinitarian theology, which most often concentrate on the structure and method of the treatise in the *Summa theologiae*, do not however generally attribute equal importance to the method of the treatise in the *Summa contra Gentiles*.[4] Those works which do examine the Trinitarian theology of the *Summa contra Gentiles* more closely have in general only considered certain particular aspects, the chief among them being the doctrine of the Word.[5] Given the occasional difficulties raised by the reception of St. Thomas's Trinitarian doctrine (the relationship between the "immanent Trinity" and the

[2] Thomas has already provided an explanation on this matter, starting with the person, in the Disputed Questions *De potentia* (q. 8, a. 1, sol.). Amongst the many works available, that of François Bourassa is particularly recommended: "Note sur le traité de la Trinité de la Somme théologique de saint Thomas," *Science et Esprit* 27 (1975): 187–207.

[3] Book IV of the *Summa contra Gentiles*, which contains the treatise on the Trinity, was undoubtedly written in 1264–65. The *Prima pars of the Summa theologiae* would seem to have been written during Thomas's stay in Rome, between 1265 and 1268, and therefore only a few years separated the two treatises. For a chronological study, see René-Antoine Gauthier, *Saint Thomas d'Aquin, Somme contre les Gentils, Introduction* (Paris: Éditions universitaires, 1993), pp. 101–8; J.-P. Torrell, *Saint Thomas Aquinas*, vol. 1, *The Person and His Work*, pp. 101–4 and 146.

[4] For an examination of the principal stages in the development of the treatise on the Trinity in the *Summa contra Gentiles*, the reader is directed to Robert L. Richard, *The Problem of an Apologetical Perspective in the Trinitarian Theology of St. Thomas Aquinas* (Rome: Gregorian University Press, 1963), pp. 137–203.

[5] Numerous works examine the doctrine of the Word in the *Summa contra Gentiles*. We will mention: Hyacinthe Paissac, *Théologie du Verbe, Saint Augustin et Saint Thomas* (Paris: Cerf, 1951), pp. 162–81; Louis-Bertrand Geiger, "Les

"economic Trinity," the danger of seeing the treatise on the Trinity in isolation, the role of theological reason in the context of documentation on revelation, etc.),[6] the *Summa contra Gentiles* proves to be particularly instructive in the clarification of Thomas's view of the task of the theologian who wishes to explain belief in the Trinity.

General Method and Positioning of the Treatise on the Trinity

The body of Trinitarian doctrine is found in the fourth Book, devoted to the "manifestation of that truth which transcends reason,"[7] while those truths which human reason is able to demonstrate and analyze have been the study of the first three Books. In either case, Thomas has a twofold purpose: To present the truth and

---

rédactions successives de *Contra Gentiles* I, 53 d'après l'autographe," in *Saint Thomas d'Aquin aujourd'hui, Recherches de philosophie 6* (Paris/Bruges: Desclée de Brouwer, 1963), pp. 221–40; César Izquierdo, "La teología del Verbo en la *Summa contra Gentiles*," *Scripta theologica* 14 (1982): 551–80; *Vruchtbaar Woord: Wijsgerige beschouwingen bij een theologische tekst van Thomas van Aquino (Summa contra Gentiles boek IV, hoofdstuk 11)*, ed. Jan A. Aertsen et al. (Leuven: Leuven University Press, 1990); R.-A. Gauthier, *Saint Thomas d'Aquin, Somme contre les Gentils*, pp. 105–8. For other aspects of Trinitarian theology, let us mention Javier Prades, *"Deus specialiter est in sanctis per gratiam": El misterio de la inhabitación de la Trinidad en los escritos de santo Tomás* (Rome: Gregorian University Press, 1993), pp. 172–97; Yves Floucat, *L'intime fécondité de l'intelligence: Le verbe mental selon saint Thomas d'Aquin* (Paris: Téqui, 2001). Finally, mention should be made of the study of the biblical sources of the treatise on the Trinity, carried out by José A. Fidalgo Herranz, *La SS. Trinidad en la Suma contra los Gentiles: fuentes bíblicas*, Diss. Universidad de Navarra, Pamplona, 1984; an extract from this doctoral thesis may be found in *Excerpta e dissertationibus in sacra theologia*, vol. 8 (Pamplona: Ediciones Universidad de Navarra, 1986), pp. 329–402 (list of biblical texts, examination of exegetical method, and analysis of certain important passages).

6 For a well-documented examination of contemporary criticism often leveled at St. Thomas's Trinitarian theology (with a brief discussion of the alternatives offered), see Leo Scheffczyk, "Die Trinitätslehre des Thomas von Aquin im Spiegel gegenwärtiger Kritik," *Studi tomistici* 59 (1995): 163–90.

7 *SCG* I, ch. 9 (#56). The text and numbering system is taken from the edition by Ceslas Pera et al. (Turin: Marietti, 1961): *Liber de veritate catholicae fidei contra errores infidelium* otherwise known as the *Summa contra Gentiles* [referred to as *SCG*].

to dispel the errors which oppose it. In both cases, the second aspect (the refutation of errors) is fully part of the task of theological wisdom. Its role is not purely one of repudiation: As is evident in the exposition of heresies in the treatise on the Trinity, detailed examination of error is one of the stages in the pursuit of truth, giving access to a better understanding of that truth.[8]

The first difficulty concerning the doctrine of God lies in the division of the treatise *De Deo* into two parts (God as One in the first Book and God as Trinity in Book IV). This separation of the treatise on God into two sections, in the *Summa contra Gentiles,* is chiefly a consequence of the fact that Thomas wants to use two *distinct* methods to reveal the truth of the faith and defend it as well as possible. In the first case, the truth of faith will be established and confirmed by necessary reasons and demonstrative proofs, while in the second case (the Trinity) the only decisive authority is that of the documents of the faith received by the Church. The reasoning processes followed and comparisons made in the latter are not therefore susceptible to proof: Their value lies rather in allowing believers the opportunity to deepen their faith *(ad fidelium quidem exercitium et solatium).*[9] It should be noted however that the treatise on God in Book I does not constitute a purely philosophical examination conducted without reference to Scripture. Scriptural references are less numerous but certainly present (often placed at the culmination of a reasoned argument, before errors connected with the point in question are identified) and typically introduced by a formula indicating that Holy Scripture "confirms" the truth which has just been proven by rational means, or "bears witness" to it. What Thomas is doing in such instances is proving the truth *of faith,* as taught by Scripture, by means of rational argument.[10] Belief in the Trinity, on the other

---

[8] See R.-A. Gauthier, *Saint Thomas d'Aquin, Somme contre les Gentils,* pp. 147–63.

[9] *SCG* I, ch. 9 (#54). The phrase quoted recalls an Augustinian theme (Trinitarian theology as a spiritual exercise): see particularly Augustine, *De Trinitate* XIII, XX, 26; XV, I, 1; XV, VI, 10.

[10] See for example *SCG* I, ch. 14 (#119); ch. 15 (#126); ch. 20 (#188); and so on. The treatise on Creation in Book II makes it evident that Thomas is adopting a theological standpoint rather than that of a philosopher (*SCG* II, ch. 4).

hand, is based solely on revelation, but this does not mean that theological reasoning is discounted. Firstly, the theologian may provide a rigorous demonstration of the invalidity of arguments against the faith taught by revelation (they are false or at least non-necessary).[11] Secondly, theological argument can highlight similarities in this context *(similitudines, verisimilitudines)* or "plausible reasons" *(rationes verisimiles),* in other words can make full use of analogies which allow an explanation of faith in three divine persons, principally by means of Augustine's "psychological" approach (the Word and Love),[12] by presenting faith as "the friend of reason in plausibility" in the words of Father Chenu.[13] Thus, it is the type of knowledge called upon, in accordance with the intention of demonstrating the truth of the Catholic faith, which dictates the division of the work and of its parts.

If we examine the general plan of the *Summa contra Gentiles,* we notice that, within this first structure (truths of the faith accessible or non-accessible to reason), Thomas develops a second: that of the principle-end incorporated into the scheme of origin–return *(exitus–reditus)* which directed his commentary on the *Sentences* and was later to dictate the organization of the *Summa theologiae.* The two structures are intimately connected, forming a whole, with theological content set out as follows:[14]

1. God in Himself (Book I) and that which is "believed about God and transcends human reason," in other words, the Trinity (Book IV, ch. 2–26);

---

[11] *SCG* I, ch. 7; ch. 9 (#52); IV, ch. 1 (#3348).

[12] *SCG* I, ch. 8 (#48); ch. 9 (#54); cf. *Super Boetium de Trinitate,* q. 2, a. 3, on the use of philosophy in sacred doctrine: ". . . secundo ad notificandum per aliquas similitudines ea quae sunt fidei, sicut Augustinus in libro De Trinitate utitur multis similitudinibus ex doctrinis philosophicis sumptis ad manifestandum trinitatem" (Leonine edition, vol. 50, 99).

[13] "Amie de la raison dans des vraisemblances." See Marie-Dominique Chenu, *Introduction à l'étude de saint Thomas d'Aquin* (Montréal/Paris: Institut d'Etudes médiévales/Vrin, 1984), p. 252.

[14] *SCG* I, ch. 9 (#57) and IV, ch. 1 (#3349). It will be seen here again that the fundamental structure of the work is governed by the theological order *par excellence,* that of the *exitus–reditus*: God in Himself and the relationship of creatures to God (God the principle and God the end); cf. II *Sent.,* prol.; *SCG* II, ch. 4.

2. The procession of creatures *a Deo* (God as origin, Book II) and that which God "does which transcends human reason," in other words, the Incarnation and all that results from it (Book IV, ch. 27–78);

3. The ordering of creatures to God as end (Book III) and that which is "hoped" of God "at man's ultimate end," in other words, the resurrection of the body, the final happiness of souls, and all that follows on from these (Book IV, ch. 79–97).

The connection between these two structures suggests particularly that the treatise on the Trinity, linked to the treatise on God in Himself, should also allow for an explanation of the work of the Trinity *ad extra* because the Trinity is the origin and end of creatures. Trinitarian doctrine dominates this section and to a certain extent is manifested in it. Thomas explains that the processions within the Trinity take place in a circular manner *(concluditur circulo)* since there is, in the procession of Love, a "return" to the substance from which the first procession came (procession of the Word).[15] With the procession of the Holy Spirit, the immanent process in God "comes to a close," and becomes in turn the princi-

---

[15] *SCG* IV, ch. 26 (#3631): "Ulterius autem non procedit intra se, sed concluditur circulo, dum per amorem redit ad ipsam substantiam a qua processio incoeperat per intentionem intellectam; sed fit processio ad exteriores effectus, dum ex amore sui procedit ad aliquid faciendum." This refers precisely to the mens created which knows itself and loves itself; the attribution of this process to God the Trinity is put more plainly: "Ulterius autem intra divinam naturam nulla processio invenitur, sed solum processio in exteriores effectus" (ibid., #3632). However, in the Disputed Questions *De potentia*, Thomas does not hesitate to apply the image of the circle to God himself, as he had done in his commentary on the *Sentences*: "Est ergo tam in nobis quam in Deo circulatio quaedam in operibus intellectus et voluntatis; nam voluntas redit in id a quo fuit principium intelligendi. . . . Sed in Deo iste circulus clauditur in seipso. Nam Deus intelligendo se, concipit Verbum suum, quod est etiam ratio omnium intellectorum per ipsum . . . et ex hoc Verbo procedit in amorem omnium et sui ipsius" (*De potentia*, q. 9, a. 9, which is evidently a reworking of *SCG* IV, ch. 26). We see here very clearly the idea of an intra-Trinitarian circle governing the procession and return of creatures to God. Cf. the earlier work by Albert the Great, *Super Dionysium de divinis nominibus*, ch. 4, #109 (Cologne edition, vol. 37/1, 207) and I *Sent.*, d. 11, a. 1. (ed. Borgnet, vol. 25 [Paris: Louis Vivès, 1893], 335 ss).

ple of the procession of effects taking place outside of God. The procession of creatures, using the image of the circle, is more particularly linked to the Holy Spirit as Love, since it is through love that a perfect agent is prompted to act.[16] Trinitarian doctrine thus throws light of special significance on the structure of "principle-end" governing the *Summa contra Gentiles*. We may note here not only that the theme of the origin–return is brought out in this context, but that it also makes an appearance in other chapters, particularly in connection with the production of spiritual creatures and in the question of the suitability of the Incarnation.[17]

The link between these two sections introduces a difficulty raised by several studies on the subject, for in Book III Thomas deals extensively with the vision of God, the law and grace, in that part dedicated to the *ordo in finem* within the context of truth which may be demonstrated by reason.[18] But are we not here addressing realities which belong exclusively to the domain of faith? This problem is closely concerned with Trinitarian theology, and without entering into detailed discussion about the purpose of the *Summa contra Gentiles* or its intended audience, it will be worth examining the internal structure of Book IV.

We have already noted the tripartite plan of Book IV and its correspondence to the structure of the first three Books. However, if we follow Thomas's purpose more closely throughout the course of Book IV, we find not only the expected tripartite structure but, at a deeper level, a complementary bipartite structure. The whole of Book IV after the treatise on the Trinity (ch. 2–26) is concerned with Christ (his humanity). Following the exposition of faith in the Incarnation (the fact and the suitability of the Incarnation of the Word: ch. 27–55), the treatise on the sacraments (ch. 56–78) is directly linked to

---

[16] This theme is developed in *SCG* IV, ch. 20 (#3570) in the context of the creative causality of the Holy Spirit.

[17] *SCG* II, ch. 46 (#1230): *motus circularis, reditus ad principium;* IV, ch. 55 (#3937): union of mankind with the first principle *ut quadam circulatione perfectio rerum concludatur.*

[18] See the analysis and discussion of these problems by René-Antoine Gauthier, "Introduction historique," in *Thomas d'Aquin, Contra Gentiles,* vol. 1 (Paris: Lethielleux, 1961), pp. 7–123, especially 100–20.

the passion and the death of Christ, since through the sacraments we become part of the redemptive act accomplished by the passion of Christ.[19] We find the treatise on the resurrection and last things (ch. 79–97), however, coupled with faith in the resurrection of Christ, since our resurrection is an effect of the resurrection of Christ.[20] This schema, associating the sacraments strictly with the death of Christ, and the treatise on the last things with the resurrection of Christ, is adhered to so scrupulously by St. Thomas that the resurrection of Christ is hardly mentioned in his presentation of the sacraments.[21] Thus, it appears that Book IV covers precisely and exclusively faith in the Trinity and in the humanity of Christ, with its effects. The *Trinity* and *Christ:* These are exactly what St. Thomas is thinking of in the texts presenting the structure of the *Contra Gentiles,* when he speaks of those truths held by faith alone or inaccessible to reason. These two fundamental articles of faith dictate the structure of Book IV and the ensuing fundamental division of the work into two parts. They recall, moreover, the constant teaching of St. Thomas, present for example from the very first chapters of the *Compendium theologiae:* "All our understanding of the faith *(tota fidei cognitio)* thus rests upon these two points: the divinity of the Trinity and the humanity of Christ. This is no surprise, for the humanity of Christ is the path leading to divinity."[22]

There is no reason to think, because of this, that St. Thomas set out with one plan in mind but actually followed another. Truths such

---

[19] See *SCG* IV, ch. 56 (#3962): The sacraments are introduced and presented in the immediate aftermath of Christ's death as being the "quasi universal" cause of the salvation of mankind, this cause being "applied" to each of its effects. There is no mention here of the resurrection of Christ.

[20] *SCG* IV, ch. 79 (#4128–29): We share in the effect of the death of Christ through the sacraments, in that we receive forgiveness for sins, and we share in the effect of the resurrection of Christ in that we will be freed from death in the future resurrection.

[21] A word search in the *Index thomisticus* confirms this observation: The terms *resurgere* and *resurrectio* do not feature in the treatise on the sacraments.

[22] *Compendium theologiae* I, ch. 2: "Circa hec ergo duo tota fidei cognitio versatur, scilicet circa divinitatem Trinitatis et circa humanitatem Christi: nec mirum, quia Christi humanitas via est qua ad divinitatem pervenitur" (Leonine edition, vol. 42, 83); cf. *De articulis fidei,* ch.1: "In primis igitur vos scire oportet quod tota fides christiana circa divinitatem et humanitatem Christi versatur" (ibid., p. 245).

as the vision of God, the final beatitude, the law, grace, prophecy, and so forth may be addressed in the section dealing with matters which can be argued and analyzed by human reason, but only from one point of view, or in the form of a preliminary examination which achieves consummation in the sections on the Trinity and on Christ, when the Trinitarian and Christological foundations and consequences are set out. We will identify some of these points later. The interplay at work within Book IV lies not so much between truths held by faith alone and those which are accessible to reason, but rather in the connection between the tripartite schema referred to in the Book's Prologue (which reminds us of the first three Books and of the *exitus–reditus*) and the fundamental bipartite structure of the understanding of faith (the Trinity and Christ). As regards the internal organization of the work, we should note finally that the mainstay of Book IV's treatise on the Trinity is chapter 42 of Book I, which deals with divine unity. This is evident from the close correspondence between topics covered (reference to Arians, elimination of the possibility of plurality of gods, examination of traditional scriptural terms of expression, etc.). It is obvious here that Thomas develops his Trinitarian theology with constant reference to divine unity and that one of the principal concerns of his Trinitarian treatise will be to show that the confession of a true Trinity of persons will in no way undermine belief in the absolute divine unity.[23]

Plan and Method of the Treatise on "The Confession of the Trinity"

From its start, the treatise on the Trinity refers to the veiled nature of our knowledge of the faith, setting the tone for the fourth Book.

---

[23] This concern is evidently aroused by Sabellianism, but it is also particularly striking to find it in the refutation of Arianism, which Thomas accuses outright and in a manner which is initially rather surprising, of proposing a plurality of gods, see *SCG* I, ch. 42 (#355); IV, ch. 6 (#3387); according to this position, the central problem of Arianism lies in the unity of divine essence. See Peter Worrall, "St. Thomas and Arianism," *RTAM* 23 (1956): 208–59 and 24 (1957): 45–100, especially 23 (1956): 235–38.

In the Prologue which introduces it, we note Thomas's unwavering insistence upon the imperfection of our knowledge of the Trinity. Such knowledge is only given through listening to revelation (Rom 10:17), and represents not a clear vision but a limited grasp, "believing without comprehending." Little in the way of mystery has been revealed to us *(pauca nobis revelantur)*, adds Thomas, and that which Scripture teaches us is revealed to us in the form of obscure images and words, so that only the studious *(soli studiosi)* may succeed, with difficulty, in grasping some of it, while other believers may venerate the mystery in a veiled form *(alii vero quasi occulta venerentur)*. Either way, derision and criticism on the part of those who are opposed to the faith will have no effect.[24] This emphasis on the primacy of faith (the only way to enter into the mystery of the Trinity and of Christ) and on the limited reach of our understanding as believers, which Thomas formulates in terms similar to Hilary of Poitiers and to Pseudo-Dionysius,[25] is the dominant tone of the Trinitarian theology. It is partly dictated by the stated purpose of the *Summa contra Gentiles*, but equally is part of the unfailing teaching of St. Thomas who here gives it a very special emphasis.[26]

On this basis, the Trinitarian doctrine consists of three parts: the generation of the Son (ch. 2–14), the procession of the Holy Spirit (ch. 15–25), and a concluding chapter which shows that there can be

---

[24] *SCG* IV, ch. 1 (#3345); these observations refer to Job 26:14, which heads the Prologue, and are a reworking of points made in *Super Boetium de Trinitate*, q. 2, a. 4.

[25] Like Hilary, Thomas emphasizes the incomprehensibility of the mystery which should exclude any presumption in our search for knowledge (*SCG* I, ch. 8, #50; cf. *SCG* IV, ch. 1, #3348). St. Hilary, *De Trinitate* II, 10–11 (PL 10, 58–59; CCSL 62, 48–49); presumption will be characteristic of the attitude of heretics (*SCG* IV, ch. 4, #3358). Without identifying precise passages, we can detect an atmosphere of Dionysian thought in the mention of mediation by angels for the revelation of mystery, the obscure nature of scriptural comparisons and words, the "veils" which hide the mystery, and so on (*SCG* IV, ch. 1, #3345–3346); the mention of obscurity and veils may also more precisely refer to points made by Thomas in his commentary on Boethius (*Super Boetium de Trinitate*, q. 2, a. 4). On this theme, see Serge-Thomas Bonino, "Les 'voiles sacrés': à propos d'une citation de Denys," *Studi Tomistici* 45 (1992): 158–71.

[26] See especially I *Sent.*, d. 2, q. 1, a. 4; d. 3, q. 1, a. 4; *Super Boetium de Trinitate*, q. 1, a. 4; *ST* I, q. 32, a. 1.

no other procession in God (ch. 26). We can see straightaway that the entire exposition is founded on the two divine *processions* and on the *persons*. We note also that there is no section devoted to the Father alone. The Father is in fact present throughout as the principle of the Son and of the Holy Spirit, the "principle of all divine procession."[27] In this sense, the Father is in a way the starting point for the whole treatise, not because the person of the Father may be understood outside of his relation with the Son (the doctrine of the constitution of the divine person by his relative property would evidently not permit this), but in the sense that the study of the two processions begins with "God" who engenders the Son and "God" who, with his Word, is the spirator of Love, that is, the Father in his relation to the Son and to the Holy Spirit. It is not exactly the *ordo doctrinae* of the *Summa theologiae* (processions–relations–persons) which determines the form of the treatise here, but more precisely the *truth* of the real procession of the Son and of the Holy Spirit as divine persons. Thomas's intention, in accordance with the overall aim of the *Summa contra Gentiles,* is not so much to write a scholarly exposition of the understanding of the faith (although many features of such a work are present) as a *manifestation of the truth of the Catholic faith.* The aim will have been accomplished once it is demonstrated that there are three subsistent persons in the divine nature: the Father, the Son, and the Holy Spirit, and that these Three are one God.[28] This is what the treatise on the Trinity is setting out to do.[29]

If we examine more closely the internal arrangement of each section, we will notice that foremost in Thomas's mind is an emphasis on Scripture,[30] revealed in the following three ways:

---

[27] *SCG* IV, ch. 26 (#3632).

[28] *SCG* IV, ch. 26 (#3626).

[29] This is already indicated in the Prologue, which refers to this section as being the *confession* of the Trinity: *SCG* IV, ch. 1 (#3349); cf. ch. 7 (#3424) and 3426; ch. 8 (#3439); and so on.

[30] The Prologue of Book IV indicates that Scripture should constitute the *principium* of a theologian's thinking (ch. 1, #3348). The treatise on the Trinity demonstrates that this role of *principium* represents far more than a mere starting point: Scripture is the heart and soul of all Thomas's thinking in these chapters, to the extent that everything is structured around it.

1. The basic facts provided by Scripture (ch. 2–3 and 15). Scripture teaches about *generation* in God; a *Father* and a *Son*; a Son who is *God*. It also refers to the *Holy Spirit* as being of the same rank as the Father and the Son, and to the *procession* of the Holy Spirit. This is the basis of the treatise. At this stage, Thomas restricts himself to establishing the presence of these fundamental facts in scriptural teaching by the use of various biblical texts. Using terms borrowed from patristic sources, he then goes on to maintain that these basic elements may be interpreted in different ways, and that everything depends upon what one reads into Scripture, and into the confession of faith.[31] This is why he develops the two following approaches.

2. The reading of Scripture received by the Catholic faith in the face of heresy (ch. 4–9 and 16–23). We now enter into a vast section organized in three stages around a very large number of biblical texts: The presentation of the heresies and of their scriptural arguments, the exposition of the Catholic reading of Scripture, and finally the reply to the exegesis used in defense of the heresies. We will return to this later.

3. A discussion of rational objections to the faith (ch. 10–14 and the end of chapters 16 and 23). It might seem that Thomas has now abandoned direct explanation of scriptural texts, since he is addressing difficulties encountered by reason in accepting the generation of the Son and the procession of the Holy Spirit. But, in order to reply to these objections and demonstrate that they are not in any way necessary, Thomas inserts two long expositions (ch. 11–13

---

[31] *SCG* IV, ch. 4 (#3358). This approach is commonly found in patristic writing: see especially St. Hilary of Poitiers, *De Trinitate* II, 3 (PL 10, 51–52; CCSL 62, 39). Speaking here of "perverse men who, presumptuously measuring the truth of this doctrine by the yardstick of their own judgment, have formed vain and varied opinions on the matter," Thomas is directly echoing St. Hilary (ibid.). Moreover, St. Hilary continues his exposition by indicating the heresies which will preoccupy Thomas. See also Vigilius of Thapsus, *Contra arianos, sabellianos et photinianos*, Book I, ch. 3–5 (PL 62, 181–83).

and 19–22) intended to show how one may grasp, imperfectly but in a real sense, the truth which Scripture teaches about the Son and the Holy Spirit in their relation to the Father and in the divine economy. It is here, still rooted in biblical ground,[32] that we find the doctrine of the Word and of Love.

The section dedicated to the *Filioque* (ch. 24–25) has certain special features (notably in the form of appeals to the authority of the Fathers, the Church Councils, and the Pope), but is in the same way based on biblical exposition, then discusses objections drawn from Scripture before continuing the debate within the field of conciliary tradition and rational argument.[33]

Many of the points raised here may be compared with, and confirmed by, the section dedicated to faith in Christ, for the two principal sections of Book IV in fact adopt the same approach. In any case, we inevitably arrive at two conclusions.

Firstly, Thomas's whole submission is subject to the various levels of scriptural reading which we have just outlined. This is extremely revealing in terms of his theological method, and shows us clearly that, for Thomas, the Trinitarian theology of *Contra Gentiles* consists in essence of a reflection through Scripture and on Scripture, together with its associated theological resources such as reason and tradition. In this sense, to the extent that biblical reflection includes historical research (heresies, with the references indicated by the patristic writings), dogmatic authority (the faith of the Church, councils, the Pope), and rational argument, we can conclude that Scripture is not only the starting point but, at various levels and stages of development, is the core of all the Trinitarian doctrine.

Secondly, as each doctrinal point is dealt with, Thomas's method is such that the errors or challenges to the faith create the context in which he inserts and presents the Catholic reading of Scripture.

---

[32] The exposition on the Word in chapters 11–13 is interwoven with biblical reference throughout; ch. 19–22 on Love are in turn pure biblical theology, entirely centered around Scripture.

[33] *SCG* IV, ch. 24 (#3606–8); ch. 25 (#3621–22).

This, to a theologian, was an invitation to make full, direct use of doctrinal history.

The Study of Errors about the Trinity

Regarding the Son, Thomas discusses at length three errors in particular (ch. 4–9): that of Photinus who sees in Jesus a mere man brought up to participate in divinity; that of Sabellius who denies that the Son is a subsistent person distinct from the Father; and that of Arius who holds that the Son is inferior to the Father. Regarding the Holy Spirit, he examines the Pneumatomachi or semi-Arians who insisted that the Spirit was a creature, or denied that he was a subsistent person (ch. 16–18 and 23), before going on to discuss the question of the procession of the Spirit *a Filio* (ch. 24–25). It would be a mistake to see this section on errors as being of only marginal importance. In concrete terms, it constitutes a good third of the treatise, and is responsible for the doctrinal approach adopted. We should note here, putting aside the problem of the *Filioque,* that the treatise on the Trinity makes no mention of those more specifically medieval errors often discussed by Thomas in his other works (Gilbert de la Porrée, Joachim of Fiore, etc.). We find no reference to the Trinitarian heresies present in the Cathar movements of St. Thomas's time: These errors, moreover, may all be traced back one way or another to the main heresies of antiquity.[34] It is also worth pointing out that Thomas presents the heresies *before* outlining the Catholic reading of Scripture and the understanding which can be derived from it.[35] These heresies dating from antiquity, in which Thomas sees the greatest challenges to faith in the Trinity, thus constitute the starting point for his reflections on

---

[34] See especially Georg Schmitz-Valckenberg, *Grundlehren katharischer Sekten des 13. Jahrhunderts, Eine theologische Untersuchung mit besonderer Berückstchtigung von 'Adversus Catharos et Valdenses' des Moneta von Cremona* (Munich: Schoeningh, 1971), pp. 136–43 and 152–57.

[35] With the exception of the section on the *Filioque,* which begins with an exposition of the Catholic reading of Scripture. We can see once again the special place accorded to this doctrinal point in terms of methodology.

Scripture. Overall, this methodological choice may be seen as significant in two ways.

On one hand, the purpose of the *Summa contra Gentiles* being to show the truth of the faith by dispelling error,[36] the refutation of Trinitarian heresies must be a prominent feature of the work's overall plan. The presentation of errors and references to those who put them forward are not always as complete and detailed in the first three Books as in the fourth, but are always treated as issues of fundamental importance. Further, errors are not only dispelled by refuting arguments which have been drawn on a piecemeal basis from Scripture: It is through demonstrating the close correspondence between the Catholic faith and Scripture that the most searching and complete answers to error are provided. It is clear here that, for Thomas, demonstrating the truth and dispelling errors represent two sides of the same coin.[37]

On the other hand, as we pointed out earlier, in methodological terms it is the heresies which make up the explanatory context within which Thomas proposes the Catholic reception of Scripture. He thus goes so far as to show that the Catholic faith, by confessing with Arius the plurality of persons and, with Sabellius, confessing their unity of nature, follows the "middle path" *(media via incedens).*[38] He also explains that heresies themselves bear an element of truth in that they contradict not only the truth, but also each other.[39] By the end of the exposition concerning the Son, Thomas is able to show that the Catholic faith is the only one to confess the *true generation of a Son in God.* This approach appears to throw a great deal of light on the beginning of the *Summa theologiae,* which

---

[36] *SCG* I, ch. 2 (#9).

[37] The *Summa contra Gentiles* explains this twofold task by means of the theme of wisdom; see R.-A. Gauthier, *Saint Thomas d'Aquin, Somme contre les Gentils,* pp 143 63 ("le métier de sage"). The *Summa theologiae* was also to adopt this twin approach in showing that sacred doctrine is an argumentative science (*ST* I, q. 1, a. 8); the second aspect (refutation of error) is however less prominent in this work.

[38] *SCG* IV, ch. 7 (#3426).

[39] Ibid. Here Thomas, following Aristotle (*Nicomachean Ethics* I, 1098 b 11–12) explains an aspect already brought out by St. Hilary of Poitiers (*De Trinitate* I, 26; VII, 7).

addresses the views of Arius and Sabellius in the very first article of the Trinitarian treatise on the actual reality of procession in God. This does not suggest that, at its heart, the Catholic faith depends on heresies, but that, as Thomas explains elsewhere, the heresies led the Church Fathers to deepen their understanding of revelation and to communicate it with greater precision.[40] Thomas not only takes them into account, but sees them as providing the first opportunity for showing the truth of the faith. In so doing, he is displaying a more dispassionate version of the method used by the Church Fathers, particularly Hilary of Poitiers who is undeniably one of his major sources in this area.[41] An examination of contents and method also points clearly to the influence of Augustine and probably to Vigilius of Thapsus following on from Hilary (recognition of given scriptural basis and of a common confession of faith, then elimination of errors which in any case cancel each other out, and finally exposition of the Catholic faith at the end of the refutation of Photinus, Sabellius, and Arius).[42] The method of the treatise on the Trinity seems largely indebted here to the patristic documents consulted by Thomas.

As regards content, Thomas runs through his discussion of heresies fairly deeply, treating each in the same way: presentation of the heretical point of view, its theological premises, scriptural arguments put forward by proponents of the heresy, names of people having subscribed to the heresy, exposition of the true meaning of Scripture, then finally resolution of the scriptural arguments presented.[43] Within each chapter the themes are also arranged so that the heretical issues concerned may be placed in context and understood in

---

[40] *Contra errores Graecorum,* prol.; *De potentia,* q. 9, a. 5.

[41] Hilary undoubtedly exerts less influence than is suggested by Joseph Wawrykow, "The *Summa Contra Gentiles* Reconsidered: on the Contribution of the *De Trinitate* of Hilary of Poitiers," *The Thomist* 58 (1994): 617–34. It is however of great importance.

[42] See Gilles Emery, "Le photinisme et ses précurseurs chez saint Thomas: Cérinthe, les ébionites, Paul de Samosate et Photin," *RT* 95 (1995): 371–98.

[43] Slight variations may be identified here and there, but the approaches adopted for the discussion of Photinus, Sabellius, Arius, and Macedonius are basically identical.

detail. With Arianism, for example, Thomas lists one doctrinal point after another as follows: the non-identical nature of the Son and the Father, the non-eternal nature of the Son, and the non-divinity of the Son.[44] In the exposition of scriptural arguments put forward by the heresy, the starting point is consequently the Arian denial of the identical nature of the Father and the Son (the Son is not *verus Deus*), and after a delineation of the thesis of the inferiority of the Son, the heretical argument arrives at its final and principal conclusion: The Son, as far as Arianism is concerned, is only a creature.[45]

We should also note that before launching into the exposition of the scriptural texts cited by the heresy, Thomas takes care to set out the biblical presuppositions held by the heretical viewpoint. He shows, for example, that the Photinians, when thinking of Jesus, could never forget the frequent attribution in Scripture of the words "son" or "god" to angels or to men.[46] He suggests that the position of Arius is motivated by the fact that neither the Sabellian nor the Photinian viewpoint[47] complies with Scripture, explaining that Scripture compelled him, besides, to call the Son "God," and so on. Thomas is also scrupulous in comparing one error with another, and comparing all with the Catholic faith, in order to demonstrate the points in common and the differences.[48] He applies himself equally to demonstrating, beyond a scriptural context, the philosophical roots of the errors, thus presenting Arianism as a reading of Scripture which is contaminated, in its understanding of the supreme unity and of emanation, by a current of Platonic thought.[49] The Arians did not wish to believe, and *they were unable to understand,* their standpoint being thus dictated by a problem of faith and also by an

---

[44] *SCG* IV, ch. 6 (#3387).

[45] *SCG* IV, ch. 6 (#3389–99).

[46] *SCG* IV, ch. 4 (#3359).

[47] *SCG* IV, ch. 6 (#3387).

[48] See for example the summing up and concluding remarks in *SCG* IV, ch. 7 (#3425–26); ch. 9 (#3445).

[49] *SCG* IV, ch. 6 (#3400). Thomas notes here that the position of Arius and that of Eunomius, derived from Platonic writings, is consonant with that of Avicenna. This explanation of the origins of Arianism had already been formulated in the *Super Boetium de Trinitate*, q. 3, a. 4.

impediment of a philosophical nature.[50] All this confirms that Thomas's purpose was not simply to reject the error, but involved a deeper desire to grasp the reason behind it, and the impulses and arguments feeding it, so that he could understand it, confront it on its own terms, and then be in a better position to show the truth of the Catholic faith.

Much work remains to be done in the identification of Thomas's sources. Enjoying the freedom afforded by a work which was not intended to be scholarly, and wishing to compile a series of personal reflections (despite the abundant documentation), Thomas generally makes no explicit mention of authors.[51] The list of named heretics present in each section is clearly borrowed from the *De haeresibus* of St. Augustine. Thomas has certainly drawn his documentation on Photinus (and Cerinthus, the Ebionites, and Paul of Samosata) from Hilary, Augustine, and Vigilius of Thapsus in particular.[52] It would not be difficult to show that these same authors are the sources of the information given on Sabellius. As regards Arius, the *Summa contra Gentiles* repeats and extends the documentation listed in the *Super Boetium de Trinitate*. Arius features so often in the writings of the Church Fathers to which Thomas had access that detailed analysis in this area would prove extremely complex. However, because of the texts mentioned in the anti-Arian article of the *Super Boetium de Trinitate* (11 arguments and 9 contra, which all present biblical texts and which are all repeated in the *Summa contra Gentiles*),[53] it is possible to identify the massive and dominant presence of Augustine. As for heresies concerning the Holy Spirit more directly, in addition to the

---

[50] *SCG* IV, ch. 6 (#3387): "Non enim intelligere poterant, nec credere volebant."

[51] There is no explicit reference to the Church Fathers in chapters 3–9, apart from a mention of St. Hilary *(De Synodis)* in chapter 8 (#3436). The rest of the treatise on the Trinity shows the same reluctance to cite sources, with the exception of the two chapters on the *Filioque*. We also find three explicit references to Aristotle and one to the "philosophi." This is all St. Thomas explicitly tells us in his treatise on the Trinity.

[52] See G. Emery, "Le photinisme," footnote 42.

[53] *Super Boetium de Trinitate,* q. 3, a. 4; see editor's notes in the Leonine edition, vol. 50, pp. 114–18.

material already present in the *Super Boetium de Trinitate*[54] and its references to Augustine, a detailed study (which also still remains to be done) would probably point to an important contribution from St. Ambrose *(De Spiritu Sancto)*.[55] It is in any case clear that Thomas did not content himself with the material he found in Peter Lombard's *Sentences,* but carried out his own extensive research (in connection with his work for the *Catena aurea?*) such that the biblical arguments presented against heresies seem essentially an extension of patristic exegesis.

Scripture: Its Function and Thomas's Exegetical Method

Scripture takes pride of place in Thomas's purpose, following the three-part arrangement described above. In purely statistical terms, there are far more biblical texts discussed and cited here than is customary in Thomas's other treatises on the Trinity. According to the study carried out by J. A. Fidalgo Herranz, there are 462 biblical references in the Trinitarian treatise of the *Summa contra Gentiles* (Book IV, ch. 1–26), that is, a little less than one-third of the total number of biblical references present in the work as a whole.[56] The Johannine writings and the Pauline corpus, as is the case in Thomas's

---

[54] Compare for example *SCG* IV, ch. 6 (#3516) and *Super Boetium de Trinitate,* q. 3, a. 4, arg. 11; ch. 6 (#3617) and arg. 4; ch. 6 (#3521) and arg. 3; ch. 17 (#3526) and contra (second series) 2; ch. 1 (#3527) and contra (second series) 1; and so on.

[55] For example, the discussion of Am 4:13 and Zech 12:1 (*SCG* IV, ch. 16, #3514; ch. 23, #3592) could be derived (directly or indirectly) from St. Ambrose, *De Spiritu Sancto* II, 6 (PL 16, 753–55); for the discussion of Jn 16: 13 (*SCG* IV, ch. 16, #3515), see also *De Spiritu Sancto* II, 12 (PL 16, 770–73); compare also *SCG* IV, ch. 1 (#3530) and *De Spiritu Sancto* III, 19, n. 149 (PL 16, 811); ch. 17 (#3531) and *De Spiritu Sancto* II, 5 and III, 18, n. 139; and so on. Whether Ambrose is Thomas's direct source here or not, we see the same arguments with the same biblical texts in each case.

[56] J. A. Fidalgo Herranz, *La SS. Trinidad,* pp. 145–46 (biblical references table) and 174–78. The author counts 127 Old Testament citations and 335 from the New Testament in *SCG* IV, ch. 1–26. Such wearisome calculations may perhaps warrant some adjustment in their finer points, but at least give an idea of the central and influential position occupied by Scripture in these chapters.

other doctrinal treatises, head the list.[57] As is only to be expected from Thomas's approach to reading Scripture, there is no shortage of references to the Old Testament (the Psalms and Wisdom books are the most prominent),[58] for faith in the Trinity is already present, in a veiled but real form, in the Old Testament.[59] We will only be looking at one aspect of all this very important scriptural information: the approach to the reading of Scripture in the dossier of heresies.

As we noted earlier, it is first and foremost by setting out the true meaning of Scripture that Thomas hopes to dispel the erroneous interpretation of certain particular passages cited by the heretics. Thomas generally introduces these elucidations of the Catholic understanding by bringing out the meaning "which clearly emerges for those who give diligent consideration to the words of Holy Scripture" or by highlighting biblical accounts which are "self-evident" and the authority of which is in direct opposition to heretical opinion.[60] His initial method of using Scripture is to select certain passages or themes and place them in the context of the overall meaning of Scripture, drawing together the many interwoven threads and setting himself the task of tracing all the connections between them. At this initial stage, Thomas is aiming principally at demonstrating that the Son is true God, distinct from the Father and of the same nature as him, for all eternity. In the same way, he limits himself at this stage to establishing that the

---

57 J. A. Fidalgo Herranz counts 139 Johannic citations (121 from St. John's Gospel, 16 from the First Letter of John and 2 from the Revelation to John) as well as 135 Pauline citations (including 44 from the First Letter to the Corinthians), which represent nearly three-fifths of the biblical section.

58 There are 33 citations of the Psalms, 17 of Proverbs, and 12 of Ecclesiasticus. See J. A. Fidalgo Herranz, *La SS. Trinidad*, pp. 145–46.

59 See especially I *Sent.*, prol.; III *Sent.*, d. 25, q. 2, a. 2, qla 4; *ST* II–II, q. 2, a. 8 (the need for an explicit understanding of the Trinity on the part of the *maiores* before the coming of Christ). The reader will furthermore be familiar with the splendid Prologue to the commentary on the Psalms, which describes the contents of the Book as being "the general subject matter of all theological knowledge" (In *Psalmos Davidis expositio*, Proœmium; editio parmensis, vol. 14 [Parma: P. Fiaccadori, 1863], p. 148).

60 *SCG* IV, ch. 4 (#3368); ch. 5 (#3379); ch. 7 (#3402); ch. 17 (#3526). These sections concern chapters 4 (second part), 5 (second part), 7 and 17–18 (with ch. 24, first part, for the *Filioque*).

Holy Spirit is true God and a subsistent person. There is no attempt, in these chapters concerning the fundamental tenets of the faith, to address the doctrine of the Word and of Love, with all the consequent ramifications. At the next stage, he takes one by one the scriptural passages quoted as arguments against the Catholic faith (following the patristic dossier examined earlier), showing that the heretical exegesis is invalid and inconsistent with scriptural meaning in its context, while the Catholic faith is in keeping with the teaching in these passages.[61]

The first characteristic of the exegesis practiced here by Thomas is its heavy dependence upon patristic sources. A detailed study could no doubt provide evidence of far more borrowings than the few examples given above. The second characteristic is the literal method of reading Scripture. A literal reading in this context is in accordance with the hermeneutical principles constantly cited by Thomas: The literal sense of Scripture is the only sense which is properly conducive to argument *(ex quo solo potest trahi argumentum)*.[62] This is why "in order to dispel error, it is essential to adopt a literal approach."[63] Thomas's method thus exploits all the resources of a literal reading on its own terms, particularly that of very frequent recourse to context *(circumstantia litterae, contextus litterae)*,[64] and to words preceding or following the text in question,[65] in order to provide the overall interpretation of a passage which makes up a whole. If necessary, Thomas gives several possible interpretations,[66] explains the general sense of a mode of expression found throughout the Bible,[67] or discusses a

---

[61] This second stage involves chapters 8, 9, and 23 (with ch. 25, first part, for the *Filioque*).

[62] *ST* I, q. 1, a. 10, ad 1.

[63] I *Sent.*, prol., a. 5, sol. "Ad destructionem autem errorum non proceditur nisi per sensum litteralem, eo quod alii sensus sunt per similitudines accepti et ex similitudinariis locutionibus non potest sumi argumentatio."

[64] The two expressions are referred to in *SCG* IV, ch. 8 (#3430).

[65] See for example *SCG* IV, ch. 8 (#3431; #3433; #3435).

[66] *SCG* IV, ch. 8 (#3436); ch. 23 (#3597).

[67] For example in the case of exclusive expressions (exclusive mentions of whichever divine person), in *SCG* IV, ch. 8 (#3428–29); ch. 23 (#3596); ch. 25 (#3622); or for the interpretation of divine knowledge in the sense of "making known," ch. 8 (#3435); ch. 23 (#3600).

problem of textual criticism or of the Latin translation from the
Greek.[68] His reading of Scripture is of course theological and doctrinal, intended to bring out the dogmatic content of the wording.

We find a splendid illustration of this in chapters 7 and 17
which describe the works of the Son and of the Holy Spirit as
attested by Scripture (creation, sanctification, forgiveness of sins,
inspiration, vivification and resurrection, revelation of mysteries,
inner teaching, inhabitation, gift of beatitude, etc.) in order to
demonstrate their divinity. Paying attention to context and to the
language of Scripture, Thomas brings together a succession of themes,
seeking to emphasize the "self-evident" or "obvious" teaching in
Scripture. It is basically through this vast array of biblical accounts
that the error of heretical opinion is demonstrated,[69] and this is the
foundation for Thomas's entry into a detailed refutation of scriptural
arguments cited by the heretics, for "truth cannot be against truth."[70]

Finally, it should be pointed out that with the exception of the
question of the *Filioque,* Thomas at no point calls upon the authority
of the Church, the Councils, or the Fathers. Throughout all these
pages, Scripture provides its own interpretation. This methodological
characteristic evidently does not exclude the authority of the Church,
as is clear from the numerous references to the "Catholic faith" which
implicitly point to Church authority. But what Thomas wants to
demonstrate is *the conformity of the Catholic faith to the teachings of
Scripture.* The specific point he intends to make is that of the Catholic
Church being taught by the documents of Scripture *(Sacrae Scripturae documentis Ecclesia catholica docta).*[71] This clear affirmation of
the primacy of Scripture, both in practice and in theory,[72] should be

---

[68] See *SCG* IV, ch. 17 (#3527), regarding Phil 3:3; we also find a reference to
Hebrew in ch. 7, regarding Jer 23:6 (#3408).

[69] See the introductions to: ch. 4 (#3368); ch. 5 (#3379); ch. 7 (#3402).

[70] *SCG* IV, ch. 8 (#3427).

[71] *SCG* IV, ch. 7 (#3424).

[72] An implied reference to Pseudo-Dionysius in chapter 25 (#3621) recalls this:
"Cum de Deo nihil sit sentiendum nisi quod in Scriptura traditur." Cf.
Dionysius, *De divinis nominibus,* ch. 1, § 1 and § 2 (PG 3, 587–88; *Dionysiaca,* ed. Philippe Chevallier, vol. 1 [Paris/Bruges: Desclée de Brouwer, 1937],
pp. 7 and 12–13).

understood first and foremost in the light of the foundations of Trinitarian theology (only Scripture provides us with knowledge of the Trinity which is received in faith) and because of the acknowledged significance of heresies concerning the Trinity. There is no point in employing arguments relying on the authority of the Church when faced with doctrines which reject this authority: The debate should rather be located within a context recognized by the interlocutor as being authoritative.[73] The heresies being addressed by Thomas, however, and countered through the Catholic faith, claim to have their roots in Scripture. We should note, though, that the Fathers and the Councils (especially those of Nicea and Constantinople I) are never absent from the background discussion, and the Councils' deliberations on matters of faith are actually at the heart of Thomas's writing. It would seem appropriate at this point to suggest that Thomas is here setting out *to provide his own, personal account of Patristic and Conciliar writings, based on scriptural and doctrinal sources.* If therefore the heresies are dispelled, it is *because the doctrines involved are not what Scripture teaches.* This is an excellent illustration, in the characteristic style of the *Summa contra Gentiles,* of Thomas's habit of equating sacred doctrine (theology) with Holy Scripture.

Approaches to a Theological Understanding of the Mystery

The references to Scripture are not limited to this first anti-heretical section, but are also found at the heart of what is the more truly speculative discussion in the Trinitarian treatise.

Immediately after having stated the rational arguments against the Catholic faith, and before he resolves them, Thomas inserts a weighty section intended to demonstrate how the generation should be understood, and what Scripture teaches concerning the Son (ch. 11–13), and how, enlightened about the Holy Spirit by Scripture,

---

[73] This principle governing discussion with non-Catholics is set out in an especially detailed manner in the *De rationibus fidei*, Prologue. It also provides the explanation for Thomas's references to Councils of Antiquity in the discussion of the *Filioque*: such authorities were recognized by the Eastern Church.

we should grasp this truth (ch. 19–22). The aim of this section on
the Word (and Wisdom) and Love is to provide a positive demonstration that truths of the faith cannot be undermined by reason.[74]
In other words, when we seek a deeper understanding of Scripture
we are simultaneously in a position to refute those arguments which
attack faith from the standpoint of reason. The two processes are
intimately linked. This section on the Word and Love therefore
plays the same role in respect to rational argument as does Catholic
exegesis in respect to heretical exegesis. The structure of the chapter
on the Word is itself determined by the first verses of the Gospel
according to St. John, and the doctrine of the Word and of Love is
applied in great detail throughout several chapters to very many
biblical passages concerning the Son and the Holy Spirit. Thomas
sees those parts of his Trinitarian doctrine relying most heavily on
speculative arguments as nothing more than an "exercise" which
begins and ends with Scripture.

The in-depth discussion involved here is not intended to convince non-believers, but is aimed at the faithful who wish to arrive
at a better understanding of the truth of their faith.[75] At the start of
each of these expositions, Thomas reminds us that it will provide
only a limited grasp, which is all that mankind can hope for, of the
truth taught by the documents of revelation. The characteristic
expression used in the *Summa contra Gentiles* to describe this concept of faith-based reason is, after St. Augustine, *utcumque mente
capere (utcumque concipere, utcumque accipi)*.[76] This formula sug-

---

[74] *SCG* IV, ch. 10 (#3460).

[75] *SCG* I, ch. 9 (#54): *ad fidelium exercitium et solatium.*

[76] *SCG* IV, ch. 1 (#3348). The expression is used as a marker at the beginning
and ending of the exposition of the doctrine of the Word: ch. 11 (#3468) and
ch. 13 (#3496). See also ch. 19 (#3557). This expression reminds us of the
incomprehensibility of the mystery and is associated with the aim of defending
the faith in the face of errors. The term *utcumque* appears elsewhere, often in
the context of the knowledge of God, to dispel any presumption of perfect
knowledge and to emphasize the role of similitudes; see for example *SCG* II,
ch. 2 (#859); III, ch. 49 (#2270); ch. 113 (#2873); IV, ch. 21 (#3575). On
Augustine *(De Trinitate and Homilies on John)*, see Aquinas's *Catena aurea*
(Turin: Marietti, 1953): *Catena in Matth.* 3:17 (vol. 1, 55) and *Catena in Ioan.*
14:26 (vol. 2, 524).

gests the imperfection of our knowledge of the Trinity and directs us to the similitudes (word and love) which offer access to a certain degree of understanding about the mystery of the Trinity.

Despite the fact that the Thomist doctrine of the Word and of Love undeniably has its roots in the Augustinian heritage, we should note that Thomas does not introduce it with an analysis of the tripartite structure of the image of God in man, as he did in his commentary on the *Sentences* (memory–understanding–will and *mens–notitia–amor*).[77] This doctrine of the image is found at the very end of the Trinitarian treatise of the *Summa contra Gentiles,* next to the vestiges of the Trinity, and is intended to show that there cannot be more than three persons in God.[78] It would seem that we can detect a change in emphasis here on Thomas's part, in comparison with certain contemporary writings which were still attributing primary importance to the image and the vestiges as means of coming to know God.[79] The doctrine of the image as such, examining the representation of the Trinity in the soul in terms of its tripartite structure, is no longer truly a starting point but rather a point of arrival. We should note that the *Summa theologiae* was to adopt the same attitude, placing the study of the image within the treatise on the Creation and within the context of anthropology.[80]

Thomas bases his exposition rather on a vast survey of the degrees of emanation present in beings in accordance with the hierarchy of natures, calling to mind a structure already established by St.

---

[77] I *Sent.,* d. 3, q. 3–5; this, following the structure of the *Sentences,* was the starting point for the Trinitarian theology (with the theory of the vestiges of the Trinity, ibid., q. 2). Thomas later examined it very carefully in the *De veritate,* q. 10.

[78] *SCG* IV, ch. 26 (#3631–33). The question of the Son being an uncreated Image is considered earlier in the text (ch 11, #3474). Thomas also emphasizes the radical difference between the perfect Image which is the Son, and the created image which is man, and through which we cannot know the *quid est* of God (ch. 7, #3416).

[79] We might consider, for example, Bonaventure's *Itinerarum mentis in Deum,* even though this work does not belong to the same genre as the *Summa contra Gentiles.*

[80] *ST* I, q. 45, a. 7 and q. 93.

Albert:[81] inanimate beings, plants (vegetative life), sentient life, intelligent life. Such, in very explicit terms, is the *principium* which needs to be expounded in order to build the doctrine of the Word.[82] Its aim is to show that the higher the position in the hierarchy of natures, the more intimate, interior, and immanent to that nature is the emanation found. At the top of the ladder is intelligent life: Thomas works through this progressive intimacy in man and in angels, arriving at the consubstantiality and at the unity to be considered between the Intellect and its Word in God. The divine generation can therefore be demonstrated by means of the conception of the Word, through eliminating all the other kinds of emanation. The doctrine of Love is directly related to the exposition on the Word.[83] This detailed analysis of the emanations, which starts by looking at the *nature* of things and ascends to intelligent life, evidently does not leave out the doctrine of the image which is dealt with at the end. Removed from the problems inherent to Augustinian triadology (problems of *mens*, of memory, etc.), it provides Thomas rather with the foundation for a fruitful harvest which he intends to exploit with rigor.

This method was not to be used again in exactly the same form until the *Compendium theologiae*,[84] but is also used in very abbreviated forms to determine the approach of the *De potentia* and the *Summa theologiae*. When introducing the question of the procession or of the immanent communication of the divine nature in the

---

[81] Thomas has already provided a shorter outline of this analysis in the same context in the *De veritate*, q. 10, a. 1, sol. Within a similar thematic context (procession, theophany), see Albert's Prologue to the commentary on Dionysius' *Celestial Hierarchy* (Cologne edition, vol. 36/1, p. 1).

[82] *SCG* IV, ch. 11 (#3461). The Augustinian triadic patterns are not present in this chapter.

[83] *SCG* IV, ch. 19 (#3558–59).

[84] *CT* I, 52: Here the method is subject to several instances of fine tuning: On one hand, analysis of the emanations is directly linked to a distinction of the persons by means of their relations; on the other, Thomas presents the procession according to the operation of the intellect, and according to the operation of the will, within the same synthesis. In addition, Thomas no longer speaks of the "life of plants" but more precisely of the "powers of the vegetative (sensitive) soul."

Trinity, Thomas maintains from the start that the best example is to be found in the operation of the intellect *(in operatione intellectus congruentissime invenitur; maxime patet in intellectu).*[85] This way of presenting the foundations of theological knowledge of the person of the Son also reveals the fact that, in contrast to his approach in the commentary on the *Sentences,* Thomas now considers the name "Word" as being the most fruitful path to follow in order to grasp the first procession (the name "Son" was to be added to the exposition of the Word in due course).[86]

This methodological progression is linked to a marked progression in the understanding of what a word is. It is in the *Summa contra Gentiles* that Thomas's conception of the mental word *(intentio intellecta* is here the characteristic expression) begins to be concerned exclusively with what the intellect expresses or produces in its act of understanding.[87] Although Thomas pays hardly any attention to the problem of the essential or personal signification of the name of Word (no more, besides, than to the same problem concerning the name of Love), it is clear that this understanding opens the door to the exclusively personal signification of this name in God, since *verbum* through its own internal constitution implies a relationship with its source: the intellect which utters the word.[88] Following the works of Father Paissac and Father Geiger, critical studies have underlined the central importance of the *Contra Gentiles* in Thomas's doctrinal evolution, pointing out that the exposition has perhaps not yet reached the full stage of development which it would assume in Thomas's later work. Thus, in the words

---

[85] *De potentia,* q. 2, a. 1; *ST* I, q. 27, a. 1.

[86] *SCG* IV, ch. 11, #3476 (Son) and 3477 (generation and nativity). We should note here that Thomas even establishes the identity of *Verbum* and *Filius* in God with reference to the previous identification of *Verbum* and *Imago*. This sequential citing of the names of the Son is not without significance: it is a very clear expression of the central role of the doctrine of the Word.

[87] *SCG* I, ch. 53 and IV, ch. 11. See studies listed above in note 5.

[88] *SCG* IV, ch. 11 (#3473). The expressions are very clear: "Est autem de ratione interioris verbi, quod est intentio intellecta, quod procedat ab intelligente secundum suum intelligere, cum sit quasi terminus intellectualis operationis. . . . Comparatur igitur Verbum Dei ad Deum intelligentem, cuius est Verbum, sicut ad eum a quo est: hoc enim est de ratione verbi."

of Father Geiger, "Thomas does not yet state, as he does later, that the word is produced in all intellection, but he broadens the field considerably" and he "does not prove that God, in his understanding, expresses a Word, an *intentio intellecta.*"[89] These problems directly concern the extent of the analogy, and thereby the value of St. Thomas's theological method. It will be useful for us to identify briefly some of these elements.

St. Thomas certainly does not claim that the *real distinction* between the divine Word and the Father who utters it can be proved by reason (that would mean proving something which only faith can teach us), but the reasoning showing the existence of a Word in God (irrespective of the form which its reality in God takes, that is, of the problem of its personality and of its real relationship with the entity from which it proceeds) would however seem to include all the rigor of mature Thomist thinking. Given that any known thing, since it is known, must be present in the subject who knows it, Thomas's meticulous argument establishes that our intellect, when it is aware of itself, is in itself not only identical to itself through its essence but also as apprehended by itself in the operation of intelligence. Thus, Thomas had no difficulty concluding that God must be in himself as the known is in the knower *(ut intellectum in intelligente)* since God has perfect knowledge of himself.[90] Theological reason seems perfectly capable here of establishing the existence of a *verbum* in God, since the word or *intentio intellecta* is that by which the known is in the knower (irrespective of the question whether this Word is really distinct or not really distinct from God's intellect forming it). The theological

---

[89] L. B. Geiger, "Les rédactions successives," pp. 238 and 239. For C. Izquierdo ("La teología del Verbo," p. 568), the themes of person and relation are insufficiently explored in the *Summa contra Gentiles*, and an explicit treatment of the fundamental theme of the personality of the Word is held to be lacking. The doctrine of the person is certainly not examined in its full dimensions in this Trinitarian treatise, but is undoubtedly present in detailed form regarding the Word, with the doctrine of relations, in chapters 10 and 14 (#3451–57 and 3502–8). These chapters, as has been mentioned, are essential for the understanding of chapter 11.

[90] *SCG* IV, ch. 11 (#3469).

treatise on the Trinity does not deal directly with the necessary presence of the word in all processes of intellectual understanding, for its focus is narrowed more precisely to the knowledge *of self* in order to consider by analogy a true Word in God. Thomas limits himself here to establishing the word as "that which the intellect conceives of the thing which is known" (the known as it is present in the knowing intellect, without entering into a detailed discussion of the relationship between the intelligible *species* and the word), stating that "anything known, since it is known, must reside in the one who knows. . . . And the known thing, in the knowing subject, is the *intentio intellecta* or the word."[91]

It is in the first Book, in the third version of the famous chapter 53, that Thomas goes into greater detail. Here, Thomas distinguishes the word from the intelligible *species* very clearly, and gives two reasons for stipulating the necessary presence of the word in our operation of intellectual understanding *(et hoc quidem necessarium est)*. One reason is given as being due to the immaterial nature of the thing known in the understanding: Our intellect, knowing things removed from their material conditions, cannot accomplish its activity without forming an *intentio* of the thing known, that is to say a word, which is the *ratio* which our definition of things signifies. At this level it would seem that Thomas is confirming at least the need for a word in our understanding of material reality each time we form a definition or grasp the essence of a thing. The other reason, which is actually the first given by Thomas, is no less important: The formation of a word is necessary because of the fact that our intellect understands a thing irrespective of whether it is present or absent.[92] But Thomas explains that the *species intelligibilis* is exclusively that by which *(quo)* the intellect is formed, that which prompts the intellect into an act of understanding. It is not the end of the activity of understanding but rather its principle; the word alone is this immanent end. Without this word or *intentio*

---

[91] *SCG* IV, ch. 11 (#3466 and 3469).

[92] *SCG* I, ch. 53 (#443): "Et hoc quidem necessarium est: eo quod intellectus intelligit indifferenter rem absentem et praesentem."

intellectua, the presence of the object in the knowing subject (a presence in the manner of a term formed by the intellect, a term in which the process of understanding is achieved) would be missing. Therefore, because a thing is understood in an identical way whether it is present or absent, the word in which the thing is understood appears to be necessary in order to build the relationship between the intellectual activity and the object concerned, and to ensure the achievement of the act of understanding. In this minutely precise context (the question is about the divine understanding of a multitude of intelligible objects), Thomas does not stipulate in explicit terms the universal need for the word in every intellectual act[93] (and there is no question of more specific problems such as the vision of the divine essence, or angelic knowledge), but the far-reaching function of the word is nonetheless apparent. Thomas is thus able, and by rigorous argument, to propose a word in God in terms of a divine "attribute," by analogy. This exposition lays the foundation upon which Trinitarian theology will be able to base its understanding of the first procession.

The Trinitarian treatise, for its part, addresses the question of the Word of God more directly in terms of a divine person, after having recalled the meaning of the name "word." Thomas's aims are no less rigorous, and a highly structured sequence is followed: There is a Word in God; this Word is eternal; he is truly God, really identical to the divine *esse,* to the divine essence and the divine substance, he is a reality subsisting in the divine nature; his nature is specifically and numerically the same as that of God "who utters the Word"; the only relation distinguishing him from the Father is that of origin; he is the Image and the begotten Son. After this, Thomas considers certain biblical expressions in order to demonstrate their application to the Word *(conceptio, partus, generatio ex utero, in sinu Patris)* and ends his exposition by justifying the attribution to the Father alone of the var-

---

[93] The claim was to be made more clearly in the Commentary on St. John 1:1 (ed. Raffaele Cai [Turin/Rome: Marietti, 1952], #25). English translation: St. Thomas Aquinas, *Commentary on the Gospel of St. John,* trans. James A. Weisheipl and Fabian R. Larcher, vol. 1 (Albany, NY: Magi Books, 1980), pp. 31–33.

ious aspects of generation.[94] Thomas follows this exposition with a chapter on the Word as Wisdom, and then with a chapter on the unicity of the Word in God. The fundamental characteristic of this approach, apart from its rigorous adherence to sequential structure, lies in its close connection with Scripture. The setting out of the prerogatives of the divine Word thus reads like a sort of commentary on the opening verses of St. John's Gospel, with Thomas linking each Johannine phrase with a corresponding doctrinal point: "The Word *was* with *God*" (existence of a Word in God), "*In the beginning* was the Word" (eternity of the Word), "the Word was *God*" (divinity of the Word), "the Word was *with* God" (distinction between the Father and his Word). This is very close to being a doctrinal commentary on Scripture. This close connection is maintained in the rest of the text: Thomas is always bent on clarifying the pronouncements at the heart of biblical revelation concerning the Son. In the end, the merits of this analysis are demonstrated by the replies to rational arguments against Catholic faith in the person of the Son, for it is through his doctrine of the Word that Thomas dispels almost all the objections.[95]

---

[94] This is the internal plan of ch. 11, from #3469 to #3479. However, there is here a difficulty in the text. It will be helpful to look at the footnoted examination of the "interpolation" in chapter 11 in the Leonine edition (vol. 15, p. 35; cf. pp. XXIV– XXV; Marietti edition, vol. 3, p. 269, note 2). This refers to a passage of over 200 words demonstrating the equal status of the Father and the Son, as much by the notion of the Word as by the notion of the Son. The external criteria of the Leonine edition (handwritten tradition) which led to this passage being considered as an "interpolation" have been thoroughly reviewed by Father Gauthier, who suggests a new provisional theory, and thereby a reconsideration of the authenticity of this passage (see R.-A. Gauthier, *Saint Thomas d'Aquin, Somme contre les Gentils,* 23–35). Father Gauthier kindly confirmed this in a written communication dated 30 July 1995. The internal criteria of the Leonine edition would also seem to merit discussion and further analysis.

[95] *SCG* IV, ch. 14. All the principal arguments are refuted through reference to the Word, and in a particularly striking manner. Even the response to the problem of generative power (does the Son lack the power to beget, since he does not do so?) is based upon the doctrine of the Word, for Thomas sees the *potentia generandi as potentia ad intelligendum* (*potentia intelligendi seipsum*; ch. 13, #3488). This way of addressing the problem with reference to the intellect rather than to the nature is an entirely new, if not unique, feature in Thomas's writings. We find an echo in the *De potentia* (q. 9, a. 9, ad 1), but Thomas does not develop it in the *Summa theologiae.*

This role attributed to the doctrine of the Word shows very clearly that it is henceforth in Thomas's view the best route to a faith-based understanding of the person of the Son.

In a similar way, Thomas develops the theme of love when seeking to demonstrate how the procession of the Holy Spirit should be understood, and once again introduces ideas which are unprecedented in his theological writings. He abandons the theme of the mutual love of the Father and Son, outlined by Augustine and developed by Richard of St. Victor, and still highly regarded by thirteenth-century authors. This theme of the mutual love or the bond of love uniting the Father and the Son, which is found at the center of Thomas's pneumatology in his commentary on the *Sentences,* is totally absent in the *Summa contra Gentiles.*[96] The theological route will from now on pass via the love with which God loves himself, offering a more metaphysically sound basis and allowing a better exposition of the operation of the will which gives rise to procession. Thomas's explanations follow on from what has already been established in connection with the Word, and develop a comparable and equally rigorous structure. There is will in God, this divine will is God himself, his will is in operation, and there is therefore a love in God; this love with which God loves himself is God, and it proceeds from God who loves himself and from the Word of God. Thomas can therefore show that "God proceeding through love" is not begotten, is not the Son, but is the Holy Spirit.[97] Once again, despite the absence of biblical texts which authoritatively and explicitly teach that the Holy Spirit is in its person, Love, Thomas inserts into his exposition two passages from St. Paul which allow him to establish a relationship between the impulse of love and the Holy Spirit (Rom 8:14 and 2 Cor 5:14).

The explanations concerning the Holy Spirit are based on the presence of "God as loved" within "God who loves himself," in the

---

[96] It should be made clear that Thomas does not reject this theme of the Spirit as the mutual Love of the Father and the Son: It is to be taken up and developed in the *Summa theologiae* (*ST* I, q. 37, a. 2). But he no longer uses it as the principal vehicle for the admission of the person of the Holy Spirit to theological understanding, and the *Summa contra Gentiles* has no need of it.

[97] This, in a few words, is a summary of the contents of chapter 19.

same way that "God as known" is present within God who knows himself (the doctrine of the Word).[98] As in the case of the Word, Thomas's understanding undergoes a transformation: His concept of love is now firmly understood as an "affection toward" *(affici ad aliquid)*, an impulse *(impulsio, impulsus)*, a movement toward the thing loved, and no longer as a sort of informing of the will by goodness (which was the more "static" perspective adopted in the *Sentences*).[99] Within the will of someone engaged in the action of loving, he detects a dynamic presence of the thing loved (that which I love is present in my will by moving me toward it), which Thomas compares to the end of a movement present in the principle of the movement which displays proportion and affinity toward it.[100] Despite the lack of terminology such as *"attractio"* *(Compendium theologiae)* or *"impressio"* *(Summa theologiae)* to name the reality which proceeds within the loving will,[101] he is certainly referring to the same thing here, and his statements are absolutely clear: When the *mens* loves itself, "it reproduces itself as the thing loved within the will" *(seipsam producit in voluntate ut amatum)*.[102] It is through this affection or impulse of love that the presence of "God loved" in "God who loves himself" is verified, and this is henceforth the preferred route for the understanding of the person of the Holy Spirit.

This doctrine of the Holy Spirit as Love–impulse is exploited to the full in order to reply to objections lodged against the Catholic

---

[98] With one fundamental difference: The word is in the intellect through specific similitude, whereas love is in the will as an impulse.

[99] Regarding the evolution of St. Thomas's thinking on this, see Henri D. Simonin, "Autour de la solution thomiste du problème de l'amour," *AHDLMA* 6 (1931): 174–274.

[100] *SCG* IV, ch. 19 (#3560). We note here that this loving impulse implies the presence of a "term" *(sicut terminus motus)*.

[101] See *CT* I, ch. 46 *(attractio)* and *ST* I, q. 37, a. 1, sol. *(impressio, affectio)*; there is already a mention of *impressio* in this context in *De potentia*, q. 10, a. 2, ad 11. In the *Summa theologiae* Thomas explains in greater detail the language problems connected with the meaning of love (we lack a proper vocabulary to describe and distinguish the essential love and the notional love). Such problems do not occupy Thomas's attention in Book IV of the *Summa contra Gentiles* for he is writing exclusively about the notional and personal dimension, without entering into a discussion of the essential meaning of divine love.

[102] *SCG* IV, ch. 26 (#3631).

faith with regard to the person of the Spirit[103] for, just as with the doctrine of the Word, its precise aim is to show how the Catholic faith should be understood so that it might be defended against the "attacks of unbelievers."[104] This "apologetic" dimension of the doctrine of the Word and of Love in the *Summa contra Gentiles,* we should remember, does not mean that we should take it to be a treatise addressed to non-believers. It is abundantly clear that these chapters are aimed at the studious faithful according to the project of a Christian wisdom, such as Thomas understands it, since the similitudes used in the Trinitarian doctrine could never be intended to persuade non-believers.[105]

This consummate teaching, formulated here by Thomas for the first time, is not only concerned with what is known as the "immanent Trinity": Thomas develops and extends it to encompass what is conventionally known as the "economic Trinity," the Trinity in terms of its presence and operation in the world. Using his doctrine of the Word, Thomas continues his exposition and shows how the Son is the expression of other realities[106] and the reason for all that which God does,[107] and he is thereby able to take in the scriptural teaching concerning the creative action of the Son, his work in sustaining all things in being, and the existence of creatures which are alive in the Word, as well as the causality of the Word in our human understanding and especially in the understanding through which we are drawn to God.[108] The chapter on the Son as Wisdom, for its part, finishes with the manifestation of the Father accomplished by the Word.[109] All that is missing from the picture is a detailed explanation of the effects of the incarnation of the Word, and this is found later in the section on Christology.

---

[103] *SCG* IV, ch. 23.
[104] *SCG* IV, ch. 19 (#3557); cf. ch. 10 (#3460).
[105] *SCG* IV, ch. 9 (#3454).
[106] *SCG* IV, ch. 11 (#3474).
[107] *SCG* IV, ch. 13 (#3490–91).
[108] *SCG* IV, ch. 13 (#3491–95).
[109] *SCG* IV, ch. 12.

In a similar fashion, Thomas devotes three long chapters (ch. 20–22) to the action of the Holy Spirit in the world, employing a comparable structure which recalls the *exitus–reditus* movement mentioned above: the work of the Spirit in creation *(Amor est causa creationis rerum)* and divine governance, the action of the Spirit in rational creatures, and the work of the Spirit in our return to God. Thomas is here systematically presenting and developing a huge number of biblical themes on the action of the Spirit, from the first creation to beatitude, and based around the divine love–impulse and divine friendship.[110] All the works of God in the world, whether in the order of creation or in the order of grace, are thus placed under the auspices of the Holy Spirit.

This vast fresco devoted to the Holy Spirit in the creation and in the economy of salvation may be explained in two ways. In one sense, it demonstrates and confirms the validity of Thomas's teaching on the Spirit as Love–impulse, for all the work of the Spirit, as taught by the biblical texts Thomas cites, can actually be understood in the light of Love. In another sense, the economic dimension of the mystery of the Trinity is for Thomas an integral part of his subject matter. He brings in here, as he does when writing about the Son, the Trinitarian foundation of the truths of the faith dealt with in Books II and III (the creation and divine government, the search for eternal blessedness, the law, freedom, grace, prophecy, etc.). This point is of vital importance for an appropriate understanding of the theology developed by Thomas in the *Summa contra Gentiles*. For example, the treatise on the law or on grace in Book III is only intended to be an initial treatment, with the second part being supplied in Book IV: here in the section on the Trinity and later in the Christology section. It follows therefore that any

---

[110] *SCG* IV, ch. 20–22. Creation, divine government, exercise of divine lordship, and vivification: charity, inhabitation by the Holy Spirit, and the whole Trinity in people of goodwill, revelation of mysteries, bestowing of gifts, preparation for beatitude, filial adoption, forgiveness of sins, renewal, and purification; contemplation, joy and consolation, fulfillment of the commandments, freedom of the children of God, mortification. All of these themes are fully developed with reference to Scripture, using the doctrine of Love.

reading of a treatise on the law or on grace by Thomas which ignores its Trinitarian foundation, amounts to a distortion of his meaning. Despite the perfectly valid arrangement of the treatises in separate sections, the *Summa contra Gentiles* must be read in its entirety and understood as a whole.[111]

The Question of the *Filioque*

The exposition on the procession of the Spirit *a Filio* which occupies chapters 24–25 merits close examination for, despite its significant distinguishing features, this little treatise is altogether characteristic of Thomas's method in the *Summa contra Gentiles*. It should be understood that the following observations are concerned only with St. Thomas's method of working. A further study will be necessary to examine in greater depth the question of the *Filioque* in Thomas's work, and to reach any conclusion about its significance for the current ecumenical dialogue.[112]

The procession of the Spirit *a Filio* is presented as a special problem which Thomas deals with separately, once he has dispelled the errors directed toward the divinity and the personhood of the Holy Spirit. The discussion is presented as a clarification of the "procession" of the Spirit mentioned among the basic tenets of the faith, from chapter 15, with Jn 15, 26 ("the Spirit of truth who comes from the Father," a passage which is evidently at the center of the debate).[113] As is the case in other sections of the Trinitarian doctrine of the *Summa contra Gentiles,* Thomas is here concerned with demonstrating the truths of the faith in the face of error. In view of this, the "polemical" tone of certain passages should come as no surprise. It should also be pointed out that Thomas does not

---

[111] Without, that is, turning Book IV into a sort of appendix: The intrinsic connection with the preceding Books should be underlined. This point has been emphasized, regarding the question of grace, by Alfonso C. Chacon, "El tratado sobre la gracia en la *Summa contra Gentiles,*" *Scripta theologica* 16 (1984): 113–46, cf. 139–44.

[112] See chapter 6 below.

[113] *SCG* IV, ch. 15 (#3512); cf. ch. 24 (#3607); ch. 25 (#3621–22).

intend to provide a complete picture of the procession of the Spirit at this point. Questions which concern the Father more directly (for example, the procession of the Spirit *principaliter a Patre, or a Patre per Filium*) are not discussed: The only matter which directly attracts Thomas's attention in these chapters is the Holy Spirit's relation of origin toward the Son, in the sense of the truth of the faith confessed by the Catholic Church. Although Thomas addresses the question of the unity of the Father and the Son as principle of the Holy Spirit, for example,[114] he does so exclusively from the point of view of the *Filioque,* without considering the other problems generally linked to this question (one or two *spirantes/ spiratores,* etc.).

In terms of method, the first distinguishing feature lies in the fact that Thomas does not introduce the discussion by means of an exposition of opposing arguments (as he has done in the case of all other doctrinal points), but by means of an exposition of the biblical and Conciliar foundations, and of the rational arguments in favor of the *Filioque* (ch. 24). It is only after this that he considers the objections, within the three domains mentioned, and answers them (ch. 25). In this single instance, Thomas thus judges it more opportune to present a scriptural and theological exposition first, thereby putting readers in possession of the elements necessary to understand the objections of "certain people" (curiously, Thomas does not explicitly mention the Eastern Christians being referred to)[115] and respond to them.[116] This manner of proceeding in itself suggests the special importance of the question of the *Filioque.* The second distinguishing feature lies in the use of authorities: It is no longer simply Scripture and reason, but also the Councils (and on another level, the Church Fathers), which are called upon. This is

---

[114] *SCG* IV, ch. 25 (#3625)

[115] Despite the reference to the "doctors of the Church, including the Greeks" (#3609). Previously, Thomas has always identified and named the chief proponents of the errors he is discussing.

[116] This might also suggest that it is not the opposition to this doctrine which has led to the clear statement of the tenets of faith, but that the *Filioque* constitutes a doctrine which is in some way independent of its refutation by "certain people."

clearly understandable, since these are the authorities which are accepted by those who contest the *Filioque*[117] and which therefore can be cited in support of the question. This is why the tripartite structure, which was to be taken up and exploited so enthusiastically by "apologetics" manuals, is so much in evidence here, dictating the treatment of the two chapters devoted to the procession of the Spirit *a Filio*: Scripture, the Councils, and the Fathers, followed by rational arguments.

The theological material emphasized by Thomas demonstrates the close connection between the *Contra Gentiles* and the *Contra errores Graecorum*. We also notice that, within each domain of authority, Thomas makes use of a selection of the principal arguments (a far greater number of arguments based on tradition and on reason were to be used in the *De potentia*[118]). Firstly, on the scriptural level, Thomas bases his affirmation of the *Filioque* on three themes: The Holy Spirit is the Spirit of the Son (Rom 8:9 and so on), he is sent by the Son (Jn 15:26), and he receives from the Son or "of that which is of the Son" (*de meo accipiet*: Jn 16:14).[119] This section corresponds, in the same order, to chapters 1 to 3 of the second part of the *Contra errores Graecorum*.[120] This choice of texts in itself is hardly original. The passages are those already cited by the *Sententiae* of Peter Lombard[121] and are to be found in Bonaventure, for example.[122] Thomas's special contribution lies rather in the systematic exegesis of these themes, in terms of the relation of eternal origin which accounts for the personal distinction between the Son and the Holy Spirit, and which is developed by Thomas in chapter

---

[117] Putting aside the authority of the Pope "which is sufficient in itself," Thomas explains (ch. 25, #3624).

[118] *De potentia,* q. 10, a. 4.

[119] *SCG* IV, ch. 24 (#3606–8).

[120] This work continues the exposition using the connected themes which the *Summa contra Gentiles* leaves aside: the operation of the Son through the Holy Spirit, the theme of the Holy Spirit as image ("imprint," "seal") of the Son, the procession *a Patre per Filium*, and so on. Cf. *Contra errores Graecorum* (Leonine edition, vol. 40, pp. 88–93).

[121] Peter Lombard, *Sententiae,* Book I, dist. 11 and 34.

[122] St. Bonaventure, I *Sent.,* d. 11, a. 1, q. 1, contra 7–9.

25 in the analysis of relative opposition. We should equally note the central position of Jn 16:14 *(De meo accipiet)*, the importance of which Thomas was to underline increasingly in this context. The *Summa theologiae* was to see it as the principal biblical passage which teaches the procession of the Holy Spirit *a Filio*, in terms of its meaning if not in an explicit manner, and the *Commentary on St. John* was to devote a great deal of attention to it.[123]

The patristic texts presented by Thomas are also indications of the options being chosen within the context of a larger framework, which was to be developed in the *De potentia* and in the *Summa theologiae*. To begin with, Thomas establishes the authority of three Greek Fathers in support of the *Filioque*: Athanasius (the *Quicumque* Creed of Pseudo-Athanasius), Cyril (the letter *Salvatore nostro* to Nestorius), and Didymus (*De Spiritu Sancto*, translated by Jerome).[124] These three authors were already mentioned by Abelard and by Peter Lombard's *Sententiae*.[125] Thomas's individual contribution here is evident in the choice of a different text from Didymus to that presented by Peter Lombard,[126] in order to better emphasize the affirmation of the distinction in terms of origin, as well as in a quotation of Cyril's Letter to Nestorius taken from the *Collectio Casinensis* which would henceforth constitute Thomas's reference text for the Decrees of Ephesus.[127] In a direct extension of the *Contra errores Graecorum,* Thomas here makes use of Cyril's text to establish the full legitimacy of the vocabulary of the *processio* which he judges to be the most appropriate for signifying the origin of the Holy Spirit *a Filio*.[128] The value of these

---

[123] *ST* I, q. 36, a. 2, ad 1; *Super Ioan.* 16:14 (#2114–15). The commentary on the *Sentences* paid little attention to it.

[124] *SCG* IV, ch. 24 (#3609).

[125] Peter Lombard, *Sententiae,* Book I, dist. 11, ch. 2 (vol. I/2, pp. 116–17); Peter Abelard, *Theologia "Scholarium"* II, pp. 157–59 (CCCM 13, 483–85).

[126] The text from Didymus cited by Peter Lombard is found in Thomas's *Catena in Ioan.* 16:13 (Marietti edition, 540; cf. PL 23, pp. 133–34), while that cited by the *Summa contra Gentiles* appears in the *Catena in Io*, 16, 14 (Marietti edition, 541; cf. PL 23, p. 135).

[127] *Acta Conciliorum Œcumenicorum,* vol. I/3, ed. Eduardus Schwartz (Berlin/ Leipzig: De Gruyter, 1929), p. 32, with the variant reading indicated in the critical apparatus [referred to as *ACO*].

[128] *SCG* IV, ch. 24 (#3640); *Contra errores Graecorum* II, ch. 26–27.

dicta of the Fathers is reinforced by the authority of the Councils, since Thomas also takes care to point out (something which Peter Lombard did not do) that Cyril's Letter was received by the Council of Chalcedon, thereby enhancing its authority amongst the Greeks.[129] He similarly calls upon the authority of the Second Council of Constantinople in a passage in which the Fathers of the fifth general council state that they "follow wholly" and "receive" the exposition of faith declared by several Fathers and Doctors, including St. Augustine. Thomas points this out in order to underline the authority of Augustine who frequently maintained the fact of the procession of the Spirit *a Filio* (Thomas mentions especially Augustine's *De Trinitate* and *Super Ioannem*).[130] This last reference, as Ignaz Backes noted earlier, is probably directly or indirectly derived from the *De processione Spiritus sancti of Alcuin*, who even then had been devoting considerable and detailed attention to Conciliar documents.[131]

The same attention to Conciliar documentation is also evident in the response to the argument regarding the prohibition of addenda to the Council, formulated on pain of anathema notably at Ephesus and Chalcedon, and featuring regularly in the *Filioque* controversy since Photius.[132] In essence, Thomas replies by showing that the *Filioque* is not an intrinsically foreign modification or addition to the Symbol of Constantinople, but states explicitly what the Conciliar

---

[129] *SCG* IV, ch. 24 (#3609): "Cyrillus etiam, in Epistola sua, quam Synodus Chalcedonensis recepit. . . ." Cf. *ACO* II/3, ed. E. Eduardus Schwartz (Berlin/ Leipzig: De Gruyter, 1936), p. 137. Was Cyril's "Salvatore nostro" one of the Synodal letters received by Chalcedon? This is a matter for debate: See the comments in the Marietti edition, vol. 3, pp. 433–34.

[130] *SCG* IV, ch. 24 (#3611).

[131] Ignaz Backes, *Die Christologie des hl. Thomas von Aquin und die griechischen Kirchenväter* (Paderborn: Schoeningh, 1931), pp. 30–31. Cf. Alcuin, *Libellus De processione Spiritus sancti,* ch. 1 (PL 101, p. 73).

[132] *SCG* IV, ch. 25 (#3623); Thomas writes that the prohibition is found "in quibusdam conciliis." He was to cite Ephesus and Chalcedon deliberately on this subject in *De potentia*, q. 10, a. 4, arg. 13. Cf. Photius, *De Sancti Spiritus mystagogia*, n. 80 (PG 102, 363–66). On the principle of the sufficiency of the Council and of the Nicene Creed in particular, which appeared before the First Council of Constantinople, see André de Halleux, *Patrologie et œcuménisme: Recueil d'études* (Leuven: University Press/Peeters, 1990), pp. 3–24 ("Pour une profession commune de la foi selon l'esprit des Pères").

text implies. This understanding of the relationship between the Latin confession and the Symbol of Constantinople, involving an explicit statement of the implicit, was something Thomas had already been formulating in his commentary on the *Sentences* (following Albert, notably).[133] He also reminds the reader of the sufficiency of the authority of the Roman pontiff in matters of faith, for "he is the one who convoked and confirmed the councils of antiquity."[134] But, and this is something new, he relies primarily on a quotation from the Council of Chalcedon explaining that the Fathers of Constantinople only corroborated the Nicene doctrine by declaring their faith concerning the Holy Spirit, through scriptural accounts, when confronted by those who were trying to deny that the Holy Spirit is Lord.[135] Thomas is thus able to establish, within the Conciliar tradition itself, the principle of clarification of the faith, and applies then this principle to the affirmation of the *Filioque*. G. Geenen showed earlier that this Chalcedonian text cited by the *Summa contra Gentiles* can also be identified, despite slightly variant readings, by consulting the Decrees of Chalcedon in the *Collectio Casinensis*.[136] Without wishing to anticipate the findings of a more extensive study, it would seem that Thomas was the first person to use this *determinatio* of Chalcedon as a textual reference, since it does not usually appear in the scholarly works of his contemporaries.[137]

Whatever there might be in the way of particular problems (notably concerning the interpretation of Cyril's and Didymus's texts

---

[133] *SCG* IV, ch. 25 (#3524); cf. I *Sent.*, d. 11, exp. text. See also Albert, I *Sent.*, d. 11, a. 9.

[134] *SCG* IV, ch. 25 (#3624). Thomas overestimates the role of the pope in ancient councils.

[135] *SCG* IV, ch. 25 (#3624); *ACO* II/3, 137. The reference was to be repeated in *De potentia*, q. 10, a. 4, ad 13 and in *ST* I, q. 36, a. 2, ad 2.

[136] Godefridus Geenen, "En marge du concile de Chalcédoine, Les textes du quatrième concile dans les œuvres de saint Thomas," *Angelicum* 29 (1952): 43–59, especially 54.

[137] G. Geenen ("En marge du concile," 45, note 3) mentions here the results of unpublished research by Father Gallet on the sources of St. Thomas's Trinitarian theology; this research, written in 1942, failed to find this Chalcedonian text in the works of Abelard, Peter Lombard, Alexander of Hales, St. Bonaventure, and St. Albert.

in a "theological" rather than simply "economic" sense), everything
goes to show that, here as in the case of other problems of Trinitarian
theology addressed by the *Summa contra Gentiles,* Thomas's research is
of the highest order. In order to demonstrate the truth of the Catholic
faith, he sought to make use of references from the best patristic and
conciliar sources, updating to a considerable extent the relevant material found in his commentary on the *Sentences.*

As regards the "evident reasons" demonstrating the truth of the
procession of the Holy Spirit *a Filio,* we might perhaps have expected
to find Thomas's line of thought leading us ultimately to the argument drawn from the origin of Love *"a Verbo,"* as happens in the
Compendium theologiae which uses this argument as the principal
means of explaining the *Filioque.*[138] Such an approach would have
been appropriate, following the rigorous exposition on the Word
and Love which informs our understanding of the divine persons.
This argument, linking the operation of the will to the operation of
the intellect (we can only love that which we have conceived first
through the "word of the heart") is certainly present in the *Summa
contra Gentiles,* but appears only as part of a series of eight arguments
produced by Thomas.[139] Leaving aside the merits of these arguments
which deserve close analysis, it is undoubtedly the theory of the distinction of divine persons solely by relative opposition regarding origin which dominates the exposition as a whole. Out of all of
Thomas's works, this is one of the most complete and detailed explanations of relative opposition (distinction by opposition, kinds of
opposition, foundations of the opposition, the necessity of relative
opposition according to origin for a real distinction between the Son
and the Holy Spirit).[140] This line of reasoning was already present in
the commentary on the *Sentences* (following Albert) but in a very
much briefer form.[141] Thomas develops it to its full extent in the
Summa contra Gentiles, and takes it up again in his later works. There
is no doubt that, for Thomas, once the real distinction between the

[138] *CT* I, ch. 49.
[139] *SCG* IV, ch. 24 (#3617).
[140] *SCG* IV, ch. 24 (#3612).
[141] I *Sent.,* d. 11, q. 1, a. 1; cf. Albert the Great, I *Sent.,* d. 11, a. 6, contra 1–5.

Son and the Holy Spirit required by faith has been received, there is in the fullest meaning of the word a *necessity* for the procession of the Holy Spirit *a Filio*.[142]

The necessity of *Filioque* for the distinction of persons (without *Filioque* there would be, in Thomas's opinion, a return to a form of *Sabellian modalism*) explains the pejorative tone of some of the responses to objections formulated against the Latin doctrine.[143] For Thomas, the position adopted by experienced theologians who reject the *Filioque* is from a rational viewpoint "incomprehensible," so essential does it seem for a sound interpretation of the faith. It would be interesting to find out whether, quite apart from the problem of his understanding of Cappadocian triadology, Thomas was aware of other historical and ecclesial reasons that might have been partly responsible for the very determined refusal of the *Filioque*. However, in accordance with his declared purpose, he keeps strictly within the confines of doctrinal argument in its true sense. The theological weakness which, in Thomas's eyes, characterizes the rejection of the *Filioque*, does in any case explain why he does not conduct detailed analyses of the rational arguments which oppose this doctrine. He only mentions two (the simplicity of the Holy Spirit and the sufficient perfection of the Father) and two moreover which have been commonly voiced since the beginning of the controversy,[144] pointing out that they are easy to answer, "even for someone having little exercise in theology."

It is apparent here that Thomas has not sought to provide a complete list of all the arguments drawn from Scripture and tradition, together with all the rational arguments possible, but has limited himself to picking out the most significant. In doing so, however, he confronts the "error" he is seeking to refute in its own

---

[142] Expressions stating this necessity are repeated throughout ch. 24 ("necesse est," "non possunt nisi," and so on).

[143] See ch. 24 (#3610: *ridiculosum*); ch. 25 (#3621: *vix responsione digna*); ch. 15, #3622: *frivolum*), and so on.

[144] *SCG* IV, ch. 25, #3625; cf. I *Sent.*, d. 11, q. 1, a. 1, arg. 7 and 9. See Photius, *De Sancti Spiritus mystagogia*, n. 4 and 44–45; cf. *Libellus*, n. 1 (PG 102, 283–84; 321–24; 391–92).

terms. Therefore we will not find in the *Summa contra Gentiles* a complete discussion of this topic (the *Contra errores Graecorum* and the *De potentia* are in many respects more comprehensive), but rather the fundamental structure to be applied in the analysis of the problem which is presented, together with a discussion of the principal issues involved. When arguments attacking the Catholic faith seem to Thomas to show little coherence, he pays little attention to them. The *Summa contra Gentiles* differs quite markedly from contemporary treatises, which pay more attention to the detailed arguments of the controversy, repeating more laboriously the convoluted discussions held between the Greek and the Latin Church.[145] But on the other hand, the work demonstrates the great care employed by Thomas in updating his patristic documentation, despite the constraints characteristic of the medieval approach in such matters. This active historical research, combined with a speculative analysis which throws full light on the significance of the doctrine of relative opposition, constitutes one of the major features of the method used in the *Summa contra Gentiles* in comparison with Thomas's earlier works.

Problems of Trinitarian Theology

The treatment of the more technical elements of Trinitarian theology involves a array of individual features which will repay consideration, if we are to understand Thomas's purpose in writing about the Trinity in the *Summa contra Gentiles,* as opposed to his purpose in the commentary on the *Sentences* or especially in the *Summa theologiae.* The doctrine of relation just mentioned offers the first example. This doctrine is divided across two sections. Firstly, in chapter 14 (on the Son) we find a selection of insights into the nature of relation in God: The selection is limited to examples which corre-

---

[145] See for instance the *Tractatus contra Graecos* (PG 140, col. 487–510 on the *Filioque*), written by a Dominican brother of Constantinople in 1252, and which Thomas probably knew; cf. Antoine Dondaine, "*Contra Graecos,* Premiers écrits polémiques des Dominicains d'Orient," *Archivum Fratrum Praedicatorum* 21 (1951): 320–446, here 387–93.

spond to the rational problems which Thomas wishes to resolve (plurality and reality of the relations, subsistence of the divine relation, real identity of relation and essence, absence of inferiority or imperfection of the Son).[146] Then in chapter 24 he provides a long, detailed development of the general theory of distinction by relative opposition according to origin, in order to apply it to the *Filioque*, and it is also at this point that he demonstrates in greater detail the constitution of the person by the relation of origin.[147] This contextual usage of relative opposition according to origin is at first sight surprising when we bear in mind the central role of opposed relations in Thomas's Trinitarian theology. On one hand, Thomas places the exposition of the relation, in both cases, amongst the rational problems and arguments. On the other, he develops this theme only as and when required by the precise argument called for by the point under consideration. In his exposition on the Son, it is enough to show that the Son is distinguished from the Father solely by a relation of origin and to state the prerogatives of this relation in God in order to reply to rational objections.[148] It is only in the question of the *Filioque* that he fully develops all the consequences of relative opposition. It is evident that, while the *Summa theologiae* sees the general theory of relation as a logical and pedagogical prerequisite for the theological understanding of the divine person, the *Summa contra Gentiles* calls upon it as and when required by a particular problem. The *Summa contra Gentiles* shows clearly here how

---

[146] *SCG* IV, ch. 14 (#3502–8); Thomas is here replying to arguments formulated earlier in ch. 10 (#3451–57). The theme is also present in ch. 11 (#3473). We note that Thomas does not introduce the theme of real relations within the scriptural discussion of the Sabellian heresy, but in chapters 10 and 14.

[147] *SCG* IV, ch. 24 (#3612 and 3613).

[148] The very term *oppositio* or *opposita*, apart from a mention intending to show that there is an opposition between *generans* and *genitum*, *genitum*, and *ingenitum* (ch. 10, #3459 and ch. 14, #3510: where there is distinction, there must be opposition), does not play a decisive role before ch. 24 on the *Filioque*. The term *constituere*, in the sense of the constitution of the divine person, only appears in the context of the *Filioque* (ch. 24, #3613). The importance of such points of vocabulary should not however be exaggerated, for the notion of the relation, the mutual relationship, the person and relation are themes already present in the section devoted to the Son.

the doctrine of relation fits into Trinitarian theology (rational arguments and difficulties in the context of faith), and identifies the problems which it addresses in its various aspects.[149]

A similar problem arises in connection with the concept of the person. When he speaks of the divine person during the course of his treatise on the Trinity, Thomas is thinking of a *distinct* reality which subsists, in accordance with a relation, since the divine relation is what subsists.[150] He is thus able to show that the Father and the Son are divine persons, without prejudice to divine unity, and equally that the Holy Spirit is a person. His insistence on subsistence is such that, each time he affirms the personality of the Holy Spirit in chapter 18 (devoted entirely to showing that the Holy Spirit is a person), he says very precisely "a subsistent person" *(persona subsistens)*. Boethius's definition of the person, generally present in all Thomas's Trinitarian treatises from the commentary on the *Sentences* right up to the *Summa theologiae*, is not explicitly referred to, but only indirectly during an argument countering the faith that describes the person as *"res subsistens in intellectualibus naturis."*[151] Associated problems, such as the relationships between *persona* and *hypostasis*, for example, are not discussed.[152] It is not until the section on Christology, in the context of the theory of the *homo assumptus* and that of Nestorius, that Thomas formally examines Boethius's definition of the person, and discusses the relationship between person, hypostasis, and suppositum.[153] It is evident here once again that the *Summa contra Gentiles* does not intend to offer a complete manual of theology, but that

---

[149] This also calls to mind an aspect of the historical development of the problem: substantiating the doctrine of relation under the cross-fire of Arian thinking (for example, the Cappadocians confronted by Eunomius), and the development of relative opposition in the Latin Church on the question of the *Filioque* (Anselm).

[150] *SCG* IV, ch. 14 (#3502).

[151] *SCG* IV, ch. 10 (#3451).

[152] The word "hypostasis" is totally absent from the Trinitarian treatise: It does not appear before the section on Christology.

[153] *SCG* IV, ch. 38 (#3761–70). The discussion is moreover in exactly the right place, for Boethius also attempts his definition of the person within a Christological context, when addressing associated problems (*Liber de persona et duabus naturis contra Eutychen et Nestorium,* ch. 3 [PL 64, 1343]).

Thomas is concentrating on what he believes necessary in order to demonstrate the truth of the faith in the face of error: That the Father, the Son, and the Holy Spirit are three persons, truly distinguishable by their relations of origin, and subsisting in a single divine nature. Such decisions are clear indications of a methodological approach adopted and determined by Thomas's precise intentions and subject matter.

These methodological characteristics are even more marked when taken in comparison with other concepts of Trinitarian theology, predominant in Thomas's other works of synthesis, but remaining very much in the background in the *Summa contra Gentiles*. The themes of notions, properties, and notional acts, discussed at length in the other works, are touched on briefly in chapters 24 and 26,[154] but Thomas does not address the problems of the schools associated with these conceptual tools and he even avoids the vocabulary adopted by them. There is no discussion of notions and notional acts as such (in terms of vocabulary, no mention of *notio, notionalis, or notionaliter*); three brief mentions of *proprietas* are present, but do not include any analysis of the relationship between property, relation, and person;[155] the problem of the essential or personal signification of the names "Word" and "Love" is not discussed; and so forth. The total absence of the theme of appropriation (even the term is absent from the Trinitarian treatise) is also particularly striking, for Thomas makes extensive use of it, albeit in an implicit manner, in the expositions on the work of the Son and of the Holy Spirit *ad extra*.[156] All of this bears eloquent witness to the difference between a personal work, which is what the *Summa contra Gentiles* is, and Thomas's more scholarly works. A demonstration of the *truth of the faith*, which is the task Thomas

---

[154] See *SCG* IV, ch. 24 (#3613); ch. 26 (#3626).

[155] *SCG* IV, ch. 5 (#3378); ch. 25 (#3622).

[156] The vocabulary of appropriation, in its Trinitarian sense, only appears in ch. 46 when Thomas explains that the formation of the body of Christ and the work of incarnation are attributed and appropriated *(appropriatur)* to the Holy Spirit (ch. 46, #3828); however, there is no explanation here of the method of appropriation.

sets himself in the *Summa contra Gentiles,* can afford to tread more lightly over such technicalities. An awareness of this would seem to be particularly helpful in our efforts to adopt a truly Thomist perspective on the function of these tools of thought, and a comparison between the *Summa contra Gentiles* and the *Compendium theologiae* turns out to be highly instructive in this respect. The *Compendium theologiae* firstly takes up the basic elements of the Trinitarian doctrine of the *Summa contra Gentiles,* and in a later section turns to the problems which we have just mentioned, and which the *Contra Gentiles* leaves aside.[157]

These observations are an invitation to read the *Summa contra Gentiles* without classifying it and its Trinitarian treatise (and the same applies to the treatise on Christ) in the same genre as a commentary on the *Sentences,* a manual or comprehensive survey of theology in the full sense. The biggest single error in attempting to understand the *Summa contra Gentiles* would be to see it as the same synthesis of *intellectus fidei* as the *Summa theologiae.* The *Summa contra Gentiles,* as is demonstrated by the Trinitarian section, has a precise aim which circumscribes minutely, following a set structure and methodology, the subject matter to be discussed and the inherent objective: the truth of that which the Catholic faith confesses. In terms of the present discussion everything leads to the substantiation of the following points, and Thomas methodically dismisses anything which is not strictly necessary to do so: The Father, the Son, and the Holy Spirit are three persons who subsist in the divine nature, they are one God, they are truly distinguishable only in their relations of origin, according to which the Son proceeds from the Father, and the Holy Spirit proceeds from the Father and from the Son.

Conclusions

In order to grasp the Trinitarian thought of the *Summa contra Gentiles,* and incorporate it into a synthesis of Thomas's Trinitarian doc-

---

[157] See *CT* I, ch. 37–56 (the section culminates, as in the *SCG,* with a chapter showing that there cannot be more than three persons in God) then ch. 57–67 (properties, notions and relations, personal or notional acts, and so on).

trine, the structure imposed upon the work and ensuing connections within it must be borne in mind. The treatise on "the confession of the Trinity" concerns the knowledge of faith in the Trinitarian God in terms of his inmost or immanent mystery (corresponding to what Book I did for the God as One), but it also traces the Trinitarian roots and activity in the entire divine work *ad extra*, from the Creation to our pathway or return to God (corresponding to what Books II and III did for God as One). In this treatise, which focuses exclusively on demonstrating the truth of our faith in the Trinity, the economic Trinity is featured on two levels: In the confrontation with error, it allows the substantiation of the truth of faith in the divine persons who reveal themselves through their action in the world; in the context of rational difficulties, Thomas shows us that a doctrine on the Trinity, which he develops resolutely around the Word and Love, finds its culmination in its capacity to account for the work of the divine persons in its entirety. The economic Trinity thus constitutes an essential part of Thomas's subject matter.

Thomas's conception of theological research on the Trinity is entirely based around Scripture. In theory as in practice, Thomas's understanding both of the exposition of the faith and of the speculative task of theology, with regard to the Trinity, is one based on the reading of Scripture at various levels. The fact is very significant: It is in his most "biblical" treatise on the Trinity that Thomas first works out his fully mature doctrine on the Word and on Love, which constitutes the heart of his speculative approach to the Trinitarian mystery. The *Summa contra Gentiles* shows us equally that Thomas sees the history of errors and heresies as an excellent opportunity for offering an exposition of the faith, and his very method owes much to the Church Fathers. The same point would be evident in Thomas's writings in the field of preaching, for even within the context of the homily, the same approach is strikingly present.[158]

---

[158] See especially *In Symbolum Apostolorum*; for errors concerning the Trinity: art. 2 (Photinus, Sabellius, and Arius, as in the *Summa contra Gentiles*) and art. 8 (error regarding the Spirit seen as a creature, and on the *Filioque*). Latin text: St. Thomas Aquinas, *Opuscula theologica,* vol. 2, ed. Raimondo Spiazzi (Turin: Marietti, 1954), #888–90, 959, and 962.

Despite the difference in genres and methodologies involved, the *Summa contra Gentiles* can serve as a useful reference in the identification of the goal of the *Summa theologiae* in terms of Trinitarian theology. The *Summa theologiae* is essentially concerned with showing how the mystery accepted in faith may be grasped by the faith-based reason. This project of the *intellectus fidei,* set within a more directly pedagogical genre, corresponds fairly precisely (although in a more developed form) with the last section of Trinitarian thought in the *Contra Gentiles* (*"utcumque"* grasp of the mystery, problems of reason, doctrine of the Word and of Love, relation and person, etc.). The scriptural aspect and the confrontation between the Catholic faith and heresies are far less important. What is more, the *ordo doctrinae* of the *Summa theologiae* results inevitably in general theories being presented as prerequisites for the examination of the divine persons taken individually, while the *Summa contra Gentiles* validates them by direct application to the problems relating to each divine person. In addition, the connection between the "immanent Trinity" and the "economic Trinity" is perhaps less immediately obvious because of the complex structure of the *Summa theologiae*. For all these reasons, the *Summa contra Gentiles* is a work offering an extraordinary opportunity to gain insight into the full breadth of Thomas's thinking regarding the Trinity, and is a great aid in our reading of his other works.

CHAPTER FOUR

The Treatise on the Trinity in the *Summa theologiae*

T HE TREATISE on the Trinity (*Prima pars,* q. 27–43) is at the same time one of the most important and one of the most difficult of the *Summa theologiae*.[1] Its importance is manifest: The specifically Christian understanding of God, as well as the Christian understanding of the relationship the world holds with God (which is treated in the following part of the *Summa*), depends on the correct understanding of this treatise. This treatise, however, is not easily accessible, notably because of its highly speculative character and because of the many technical notions that it employs. Without providing a complete examination of this treatise, we propose to present briefly here its principal elements, by way of an introduction that will serve, we hope, to guide the reading of these questions.

The Theological Intention of the Treatise on the Trinity

In order to be able to understand correctly the purpose of St. Thomas in his questions on Trinitarian theology, it is important first to perceive the general intent that governs the writing of this treatise. St. Thomas has not placed the formulation of this intention at the beginning of his treatise, in the manner of epistemological and

---

[1] Translation by Teresa Bede and Matthew Levering.

methodological prolegomena, but he reveals it in the course of his treatise, following a procedure that one can observe in the other parts of the *Summa*: The epistemological elements appear in the body of the theological reflection.[2] Notably, St. Thomas refuses to subordinate Trinitarian theology to other theological and anthropological interests, as one often observes in essays on the Trinity today.[3] In order to read correctly the Trinitarian treatise of the *Summa theologiae*, it does not suffice therefore to pose the question of the method and content of the Trinitarian theology. First it is necessary to respond to this question: What is the goal of a speculative study on the Trinity? This question requires a reflection on the nature of revelation as well as on the conceptual instruments by which the theologian sets forth revelation by means of the resources of human reason.

The Revelation of the Trinity

In the first article of the *Summa theologiae*, St. Thomas explains that the philosophical sciences, which offer a knowledge of God according to human reason, do not suffice for the salvation of man. Salvation requires a sacred teaching *(sacra doctrina)* in which God is known according to revelation. The necessity *(necessarium)* of this doctrine is based upon the goal of human life: "Man is directed to God, as to an end that surpasses the grasp of his reason. . . . But the end must first be known by men who are to direct their thoughts and actions to this end. Hence it was necessary for the salvation of man that [certain truths] which exceed human reason should be known to him by divine revelation."[4] It is this same reason that St. Thomas puts forward when he explains the "necessity" of the revelation of the Trinity:

---

[2] For Trinitarian theology, see in particular question 32; but other elements are discussed elsewhere in the treatise (notably in questions 39–41, as well as in other questions).

[3] This "functionalization" of Trinitarian discourse appears in numerous modern and contemporary treatises on the Trinity; see for example Anne Hunt, *What Are They Saying About the Trinity?* (New York: Paulist Press, 1998).

[4] St. Thomas Aquinas, *ST* I, q. 1, a. 1.

The knowledge of the divine persons was necessary to us on two grounds. The first is to enable us to think rightly on the subject of the creation of things. For by maintaining that God made everything through his Word we avoid the error of those who held that God's nature necessarily compelled him to create things. By affirming that there is in him the procession of Love, we show that he made creatures, not because he needed them nor because of any reason outside him, but from Love of his own goodness. . . . The second reason, and the principal one, is to give us a true notion of the salvation of mankind, a salvation accomplished by the Son who became flesh and by the gift of the Holy Spirit.[5]

The Trinitarian faith is therefore required in order to understand properly the divine act of creation and, by extension, all of God's activity in the world (the exercise of divine providence, human life under the action of God). More precisely, St. Thomas puts in the first place *(principalius)* the *soteriological* dimension of Trinitarian doctrine. This soteriological dimension, for St. Thomas, is first of all contemplative in nature, like the *sacra doctrina* itself.[6] Trinitarian faith is the reception of the gift of God who reveals himself as he is. Trinitarian theology therefore constitutes a speculative or contemplative[7] study that has as its subject the mystery of God the Trinity in whom man finds his salvation, his end, and his happiness. For this reason, the reading of St. Thomas's Trinitarian theology should lead us to bring to light the Trinitarian dimension of creation and, above all, the salvific dimension of the revelation of the mystery of the Trinity (divine missions).

---

[5] *ST* I, q. 32, a. 1, ad 3.

[6] *ST* I, q. 1, a. 4. There is no reason to oppose here the "speculative" dimension and the "soteriological" dimension, since these two aspects, as we will see, are rightly linked.

[7] For St. Thomas, the words "contemplative" and "speculative" are practically equivalent; see Servais Pinckaers, "Recherche de la signification véritable du terme *spéculatif*," *Nouvelle Revue Théologique* 81 (1959): 673–95.

The Prerogatives of Faith

Only the reception of revelation, in other words only faith, gives us access to knowledge of the Trinity. This exclusive role of faith, as contrasted with natural reason, constitutes a common trait of Trinitarian theology since its origins, but it provoked a renewal of interest in the Middle Ages due to Peter Abelard. Abelard had attempted to identify the properties of the three divine persons with the attributes of power (Father), wisdom (Son), and goodness (Holy Spirit).[8] In consequence, according to Abelard, the philosophers and all men of good sense who have known the power, wisdom, and goodness of God have borne testimony to the Trinity, especially Plato, "the greatest of philosophers." Plato, according to Abelard, even "taught what is essential concerning the Trinity" (the Platonic doctrine of God the Father of the world, of the *Nous*, and of the world soul).[9] Such overly enthusiastic Platonism led the majority of later authors to affirm very clearly the limits of the knowledge of the Trinity outside of faith.

Like all his contemporaries, St. Thomas explains that the existence of a Trinity of persons cannot be known by natural reason: Only faith makes known the Trinity. When he explains that the philosophers could not reach the knowledge of the Trinity through natural reason, however, St. Thomas does not find the reason for this in original sin, as Alexander of Hales holds,[10] nor in the "opposition" of Trinitarian faith and the natural principles of reason, as St. Albert the Great would have it.[11] St. Thomas's response is founded on two principles: the proper mode of human knowledge, and the nature of the causality of God.

---

[8] Abelard, *Theologia Summi Boni,* Book I, ch. II (Petri Abaelardi Opera Theologica, vol. 3 (CCCM 13), ed. Eligius M. Buytaert and Constant J. Mews [Turnhout: Brepols, 1987], pp. 86–90); ch. V (pp. 92–94).

[9] Abelard, *Thelogia Summi Boni,* Book I, ch. V (pp. 98–99); Book III, ch. V (pp. 200–1). See chapter 1 above: "The Threeness and Oneness of God in the Twelfth to Fourteenth Century Scholasticism."

[10] *Summa fratris Alexandri,* tract. intr., q. 2, m. 1, c. 3, sol. (vol. 1 [Quaracchi: ed. Collegii S. Bonaventurae, 1924], p. 19, #10,).

[11] Albert the Great, I *Sent.,* d. 3, a. 18, sol. (*Opera omnia,* vol. 25, ed. Auguste Borgnet [Paris: Vivès, 1893], p. 113).

Through natural reason man can know God only from creatures; and they lead to the knowledge of God as effects do to
their cause. Therefore by natural reason we can know of God
only what characterizes him necessarily as the source of all
beings. Now, the creative power of God is common to the
whole Trinity; and hence it concerns the unity of the essence,
and not the distinction of the persons. Therefore, by natural
reason we can know what concerns the unity of the essence,
but not what concerns the distinction of the persons.[12]

Nature here is considered as the principle of the action and, therefore, as the "specific essence." God acts in virtue of his nature which is
common to the three persons (without which one would undermine
the divine unity), and this is why the creative cause is demonstrated
under the aspect of this nature, but not under the aspect of the properties of the persons. St. Thomas develops a remarkable Trinitarian
doctrine of creation in the light of faith which makes known the Trinity, but this Trinitarian dimension cannot be discovered by man's natural reason. St. Thomas is very firm: The knowledge of the Trinity
rests exclusively on the reception of revelation in the history of salvation, by faith. Philosophical reasoning can reach the knowledge of the
essential attributes of God, but cannot go beyond.[13]

The Exclusion of Necessary Theological Reasons
Thomas Aquinas equally objects to the apologetic project of "necessary reasons" through which certain theologians try to show the
necessity of the Trinity for reason informed by faith. This project of
necessary reasons was inaugurated by St. Anselm of Canterbury
and pursued by Richard of St. Victor, but it is more directly the
Franciscan theologians that St. Thomas opposes. Following the
Summa Fratris Alexandri, St. Bonaventure had sought to show the
existence of the divine Trinity through arguments drawn from the
perfect goodness of God, from his beatitude, from his joy, from his

---

[12] *ST* I, q. 32, a. 1. For the originality of this response, see G. Emery, *La Trinité
créatrice*, pp. 345–51.
[13] Ibid.

liberality, and from his primacy. St. Bonaventure explained that it is necessary to recognize a Trinity of divine persons and that these speculative arguments allow one to demonstrate the Trinity in a convincing manner.[14]

Thomas Aquinas vigorously argues against such an apologetic project in Trinitarian theology: St. Bonaventure's reasons are probable arguments, but they have no force of necessity. For St. Thomas, the attempt to elaborate necessary reasons in Trinitarian theology places faith in danger: "Whoever tries to prove the Trinity of persons by natural reason, derogates from faith."[15] Such an attempt neglects the dignity of the faith—since faith concerns realities that are found beyond reason—and it suggests to unbelievers that Christians confess the Trinity because of reasons that are in reality very fragile (the theme of the *irrisio infidelium*).[16] St. Thomas's response implies a very clear distinction between the domain of the faith and the domain of natural reason: The clarity of this distinction constitutes one of the characteristic traits of St. Thomas in contrast notably with St. Bonaventure. The reasons deployed by theology in order to elucidate the mystery of the Trinity are therefore never necessary arguments, but rather "adaptations" or "probable arguments,"[17] that is to say "arguments capable of showing that what is proposed to our faith is not impossible."[18]

The epistemology of St. Thomas, as regards the Trinity, is therefore characterized by two fundamentally connected theses: (1) the strict exclusion of necessary reasons for establishing the Trinity;[19] (2) the impossibility of conceiving of the Trinity by deducing it from divine unity, that is to say the impossibility of thinking of the plurality of persons as a derivation from essential attributes.[20] This second thesis, too little known even today, constitutes one of the absolutely fundamental traits of St. Thomas's Trinitarian theology.

---

[14] See chapter 1 above.

[15] *ST* I, q. 32, a. 1.

[16] Ibid.

[17] I *Sent.,* d. 3, q. 1, a. 4, ad 3; *SCG* I, ch. 8–9.

[18] *ST* II-II, q. 1, a. 5, ad 2.

[19] See R. L. Richard, *The Problem of an Apologetical Perspective,* pp. 137–330.

[20] See H. C. Schmidbaur, *Personarum Trinitas.*

Aquinas excludes, with more rigor than most of his contemporaries, the epistemological confusion between our knowledge of the divine essence and our knowledge of the personal plurality in God. He refuses, with the greatest firmness, to conceive of the personal plurality of God as the fruit of an essential fecundity of the divine being. Consequently, it is necessary to state precisely the role of human reason in Trinitarian theology.

The Purpose of Trinitarian Theology and the Function of Analogies

The treatise on the Trinity develops several themes applied to God by analogy ("person," "relation"); the properties of persons are likewise elucidated by means of analogies taken from anthropology ("word," "love," etc.). The function of these analogies gives St. Thomas the opportunity to clarify the purpose of his Trinitarian doctrine. Thus, as regards the notion of "person" in the Trinity, he explains that the use of this notion was imposed "because of the urgency of arguing with heretics."[21] One finds here, in the *Summa theologiae,* the purpose that St. Thomas had systematically put to work in the *Summa contra Gentiles.*[22] The elaboration of a speculative reflection on the Trinity, with the use of analogies and philosophical resources, is guided by a double motive: the defense of the faith against errors, and the contemplation of revealed truth. Trinitarian theology has as its goal to show that the Trinity is *reasonably thinkable,* and therefore that arguments against the Trinitarian faith are not compelling (they are not necessary).[23]

When St. Thomas manifests the truth of the Trinitarian faith through "probable arguments" or "adaptations," he shows—without proving the faith—that the arguments of heretics (Arianism, Sabellianism), or the arguments of those who reject the Trinity, are not compelling, since he establishes an alternative. Trinitarian theology

---

[21] *ST* I, q. 29, a. 3, ad 1: cf. *De potentia,* q. 9, a. 5.

[22] See chapter 3 above.

[23] *Super Boetium de Trinitate,* q. 2, a. 3: "As those things which are of faith cannot be demonstratively proven, so certain things contrary to them cannot be demonstratively shown to be false, but they can be shown not to be necessary."

thus offers believers a foretaste of what they hope to see in the beatific vision of God: This is the essentially contemplative dimension of Trinitarian theology. If one rejects this use of speculative reason, one could indeed *affirm* the Trinity, but one could not *manifest* (that is to say make more manifest to our mind) the truth of the Trinitarian faith. Such is the function of "similitudes" *(similitudines, verisimili-tudines)* or "probable reasons" *(rationes verisimiles)*, in other words analogies which allow for rendering account of faith in three divine persons, principally the Augustinian analogy of the word and of love.[24] This purpose of Trinitarian theology, which St. Thomas takes from St. Augustine, is ambitious and modest at the same time: to manifest the truth "to the exercise and consolation *(exercitium et solatium)* of the faithful."[25]

For this reason, the correct interpretation of the Trinitarian treatise of the *Summa* must remove all rationalism. It is by a grave error of reading that certain authors have thought they found in St. Thomas an attempt to establish rationally the Trinity.[26] Rather, St. Thomas proposes a speculative or contemplative exercise allowing a modest understanding of "something of the Truth" *(aliquid veritatis)*,[27] in developing "similitudes" and "adaptations" (probable arguments) that suffice for excluding errors, because they show that Trinitarian faith can be reasonably thought, without seeking to convince those who do not share Trinitarian faith, and without in any manner substituting for faith.

The Plan of the Treatise on the Trinity

The Diverse Approaches to the Trinitarian Mystery in St. Thomas

St. Thomas treated Trinitarian faith in most of his great works. Each time, he gave a different structure to his account, according

[24] Ibid. Cf. *SCG* I, ch. 7–9; *ST* I, q. 1, a. 8, ad 2.
[25] *SCG* I, ch. 9. Cf. S. Augustine, *De Trinitate* XIII, XX, 26; XV, I, 1; XV, VI, 10.
[26] See R. L. Richard, *The Problem of an Apologetical Perspective,* pp. 1–60.
[27] *De potentia,* q. 9, a. 5.

to its circumstances and the particular purpose of the work. In his commentary on the *Sentences*, the structure of the treatise on God was given by the text of Peter Lombard. The general organization of the treatise does not reveal, therefore, the proper intention of St. Thomas, although this intention appeared in the prologues (and in the internal order of the questions within each distinction) where one can observe the central place of the notion of "procession" and of the structure of *"exitus–reditus."*[28] The Trinitarian treatise of *Summa contra Gentiles* is structured in a much clearer way, in two main parts: The generation of the Son (Book IV, ch. 2–14) and the procession of the Holy Spirit (ch. 15–25); a chapter of conclusion (ch. 26) shows that there is no other procession in God. Each of these two main parts contains the following three stages: (1) the fundamental givens of Scripture; (2) the Scripture interpreted by Catholic faith in contrast to the heresies; (3) discussion and refutation of objections against Catholic faith in the Trinity. It is in this third stage that St. Thomas exploits the doctrine of the Word and of Love, as well as the other major speculative themes. This structure is governed by the specific purpose of the *Summa contra Gentiles*, which seeks to manifest the truth of the Catholic faith, on the basis of the testimonies of Scripture, by removing errors opposed to these testimonies.[29]

The plan of the Trinitarian treatise of *Compendium theologiae* can be associated with that of *Summa contra Gentiles*. The *Compendium* first presents the doctrine of the Word (I, ch. 37–44), then the doctrine of Love (I, ch. 45–49), and then shows how the doctrine of relation allows one to conceive of the plurality of persons in the unity of essence (I, ch. 50–67, with the doctrine of properties and of notional acts). The treatise contains three parts: The first manifests faith in the Son (the Word), the second manifests faith in the Holy Spirit (Love), and the third shows that the three divine persons are not three gods but one single God.[30]

---

[28] See G. Emery, *La Trinité créatrice*, pp. 249–344.
[29] See chapter 3 above: "The Treatise of Saint Thomas on the Trinity in the *Summa contra Gentiles*."
[30] Cf. *CT* I, ch. 36.

Closer to the *Summa theologiae*, the disputed questions *De potentia* are particularly instructive. After having treated the generative power of God (q. 2), St. Thomas devotes three questions to Trinitarian faith: Question 8 deals with relations, question 9 deals with the persons, while question 10 is devoted to processions. St. Thomas does not present the testimonies of Scripture, as he had done in the *Summa contra Gentiles*, but rather he organizes and makes precise the theological notions that allow one to think of the Trinity in its unity. The point of departure is furnished by faith in the three divine persons. On this basis, St. Thomas explains, the personal plurality in God requires one to pose the *relations* that allow understanding of the persons: These relations are founded on the *processions*.[31] The questions *De potentia* offer an extremely developed reflection on the relations, the processions, and the persons, as well as on the relationships and the arrangement of these notions in the theological intelligence of the Trinitarian mystery.[32] As one can see, the elaboration of the Trinitarian treatise of the *Summa theologiae* benefits from clarifications brought by the disputed questions *De potentia*.

The understanding of the Trinitarian doctrine in the *Summa theologiae* is closely linked to the correct understanding of its structure. This structure is important, because it contains and reveals, on a small scale, the master ideas that guide St. Thomas's doctrinal elaboration. In the *Summa contra Gentiles*, St. Thomas separated the treatise on God into two parts: what natural reason can know of the mystery of God (Book I), and what faith reveals to us, that is to say the Trinitarian mystery (Book IV). In the *Summa theologiae*, however, as in the *Compendium theologiae*, the treatise of God constitutes a structured unity. This structure appears in the Prologues and allows one to understand the purpose of the treatise which contains

---

[31] *De potentia*, q. 8, a. 1.

[32] Unfortunately, there is no profound study of the Trinitarian theology of the *De potentia*, to our knowledge. Paul Vanier's study (*Théologie trinitaire chez saint Thomas d'Aquin: Evolution du concept d'action notionnelle* [Montréal/Paris: Institut d'Etudes médiévales/Vrin, 1953]) gave great attention to these questions and showed their originality, but the interpretation of P. Vanier is too unilateral for one to follow it; cf. G. Emery, *La Trinité créatrice*, pp. 460–61.

three parts: "The treatment of God will fall into three parts: first, what concerns the divine essence; second, what concerns the distinction of persons; third, what concerns the coming forth of creatures from God."[33] The structure of the treatise on God thus rests on a double distinction: (1) God in his immanent life and in his action as creator and savior; (2) what concerns the divine essence and what concerns the distinction of persons.

Immanent Trinity and Creative Trinity

The first distinction concerns God in his immanent life (*ST* I, q. 2–43) and God in his creative and saving action (q. 44 ff.). This distinction is founded on the exigencies of Christian doctrine set in place since the fourth century: The existence of the divine persons and the properties of these persons do not depend on creation or divine action in the world. In order to avoid considering the Son and the Holy Spirit as creatures (Arianism), it is necessary to be able to think of the divine persons and their mutual relations on the plane of divine eternity, by clearly distinguishing between the created and the uncreated. This distinction rests equally on the philosophical analysis of action. St. Thomas's reflection on God takes from Aristotle the distinction between two types of actions: the "immanent actions" that are accomplished in the agent itself (for example, to feel, to know, to will), and the "transitive actions" that are exerted on an exterior object (for example, to cut, to build, to heat up, and so on). These two types of actions should be attributed to God through analogy: God knows and loves himself (immanent action), he creates and governs the world (transitive action). The first of these actions, St. Thomas specifies further, is the reason for the second and naturally precedes it: This is why the study of creation and salvation must be preceded by a prior study of God and his immanent life.[34]

According to St. Thomas, Arianism and Sabellianism committed the error of thinking of the procession of the Son and the Spirit

---

[33] *ST* I, q. 2, prol.; cf. q. 27, prol.; cf. *CT* I, ch. 2.
[34] *SCG* II, ch. 1; cf. *ST* I, q. 27, a. 1; *De potentia,* q. 9, a. 9; q. 10, a. 1; Aristotle, *Metaphysics* IX, 8 (1050 a 23–b 2).

as a transitive action, in other words according to the manner in which an effect proceeds from its cause; but transitive action does not allow one to account for the true divinity of the persons, or for their real distinction. Arianism thought of the Son and the Holy Spirit as creatures, that is, effects of God (transitive action). For its part, Sabellianism conceived of the generation of the Son as a mode of divine action in the world: God would have taken the form of the Son when he was incarnated. This position furnishes the point of departure for the Trinitarian treatise of the *Summa theologiae* (I, q. 27, a. 1). For this reason, the Trinitarian treatise begins precisely by establishing the necessity of considering the procession of the divine persons not as a transitive action, but as an immanent action.

The study of God the Trinity in his immanent life, however, is not separated from the study of creation and the economy of salvation (the effects of God), since the doctrine of God should allow one to manifest the action of God in the world. The Trinitarian treatise should therefore show that the three persons are one single God and that they are really distinct, in virtue of the immanent processions within the divinity, and it should also show that the creating and saving action of the Trinity is founded in the properties of the Father, the Son, and the Holy Spirit. The Trinitarian treatise therefore is distinguished from the treatise on creation, but it is not separated from it. One recognizes here, in the structure of the treatise of God, what St. Thomas explains about the *subiectum* of theology: "All things are dealt with in holy teaching in terms of God *(sub ratione Dei)*, either because they are God himself or because they are relative to him as their origin and end."[35]

The Divine Essence and the Persons: The Common and the Proper

The second distinction which structures the treatise of God in the *Summa theologiae* is that of "what concerns the divine essence" and of "what concerns the distinction of persons." It is not about the division of a treatise "De Deo Uno" and "De Deo Trino" in the manner

---

[35] *ST* I, q. 1, a. 7.

of manuals of neo-scholastic theology. Neither is it about the division of a philosophical approach and a theological approach to God either, as if the first part of the treatise of God (q. 2–26) were philosophical in nature and the second (q. 27–43) properly theological in nature. The totality of the treatise of God concerns God the Trinity under the aspect of revelation: The formal object of the *Summa theologiae* is the formal object of Christian theology, that is to say God who is himself made known by revelation *(per revelationem)*.[36] The distinction between "what concerns the divine essence" and "what concerns the distinction of persons" rests principally on a demand of theological order, which stems, once again, from the controversy against Arianism. It is about the distinction between what is *common* to the three persons and what is *proper* to each person. This distinction was elaborated by St. Basil of Cesarea: "The divinity is common but the paternity and the filiation are properties; and from the combination of these two elements, that is to say from the common and from the proper, occurs in us the understanding of the truth."[37]

Following the Cappadocian Fathers and St. Augustine, St. Thomas notes therefore that Christian discourse about God is constituted by a kind of *redoublement* that "combines" two aspects: the divinity or divine essence *common* to the three persons, and the *properties* that distinguish the persons. It is this theological exigency that governs the structure of the treatise on God for Thomas Aquinas.[38] St. Thomas further specifies that, in the order of our concepts, the *commune* precedes the *proprium*: The knowledge of the divine essence precedes the knowledge of the personal properties since "what is

---

[36] *ST* I, q. 1, a. 1. For the nature of theology and its relation to philosophy in the thought of St. Thomas, see in particular Jean-Pierre Torrell, "Le savoir théologique chez saint Thomas," *Revue Thomiste* 96 (1996): 355–96; "Philosophie et théologie d'après le Prologue de Thomas d'Aquin au *Super Boetium de Trinitate*. Essai d'une lecture theologique," *Documenti e Studi sulla tradizione filosofica medievale* 10 (1999): 299–353.

[37] Basil of Caesarea, *Against Eunomius* II, 28 (ed. Bernard Sesboüé, Sources chrétiennes 305 [Paris: Cerf, 1983], pp. 120–21).

[38] See chapter 5 below: "Essentialism or Personalism in the Treatise on God in Saint Thomas Aquinas?"

common is included in our knowledge of the proper."[39] In other words, the notion of "divine person" includes the divine essence. This is the reason for which the essence common to the three persons must be treated beforehand (q. 2–26) in order then to be integrated into the study of the properties that constitute the persons (q. 27–43).

The Internal Structure of the Treatise

The purpose of St. Thomas, according to the principles that we have described, aims to account for each of the persons who are God (common essence) and who are characterized by a personal property (distinction of persons). It is then in the notion of person as "subsistent relation," as we will see later, that the synthesis of the treatise of God is effected in Thomas Aquinas's writings. Since the divine person will be conceived as a subsisting relation, the study of the *person* must be preceded by a study of *relation*, and since the real relation is founded on a procession, the study of the relation must be preceded by a prior study of *procession*. The order of our concepts, in the intelligence of the Trinitarian mystery, therefore will be the following: (1) the processions; (2) the relations; (3) the persons. One finds here the structure of reflection of the disputed questions *De potentia*.

This structure does not reflect the order of our discovery of the Trinitarian mystery, as it is set forth in *Summa contra Gentiles* (the testimony of Scripture, the confession of faith of the Church, and lastly the understanding of the faith in contrast with heresies). Neither is it a historical approach that would expose the genesis of the Trinitarian confession. The *Summa theologiae* proposes a speculative understanding of the faith *(intellectus fidei)* which exposits the notions in the inverse order of our discovery.[40] St. Thomas presents procession, relation, and person in the logical order of their conceptual sequence, so

---

[39] *ST* I, q. 33, a. 3, ad 1.

[40] In faith, we confess the three divine persons (cf. the Creed), then theology specifies that these persons are distinguished by relations and shows that these relations are founded on the processions (persons–relations–processions). The treatise in *Summa theologiae* follows an inverse order.

that, at each stage, the reader might benefit from the elements that are previously required.

The study of the persons is itself structured in a comparable fashion: Each element is placed in a way to benefit from the preceding elements, and in a manner that illumines the section that follows. This study of persons constitutes the principal part of the Trinitarian treatise: If one excepts the two introductory questions devoted to procession and to relation, the entire Trinitarian treatise is placed under this title—"the divine persons" (q. 29–43). The Trinitarian doctrine of St. Thomas is not, therefore, "abstract." It is concentrated principally on the reality of the Trinity, namely the Father, the Son, and the Holy Spirit. St. Thomas sets forth first the notion of "person," the signification of this word and the knowledge that we have of the divine persons (q. 29–32), and then he studies in detail each of the three divine persons (q. 33–38), before addressing the diverse relationships of the persons (39–43). The comparative study of the persons deals with several elements. Some of them are conceptual: The person is compared with the other aspects of the Trinitarian mystery (the essence, the properties, the notional acts of generation and of spiration: q. 39–41). Other elements of this comparison concern personal and real relations: the mutual relation of the persons, either in the Trinity in his immanent life (equality, relation of principle, order of origin, perichoresis: q. 42), or in the Trinity in his salvific action, when the Son and the Holy Spirit are sent to the saints (mission: q. 43).

The Trinitarian treatise is thus constructed according to its end which is to manifest the three divine persons in their subsistence, in their properties, in their relations, and in their action for us. Such is the structure of the Trinitarian treatise, which one can schematize in the following way, according to the explanations that St. Thomas gives in his prologues:

1. origin or processions (q. 27)
2. the relations of origin (q. 28)
3. the persons (q. 29–43)

a. the persons, considered in an absolute manner (q. 29–38)

   i. the persons according to what is common to them (q. 29–32)

   ii. the persons according to what is proper to each (q. 33–38)

      • The Father (q. 33)

      • The Son (q. 34–35)

      • The Holy Spirit (q. 36–38)

b. the persons, considered according to their relationships (q. 39–43)

   i. the persons in relationship to the essence (q. 39)

   ii. the persons in relationship to the properties (q. 40)

   iii. the persons in relationship to notional acts (q. 41)

   iv. the persons according to their mutual relationships (q. 42–43)

      • the relationships of equality and similarity of the persons (q. 42)

      • the mission of the persons (q. 43)

As we have recalled above, there is not only one but several Trinitarian treatises in the works of St. Thomas in which we can perceive differences and complementarity. The biblical foundations are particularly developed in the *Summa contra Gentiles*: Thomas does not return to them in detail in the *Summa theologiae*, but he reexamines them in his commentary of the Gospel of St. John.[41] Comparison of the two *Summae* shows that in *Summa theologiae* the exposition is principally consecrated to the notions which, in the *Summa contra Gentiles*, served to give an account of the faith in the face of the challenge of the heresies. The first article of the treatise of *Summa theologiae*, as we have seen, confirms this interpretation (q. 27, a. 1). Although the "polemical" dimension against the heresies is discreet in *Summa theologiae*, the understanding of the truth and the defense of this truth against errors constitute the two

---

[41] See chapter 7 below: "Biblical Exegesis and the Speculative Doctrine of the Trinity in St. Thomas Aquinas's Commentary on St. John."

inseparable facets of the same theological undertaking: It is in manifesting the truth that one removes errors, by a speculation or contemplation which allows one to perceive something of the mystery
of God. Trinitarian doctrine thus constitutes a foretaste of what the
theologian hopes to contemplate one day in full clarity with all the
saints in the beatific vision. This theological contemplation has at
its core the doctrine of procession, of relations, and of the person, as
St. Thomas made clear in his questions *De potentia.* As regards the
structure of this speculative effort, it expresses the resolute option of
St. Thomas in favor of the central place of the *person* and in favor of
the role of *relation* in understanding the person.

Procession, Relation, and Person

For St. Thomas Aquinas, as we have already noted in the structure
of the treatise, the persons are distinguished by the relations that
constitute these persons, and the relations are founded, in turn, on
the processions. Let us state precisely at the outset that this doctrine
ought not to be understood as a theological "superstructure": that
reflection imposed, as it were from the exterior, on the confession of
faith. For St. Thomas, the goal of this speculative reflection is to
uncover the deep meaning of the biblical revelation, as his commentary on St. John will show.[42]

The Notion of Procession

The point of departure of the Trinitarian treatise is the concept of
"immanent procession," that is, a procession which is accomplished
in the acting subject (q. 27). This placement of the notion of procession should be understood hand-in-hand with the real relation
that one must be able to posit in order to grasp the divine person.
The existence of real relations in God, for St. Thomas, is not an
arbitrary theological opinion, but rather is required by "the truth of
the faith."[43] Real relations, in creatures, do not arise from nothing:

---

[42] Cf. ibid.
[43] *Quodlibet* XII, q. 1, a. 1 (Leonine edition, vol. 25/2, 399).

When the relation is endowed with a concrete existence, it is an accident which belongs to a substance. St. Thomas interprets Aristotle's doctrine on relation in order to establish that a real relation can be caused by three grounds: quantity, action, or passion.[44] Because of the immateriality of the divine persons, it is necessary to exclude quantity; one must also exclude from God, by reason of the equality of the persons, the notion of passion properly speaking. There remains, therefore, as the only ground of real relation in God, the action, that is to say the origin.[45]

But what action is spoken of here? This action must be accomplished in God himself, since the divine persons are not constituted as such by their action in the world (Arianism or Sabellianism). Thomas uses his interpretation of Aristotelian anthropology to show, by analogy, that there can only be two types of immanent actions in God: the activity of the intelligence and that of the will. Life and other divine operations are reducible to his knowledge and his will,[46] while sensation must be excluded from God.[47] This is the reason for which the Trinitarian treatise begins by positing a procession by way of intellect *(per modum intellectus)* and a procession by way of love *(per modum amoris)*.[48]

In order to reach this result, Thomas must carry out a twofold argument. First, it is necessary to show that the procession *per modum intellectus*, that is, the speaking of the Word, is none other than the generation of the Son, and that the procession by way of love

---

[44] *ST* I, q. 28, a. 4; Cf. *De potentia,* q. 8, a. 1; *SCG* IV, ch. 24; Aristotle, *Metaphysics* V, 15 (1020 b 26–29).

[45] Ibid., St. Thomas employs in an equivalent manner the expressions *origo* and *processio*. The origin or procession has as its subject the person who is issued from another person (the Son who is engendered by the Father, the Holy Spirit who is breathed by the Father and the Son). On its side, the act of the person who is the principle of another person is called "notional act" or "notional action"; in these expressions, the term "notional" signifies that it is not an essential act common to the three persons, but an act that is the source of a personal relation within the Trinity (the act of the Father who begets the Son, the act of the Father and the Son who breathe the Holy Spirit).

[46] *ST* I, q. 18, a. 3; cf. *SCG* IV, ch. 11.

[47] *ST* I, q. 27, a. 5; cf. a. 3; *SCG* II, ch. 1.

[48] *ST* I, q. 27; cf. *De potentia,* q. 9, a. 9; q. 10, a. 1.

is none other than the procession of the Spirit, and then it is necessary to establish that these two processions are distinct (*ST* I, q. 27, a. 2–4). But, above all, one must show that intellection and willing are fruitful acts that "produce" something in the one who knows and loves. Thomas must work here a profound modification of Aristotle's anthropology. For Aristotle, the immanent operations of the intellect and the will, strictly speaking, "produce" nothing.[49] In the two cases, St. Thomas rereads Aristotle in the light of the Augustinian heritage in order to recognize the production of a "fruit" of the intelligence and of the will of God, that is, an immanent "term": such are the Word and Love, which are examined more closely in the study of the persons.[50] We are here in the order of these "adaptations" or "proba-ble arguments capable of showing that what is proposed to our faith is not impossible."[51] Trinitarian faith leads one to recognize these immanent processions in order to maintain the divinity of the per-sons (in order to avoid Arianism) and their distinct subsistence (in order to avoid Sabellianism). These two processions are not really dif-ferent from the persons, since in God the person and the act are truly one, but they are conceived by our mind as the source and as the *foundation* of the relation,[52] and they permit one therefore to mani-fest, in all truth, the existence of real relations in God.

The Relations

In his *Summa contra Gentiles*, St. Thomas started from the biblical rev-elation concerning the Father, the Son, and the Holy Spirit; he then showed how the Church understands Holy Scripture, in positing the three divine persons distinct by the relations.[53] The study of relation

---

[49] Aristotle, *Metaphysics* IX, 8 (1050 a 23–b 2).

[50] *ST* I, q. 34 and 37; *SCG* IV, ch. 11 and 19.

[51] *ST* II–II, q. 1, a. 5, ad 2.

[52] The "procession" and the "relation," while the same in reality, "are not the same in their mode of signifying: origin (or procession) is expressed as an action, e.g., fathering *(generatio)*; relation as a form, e.g., fatherhood *(paterni-tas)*" (*ST* I, q. 40, a. 2). And the "person," as we shall see below, is expressed as a subsisting subject.

[53] *SCG* IV, ch. 2–26; see chapter 3 above: "The Treatise of Saint Thomas on the Trinity in the *Summa contra Gentiles*."

then intervened, on the basis of the doctrine of the Word and Love, to remove the objections raised against the Catholic faith.[54] In a comparable way, the *Compendium theologiae* develops the doctrine of relation in order to show how the three divine persons, whose properties St. Thomas has set forth earlier, are not three gods but one single God.[55] The *Summa theologiae*, for its part, places the reflection on the relations at the beginning of the Trinitarian treatise (it is the second question: q. 28), but its purpose is entirely similar to that of St. Thomas's other works. It is to show how we can understand the three persons while confessing that they are one single God, that is to say how we can show that Christian Trinitarian faith is a strict monotheism.

The central thesis of St. Thomas is very clear: The real relations in God, founded on the processions, distinguish the persons while maintaining the substantial unity of the Trinity. The distinction of the persons is caused neither by diversity nor by a privation—that would destroy the consubstantiality and equality of the persons—but rather it stems from the relation of origin. This relation of origin happens from the sole fact that one person proceeds from another in the unity of the divine essence: The relations imply a "relative opposition" according to the origin.[56] There are four of these relations: paternity (relation of the Father to the Son), filiation (relation of the Son to the Father), "active spiration" (relation of the Father and the Son to the Holy Spirit), and procession or "passive spiration" (relation of the Holy Spirit to the Father and the Son). Of these relations, three constitute persons: paternity, filiation, and procession. For this reason, these three relations of origin are called "personal properties": Each one of them belongs properly, in an exclusive way, to one person, and constitutes this person in the unity of the divine essence which is communicated. The relation of "active spiration" (relation of the

---

[54] *SCG* IV, ch. 14 (#3502, 3504, 3506–10); ch. 24 (#3612–13).

[55] *CT* I, ch. 51–55.

[56] *ST* I, q. 28, a. 3; cf. q. 30, a. 2. The word "opposition" *(oppositio)* signifies the principle of a distinction (*SCG* IV, ch. 24, #3612). This term, of patristic origin, translates the Greek word *antithesis* used by St. Basil of Caesarea to signify that the Father is not the Son and that the Son is not the Father. See for instance Basil of Caesarea, *Against Eunomius* II, 28, (ed. Bernard Sesboüé, Sources chrétiennes 305 [Paris: Cerf, 1983], pp. 120–21).

Father and the Son to the Holy Spirit) is not a personal property, since
it is common to the Father and the Son: The Father and the Son are
not constituted as Father and Son through the spiration of the Spirit
(though the spiration of the Spirit is not absent in the generation of
the Son),[57] but they are constituted by paternity and filiation.[58]

St. Thomas studies relation by extending the thought of St.
Albert the Great.[59] The analysis of relation is founded on the Aristotelian doctrine of categories or predicaments. For St. Thomas, real
relations in our world are "accidents" that exist not "between" things
but "in" things: The relation is carried by a concrete subject in which
it exists in the mode of an accident. In extending Aristotle's thought
(*Catégories* 7 and *Metaphysics* Δ, 15), St. Thomas Aquinas distinguishes two aspects in the relation, as in each of the nine kinds of
Aristotelian accidents: (1) the being or existence of the accident *(esse)*;
(2) the definition or proper nature of the accident *(ratio)*. As regards
its *ratio*, relation presents a unique character among the accidents:
Relation does not positively affect the subject that bears it, it is not
an intrinsic determination of this subject (as is quality or quantity,
for example), but rather it is a pure relationship to another *(ad
aliud)*. The relation possesses here an "ecstatic" character, a sort of
metaphysical simplicity that permits its direct attribution to God.
But on the side of its existence *(esse)*, the relation possesses the mode
of being common to all the accidents, namely inherence in a subject
(the existence in another and through another).[60]

The transposition to God of this double aspect of relation allows
one to consider the divine person. (1) From the side of the existence,
it is necessary to recognize that the *esse* of the divine relation is the
same being as the divine substance: Under the aspect of its existence,
the relation identifies itself purely and simply with the substantial

[57] In engendering his Son, the Father gives to the Son to spirate the Holy Spirit
with him (*ST* I, q. 36, a. 3, ad 2).

[58] *ST* I, q. 28, a. 4.

[59] See Gilles Emery, "La relation dans la théologie de saint Albert le Grand," in
*Albertus Magnus, Zum Gedenken nach 800 Jahren: Neue Zugänge, Aspekte und
Perspektiven,* ed. Walter Senner (Berlin: Akademie Verlag, 2001), pp. 455–65.

[60] *ST* I, q. 28, a. 2; *De potentia,* q. 8, a. 2.

being in God, since there is not accidental being in God. (2) From the side of its definition or proper nature *(ratio: ad aliud)*, the relation is transposed in God as a pure relationship of "opposition according to origin" (paternity, filiation, and procession). Under this second aspect, the relation does not consist in a determination of the divine essence, but rather consists only in the interpersonal relationship according to origin.[61] St. Thomas shows thus that the relations are really distinct from each other, in virtue of their "opposition" (according to their *ratio*), that is to say in virtue of the pure relationship to the other according to the origin: The paternity is not the filiation; but these relations are really identical to the unique substance of God (in virtue of their *esse*).

It is thus in the theme of relation that is organized, for Thomas Aquinas, the question of the relationship between Unity and Trinity. For St. Thomas, there is not on one side the unique essence, and on another side the relation. All converges in the relation, since the divine relation contains both the element of personal distinction *(ratio)*, and the element of the divine hypostatic subsistence *(esse)*. These two aspects together constitute the theological notion of divine person. This is why priority is given neither to the essence nor to the mutual relationships, but to the *person* who reunites these two dimensions.

The Person

The point of departure of the study of the person resides in the famous definition of Boethius, issuing from the Theopaschite Christological controversy, in the context of the rejection of Nestorianism and Monophysitism: "The person is an individual substance of a rational nature" *(persona est rationalis [rationabilis] naturae individua substantia)*.[62] St. Thomas starts from the concept of individual. The person is an individual of the genre of the substance, in the sense

---

[61] *ST* I, q. 28, a. 2; *De potentia*, q. 8, a. 2.

[62] *ST* I, q. 29, a. 1. Boethius, *Against Eutyches and Nestorius,* ch. 3 (English translation in: Boethius, *The Theological Tractates,* pp. 84–85). See Corinna Schlapkohl, *Persona est naturae rationabilis individua substantia: Boethius und die Debatte über den Personbegriff* (Marburg: N. G. Elwert Verlag, 1999), pp. 199–217.

of the Aristotelian *substantia prima* (the concrete subject, the suppposit, the hypostasis). An individual substance is characterized by a proper mode of existence *(modus existendi)*: It exists by itself and in itself, and not in another or through another. This "existence by itself" constitutes the fundamental characteristic of the substance, and therefore of the person. Examining the definition of Boethius, St. Thomas explains that the "individual substance" is the *genus proximum* of the definition of the person, while the *differentia specifica* is found in the "rational nature." The expression *rationalis natura* does not designate the activity of the intelligence, but the power or faculty of rational knowledge (which fits, by analogy, God, angels, and men). The "nature" means the principle of action (the principle of movement and of rest), and therefore the essence. As regards rationality, which implies the will and liberty, it characterizes the mode of being and of action proper to beings who freely move themselves toward the end which they know by their intelligence. At the heart of this definition of the person is found therefore the theme of *freedom of action*: "Rational substances have control over their actions, and are not only acted upon as other beings are, but they act by themselves."[63]

St. Thomas defines the person by three marks: individuality (distinction), substance (existence by itself), and rationality with the will (to act freely by oneself). This is the reason why "*Person* means that which is the most perfect *(perfectissimum)* in the whole of nature."[64] The psychological traits of the person (knowledge, freedom, responsibility) are founded in an ontological understanding (substance). Applied to God, this definition guarantees the divinity of the three persons (divine intellectual nature) against Arianism, their real distinction and their proper subsistence (individual substance) against Sabellianism, and it grounds their action (intelligent and free individual substance).

It is here that the previous analysis of relation intervenes. The word "person," when applied to God, signifies the divine essence

---

[63] *ST* I, q. 29, a. 1.
[64] *ST* I, q. 29, a. 3.

and the relation. More precisely, *"Divine person* signifies relation as something subsisting *(relatio ut subsistens)"* or "relation by way of substance which is a hypostasis *(relatio per modum substantiae quae est hypostasis),"* that is to say, the relation in the mode of first substance.[65] As we have seen, the relation is not an accident in God, but it is identical to the divine substance itself.[66] Thus, the relation subsists in virtue of the divine essence to which it is identical, and it distinguishes the persons in virtue of the relationship *ad aliud* that constitutes its *ratio.* In contrast to men, the divine persons are individuated by the relations, and they are constituted by these relations (the relation is identical to the divine essence). The capacity of subsistence does not belong to the relation under the aspect of the relationship to the other *(ratio),* but it belongs to the relation in so much as this relation is divine *(esse).*[67] St. Thomas explains, in similar terms, that the person designates in God "the distinct subsistent in the divine nature" *(subsistens distinctum in natura divina),* by specifying that this "distinct subsistent" is the relation taken in the integrality of its constitution in God, in its *esse* (divine substance) and in its *ratio* (relationship *ad aliud* that distinguishes).[68] It is therefore in the "subsisting relation," which guarantees a strict Trinitarian monotheism, that St. Thomas effects the synthesis of his doctrine on God the Trinity.

The Three Divine Persons

The first three questions have posed the pillars of Trinitarian theology. On this foundation, St. Thomas considers the three persons in their properties, that is to say in the proper traits that constitute and distinguish each of these persons. In this section, the explanations of St. Thomas seek to manifest the persons within the Trinity *(theologia)* and then, in light of the properties of the persons, to clarify their action in the world *(oikonomia),* conforming to the motive of the revelation of the Trinity which we have recalled above.

---

[65] *ST* I, q. 29, a. 4.
[66] *ST* I, q. 28, a. 2.
[67] Cf. *De potentia,* q. 10, a. 3.
[68] *De potentia,* q. 9, a. 4.

The Person of the Father

The name "Father" must pass through a work of purification in order to be applied to God, since one must exclude corporal genera- tion, the sexual difference, change, aging, and so on.[69] What remains in the notion of *Father*? Two major traits must be retained which constitute the two properties of the first person of the Trinity: (1) the Father is the one from whom the Son is engendered; (2) the Father does not have an origin. The first of these traits is expressed by the notion of "paternity," and the second by the notion of "innascibil- ity." These two properties contain the essentials of what Trinitarian doctrine places under the word "Father": It is around these that St. Thomas organizes his study of the Father (q. 33).

These two properties are exposited by St. Thomas by means of the notion of "principle" that is omnipresent in the question devoted to the Father: This notion dominates the entire theological discus- sion. St. Thomas places this notion in the foreground because of its conceptual precision. "Principle" does not imply, in itself, any poste- riority or any inequality with the reality that comes forth from this principle. There are indeed principles that imply a certain inequality or posteriority, because the notion of principle is analogous (there are several ways to be principle), but inequality is not included in the formal notion of this term. "The word 'principle' means simply that from which something proceeds."[70] Applied to God, in Trinitarian theology, this name designates the divine person with a relationship *(ordo)* toward another person who proceeds from him.[71] St. Thomas integrates into the study of the name "principle" the results of his doctrine of relation. The "principle" designates the divine person *under the aspect of the relation* that it holds with the person who pro- ceeds from it. Paternity, in God, designates therefore the relation that the Father holds with the Son, that is to say the Father under the aspect of his relation to the Son. This relation includes all the goods that the Father communicates to the Son through generation

---

[69] See *SCG* IV, ch. 11 (#3478–79).
[70] *ST* I, q. 33, a. 1; cf. q. 42, a. 2.
[71] Ibid.; cf. *ST* I, q. 42, a. 3.

(divine being, wisdom, love, power of action, and so on), except, precisely, the fact of being Father. It is, for this reason, an exclusive property of the Father.[72]

St. Thomas takes particular care to show that the name "Father," in God, first concerns the interpersonal relation of the Father to the Son, and not the relation to creatures: The name *Father* first signifies the eternal relation of the Father to his only Son. The paternity of the Father exists in the most eminent and perfect way in his relation to the only Son, since the Father gives to the Son his entire nature and all his love in the divine unity, while creatures only receive a participation in this divine fullness. This does not signify that the name "Father" is foreign to the relation that God holds with us: While we recognize God as Father of creatures or as Father of men, or while we pray to him as "our Father," the relation that creatures hold with God the Father must be understood as a "similitude" of the eternal relation of the Son to the Father, that is to say as a derivation or a "participation" in the personal relation of the Son to the Father.[73]

The study of the name *Father*, like the study of the other names of the divine persons, thus comprises a double aspect. (1) It concerns first of all an intra-Trinitarian relation, of person to person, within the divine eternity. This intra-Trinitarian relation is primary. (2) By analogy and derivation, it concerns in the second place the economy, the action of God in the world. This economic significance of the name "Father" is also analogical, since it comprises diverse modes of realization: God is Father of all beings by creation (he is the principle of the created world), he is Father of the men that he creates to his image, and he is the Father of the saints by grace. In all cases, the paternity of God toward his creatures appears as an extension, by a free gift, of his eternal paternity toward his Son. Under this aspect, the paternity of the Father toward the eternal Son is the root of his creating and saving action. St. Thomas has set this forth with more details in his *Scriptum* on the *Sentences*. The

---

[72] *ST* I, q. 33, a. 2.
[73] *ST* I, q. 33, a. 3.

Father communicates to his Son, from all eternity, all the goods of divine life; to his creatures, he communicates a participation in the divine life (creation and salvation). The first communication (eternal generation) is the principle, cause, and reason of the second communication (creation and salvation). The intra-Trinitarian relation of the Father to the Son, that is to say paternity, is therefore the source of God's action in the world.[74]

It is again with the notion of "principle" that St. Thomas explains the property of innascibility that characterizes the Father. The Son is—with the Father—the principle of the Spirit, and the three persons are together the principle of creatures. But it belongs to the Father alone to be the principle "without principle."[75] More precisely, according to St. Thomas, the notion of innascibility is a "negative" notion: It signifies that the Father does not have a principle, that he is not engendered (it therefore signifies a negation). This question of innascibility reveals a divergence between the Franciscan Trinitarian theology of St. Bonaventure and the Dominican school of St. Albert and St. Thomas. For St. Bonaventure, innascibility contains a negative aspect (the Father does not have a principle), but it equally contains a positive aspect: Since he is without principle, the Father possesses "fecundity" and therefore he is the source of other persons. The innascibility designates, for St. Bonaventure, the "fontality" *(fontalitas)* or "fontal plenitude" *(fontalis plenitudo)* of the Father, that is to say his fecundity toward the other persons.[76] St. Thomas rejects this teaching of St. Bonaventure: "hoc non videtur verum." The Father's fontal plenitude is not signified by the innascibility, but by the paternity and by the spiration which manifest the Father as the principle of the Son and of the Spirit.[77]

This divergence, though it appears secondary, in reality reveals a fundamental and characteristic trait of the Trinitarian theology of St. Thomas. For Bonaventure, the personal distinction of the Father is inchoatively posed by the innascibility, and is achieved

---

[74] See G. Emery, "Le Père et l'oeuvre trinitaire de création," pp. 85–117.

[75] *ST* I, q. 33, a. 4.

[76] St. Bonaventure, I *Sent.,* d. 27, p. 1, a. un., q. 2, ad 3; d. 28, a. un., q. 2.

[77] St. Thomas, *ST* I, q. 33, a. 4, ad 1.

through the paternity: "The Father engenders *because he is innascible.*"[78] One recognizes here the theme of primacy *(primitas)* that is dear to Bonaventure. But, for St. Thomas, this Bonaventurean thesis means that the Father would be in a certain manner constituted as Father prior to his relation of paternity. St. Thomas therefore rejects this thesis because in it he finds a pre-relational conception of the Father. What is at stake in the debate on the negative character of the innascibility of the Father is clear: It is about the doctrine of the person as subsisting relation, that is to say about the exclusive role of the relations for distinguishing and constituting the persons.

The Person of the Son

The study of the person of the Son is undertaken by the examination of two names which express his personal property: *Word* and *Image*. One may be surprised at first by the fact that St. Thomas does not devote an article to the name "Son" (while he devotes one question to the name "Father" and an article to the name "Holy Spirit"). But, on the one hand, the name "Son" was already studied in the study of the name "Father," since these two correlative names mutually imply each other. On the other, it is in the study of the name "Word" that St. Thomas presents his teaching on the name "Son." The doctrine of the Word has no other end than to manifest what is, in God, the filiation of the Son. St. Thomas therefore first sets forth the doctrine of the Word, and he then shows how this name "Word" allows one to understand who the "Son" is within the Trinity.

The doctrine of the Word, along with that of Love with which it is intimately connected, is the heart of Aquinas's Trinitarian theology. Its importance is indicated as early as the first article of the treatise of *Summa theologiae*: In order to set forth the Trinitarian faith, one must be able to account for *immanent* processions; according to St. Thomas, it is in the operation of the intellect that one finds, in

---

[78] St. Bonaventure, I *Sent.*, d. 27, p. 1, a. un., q. 2, concl. and ad 3; d. 28, dubium 1: "Unde distinctio personae Patris quasi inchoatur in innascibilitate et consummatur in paternitate;" cf. II *Sent.*, *Praelocutio.*

the clearest and most manifest way, such an immanent procession.[79] The study of Love will be developed in an analogous manner. This doctrine serves to show the existence of immanent processions in God (*ST* I, q. 27, a. 1), to specify the mode and number of the processions (q. 27, a. 2–5); and thereby to render account of the relations of origin that distinguish and constitute the persons (q. 28–29, q. 40). It allows one also to determine the personal property of the Son (q. 34–35) and the personal property of the Spirit (q. 37–38), and to explain the action of these persons in the world (q. 34, a. 3; q. 37, a. 2, ad 3), in particular the sending of the Son and the Spirit to men in the gift of grace (q. 43).

This doctrinal elaboration exploits the analogy drawn from the human soul, in the order of *similitudines* whose function has been specified above. The reflection of St. Thomas here shows progress. In his commentary on the *Sentences*, he was not yet in possession of his mature doctrine. In this commentary, the generation of the Son was principally understood as a procession "by the mode of nature": The theme of the intellectual procession is found at a second level. St. Thomas still recognized an essential sense of the name *Verbum* in God, and he conceived the Holy Spirit as "a subsisting act" or "a subsisting operation of love" that proceeds in God.[80] Progressively elaborated beginning with the *De veritate*, St. Thomas's doctrine reaches its first maturity in the *Summa contra Gentiles*.[81] The subsequent works (*De potentia, Compendium theologiae, Summa theologiae, Lectura in Ioannem*) develop the path opened by the *Summa contra Gentiles*.

Thomas Aquinas, as already noted, modified the thought of Aristotle by positing, following St. Augustine, a fecundity of the

---

[79] St. Thomas, *ST* I, q. 27, a. 1: "maxime patet in intellectu." When our intellect knows, it produces in itself (immanent procession) a concept of the thing known. Cf. *SCG* IV, ch. 11; *De potentia*, q. 8, a. 1; q. 9, a. 9; q. 10, a. 1. St. Thomas gave a summary of his doctrine of the Word and of Love in his short work, *De rationibus fidei*, ch. 3–4. For an introduction to this doctrine, and for bibliographical information, see my translation: Thomas d'Aquin, *Les raisons de la foi*, pp. 35–40 and 66–79.

[80] For the explications of the commentary on the *Sentences*, see G. Emery, *La Trinité créatrice*, pp. 414–22 and 430–34.

[81] See chapter 3 above.

immanent activity of knowledge and of love. His purpose consists in showing that the *verbum* and the *amor* include a relation of origin with regard to a principle; it is this relation of origin that allows the manifestation of the distinction of the persons, and therefore the precision of the property of the Son and of the Spirit. In a second stage, Thomas shows that Word and Love, in God, have the existence and the nature of God himself: This aspect, joined with the preceding, will allow the manifestation of the hypostatic subsistence of the persons and their divine consubstantiality.[82] Here we again find the two aspects of relation explained earlier.

The doctrine of the Word is founded on the analysis of language: The vocal word exteriorly pronounced *(verbum exterior)*, according to St. Thomas, signifies the "interior word" which is the concept *(verbum interior, verbum mentis, intentio intellecta, conceptio, conceptus)*. The word, according to this analysis, is the concept formed by the intellect: This word expresses the thing known and possesses a relationship of origin to the intellect which forms it interiorly. Our vocal words do not immediately signify the known reality: They signify our interior word which expresses this known reality.[83]

Beginning with the *Summa contra Gentiles*,[84] and in a manner that is completely his own among his contemporaries, St. Thomas clearly distinguishes the *species intelligibilis* which places the intellect in the act of knowing (the *species*, the outcome of the abstraction, is that by which the intellect knows), and the *verbum* which appears in a subsequent stage when the intellect forms or produces a conception of the thing known. While the *species intelligibilis* is the principle of the activity of intellectual knowledge, the *verbum* is for its part the immanent term of the activity of intellectual knowledge, the term formed by the intellect, which makes the objective presence of the thing known in the knower, and in which the process of knowledge is completed: The word is that "in which" *(in quo)* the

---

[82] *ST* I, q. 34, a. 1–2; q. 37, a. 1.

[83] *ST* I, q. 34, a. 1; cf. *Lectura in Ioannem* 1:1 (ch. 1, lect. 1); *SCG* I, ch. 35.

[84] *SCG* I, ch. 53; *SCG* IV, ch. 11.

intellect knows.[85] The theme of the production or of the real formation allows one to show, by analogy, that the divine Word is conceived by the Father and is really distinct from him.[86] St. Thomas
therefore can establish that the name "Word" is said properly in
God and not by a metaphor or by a convention of language, and
that this name is exclusively attributed to the Son whose personal
property it signifies.[87]

Thus it is from the study of the name "Word" that St. Thomas
explains the generation of the "Son" in God. Generation is the birth
or the procession of a being in a specific nature similar to that of its
parent. And since God is of purely spiritual nature, the divine generation is accomplished according to the highest vital act, which is
the act of the intellect. When God knows himself, he engenders a
Word who proceeds from the divine intellect and who is the perfect
expression of what is found in the divine intellect:

> So in this manner the procession of the Word in God is gen-
> eration; for he proceeds by way of intelligible action, which
> is a vital operation; and from a conjoined principle; and by
> way of similitude, inasmuch as the concept of the intellect is
> a likeness of the object conceived; and he exists in the same
> nature, because in God the act of understanding and his
> existence are the same, as shown above (q. 14, a. 4). Hence
> the procession of the Word in God is called *generation*; and
> the Word himself proceeding is called the Son.[88]

It is equally by means of the notion of "Word" that St. Thomas
exposits the name "Image" attributed to the Son. The notion of
image contains two principal elements, which St. Thomas receives
from St. Hilary of Poitiers: (1) the image must possess the same specific nature as its model (it must resemble the model according to
the specific nature of this model); (2) the image must derive from
the model (it must take its origin from the model itself). St. Thomas

[85] *Lectura in Ioannem* 1:1 (ch. 1, lect. 1).
[86] *ST* I, q. 34, a. 1; *SCG* IV, ch. 11; *Lectura in Ioannem* 1:1 (ch. 1, lect. 1).
[87] *ST* I, q. 34, a. 1 and 2.
[88] *ST* I, q. 27, a. 2.

easily shows that the Word confirms these two elements, since the Word is the perfect expression (similitude in the divine unity) of all that is found in the intellect of the Father, and since he proceeds from the Father. Therefore, since he is the Word of the Father, the Son is the Image of the Father and, for this same reason, the name "Image" is a proper name that one attributes exclusively to the Son.[89] By expositing the names "Word" and "Image" that the Scriptures attribute to the Son, St. Thomas brings out the elements required for understanding with precision the notion of "filiation," which is the personal property of the Son.

The theme of the Word is not limited to manifesting the property of the Son in the divine eternity, but it equally clarifies the action of the Son in the world (creation and salvation).[90] The Word engendered by the Father expresses all that is in the intellect of the Father:

> Because God by one act understands himself and all things, his one only Word is expressive not only of the Father, but of all creatures. And as the knowledge of God is only cognitive as regards God, whereas as regards creatures, it is both cognitive and operative, so the Word of God is only expressive of what is in God the Father, but is both expressive and operative of creatures; and therefore it is said (Psalm 32:9 [33:9]): "He spoke, and they were made" because in the Word is implied the operative idea of what God makes.[91]

Because the Word expresses all that is in the Father, the Word also expresses the creatures that preexist in the Father. And since the knowledge of God is the cause of creatures, the Word is not only the exemplary expression of creatures, but he is also the efficient cause that produces creatures: The Father accomplishes all things through his Word (cf. Jn 1:3). This doctrine of the Word in addi-

---

89 *ST* I, q. 35. See also Thomas's Commentary on Colossians 1:15 (#30–35).

90 *ST* I, q. 34, a. 3; cf. *SCG* IV, ch. 12–13.

91 *ST* I, q. 34, a. 3. Cf. *Lectura in Ioannem,* ch. 1, lect. 1 (#27): "The divine Word is expressive of all that is in God, not only of the persons but also of creatures."

tion permits the understanding of the mission of the Son in the soul of saints (q. 43), and it also allows the manifestation of the fittingness of the incarnation of the Son, in the *Tertia pars*: The doctrine of the Word constitutes the point of principal contact, the pivot, of Trinitarian theology and of Christology.[92] Thus the name "Word" furnishes the key to showing not only the personal property of the Son, his relation to the Father, and his subsistence within the Trinity, but also his action in creation and in the exercise of providence, in particular in the incarnation.

The Person of the Holy Spirit

Three questions are devoted to the Holy Spirit (q. 36–38): It is the Holy Spirit who, materially, receives the greatest attention in the study of the divine persons. The first question examines the name "Holy Spirit" and, in particular, the procession of the Holy Spirit *a Patre et a Filio* (q. 36).[93] The heart of St. Thomas's speculative doctrine is found in q. 37: As St. Thomas expounded the personal property of the Son by means of the doctrine of the Word, it is with the theme of Love that he explains how one must conceive the procession and the property of the Holy Spirit. The explanation in the *Summa theologiae*, like that in the *Summa contra Gentiles*,[94] rests on the theme of the love through which God loves himself. As God knows, so God wills and loves.[95] And as the intellect in action forms a word, so the will in action causes to arise in itself an "impression" *(impressio)* of the being who is loved. Thomas conceives this impression as an "affection toward" *(affectio)*, an impulse *(impulsio, impulsus)*, a surge or an attraction *(attractio)* to the beloved thing.[96] In the will of the lover arises at the same time a

---

[92] Cf. *ST* III, q. 3, a. 8.

[93] For the teaching of question 36, see chapter 6 below.

[94] *ST* I, q. 37; *SCG* IV, ch. 19. On the doctrine of the property of the Holy Spirit (love, gift, communion), see the contributions of Francois Bourassa, *Questions de théologie trinitaire* (Rome: Gregorian University Press, 1970); "Sur la propriété de l'Esprit-Saint. Questions disputées," *Science et Esprit* 28 (1976): 243–65; 29 (1977): 23–43.

[95] *ST* I, q. 19–20.

[96] *ST* I, q. 37, a. 1; *SCG* IV, ch. 19; *CT* I, ch. 46.

dynamic impulse toward the beloved object (what I love is present to my will as inclining me toward it).

It is this impression, affection, surge, or impulse of love, that permits the understanding of the personal property of the Holy Spirit, and it is this that one designates when one says that "the Holy Spirit is personal Love," for lack of another more precise word.[97] This point must be noted with precision. When we say that "the Holy Spirit Love in person," this name "Love" does not designate the act of loving,[98] but the *fruit* of the Father and Son's act of love, that is to say, the "impression" or the dynamic impulse that arises in the loving will of the Father and the Son.[99] This impression of love proceeds within the loving will (immanent procession); it possesses a relation of origin to the will from which it proceeds, and to the Word who is presupposed to love (the will loves what the understanding has first conceived): This allows one to show the distinction of the Holy Spirit in relationship to the Father and the Son, and thereby to manifest the relative property of the Holy Spirit. Thus, it is by this impression or affection of love that the presence of "God loved in God who loves himself" is verified. The theme of the Holy Spirit as "mutual Love of the Father and the Son" (Augustine, Richard de Saint-Victor) is connected to these explanations.[100]

It is again by means of this theme of Love that St. Thomas expounds the name "Gift" that belongs to the Holy Spirit (q. 38):

> The reason for giving gratuitously is love: the reason we
> give something to another gratuitously is that we will good
> to him. So what we first give him is the love whereby we

---

[97] *ST* I, q. 37, a. 1. The name "Amor," in God, will have two meanings: the essential love common to the three persons, and the personal love identified in the *impressio* of love that is the Holy Spirit.

[98] As noted above, this was St. Thomas's thought in his commentary on the *Sentences*: he conceived the Holy Spirit as an operation or as a subsisting act of love that proceeds in God (I Sent., d. 32, q. 1, a. 1); see G. Emery, *La Trinité créatrice*, pp. 430–34.

[99] *ST* I, q. 37, a. 1.

[100] *ST* I, q. 37, a. 2.

will good to him. Clearly, then, love has the nature of a first gift, through which all other free gifts are given. Since, then, the Holy Spirit comes forth as Love, as stated above (q. 27, a. 4; q. 37, 1), he proceeds as being the first Gift.[101]

The word "Gift" designates a relation of origin, as does the name "Love," since the gift is the gift *of someone*: It therefore signifies a personal distinction in God.[102] Thus St. Thomas can explain that the word *Donum* is a name proper to the Holy Spirit whose personal property it signifies.

This name "Gift" is found in the junction of theology and economy since, as St. Thomas notes, "The word *Gift* imports an aptitude for being given."[103] The gift of the Holy Spirit to men in the economy of salvation is the extension, free and gratuitous, of his personal property within the Trinity. By exposing the eternal property of the Spirit, St. Thomas also furnishes the key to understanding the salvific action of the Spirit. This economic dimension is equally present in the study of the word "Love." The doctrine of the Holy Spirit as Love, in manifesting the property of the Spirit within the Trinity, also allows the understanding of the Holy Spirit's role in creation and in the work of salvation:

> Even as the Father utters himself and every creature by the Word he begets, inasmuch as the Word begotten completely expresses the Father and every creature, so also he loves himself and every creature by the Holy Spirit, inasmuch as the Holy Spirit proceeds as Love for the primal goodness, by which the Father loves himself and every creature.[104]

The creation and all the works of God, inasmuch as they come forth from the free will of God, have as their principle the personal Love, the Holy Spirit by whom the Father and the Son love each other and by whom they love us.

---

[101] *ST* I, q. 38, a. 2.
[102] *ST* I, q. 38, a. 1, ad 1.
[103] *ST* I, q. 38, a. 1.
[104] *ST* I, q. 37, a. 2, ad 3.

In this manner, the theme of the Word and of Love constitutes the best way, according to St. Thomas, of manifesting the relative personal property of the Son and of the Holy Spirit, and of rendering account of Trinitarian monotheism. One cannot underestimate the importance that St. Thomas recognizes in this doctrine of the Word and of Love: "If the procession of the Word and of Love does not suffice for suggesting the personal distinction, there could not be any personal distinction in God."[105] In addition, by developing his doctrine of the Word and of Love, St. Thomas establishes the Trinitarian foundations of every divine action: He places on one side the foundations of creation and of the divine government, and he places on the other side the foundations of the union with God by grace, that is to say by the mission of the Son and of the Spirit, as we will see later. Numerous authors, following notably Karl Rahner, hold that Thomas's doctrine of the Word and of Love (the "psychological" doctrine of the Trinity, according to the questionable vocabulary of Michael Schmaus) presents an "abstract" approach to the Trinity, a Trinity "locked within himself" and detached from the economy of salvation.[106] In reality, one finds the contrary in St. Thomas's writings: The doctrine of the Word and of Love, by clarifying the properties of the persons, is closely connected to the intelligence of the Trinitarian economy.

The Persons, the Essence, the Properties, and the Notional Acts

After the study of the divine persons, St. Thomas devotes a group of questions to the relationships that the persons hold with the essence, with the relations and the properties, and with the notional acts (q. 39–41). These questions have as their goal the specification of the doctrine of the divine persons, by clarifying the diverse aspects of our understanding of the Trinitarian mystery and by providing

[105] *De potentia*, q. 9, a. 9, ad 7.
[106] Karl Rahner, *The Trinity*, trans. by Joseph Donceel (New York: Herder and Herder, 1970), pp. 18–19 and 119–20.

certain complements involving our language to the subject of the Trinity (the appropriations, for example). The detailed examination of these questions exceeds the limited purpose of our study. We will content ourselves with presenting here the principle aspects, by indicating the characteristic theses of St. Thomas.

St. Thomas's first concern, in these questions, consists in showing the unity of each person and the unity of the Trinity, against the danger of an excessive conceptualism. The realism of St. Thomas is here expressed in an exemplary manner. This purpose is inscribed in the theological debate sparked notably by the reception of Boethius in Gilbert de la Porrée (Gilbert of Poitiers), in the twelfth century. Gilbert de la Porrée, an eminent theologian who generally received great respect from his contemporaries (a respect that one perceives in St. Thomas), held the Boethian distinction between the abstract forms *(quo est)* and the concrete subject *(quod est)*, and he affirmed an analogous distinction in God. Whatever Gilbert's authentic thought was, it led to an energetic reaction from St. Bernard of Clairvaux who reproached him for posing a difference between "God" and the "divine essence," and an analogous difference between the person (for example, the Father) and the property of this person (paternity). Pope Eugenius III, without condemning Gilbert himself, prescribed "that no reasoning should make a division between nature and person in theology, and that God *(Deus)* should be called divine essence *(divina essentia)* not only according to the sense of the ablative but also according to the sense of the nominative."[107]

This prescription, invoked by St. Thomas,[108] governs all his explanations on the relationships between the person and the essence (q. 39): The person is strictly identical to the essence, and vice versa. St. Thomas also knows that Joachim of Fiore had reproached Peter Lombard for having taught the existence of a "quaternity" in God, that is say for having added the divine essence to the three persons in the manner of a "fourth reality," as if the

---

[107] Denzinger, #745–46. For more details, see chapter 1 above.
[108] *ST* I, q. 28, a. 2; cf. I *Sent.*, d. 33, q. 1, a. 1.

essence were numbered with the three persons.[109] He is therefore particularly careful to show that the divine essence is not added to the divine persons, since the persons are this essence (q. 39, a. 1–6).

In order to expound the identity of the essence and of the divine person, St. Thomas returns to his doctrine of relations.[110] Here again, St. Thomas clashes with Gilbert de la Porrée. In order to preserve the unity of the divine essence, absolutely identical in each person, Gilbert had explained that the relation is not attributed *secundum rem* in God: The relation does not modify the essence, it is not a thing *(aliquid)*, but a relationship to a thing *(ad aliquid)*; the divine persons are not opposed to each other in virtue of their essence, but rather they are distinguished according to the relation that Gilbert declared "extrinsic" or "affixed from the outside" *(extrinsecus affixa)*.[111] St. Thomas takes particular care to rectify the thought of Gilbert, by showing that the relation is identical to the divine essence and is neither accidental nor "affixed from the outside" in God (q. 28, a. 2), and that the relation is identical to the divine person (q. 40, a. 1), just as the essence is identical to the divine person (q. 39, a. 1).

St. Thomas exploits, here again, the double aspect of relation that we exposed earlier: According to its *ratio*, the relation is a pure reference to the other, which does not modify the divine essence; as regards its *esse*, the relation is identified purely and simply with the being of the divine essence: It is this divine essence. Since the persons are subsisting relations, it is the same for the persons as it is for the relations: They do not modify the divine essence, nor do they add to the divine essence, but are truly identical to this divine essence.[112] The clear affirmation of the real identity of the person, the essence, and the relation, thus constitutes a fundamental princi-

---

[109] See St. Thomas's commentary on the Decretal *Damnamus* of the fourth Lateran Council *(Expositio super secundam Decretalem ad Archidiaconum Tudertinum).*

[110] *ST* I, q. 39, a. 1.

[111] Gilbert of Poitiers, *Expositio in Boecii de Trinitate* I, 5, n. 43 (ed. N. M. Häring, *The Commentaries on Boethius by Gilbert of Poitiers,* 148); cf. II, 1, n. 37 (pp. 170–71).

[112] *ST* I, q. 28, a. 2; q. 39, a. 1; q. 40, a. 1.

ple in the entire reflection of St. Thomas who sees in it an indispensable affirmation for a true Trinitarian monotheism.

The central role of the doctrine of relation appears again in question 40, in the study of the relationships that the persons hold with the relations. St. Thomas here reprises his explanations by showing that the persons are distinguished only by the relations, and not by an "absolute" reality in God: The relations distinguish and constitute these persons.[113] On this basis, returning to the thought of Albert the Great, St. Thomas expounds a thesis entirely characteristic of his Trinitarian theology: If, when we think of the Trinity, we abstracted from the relations, the person would disappear totally from our mind (since the person is constituted by the relation).[114] St. Thomas clearly rejects any attempt to conceive of the person independently from the relations. One cannot, for example, conceive of the Father as "the primordial divine being," since it is only by his relation to the Son that the Father can be thought of as Father. This is the reason for which, in St. Thomas, the divine personal plurality never appears as the fruition of the divine essence. This thesis, among others, manifests the exceptional place of relation in the Trinitarian theology of St. Thomas, that is to say the decided option of St. Thomas for a relational understanding of the divine person.

The Mission of the Divine Persons

After having treated the relationship of the persons with the essence, with the properties, and with the notional acts, St. Thomas completes his Trinitarian treatise through the study of the "mutual relationships of the persons" (q. 42–43).[115] These mutual relationships involve the equality and the likeness of the persons (q. 42) as well as the mission of the divine persons (q. 43). This context of the study of the divine missions is completely remarkable. On the one hand,

---

[113] *ST* I, q. 40, a. 1–2.
[114] *ST* I, q. 40, a. 3; *De potentia*, q. 8, a. 4.
[115] *ST* I, q. 39, prol.; q. 42, prol.: "De comparatione personarum ad invicem."

it signifies that while treating the mission of the persons, the theologian does not cease to probe the intra-Trinitarian mystery. On the other hand it indicates that the divine persons, in their mission, are given according to their personal distinction, that is to say in their distinctive properties: The mission implies the divine persons in their mutual relationships. The structure of the treatise also manifests the personalism of grace in St. Thomas: The gift of grace appears as a personal Trinitarian communication in which the persons are given according to their relative properties.

The procession of the divine persons, as we have already noted in the doctrine of the Word and of Love, is the reason of the creation.[116] The creating activity of the three persons grounds the theme of the "vestige" *(vestigium)*, that is to say the representation of the Trinity in all creatures. However, this representation by the *vestigium* remains very imperfect and obscure, because the Trinity is here manifested only as the cause of the creatures.[117] At a higher level, the procession of the divine persons is also the reason of the grace by which creatures (human persons and angels) return to God.[118] The presence of the Trinity is here of another order, more manifest, because the saints rejoin God by loving him and knowing him: This union with God is accomplished through the mission of the Son and the Spirit.

The notion of "mission" of a divine person includes two elements: (1) the eternal procession of this person from another; (2) the gift of a created effect in time, namely sanctifying grace. Concerning the first element, St. Thomas explains that the mission does not comprise a "movement" properly speaking, since the divine persons are unchanging, but it simply implies the "procession of origin" (that is to say, the relation of origin of the Son to the Father, and the relation of origin of the Spirit to the Father and the Son in the divine eternity).[119] Here the study of the divine missions integrates the anterior explanations concerning the processions and the relations (for

---

[116] *ST* I, q. 45, a. 6, sol. and ad 1; q. 45, a. 7, ad 3: "The processions of the divine persons are the cause of creation."

[117] *ST* I, q. 45, a. 7; cf. q. 93, a. 2.

[118] Cf. I *Sent.*, d. 14, q. 1, a. 1; I *Sent.*, d. 14, q. 2, a. 2.

[119] *ST* I, q. 43, a. 1.

this reason, the speculative study of the processions and of the relations is required beforehand in order to understand the salvific action of the divine persons). Concerning the second element, St. Thomas explains that, through the mission, the divine person who is sent "begins to exist in a new way" in the saints: This new mode of presence is that of grace, by which God indwells the saints. Only sanctifying grace constitutes this "effect" (second element) which verifies the mission of a divine person.[120] In the mission, the divine person who is "sent" is also given: It comes to inhabit or dwell in men who receive the grace. The Son and the Holy Spirit, who are the subject of procession in God, are sent, and the Father (who is not sent but sends) comes with them. The three persons thus dwell in the soul of the saints.[121]

In conclusion, according to the explanations of St. Thomas, the mission of the divine person comprises a double relation: (1) a relation to the person who sends (origin); (2) a relation to the created term (new presence of the divine person in the saints, according to an effect of grace).[122] In other words, in the mission, the eternal procession of the divine person is extended to us, in time, by grace. One can speak, therefore, in order to designate the mission, of a "temporal procession."[123] Thus the treatise on the Trinity, that commences with the notion of "procession" (eternal and immanent procession: q. 27) is also completed by the notion of "procession" (temporal procession: q. 43). One finds again, in the treatise on the missions, the three key notions of the Trinitarian theology of St. Thomas: procession, relation, person.

In order to understand the inhabitation of the Trinity in the saints, when the Son and the Holy Spirit are sent to them, St. Thomas developed two lines of thought. The first, which we may call "ontological," is especially present in St. Thomas's first theological synthesis, his commentary on the *Sentences*. There he explains that the Son and the Holy Spirit impress in the soul of the saints a

---

[120] *ST* I, q. 43, a. 3.
[121] *ST* I, q. 43, a. 1, 2, and 8.
[122] *ST* I, q. 43, a. 2.
[123] *ST* I, q. 43, a. 2.

likeness of their eternal property, namely wisdom and charity. This likeness, impressed in the manner of a seal in the soul, has for its exemplary cause the eternal property of the Son and the Spirit. St. Thomas here speaks of a "sealing" *(sigillatio)* of the Son and the Spirit who give men a participation in their eternal relation to the Father, by imprinting in the saints a participation of their eternal relation.[124] By faith and charity, fruits of grace, the saints have access to the Father by participating in the relation which the Son and the Spirit hold with the Father.[125]

The second line of explanation can be called "objective." It makes precise the first by completing it, and this second line is found in the foreground in the *Summa theologiae*. By the gift of grace, the saints are united to God by knowing God and loving him. When the Son is sent on mission, the saints are "assimilated" to the Son by the illumination of their intelligence (participation in the property of the Son, through an effect of grace appropriated to the Son) which enables them to know God. When the Holy Spirit is sent on mission, the saints are "assimilated" to the Spirit through the ardor of charity (participation in the property of the Holy Spirit, by an effect of grace appropriated to the Holy Spirit), which enables them to love God.[126] The theologal activity of knowledge of God and love of God, in the saints, "imitates" or "represents" the activity of God the Father who pronounces the Word and breathes the Spirit. This theologal activity will be studied in a more developed manner in anthropology, in the study of the image of God.[127] In this manner, God is found in the saints "as the known is present in the knower and as the loved is present in the lover,"[128] that is to say, "as an object attained by some activity is present within the acting subject."[129] This doctrine of the presence of the known in the

---

[124] See notably I *Sent.*, d. 15, q. 4, a. 1.

[125] For more details, see G. Emery, *La Trinité créatrice*, pp. 402–13.

[126] *ST* I, q. 43, a. 5.

[127] *ST* I, q. 93, a. 7–8: The saints are assimilated to the divine persons, in an active way *(secundum actus)*, by participating in the procession of the Word and of Love.

[128] *ST* I, q. 43, a. 3.

[129] *ST* I, q. 8, a. 3.

knower and of the beloved in the lover, with which St. Thomas expounds the inhabitation of the divine persons, manifestly benefits from his doctrine of the procession of the Word and of Love.[130] Trinitarian doctrine furnishes here the foundation of St. Thomas's theological anthropology (doctrine of the image of God), of his moral theology (doctrine of theological virtues in particular), and of his eschatology (doctrine of the vision and of the fruition of God).

Conclusion

The Trinitarian treatise has thus accomplished its purpose: to show how faith in God the Trinity can be reasonably thought, without proving the Trinity, but rather by exposing Trinitarian faith by means of analogies that manifest to believers the intelligibility of the revelation of God the Trinity. Within this elaboration, the notion of relation as well as the doctrine of the Word and of Love occupy the central place.

In addition, the speculative doctrine of the Trinity shows the depth of God's action in the world. Whereas at first one might perhaps have suspected the speculative reflection to be deprived of interest for the economy of creation and of salvation, one discovers in reality a doctrine that accounts for, in the most profound manner, the foundations of the action of God and of the relations that the world and men hold with God. The economic doctrine of the Trinity also appears, in St. Thomas, as the last fruit of his speculative Trinitarian doctrine. For St. Thomas, it is not in ascertaining God by his relations to the world that one realizes the profundity of the action of God (as a vast theological current today, issuing from Hegel, would have it), but inversely it is in the contemplation of the

---

[130] In his commentary on the *Sentences*, St. Thomas equally emphasizes the presence of God the Trinity by the activity of the saints who attain God known and loved (see for example I *Sent.*, d. 37, q. 1, a. 2), but without offering as precise a view of the presence of God known and loved "as the known is present in the knower and as the loved is present in the lover." St. Thomas's progress in his doctrine of the Word, and above all in his doctrine of Love, exerted a decisive influence in this domain: the mutual enlightening offered by anthropology and Trinitarian theology is very clear.

transcendent being of God the Trinity that one discovers the source of the divine economy: creation, man, grace, the mysteries of the incarnation, eschatology.

The Trinitarian treatise thus shows itself to be faithful to the purpose formulated by St. Thomas: to furnish a contemplative teaching that considers God in himself and God as the principle and end of creatures. Trinitarian doctrine, by clarifying our understanding of the divine persons within the eternal Trinity, supplies equally the elements required for a correct understanding of creation, as well as for a correct understanding of salvation which is effected by the sending of the Son and the gift of the Spirit. Under this aspect, the Trinitarian treatise furnishes the foundation of all the teaching that the remainder of the *Summa theologiae* offers.

CHAPTER FIVE

Essentialism or Personalism in the Treatise on God in St. Thomas Aquinas?

T HE RELATIONSHIP between the unity of God and the distinction of persons belongs among the foremost points of controversy in the interpretation of the Trinitarian theology of St. Thomas Aquinas.[1] The discussion has for some time crystallized around the "essentialism" or "personalism" that is attributed to Aquinas's treatise. Such a problematic (in which the very terms of the alternatives already determine the kind of solution that one can adopt) is situated at the junction of many approaches and different methods of analysis because it involves not only the restitution of the thought of Thomas Aquinas from a historical perspective, but also the profoundly speculative fundamental notions of his Trinitarian theology (person, relation, essence, notional act, and so on), the relationship between theology and philosophy, and finally the very aim of Trinitarian theology. After a brief overview of the debate, we will present the general framework of a reading that investigates the Trinitarian doctrine of St. Thomas on the relationship between person and essence in God.

---

[1] Translation by Matthew Levering of "Essentialisme ou personnalisme dans le traité de Dieu chez saint Thomas d'Aquin?" *RT* 98 (1998): 5–38. English translation published in *The Thomist* 64 (2000): 521–563.

A Long and Vast Debate

When, at the end of the nineteenth century, Théodore de Régnon examined the Trinitarian synthesis of Thomas Aquinas, his analysis led him to formulate the problem of an "essential" approach as opposed to a more personal representation of the mystery of God. It provided the basis of the distinction that, since de Régnon, has become customary to introduce: that between the "Greek" conception which begins with the consideration of the persons, and the "Latin" (Augustinian) or "scholastic" conception which takes its departure in the unity of the essence or the divine substance.[2] The problem identified by this pioneer in the history of Trinitarian doctrine concerns not only the methodological priority of the divine essence in Thomas, but also the connection between essence and person in his use of the psychological analogy derived from Augustine: "All the Augustinian theory, if superb when it begins from a 'personal' God, risks dissolving when it analyzes the acts of a 'nature' identical to many persons."[3] Such is, since then, the problem constantly posed by the reading of the treatise on the Trinity in the *Summa theologiae* of Thomas Aquinas: Does his theological elaboration, very attentive to the prerogatives of the essence or nature of God, adequately take account of the tripersonal reality of God? Placed at the heart of the interpretation of the history of doctrine sketched by de Régnon, this question is intensified by the contrasts in which it is inscribed: Thomas manifests a concern for conceptual

---

2 Cf. Théodore de Régnon, *Études de théologie positive sur la sainte Trinité* (Paris: Victor Retaux, 1892–98), vol. 1, pp. 335–40 and 428–35. For the influence of de Régnon on the theology of the twentieth century, and in particular on Eastern Orthodox neo-Palamism (V. Lossky), see Michel R. Barnes, "De Régnon Reconsidered," *Augustinian Studies* 26 (1995): 51–79. Many studies have shown that the interpretation of St. Augustine by de Régnon is false; see notably Basil Studer, *Mysterium caritatis* (Roma: Pontificio Ateneo S. Anselmo, 1999), pp. 308–9. The interpretation of the Cappadocians is also inexact: The Trinitarian theology of St. Gregory of Nyssa begins with the consideration of the divine nature and not with the distinct persons; see Michel R. Barnes, *The Power of God: Dunamis in Gregory of Nyssa's Trinitarian Theology* (Washington, DC: The Catholic University of America Press, 2001), pp. 263–64.

3 de Régnon, *Études de théologie positive,* vol. 2, 214.

organization rather than a contemplative approach to the mystery of God, a recourse to a "static" metaphysics rather than to a "dynamic" thought, and so on.[4] In the extension of this schema of interpretation, the theology of Thomas Aquinas becomes the focal point of difficulties attributed to a large current of Latin medieval thought which, following Augustine, accorded primacy to the divine essence rather than to the persons and was developed on the basis of a metaphysics rather than in reference to the history of salvation.[5]

Karl Rahner has summarized this difficulty in regard to the division of the treatise on God into a treatise *De Deo uno* and a treatise *De Deo trino*: "If one begins with the basic notions of the Augustinian and western approach, a non-Trinitarian treatise *De Deo Uno* comes apparently automatically before *De Deo Trino*."[6] Rahner specifies that "this separation first occurred in St. Thomas, for reasons which have not yet been clearly explained. St. Thomas does not begin with God the Father as the unengendered origin in the Godhead, the origin of all reality in the world, but with the nature common to all three persons. And the procedure became well-nigh universal."[7] The consequence is a "splendid isolation" of the treatise on the Trinity that fails to weigh the repercussions for the doctrine of salvation: "It looks as though everything important about God which touches ourselves has already been said in the treatise *De Deo Uno*."[8] Faced with this affirmation, contemporary Trinitarian theology received the task of displaying the personal reality of God as the point of departure of the treatise *De Deo*, thereby clarifying all the other treatises of theology and demonstrating their organic unity. It

---

[4] de Régnon, *Études de théologie positive*, vol. 2, pp. 128–29, 447–51.

[5] Michael Schmaus, "Die Spannung von Metaphysik und Heilsgeschichte in der Trinitätslehre Augustins," in *Studia patristica*, vol. 6, ed. Frank L. Cross (Berlin: Akademie Verlag, 1962), pp. 503–18.

[6] Karl Rahner, *Theological Investigations*, vol. 4, trans. Kevin Smyth, "Remarks on the Dogmatic Treatise 'De Trinitate'" (New York: Crossroad, 1982), pp. 79–102 [83–84].

[7] Ibid., p. 84; cf. Karl Rahner, *The Trinity*, trans. Joseph Donceel (New York: Crossroad, 1998), pp. 16–17.

[8] K. Rahner, "Remarks on the Dogmatic Treatise 'De Trinitate,'" p. 84; *The Trinity*, p. 17.

is precisely on the basis of this critical reading of the Latin and
Thomist tradition that one understands the famous fundamental
Rahnerian axiom: "the Trinity of the economy of salvation is the
immanent Trinity and vice versa." Karl Rahner's critique has been
pursued in many studies, notably on the Christological impact of the
deficiency present in Thomas (the hypostatic union approached by
the angle where the person is identical to the divine essence, "as if
God were not Trinity").[9] Even in recent works, it is not rare to
encounter the accusation of a philosophical pre-comprehension of
God *(de Deo uno)* that arranges the Trinitarian mystery in pre-estab-
lished human categories that are incapable of taking account of the
full tripersonal Godhead.[10] At the heart of this debate (essence–persons, immanent Trinity–economic Trinity) the firm maintaining of
the unity of operation of the Trinity *ad extra* by Thomas inspires the
suspicion of a weakening of personal traits in the creative and
redemptive action of God, in favor of a certain "monism." Thomas
Aquinas, by reason of such essentialist or "unitary" representation of
God, bears therefore a large part of the responsibility in this "loss of
function" of Trinitarian faith that the authors discern for a long
period: The Trinity remained in Thomas "locked in the immanence
of its own life."[11]

---

[9] Cf. Ghislain Lafont, *Peut-on connaître Dieu en Jésus-Christ?* (Paris: Cerf, 1969),
pp. 151–57.

[10] Michel Corbin, *La Trinité ou l'Excès de Dieu* (Paris: Cerf, 1997). On the contemporary emphasis on the "living God of Revelation" in contrast to a "principally philosophical" treatise *De Deo uno* (Thomas Aquinas), see notably
Wilhelm Breuning, "La Trinité," in *Bilan de la théologie du XXe siècle,* vol. 2,
ed. Robert Vander Gucht and Herbert Vorgrimler (Tournai-Paris: Casterman,
1970), pp. 252–67; Leo Scheffczyk, "Die Trinitätslehre des Thomas von
Aquin im Spiegel gegenwärtiger Kritik," *Studi tomistici* 59 (1995): 163–90
[164–66].

[11] Gisbert Greshake, *Der Dreieine Gott: Eine trinitarische Theologie* (Freiburg im
Breisgau: Herder, 1997), p. 117. The author summarizes here a current of
interpretation of Thomas, and holds for his part that in Thomas, despite his
going beyond a pure and simple essentialism, the "unitarian" perspective
remains dominant (119). For the position of the problem, see notably Heribert Mühlen, "Person und Appropriation. Zum Verständnis des Axioms: *In Deo
omnia sunt unum, ubi non obviat relationis oppositio,*" *Münchener theologische
Zeitschrift* 16 (1965): 37–57.

Following the lead of Walter Kasper, Trinitarian doctrine today is expected to furnish an adequate Christian response to the situation of modern atheism.[12] This demand begins from the historical affirmation of the failure of a monopersonal "theism" in modern Western thought and of its progressive transformation, through deism, into atheism.[13] In this perspective, Trinitarian doctrine should emphasize the freedom of God, which is manifested in love, by strictly linking the consideration of the "essence" to the divine freedom which accords liberty to humankind in love and for love. One thus expects of Trinitarian doctrine precisely that it clarify our understanding of human life, ecclesial and social, by removing all presentations of God, which, in conceiving God as an essence posed in opposition to man, make him a "rival" for man.[14] The question of the relationship between essence and person in God, however, goes far beyond the scope of a simple arrangement of concepts because it inquires into the very purpose of Trinitarian theology. In order to integrate correctly the contribution of Thomas Aquinas, it will be important to test the correspondence between these demands and the role that Thomas assigns to theological elaboration of a treatise on the Trinity.

In this task, which stretches over more than a century of interpretations, the first requirement was to go back, beyond the manuals of the school, to the texts of Thomas Aquinas in order to identify the place of the person in his doctrine on God. Among the major works, we should place first the studies of André Malet that, from a historical and systematic perspective, applied themselves to showing the deeply rooted influence of Greek patristics in the thought of

---

[12] Cf. Walter Kasper, *The God of Jesus Christ,* trans. Matthew J. O'Connell (New York: Crossroad, 1986), pp. 294–95.

[13] W. Kasper, *The God of Jesus Christ,* pp. 294–95: "From the theological standpoint we must speak more accurately of the heresy of theism." For the nuances of the historical evolution of this vocabulary (in which the Trinitarian question has been present since Socinus), see Henri Bouillard, *Vérité du christianisme,* "Sur le sens du mot 'théisme'" (Paris: Desclée de Brouwer, 1989), pp. 219–32.

[14] Such a demand constitutes the major purpose of the work of G. Greshake, indicated above; cf. Wolfgang Müller, *Die Theologie des Dritten: Entwurf einer sozialen Trinitätslehre* (St. Ottilien: EOS Verlag, 1996).

Thomas as well as the accent placed by Aquinas on the persons in God.[15] The research of Malet, with the goal of showing the "synthesis" of person and nature in God, nonetheless remained dominated by the antinomic dialectic imposed by the controversy: One strives to establish "the primacy of person over nature"[16] in Thomas, in order to expose the "personalism" which should be opposed to the "essentialism." Despite the reservations that one could formulate on other points, the works of Malet had the merit of showing the inadequacy of the schema of opposition between Greeks and Latins for taking account of the thought of Thomas.[17] Around the same time, a vigorous overview of the Thomist doctrine of relation and of notional acts (personal acts considered as the manner of the subsistence of the person) led Paul Vanier to note the eminently dynamic and personal Trinitarian conception in Thomas: The orientation of the study was, here again, the necessity of a return to the texts of Thomas and of a historical approach in order to recover, against certain misadventures of school–Thomism, the thought of the master.[18] In his enthusiasm for the mature thought of Thomas, P. Vanier postulated the existence of a second redaction of the commentary on the *Sentences*, in order to explain the presence of the mature doctrine of Thomas in this work (notably the rejection of a "derivation" of the persons from the essence, following a perspective that Vanier qualified as "Pseudo-Dionysian"). This hypothesis has not received scholarly confirmation,[19] but it has drawn attention to the complexity of the teaching of Thomas, even in his first work of theological synthesis.

---

[15] André Malet, "La synthèse de la personne et de la nature dans la théologie trinitaire de saint Thomas," *RT* 54 (1954): 483–522; *RT* 55 (1955): 43–84; *Personne et amour dans la théologie trinitaire de saint Thomas d'Aquin* (Paris: Vrin, 1956). See also the reviews of the work by Jean-Hervé Nicolas, *RT* 57 (1957): 365–73; and by Hyacinthe Dondaine, *RSPT* 43 (1959): 172–74.

[16] A. Malet, *Personne et amour,* pp. 71–88.

[17] Cf. W. Kasper, *The God of Jesus Christ,* pp. 297–98.

[18] P. Vanier, *Théologie trinitaire chez saint Thomas d'Aquin,* pp. 105–44.

[19] See notably, on the properly theological level, François von Gunten, "Gibt es eine zweite Redaktion des Sentenzenkommentars des hl. Thomas von Aquin?" *Freiburger Zeitschrift für Philosophie und Theologie* 3 (1956): 137–68.

By the side of various works devoted to certain more limited aspects of the problem,[20] the question has been reviewed recently by Hans Christian Schmidbaur, who endeavors to show the strict "personalism" of Thomas in opposition to other theological currents of the twelfth and thirteenth centuries, with regard principally to the doctrine of processions and relation.[21] It is again the "primacy of person" that constitutes the object of the study. The manifestation of the place of person in Trinitarian theology is here, however, taken into a framework of understanding dominated by a nearly irreducible opposition between essence and relation (to such a point that, for example, the conception of a free creation by a "mono-personal" God becomes in itself contradictory). The enterprise of "rehabilitation" of the thought of Thomas in the face of contemporary critics poses then the question of the balance of Thomas's thought. It seems indeed that, on the basis of an authentic development of the value of person, the debate should lead us to reconsider the integration of the elements of the problem in Thomas.

The Creative and Redemptive Action of the Divine Persons

The Trinitarian dimension of the divine creative and redemptive activity is not the premier element in the order of the speculative exposition, but it can be useful to consider first the influence of Trinitarian faith since what is at stake is our "experience" of the Trinity[22] and the interpretation that one should give to the rule of the unity of activity of the divine persons, a rule that is sometimes suspected of hiding the divine tripersonality. This rule of the unity

---

[20] See Emile Bailleux, *Le don de Dieu,* Essai de théologie personnaliste, 2 vol. (Lille, 1958); see also Emile Bailleux, "Le personnalisme de saint Thomas en théologie trinitaire," *RT* 61 (1961): 25–42.

[21] Cf. H. C. Schmidbaur, *Personarum Trinitas;* see our review in *RT* 96 (1996): 690–93.

[22] This vocabulary can appeal to Thomas himself: cf. Albert Patfoort, "*Cognitio ista est quasi experimentalis* (I *Sent.,* d. 14, q. 2, a. 2, ad 3)," *Angelicum* 63 (1986): 3–13; "Missions divines et expérience des Personnes divines selon saint Thomas," *Angelicum* 63 (1986): 545–59.

of operation of the persons *ad extra* (a principle shared as much in
the East as in the West) is not the sole aspect of the doctrine of
Thomas on this point. If he holds firmly the unity of divine action,
in virtue of the unity of the principle of operation (the divine
nature) required by the consubstantiality of the Trinity, Thomas
maintains equally clearly this other principle: "the procession of the
divine persons is the cause and the reason of the procession of creatures." This thesis is found in all the major works of Thomas.[23] The
connection of the double rule (unity of operation *ad extra* and
causality of the Trinitarian processions) is not the result of a modern
interpretation, but is explicitly posed by Thomas.[24] Thus, the
causality of the Trinitarian going-forth *(processus)* in the order of
efficiency and of exemplarity unites the divine activity *ad extra* to
the eternal generation of the Son and to the procession of the Holy
Spirit: It furnishes from this fact the "motive" of the divine economy. The elaboration of the doctrine of the Word and of Love at
the core of the Trinity finds itself verified by its capacity to take
account of the activity of the Son and of the Holy Spirit in the
world and in favor of humankind: The Father accomplishes all
things by his Word and by his Love.[25] We touch here the necessity
of a *"redoublement"* of Trinitarian language in Thomas: The double
perspective of the common nature and the Trinitarian relations is
imperative in order to take account fully of Trinitarian faith. We
will return to this point further on.

In order to manifest the activity of the divine persons in our
favor, Thomas exploits principally three themes of his Trinitarian
doctrine. The first resides in the *very existence of Trinitarian processions:* The "first" going-forth (the Trinitarian processions) is the cause

---

[23] Outside the commentary on the *Sentences* (which contains more than ten passages developing this thesis), cf. notably *De potentia,* q. 10, a. 2, arg. 19, sed
contra 2, and ad 19; *ST* I, q. 45, a. 6, sol.; a. 7, ad 3.

[24] Cf. I *Sent.,* d. 27, q. 2, a. 3, ad 6: "Non tantum essentia habet ordinem ad
creaturam sed etiam processio personalis, quae est ratio processionis creaturarum"; d. 32, q. 1, a. 3.

[25] Cf. *SCG* IV, ch. 13 and 20–22. See chapter 3 above. The results of the elaboration of the *Summa contra Gentiles* are reprised in *ST* I, q. 34, a. 3; q. 37, a. 2;
q. 43.

and the reason of the "second" going-forth (the production of creatures, in the order of creation as in that of grace): Such is the first
meaning of the principle set forth above. What is affirmed of the
processions (understood as the "path" that leads to the person) is
equally affirmed of the *distinction* of the persons by their relations:
The relation of divine persons is the source or the principle of this
other distinction that is the whole production, by God, of creatures;
the very plurality of creatures, under this aspect, finds its rationale in
the distinction of the divine persons by their relations.[26] The second
theme is furnished by the *personal properties* of the Word and of
Love. Word and Love provide the rationale, in an eminently Trinitarian perspective, of the effects coming forth from the generosity
and from the wisdom of God: The action *ad extra* is clarified here by
the personal "term" of the fruitful immanent actions. The third
theme is the notion of "order" *(ordo)* in the Trinity. Thomas exploits
it in all his works, by means of the concepts of "principle" (the *ordo*
signifies the relation of origin), of *"auctoritas"* (the Father is without
origin), and by analysis of the language with which we formulate the
Trinitarian act (notably the preposition "through": The Father acts
through the Son and the Spirit). Thus, regarding the Father, Thomas
can affirm that the relation of origin in the Trinity (the Father is the
principle of the Son) is the source of this relation of origin that God
maintains with creatures.[27] There should be nothing surprising in
reading in St. Thomas that as the preposition "through" *(per)* designates the divine causality on the side of the realities produced by
God, "the proposition 'the Father works all things through his Son'
does not signify something appropriated to the Word, but indeed a
reality that is proper to him *(non est appropriatum Verbo, sed proprium eius)*, since the Son has from another to be the cause of creatures, that is to say from his Father, from whom he has being."[28] We

---

[26] Cf. I *Sent.,* d. 26, q. 2, a. 2, ad 2.

[27] I *Sent.,* d. 29, q. 1, a. 2, qla 2; cf. *ST* I, q. 33, a. 3.

[28] *Lectura in Ioan.* 1:3 (#76). The expression "from the side of creatures" means
here that the Son is not the formal cause of the act of the Father—that would
make of the Son a principle with respect to the Father—but a principle with
respect to creatures, following the order in the Trinity. See also *ST* I, q. 39, a. 8.

note finally that, in the order of the supernatural acts of faith and charity, Thomas does not fail to maintain a relation to the property of the person (Son and Holy Spirit) as regards exemplarity and according to the term of theological acts: This is the reason for which a divine effect can return properly, under this aspect, to a personal property in God.[29]

These brief reminders permit us to observe that Thomas proposes a theology attentive, in its very principles, to the personal dimension of creation and of the economy of salvation. Such is moreover the motive that one should assign to the revelation of the Trinity: "The knowledge of the divine persons was necessary to us on two grounds. The first was to enable us to think rightly on the subject of the creation of things. . . . The second motive, and the principal one, was to give us a true notion of the salvation of humankind, a salvation which is accomplished by the incarnation of the Son and by the gift of the Holy Spirit."[30] The knowledge of salvation given by the mission of the divine persons, along with the right understanding of the free creation by a God acting according to love, constitute the fundamental purpose of Trinitarian doctrine for Thomas. At this first level already, we do not see that the organization of the treatise on God in Thomas, starting from the consideration of what concerns the essence in order to treat next what touches the distinction of persons, would result in "stripping the Trinity to a large extent of any function in the economy of salvation."[31] The properly Trinitarian dimension is certainly developed without prejudicing the dogmatic rule of the unity of operation of the Trinity (can it be otherwise?), and without restricting the autonomy and the proper competence of philosophical knowing, legitimate and pertinent, but incapable of discerning the presence of the Trinity. There is not however here any "primacy" of the essence or of the unity of God, but indeed two aspects or two

---

29 Cf. I *Sent.*, d. 30, q. 1, a. 2 (relationship of the creature to a personal reality in God: the act of theological charity comes to an end in the similitude of the personal procession of the Holy Spirit).

30 *ST* I, q. 32, a. 1, ad 3.

31 Walter Kasper, *The God of Jesus Christ*, p. 312.

approaches that shed light on and become integrated in the consideration of the divine person. We find here a first expression of the *redoublement* of language and of approach to the mystery of God that we will explicate further on: The divine creative and redemptive activity is first considered in the treatise on God with regard to the divine attributes of knowledge, will, and power, then in the Trinitarian treatise with regard to the names of Word, Love, and Gift; likewise, the treatise on the creation begins by taking account of the creative activity as well as of the attributes common to the three persons, which permits Thomas then to pose clearly the Trinitarian principle of the creation.[32] Even more, the key concepts of the speculative synthesis on the Trinity in its immanent being (procession, relation, property, order) are those which permit Thomas to manifest the personal traits of the act of God in our favor. One perceives here the usefulness of a doctrine of the "immanent Trinity," as it is generally called today,[33] for the understanding of the economy in which the Trinitarian mystery is revealed to us.

The Essence and the Persons in the Structure of the Treatise on God

The distinction between a treatise *De Deo uno* and a treatise *De Deo trino*, we have remarked above, constitutes one of the major critiques that contemporary theology addresses to Thomist thought. Teaching the treatise on God is most often characterized today by

---

[32] *ST* I, q. 45, a. 6–7: The procession of the eternal persons is the cause and the reason of creatures. We note that the creation is reprised in detail for the angels, the corporeal creatures, and humankind; here again, the Trinitarian dimension is presented, whether in the theological exegesis of the work of Six Days (I, q. 74, a. 3), or in the study of the creation of humankind to the image of God (I, q. 93).

[33] On the condition indeed of not defining the "immanent Trinity" as being necessarily indifferent to its manifestation *ad extra* or excluding this same manifestation in human history. This strange opposition has sometimes led authors to hold that, since the Trinity is manifested in the world, "there no longer is an immanent Trinity" (for example G. Greshake, *Der dreieine Gott*, pp. 373, 381).

the rejection of this distinction and by the choice of a resolutely "theological" approach, founded upon the history of salvation (against the "philosophical" conception of a treatise *De Deo uno*). This is not the place to show the legitimacy and the usefulness of a philosophical approach establishing the *preambula fidei* that theological reflection can then take up in deepening them, but it is necessary at least to consider the fundamental structure of the treatise. In the *Summa theologiae*, Thomas announces a treatise on God in three sections *(consideratio autem de Deo tripartita erit)*: (1) what concerns the divine essence; (2) what concerns the distinction of persons; (3) what concerns the procession of creatures *ab ipso*.[34] It is necessary to note that the treatise on God, the *consideratio de Deo*, does not consist of two, but rather of *three*, sections: The divine act *ad extra*, inaugurated with the creation, is integrated around God, in accordance with the theocentric approach specific to the theologian; creatures are examined inasmuch as they have God as their principle (efficient, exemplar, and final cause).[35] The study of God as principle is not determined by the aspect of Unity or of Trinity, but rather is determined by the unique and entire reality of God (the three persons of one same essence) which is posed here in a theological synthesis resulting from the first two sections of the treatise. Regarding the first two sections, there is no question of a "one God" or of a "tri-God *[Dieu trine]*," but of God considered *under the aspect* of the essence and *under the aspect* of the distinction (that which concerns the essence, that which concerns the distinction of persons: *ea quae pertinent ad essentiam divinam, ea quae pertinent ad distinctionem personarum*). The nuance is important, because the structure announced by Thomas poses simply the opportunity for a double consideration or a double approach to the God confessed by Christian faith.

Why this double consideration in the first two sections of the treatise on God? Having considered the texts of Thomas and researched the characteristics that are proper to them, it is worth

---

[34] *ST* I, q. 2, prol. Cf. the recapitulation of the Prologue in q. 27.
[35] *SCG* II, ch. 4.

remarking that this completely traditional distinction appears at the origins of properly speculative Trinitarian theology. On the level of the history of doctrines, indeed, this methodological option appeared as the result of a principle stemming from the triadology of the Cappadocians that Thomas receives notably through Augustine and John Damascene: The necessary distinction and connection of what is *common* and of what is *proper* in the Trinity *(commune–proprium)*, following the specifications elaborated by Basil of Caesarea in order to challenge the errors of Eunomius of Cyzicus. St. Basil, attempting to take away from the name "Unbegotten" *(agennetos)* the exceptional status that Eunomius had accorded it in order to ground his radical Arianism, observes:

> The divinity is common *(koinon)* but the paternity and the filiation are properties *(idiomata)*; and from the combination of these two elements, that is to say from the common and from the proper *(tou te koinou kai idiou)*, occurs in us the comprehension of the truth. Thus, when we mean to speak of the unbegotten light, we think of the Father, of the begotten light, we think of the Son. As regards light and light there is no contrariety between them, but as regards begotten and unbegotten one considers them under the aspect of their antithesis.[36]

The binomial *common–proper*, as is known, is equally used by St. Basil in order to establish the formula "one substance, three hypostases," which becomes from then on one of the main expressions of Trinitarian orthodoxy.[37] The Arian controversy thus led

---

[36] Basil of Caesarea, *Against Eunomius*, II, 28 (ed. Bernard Sesboüé, Sources chrétiennes 305 [Paris: Cerf, 1983], pp. 120–21). For exegesis of this fundamental passage, see B. Sesboué, *Saint Basile et la Trinité* (Paris: Desclée, 1998), pp. 122–27.

[37] Cf. notably Basil, *Letter* 214, 4 (ed. Yves Courtonne, *Saint Basile, Lettres,* vol. 2 [Paris: Belles Lettres, 1961], p. 205). It is known that the formula is already posed in Marius Victorinus, *Against the Arians* II, 4 and III, 4 (Marius Victorinus, *Traités théologiques sur la Trinité*, Sources chrétiennes 68, ed. Paul Henry [Paris: Cerf, 1960], pp. 408, 450) but its establishment as one of the main expressions of orthodoxy is the work of the Cappadocians.

orthodox theology, in order to grasp correctly what the faith itself proposes ("the comprehension of the truth"), to pose the necessary distinction between what is common and what is proper in the Trinity—that is to say, the substance *(ousia)* and the property—of which Basil already notes the purely relative content (relation of opposition). It is this binomial that becomes, in Thomas, in another context than Basil and following a different orientation but on the same basis: essence (substance)/distinction of persons (relative properties).

One can thus observe, already in Basil of Caesarea, the necessity of a connection ("combination") of the proper and of the common, that is to say of a pair of notions permitting us to know the divine persons. Basil illustrates it with the example of light, which is dear to him. This is one of the first formulations of what Ghislain Lafont has called, in St. Thomas, the "law of *redoublement*"[38] that we have evoked above in regard to the creation: In order to speak the Trinitarian mystery, it is necessary always to employ two words, two formulas, in a reflection in two modes that joins here the substantial (essential) aspect and the distinction of persons (relative properties). Now this is precisely what Thomas does in the structure of his treatise on God. It is not necessary to have recourse to the quite embarrassing concept of "total essence," as Carl Sträter has done in the past,[39] in order to explicate the first section of the treatise on God. Since the relations are really identical to the essence, there is not an essence constituted by the relations: This "totality" (of our concepts), if one wishes to speak thus, would only be adequately expressed by the complex *redoublement* of our discourse joining the aspect of the divine substance and that of the relative property, this relative property being identical to the divine substance in the reality of God.

The pair essence/distinction of persons can suggest the distinction between truths accessible to the natural reason (what concerns

---

38 G. Lafont, *Peut-on connaître Dieu en Jésus Christ?* p. 130.
39 Carl Sträter, "Le point de départ du traité thomiste de la Trinité," *Sciences Ecclésiastiques* 12 (1962): 71–87.

the essence) and truths held by faith only (what concerns the distinction of persons). Here the structure of the *Summa contra Gentiles* comes to mind. However, because of the specifically theological purpose of the *Summa theologiae*, and because of the broader value of such a distinction, this explanation is insufficient. It does not suffice to project purely and simply on the *Summa theologiae* the "apologetic" perspective of the *Summa contra Gentiles*. It would be more fitting to seek an explanatory principle belonging to the aim itself of Trinitarian theology rather than to other considerations. It seems to us that one ought first to emphasize, on the basis of the distinction *common–proper*, the *priority* that the knowledge of the *common* has with us. Thomas constantly recalls: "What is essential is prior according to our understanding *(secundum intellectum)* to what is notional, just as what is common to what is proper."[40] Such an explanation is based in the first place on the path of our access to the mystery of God (one knows the divine essence through its effects: This is a prerequisite assumed by faith in the Trinity), but it is not limited to this order of progress in understanding. The conceptual priority belongs to the "common" taken in itself, not with a relationship to creatures (in which latter case, because of the relationship associated with the *common*, the *property* of the person ought to receive the conceptual priority). The order of concepts at work takes on, indeed, a properly Trinitarian reason: The understanding of the divine person presupposes the knowledge of the essence *because it integrates it* (the *proper* does not have reality without the *common*). One cannot conceive of the person without the substance or without the nature belonging to the very *ratio* of the divine person, this latter being defined as "distinct subsisting in the divine nature *(distinctum subsistens in natura divina)*"[41] or, with Boethius, as "individual substance of rational

---

[40] I *Sent.*, d. 29, q. 1, a. 2, qla 2, arg. 1 and sol.; cf. d. 7, q. 1, a. 3, arg. 4 and ad 4; also *ST* I, q. 33, a. 3, ad 1: "Communia absolute dicta, secundum ordinem intellectus nostri, sunt priora quam propria: quia includuntur in intellectu propriorum, sed non e converso."

[41] *De potentia*, q. 9, a. 4. Thomas here makes precise the signification of the *divine* person and not only of the person in general, in order to emphasize the aspect of relation. Cf. I *Sent.*, d. 23, q. 1, a. 4. This formal definition is reprised in a very similar manner in *ST* I, q. 29, a. 4 and q. 30, a. 4.

nature." The exploitation of the category of relation carries a double aspect: By its proper *ratio*, it is pure relation *(esse ad)*, but a relation equally inheres in a subject *(esse in)* that grounds its being: this "to be" of the relation, accidental in creatures, is in God the substantial *esse* of the divinity.[42]

In treating of the divine essence, Thomas thus treats of what is fundamentally required in order to account for the person and for the *esse* of the relation in God, and therefore in order to elaborate what constitutes the pinnacle of his doctrine of the divine persons: the subsisting relation. It is not, moreover, strange that, in Thomas, the structure of a treatise is clarified by the very content of the treatise that it contains in germ. This explanation, it seems to us, respects the fundamental principles of the Trinitarian doctrine of St. Thomas and shows itself equally capable of integrating the order of our knowledge of the mystery. It likewise will permit us further on to specify the relation between essence and person.

Relation, Procession, and Person

A rapid overview of the plan of questions 27 through 43 of the *Prima pars* leads one to remark of the ensemble that the aim of Thomas is entirely oriented toward person in God:

1. Origin or processions (q. 27)
2. The relations of origin (q. 28)
3. The persons (qq. 29–43)
   a. The persons, considered in an absolute manner (qq. 29–38)
      i. The persons according to what is common to them (qq. 29–32)
      ii. The persons according to what is proper to each (qq. 33–38)
   b. The persons, considered according to their relations (qq. 39–43)

---

42 *ST* I, q. 28, a. 2; q. 39, a. 1.

    i. The persons in relation to the essence (q. 39)

    ii. The persons in relation to the properties (q. 40)

    iii. The persons in relation to the notional acts (q. 41)

    iv. The persons according to their mutual relations
       (qq. 42–43)

Of seventeen questions, fifteen are placed under the title "the persons," and are entirely devoted to the persons under their diverse considerations. The question of the divine missions (q. 43), which opens the great movement of the Trinitarian economy of grace and which attaches the *Secunda* and the *Tertia pars* to the Trinitarian treatise, is itself approached from the aspect of the mutual relations of the persons: On the simple level of structure, could one say more clearly that the missions of the persons offer a participation in the Trinitarian communion?[43] The two sole exceptions are the question on procession and that on relation (q. 27 and 28); these two questions do not have, however, any other goal than to lead to an understanding of person, as Thomas explains in q. 29, Prologue: "Having seen what ought first to be recognized *(quae praecognoscenda videbantur)* on the subject of processions and of relations, it is necessary to come to the persons." It is thus to the divine person, to each one of them and to their relationship of mutual communion, that Thomas wishes to lead us.[44] This plan manifests a resolute option in favor of a doctrine governed by the notion of person. Now this project is only effectively completed because of the integration of the consideration of the essence in that of the person, requiring the prior explication of "what concerns the essence" in order to clarify the mystery of the three divine persons. In other words, by making use of the "law of

---

[43] This structure accounts for the effect of the mission that Thomas, like Irenaeus of Lyons or Basil of Caesarea, formulates thus: The Holy Spirit makes known the Son, and the Son manifests the Father (*In Ioan.* 16:14, #2107).

[44] Cf. François Bourassa, "Note sur le traité de la Trinité dans la Somme théologique," *Science et Esprit* 27 (1975): 187–207; Hans Jorissen, "Zur Struktur des Traktates 'De Deo' in der *Summa theologiae* des Thomas von Aquin," in *Im Gespräch mit dem dreieinigen Gott: Elemente einer trinitarischen Theologie,* ed. Michael Böhnke und Hanspeter Heinz (Düsseldorf: Patmos, 1985), pp. 231–57.

redoublement" evoked above, the synthesis occurs within the notion of person that Thomas goes on to clarify by means of the notion of subsisting relation or of distinct subsisting in the divine nature.

The sequence of questions—processions–relations–persons—is thus easily explained. Procession or origin is perceived as the path that leads to the person: It signifies the relation, either in the "active" mode of a notional act (generation, spiration) or in the "passive" or rather "receptive" mode that we perceive as the foundation of the relation.[45] The concept of procession thus prepares for that of relation. For its part, the relation that distinguishes the Three in God furnishes the key to the theological understanding of the mystery: relative opposition according to origin. It only remains then for Thomas to display the bundle of Trinitarian relations in the communion of distinct persons. The methodical order followed by Thomas thus implements a rigorous use of concepts where each presupposes the preceding one.

The linking of these concepts, in this precise order, does not represent, however, the only approach of Thomas Aquinas. In the *Summa contra Gentiles*, for example, he poses first the reality of three persons and the truth of procession, and only turns to relation in order to clear up the objections that human reason can oppose to Trinitarian faith, or in order to establish the procession *a Patre Filioque* at the end of his exposé.[46] And, in this latter case, he observes the order of exposition: person–distinction–opposition–relation. Similarly, in the Disputed Questions *De potentia*, Thomas follows the sequence: person–distinction–relation.[47] In these two works, indeed, Thomas starts from the premier given of the Catholic faith: "three persons of one sole essence." In the *Summa theologiae*, the inverse sequence appears as the exact expression of the *ordo disciplinae* required by the general Prologue. This observation could

---

[45] The privilege of constituting the person, properly speaking, does not belong to the notional act or to the procession, but to the personal property that is the relation possessed by the person: cf. *ST* I, q. 40, a. 4.

[46] *SCG* IV, ch. 10–14 and ch. 24.

[47] *De potentia*, q. 8, a. 1 (on the reality of relations in God, at the beginning of three questions on Trinitarian theology).

seem elementary, but it seems to us fundamental for grasping the aim of Trinitarian doctrine in Thomas.

On the one hand, the "point of departure" of the treatise on God (that is, what concerns the essence) and that of the section on the distinction of persons (that is, procession and relation), in the *Summa theologiae*, are explained by pedagogical arrangement: This point of departure is posed for conceptual reasons of organization and only finds its full meaning in the later integration that it prepares. The methodical organization proposed by Thomas ought to be appreciated according to its point of arrival: The persons in God.

On the other hand, the organization of the material ought to be grasped in the light of a deliberately modest and limited theological aim, which Thomas explains elsewhere in these terms:

> The plurality of persons in God belongs to those realities that are held by faith and that natural human reason can neither investigate nor grasp in an adequate manner; but one hopes to grasp it in Heaven, since God will be seen by his essence, when faith will have given way to vision. However, the holy Fathers have been obliged to treat it in a manner developed because of objections raised by those who have contradicted the faith in this matter and in others that pertain also to the faith; they have done it, however, in a modest manner and with respect, without pretending to comprehend. And such a search is not useless, since by it our spirit is elevated to the understanding of an aspect of the truth that suffices for excluding the errors.[48]

This observation, in the teaching of Thomas, is not at all rhetorical. It is the project that he puts strictly to work in all of his works: Trinitarian theology is sustained by a contemplative end in which the immediate motive is the defense of the faith. The *Summa contra Gentiles* explains it in detail: It is precisely in order to show that the faith is not surpassed or vanquished by human reason that

---

[48] *De potentia*, q. 9, a. 5. The question is here that of the "number" of persons in God.

the doctrine of the Word and that of Love, of relation, and so on, take place.[49] The treatise of the *Summa theologiae* equally takes its point of departure here, from the very first article: It is necessary to pose in God, following the Catholic faith, a truly immanent procession, which Arianism and Sabellianism, the two major dangers in this matter, have failed to do (q. 27, a. 1). Thomas appears to know well that the doctrine of relation and the clarification of processions go back historically to the defense of orthodoxy in the face of Sabellianism and of Arianism under their diverse forms. The *Against Eunomius* of Basil of Caesarea does not show us anything different. Thus, what one asks from the theological reflection upon the processions and the relations is to make manifest that it is not unreasonable to believe in Three persons really subsisting in the unique essence of the divinity: The Trinitarian mystery which constitutes the heart of the Christian faith resists the objections that one can address to it. The fruit of contemplation that one obtains, in making manifest the intelligibility of the faith in the connection of its mysteries, suffices for the believer who wishes "to defend" his faith, in the hope of the beatific vision. Trinitarian theology is not pursued for other motives when Thomas, in the *Summa theologiae*, guides us progressively from processions to relations and from relations to persons.

The Processions and the "Psychological Way"

The point of departure that Thomas takes in his analysis of processions is open, however, to the suspicion of "dissolution" that de Régnon raised, and which has not ceased since then to constitute a point of controversy in the interpretation of Thomas Aquinas. In exploiting the Augustinian "psychological" way of the self's knowledge and love of itself, does Thomas manage to pose in God some properly personal (notional) acts? Does the explanation of the two processions in God go beyond that of essential acts?[50]

---

[49] *SCG* IV, ch. 10, #3460; 19, #3557.

[50] See for example W. Müller, *Die Theologie des Dritten,* p. 40; M. Corbin, *La Trinité ou l'Excès de Dieu,* pp. 54–55.

We note first that the intention of Thomas is evidently to avoid posing the distinction of persons on the basis of an absolute or essential reality. This is the error for which Abelard, who had used the triad "power–wisdom–goodness" in order to make manifest the distinction of persons, was reproached, and which caused the adjustment of the doctrine of appropriations. Thomas explains this by linking such an error to Arianism and to Sabellianism. "This distinction [of persons in God] cannot be according to an absolute reality, since everything which is attributed absolutely in God signifies the divine essence; it would result that the divine persons would be distinguished by essence, which is the heresy of Arius."[51] And if one considered a procession according to the essential attributes, it would result in a procession incapable of taking account of a real relation, since an essential act in God only involves a procession and relation of reason:[52] This leads to Sabellianism. Thus, if one considered only nature and will (or knowledge and love) in seeking to understand the modes of the procession of the Son and of the Spirit, one could not go beyond a simple conceptual distinction of persons: These attributes, since their proper *ratio* should be posed in every truth, only are distinguished by reason, being in God a single reality in virtue of the divine simplicity.

The problem recurs in the question of the *Filioque*, where Thomas exploits many times this argument to establish the necessity of an *order* of processions (and therefore the procession of the Holy Spirit *a Filio*) in order to avoid Sabellianism.[53] The Trinitarian processions cannot be explained by a relationship of the divine essence toward creatures: This is again, Thomas explains, the erroneous path followed by Sabellius.[54] One surely perceives that if Thomas had been left with an "essential" perception of divine processions, it would have gone against the most elementary principles of his Trinitarian doctrine.

It is only by missing the difference between *to know* or *to understand (intelligere)* and *to speak (dicere)* or between *to love* and

---

[51] *De potentia,* q. 8, a. 1.
[52] I *Sent.,* d. 32, q. 1, a. 1; *ST* I, q. 27, a. 4, ad 1.
[53] *SCG* IV, ch. 24, #3616; *De potentia,* q. 10, a. 2; a. 5.
[54] *ST* I, q. 27, a. 1; q. 28, a. 1, sed contra and sol.; *De potentia,* q. 8, a. 1.

to spirate love, that one could find in Thomas an "essential" comprehension of divine processions. At stake is nothing less than our capacity to be able to render account of Trinitarian faith, that is to say, of a *real* distinction of three divine persons. Thomas explains it, in the *Summa theologiae*, in opposition to St. Anselm (with regard to whom, in other contexts as well, he takes care to correct the excessive accent placed on the essence in the knowledge of personal processions):[55]

> Anselm improperly took *to speak (dicere)* for *to understand (intelligere)*. It is a matter of two different things. Because *to understand* means only the relationship of the knower to the thing known; no origin is evoked here, but only a certain information in our intellect, since our intellect has need of being put in act by the form of the object known. Now in God this means a total identity, since the intellect and the thing known are absolutely the same thing, as was seen [I, q. 14]. But *to speak* means principally a relationship to the word conceived; *to speak* is nothing other than to utter a word; but by the intermediary of the word there is a relationship to the thing known, which is manifested by the word uttered to the one who understands.[56]

Thus, *to speak a word* is a process *(processus)* constitutive of the achievement of the act of intellection, without these two acts being identified or reduced the one to the other.[57] This is not the place to present Thomas's noetics and the accomplishment of the act of

---

55 Cf. notably I *Sent.*, d. 11, q. 1, a. 3, arg. 1 and ad 1; cf. Albert the Great, I *Sent.*, d. 27, a. 2, ad quaest. 2; A. Malet, *Personne et amour*, pp. 55–59.

56 *ST* I, q. 34, a. 1, ad 3.

57 In our mind, the speaking of a mental word is necessary to the achievement of the act of intellectual knowledge (no intellection without the speaking of a word): Thomas explains this as early as *Summa contra Gentiles* (Book I, ch. 53) in order to pose a word in God. But the existence of the divine Word as a distinct person (a real relation with its source) is never established as a rational necessity. Thomas emphasizes in this regard the difference of the mode of intelligence in God and in us (*ST* I, q. 32, a. 1, ad 2): This is the limit of analogy in the things that only faith allows us to grasp.

intellectual knowledge by the speaking of the word,[58] but it is necessary at least to retain three points for Trinitarian theology. First, Thomas distinguishes between the act of intellection common to the three persons in virtue of their unique essence (essential act), and the notional act of speaking which belongs properly and exclusively to the person of the Father: "So therefore, the only person who speaks in God *(dicens in divinis)* is the one who utters the Word, although each person understands and is understood, and consequently is spoken in the Word."[59] There is not any confusion between the essential act (common to the Three) and the notional act (proper to a divine person). Secondly, this Word is entirely related to the person of the Father: Thomas discerns there an origin (as the human word is spoken by the intellect, the divine Word exists *a Patre*) that the name "Word" signifies as a properly relative term. "The Word, spoken properly in God, signifies something which proceeds from another." Thirdly, this name " Word" can only belong properly to the person of the Son. At the end of a remarkable evolution,[60] Thomas can affirm without ambiguity in the *Summa theologiae*, as an exact consequence of the preceding explanations of the *ratio* of word and of speaking: "The name Word in God, if it is taken properly, is a personal name and *in no way an essential name. . . . It is not taken essentially, but *only personally*."[61]

The same distinction, although Thomas has not developed it with a comparable fullness, is observed in the doctrine of the procession of the Holy Spirit as Love. If one takes *Love* as a proper name of the Holy Spirit, Thomas explains, it is not a matter of love or of the act of love common to the three persons (essential love, of

---

[58] One could refer with profit to Hyacinthe Paissac, *Théologie du Verbe,* Saint Augustin et saint Thomas (Paris: Cerf, 1951); cf. Yves Floucat, "L'intellection et son verbe selon saint Thomas d'Aquin," *RT* 97 (1997): 443–84 and 640–93.

[59] *ST* I, q. 34, a. 1, ad 3.

[60] For an illuminating sketch of this evolution, see François von Gunten, "*In principio erat Verbum.* Une évolution de saint Thomas en théologie trinitaire," in *Ordo sapientiae et amoris: Hommage au Professor J.-P. Torrell,* ed. Carlos-Josaphat Pinto de Oliveira (Fribourg: Éditions universitaires, 1993), pp. 119–41.

[61] *ST* I, q. 34, a. 1.

which St. John says: "God is love," 1 John 4:8–16), but of a loving imprint which is to the notional act of love (active spiration, notion of the Father and of the Son) what the Word is to the speaking of the Father, and which is related to the essential act of love in the same way that the Word is related to the essential act of intellection. Measuring the extreme poverty of our vocabulary with regard to love, Thomas observes:

> In as far as love or dilection only means a relationship of the one who loves to the thing loved, *love* and *to love* in God are said essentially, like understanding and to understand. But in as far as we use these words in order to express the mutual relationship, of the one who proceeds by the mode of love, to its principle, of such kind that by *Love* one understands *Love proceeding* and that by *to love* one understands *to spirate Love proceeding,* then *Love* is a name of the person, and *to love (diligere vel amare)* is a personal verb, like *to speak or to beget.*[62]

Just as Thomas has identified the properly relative and therefore personal standing of the speaking of the Word, he likewise deepens his thought on love until he has established the "relative" reality of personal Love sent out by a fecund act of the Father and the Son, a mysterious impression, affection, or attraction of love which is in no way confused with an essential property of the divinity. Thus, when he introduces his Trinitarian treatise by posing a mode of procession according to intellectual act and another according to voluntary or loving act (q. 27), Thomas has in view not the essential act but indeed the personal term of a notional act. The "psychological" analogy is developed here in two phases.

In a first phase, Thomas situates *the immanent spiritual activity,* the activity which befits God and which allows one to render account of the procession of a personal "term" which is God in the midst of God, and which, as such, only can be grasped in the domain of intel-

---

[62] *ST* I, q. 37, a. 1; see above chapter 3; H.-D. Simonin, "Autour de la solution thomiste," pp. 174–274.

lectual and voluntary action. One observes that, as early as the *Summa contra Gentiles*, Thomas explained the distinction of persons by the consideration of "God" present to himself as the known in the knower and as the loved in the lover.[63] Does this approach to processions, which emphasizes immanence through the self-presence of God known and loved, mean that the psychological analogy presents the Trinitarian processions as an emanation from the divine substance ("God")? In order to respond to this question, it is necessary to take into account the stages of the analogy, which is not applied in a static manner, but follows a progression intended to gather together the diverse elements of the reality. We remark first that, in this context, Thomas emphasizes always the *distinction* that this self-presence suggests, the distinction between "God knowing" and "God known," between "God loving" and "God loved." In the intellectual analogy, for instance, the accent is not placed solely on the identity, but indeed on the reflexive self-knowledge in view of manifesting the distinction according to origin.[64] Thomas can bring out here many elements already elaborated in the treatise on the divine essence (intellectual and voluntary activity by which God knows and loves himself), and the correlatives in presence are designated by the word "God" qualified by the acts of intellection and of love. But, at this point of junction, when Thomas poses the presence of a word and of a love in God in a productive operation, it is indeed the personal reality that is in view.

It is necessary to insist here that it is not simply a matter of "God knowing" or of "God known," but of the self-presence, by a fecund emanation, of "God known present in God knowing," which allows for gathering together the aspect of the distinction,

---

[63] For this formulation, on which is based the development of the intellectual analogy for the procession of the Son and the voluntary (or loving) analogy for the procession of the Spirit, cf. *SCG* IV, ch. 11 (#3469); ch. 19 (#3560–63); *CT* I, ch. 37 and 45; *ST* I, q. 27, a. 3.

[64] *SCG* IV, ch. 11 (#3469): "Etiam intellectus noster, seipsum intelligens, est in seipso, nom solum ut idem sibi per essentiam, sed etiam ut a se apprehensum intelligendo." It is already by means of this reflexive self-understanding that Thomas establishes the prerogatives of the intellect at the summit of the degrees of life: "Nam intellectus in seipsum reflectitur, et seipsum intelligere potest" (#3465).

that of the relation of origin, and that of the unity. On the other hand, the formulation of this self-presence is not the end of the analogy, but its point of departure: Thomas does not yet employ the names of Father, Son, Holy Spirit, because it is precisely this that the analogy is called upon to manifest, since it is by the speaking of the Word and the spiration of personal Love (the outcome of the psychological analogy) that, in God, this self-presence in the distinction is verified, so that the expression "God known in God who knows" only finds its full sense in the affirmation "the Father speaks the Word," where it manifests its intelligibility. This means that, in the formulation of this analogy, "God" does not designate the divine "to be" in its indistinct unity, but indeed *God referred to God* in a distinction that is grasped according to the (notional) intellectual and loving operation. In virtue of his doctrine of relation, Thomas does not think of God as the subject of a notional act without posing immediately and simultaneously two persons from the fact of the relations that constitute them.

Then, in a second phase, he establishes the personal property of the Word and of Love, personal "terms" of a notional act, which are never confused with the "essential" activity, although they are unthinkable without this essential activity common to the three persons (each person understands and loves). This elaboration, which is clarified well in the doctrine of *relation* that it introduces with the notion of distinction according to origin, is based on the knowledge of a true immanent fecundity of "to speak" and of "to spirate Love" in God. It is entirely oriented toward the manifestation of a *real distinction of persons*, of such a kind that "if the procession of the Word and of Love does not suffice for suggesting the personal distinction, there could not be any personal distinction in God,"[65] since, in short, the second term of an alternative in this domain could only consist in a common (essential) act incapable of manifesting the truth of Trinitarian faith.

There is, therefore, no "derivation" of persons from an essential act in Thomas. This observation clarifies anew the structure of the

---

[65] *De potentia*, q. 9, a. 9, ad 7.

treatise on God: The distinction of the two sections of the treatise (what concerns the essence, then what concerns the distinction of persons) does not express a separation between a treatise on a "monopersonal" God and a treatise on God the Trinity, nor a conception of the essence which opens up into a plurality. In reality, it prevents the derivation of the persons from the essence: It is to relation, and not to essence in its proper formality, that it belongs to manifest the plurality in God.[66] The pivot of this structure is, once again, the doctrine of relation, since only this relation according to origin allows for introducing the aspect of plurality in God. This theological option is crystallized in many famous theses of Thomas's triadology that it will suffice to describe briefly.

Refusing to make the persons derive from the essence, Thomas firmly excludes the expression "the essence begets" or "the essence is begotten." The question is historically connected to the critique that Joachim of Fiore had addressed to Peter Lombard, accusing the latter of posing a "quaternity" in God from the fact of the exclusion of a notional act attributed to the essence.[67] Thomas is concerned with this problem as early as his *Commentary on the Sentences* and he examines the question most closely in his commentary on the Decretal *Damnamus* of Lateran IV. To attribute a notional act to the essence ("the essence begets," "the essence is begotten") amounts for Thomas to dividing the essence among the three persons, and therefore to opening the path to Arianism, since generation and spiration, as such, distinguish a supposit–principle from a supposit–term. It is very clearly the faith of Nicea, professing the consubstantiality of the three persons, that is found in play in

---

[66] This is a fundamental insight of the work of H. C. Schmidbaur, *Personarum Trinitas*.

[67] Thomas explains thusly the interpretation that Joachim of Fiore gave of the Master of the Sentences: "He believed that Master Peter posed the essence as something distinct from the three persons, in a manner in which the essence could have been called a fourth reality. He believed that from the fact that one says that the essence does not beget, is not begotten and does not proceed, it is distinguished from the Father who begets, from the Son who is begotten and from the Holy Spirit who proceeds." (*Expositio super secundam Decretalem* [Leonine edition, vol. 40 E, 41].)

Thomas on this point.[68] His position engages first an analysis of
language: Since the mode of signification of the term "essence" is
that of an abstract form, this term does not have of itself the faculty
of holding the place of a person: otherwise, one would signify a distinction in the essence as one signifies a distinction of supposits.[69]
In creatures (to which, precisely, our mode of signification is linked
in virtue of the constitution of our knowledge), actions are the
work of supposits: "the essence does not act, but it is the principle
of the act in the supposit." In God, the essence is really identical to
each of the three supposits or persons, but, since it is necessary to
take account of the mode of our knowledge and of our language,
the essence is grasped in the notional act on a different mode from
the person, since the person is distinct whereas the essence is common.[70] The essence is what the notional act communicates, it is
also by it (principle *quo* with the property) that the Father begets
and that the Father and Son spirate the Holy Spirit, but it cannot
itself be the subject of a productive (notional) act in God.

It is in strictly extending these explanations that Thomas proposes the famous formula: "It is because he is Father that the Father
begets *(Quia Pater est, generat),*" and not the inverse proposition
(the Father is Father because he begets). What Thomas rejects, here
again, is that the supposit to whom belongs the notional act could
be thought in a pre-relational or essential manner (as subsisting
essence), independently of his constitution as a person, that is to say
independently of his personal relation. Positively, since the subject
of attribution of a notional act is a *person as such* (acts are the work
of supposits), it is not so much the begetting which makes the

---

[68] In his brief *Exposition of the Second Decretal*, Thomas has recourse two times to
the *homoousion* of the Council of Nicea in order to establish his response to the
question.

[69] *ST* I, q. 39, a. 5; *Expositio super secundam Decretalem* (p. 41).

[70] I *Sent.*, d. 5, q. 1, a. 1: "In divinis autem essentia realiter non differt a supposito sed solum ratione, sive quantum ad modum significandi: quia suppositum est distinctum et essentia est communis. . . . Sed actus qui dicitur de supposito secundum modum secundum quem differt ab essentia, non potest de essentia praedicari; et hujusmodi est actus generandi, qui praedicatur de supposito Patris, secundum quod distinctum a supposito Filii."

Father be Father, but indeed rather the inverse: The Father is thought as subject of a personal act *because he is a person*. It is also for this reason that, in the case of the personal property of the Father, insomuch as this property constitutes the person of the Father, it ought to be thought as a precondition (it is "pre-understood") to the notional act of begetting: Here, the relative property of the first person precedes the act in the order of concepts, "as the person who acts is pre-understood to his action."[71] Otherwise, it would be necessary to renounce seeing in relation the principle of the constitution of the person and the person itself. In the case of active spiration, however, there is indeed a conceptual priority of the procession or origin, that is to say of the notional act, above the property or notion of active spiration common to the Father and to the Son. The reason for this is, however, identical since here, in the order of notions, we are already in possession of a personal concept of Father and of Son, constituted by the relations of paternity and of filiation (and not by active spiration, which is not a personal property constituting a person), and the act therefore is indeed thought as the work of supposits.[72]

These explanations raise a question: In order to emphasize the personalism of Trinitarian faith, should not Thomas begin his treatise on God by the consideration of the person of the Father, rather than by a section on the divine essence? This position, promoted notably by M. Schmaus and K. Rahner on the basis of an important consideration of Scripture,[73] is largely accepted today in the essays and manuals of Trinitarian theology: "The doctrine of the Trinity must start with the Father and understand him as origin, source and

---

[71] *ST* I, q. 40, a. 4; I *Sent.*, d. 27, q. 1, a. 2.

[72] The procession or passive origin (the "begotten 'to be'" of the Son and the "to proceed" of the Holy Spirit) presents a different case since it is conceived as the path leading to the person who proceeds: It is attributed to the person who proceeds and not to the person–source to whom belongs the active origin; cf. *ST* I, q. 40, a. 4.

[73] K. Rahner, *The Trinity*, p. 16. This is one of the major conclusions that K. Rahner drew from his foundational study on the meaning of the word "God" in the New Testament: *Theological Investigations*, vol. 1, trans. C. Ernst, "Theos in the New Testament" (New York: Crossroad, 1982): pp. 79–148 [145–47].

inner ground of unity of the Trinity."[74] The Father would appear then, from the first, as "the personal divine Being."[75] In this perspective, which appeals also to Greek thought and notably the Cappadocian Fathers, the aspect of unity in the Trinity is manifested in the extension of the primacy that belongs to the Father: The unity is then the consequence of the fact that the Father communicates all his essence to the Son and to the Holy Spirit. The advantages of such a structure of triadology, like the biblical and traditional foundations that it can bring out, are not negligible. We would wish, however, to show the speculative reason[76] that leads Thomas to chose another path from which the benefit is not less.

In exposing the constitution of the divine person by relation, Thomas rules out the possibility of conceiving a divine person outside of his personal relation. Without this relation, which requires the simultaneous understanding of the other person to which a person is referred, following the Aristotelian (and patristic) rule of the necessary simultaneity and co-understanding of correlatives, a person cannot be thought as person. This is precisely the reason for which Thomas poses the conceptual priority of the personal property of paternity, inasmuch as that constitutes the person of the Father. This thesis is expressed by the repeated affirmation of Thomas: "If one abstracts the relations in the persons, the hypostases disappear."[77] Thomas distinguishes here two kinds of abstraction, but the conclusion is identical in the two cases: If one removes the relation conceived as *proprium* from the divine person, there only remains in our mind the essence common to the Three; if one abstracts the relation grasped by our intelligence as a form, then, if it is a matter of the personal relation that constitutes the person,[78] the hypostasis disappears from our

---

[74] W. Kasper, *The God of Jesus Christ,* p. 299.

[75] Ibid.

[76] In order to be complete, it would be necessary to develop the historical themes that situate more fully the thought of Thomas in the Latin heritage that he deepens.

[77] I *Sent.,* d. 26, q. 1, a. 2; *De potentia,* q. 8, a. 4; *CT* I, ch. 61; *ST* I, q. 40, a. 3.

[78] The precision is imposed, because the persons possess many relations of which only one constitutes each person. Thus, for Thomas, if one abstracts the notions of *Unbegotten* (innascibility) or of *Spirator* (principle of the Holy Spirit), which

mind. In this second case, in taking the whole measure of the function of the *constitution of the person* which belongs to the relation, and which is not limited to the simple manifestation of a distinction already given independently of the relation (as if the personal relation happened to a person already otherwise constituted), Thomas can even add:

> If one removes the relation from our mind, there does not remain any substrate to this relation, since the relation itself is the reality that subsists. If one abstracts the relation, to speak properly, *nothing subsists,* neither what is absolute, nor what is related, nor the hypostasis, nor the essence, since the relation itself is the reality that subsists.[79]

One notes in this latter text that Thomas does not oppose the personal relation to the essence as two great irreducibles, as if the essence were posed outside of persons or beside the relation: The subsisting relation "integrates" the essential being of the divinity that it possesses properly considered as divine relation and in virtue of which it subsists. In its character of personal property, of relation constituting the person or of subsisting relation, the relation cannot

---

belong to the Father, the hypostasis of the Father stays in our mind, because innascibility and active spiration do not constitute the person of the Father. The three personal relations alone are involved here: paternity, filiation, and passive spiration (procession of the Holy Spirit); cf. *ST* I, q. 40, a. 3.

[79] I *Sent.,* d. 26, q. 1, a. 2: ". . . Remota relatione per intellectum, non relinquitur aliquid quasi substratum illi relationi, sed ipsamet relatio est *res* subsistens. Unde, abstracta relatione proprie loquendo nihil manet, neque absolutum, neque relatum, neque hypostasis, neque essentia." Thomas reprises here the teaching of Albert the Great: ". . . ipsa relatio fert secum suum suppositum, quod distinguit. Et propter hoc separata personalitate per intellectum in divinis nihil manet. Separata enim paternitate a Patre per intellectum nihil manet in re Patris . . . et ita nihil manet" (Albert the Great, *Super Dionysium de divinis nominibus,* ch 2, #25; Cologne edition, vol. 37/1, p. 60). The point of view adopted in this affirmation is that of the reality of God such as the faith teaches it, and Thomas considers the relation as form (there are no accidents in God, and what is signified there as a form is subsisting). This does not take away either the legitimacy of a distinction between what is common and proper in God, or the possibility of dialogue with believers of other religions or with philosophers who know of God only what concerns his unity or his essence.

be separated from the essence without all the reality of God vanish-
ing from our mind: *Nihil manet.*

   It is because he holds, in a rigorous manner and in its furthest
consequences, a *resolutely relational understanding of the person* that
Thomas can hardly begin a treatise on God with the person of the
Father, presenting there the attributes of the divine substance
(power, wisdom, goodness) in order to come next to the Son and
then to the Holy Spirit receiving the substance of God and everything that belongs to this latter, and in order to manifest finally at
the end the divine unity resulting from the primacy of the Father. In
proceeding thus one puts, in the place of the Thomist treatise concerning the divine essence, a treatise on the Father. This approach
certainly has the advantage of emphasizing from the beginning that
the essential attributes are considered in a person (the Father), but
one would treat in that case in an extensive manner of the Father
before having grasped the Father in his relation to the Son. The consideration would be indeed that of a person, but independently of the
relation which constitutes it, in the manner of a personal essence.[80]
In all rigor, if the structure of a treatise corresponds well to the master ideas of that treatise, such an option of method requires a *theology that can think of the person without the relation,* precisely what
Thomas Aquinas rejects. If the question is posed in terms of "essentialism" and of "personalism," one should in that case wonder which
of the structures risks more the danger of an "essentialism": that of
Thomas which poses first the divine essence in order to assume it
into the doctrine of the person as subsisting relation,[81] or that

---

[80] K. Rahner ("Remarks on the Dogmatic Treatise 'De Trinitate,'" p. 84) notes
   with clarity, but not without some debatable generalization: "It would be more
   biblical and Greek to start from the one absolutely unoriginated God, who is
   still the Father, even when it is not yet known that he is the Begetter and Spirator, because he is known as the unoriginated hypostasis, who may not be
   thought of *positively* as 'absolute,' even when he is not yet known expressly as
   relative." On the other hand, in *The Trinity,* p. 16: For St. Thomas "the first
   topic under study is not God the Father as the unoriginate origin of divinity
   and reality, but as the essence common to all three persons."

[81] Not beginning his treatise on God with the person of the Father, Thomas
   equally cannot begin with a treatise on "God" that would be distinguished
   from the Trinity. There remains then only one solution: to expose first what, in

which can think of the Father in a "non-relational" or rather "pre-relational" manner with the sole essence or divine substance with which he is identified? Without entering into the speculative ramifications of these fundamental approaches,[82] or into the historical sources that one can bring out (which lead moreover to nuancing the very sharp prejudices in favor of an exclusive "personalism" of the Cappadocian triadology in contrast to Latin theology),[83] one ought at least to conclude that the question of "personalism," in the perspective of Thomas, is measured not at the level of an opposition between person and essence but by the place that one accords to relation in the account of the person.

It remains that Thomas pays great attention to the theme of the Father as "principle without principle," "principle of all the divinity," "source" or "fount of the divinity," "primordial author," possessing the "plenitude of the fount" or "the universal *auctoritas.*"[84] With his Greek sources, he speaks equally of the Father as "Fount of deity *(fontana deitas),*"[85] and he knows that the Christian East considers the procession *a Patre* as the reference to the "First origin *(prima origo).*"[86] One could multiply the examples. But these expressions are always strictly understood by means of the doctrine

---

God the Trinity, concerns the unity of essence, and to follow this with a treatise on the persons that introduces an analysis of relation.

82 One can think here of the doctrine of the *Filioque* which, in Thomas, is found fundamentally connected to the thesis of the constitution and the distinction of the person by the relation according to origin. See chapter 6 below; H.C. Schmidbaur, *Personarum Trinitas,* pp. 353–61.

83 André de Halleux, *Patrologie et oecuménisme,* Recueil d'études, "Personnalisme ou essentialisme trinitaire chez les Pères Cappadociens?" (Leuven: University Press/Peeters, 1990), pp. 215–68. A. de Halleux concludes that the principle of unity and the Trinitarian principle have equal importance in the doctrine of God of the Cappadocians who "are at the same time, and totally, personalists and essentialists" (pp. 265–66). This study, like many others of the same author, gives important foundations for the rediscovery of a complementarity between the approaches called Greek and Latin to the mystery of the Trinity.

84 The occurrences of these expressions, which one can easily retrieve by means of the *Index Thomisticus,* are very numerous, and in the majority of cases from the *Commentary on the Sentences.*

85 I *Sent.,* d. 11, q. 1, a. 1, arg. 1; d. 28, q. 1, a. 1; *In librum beati Dionysii De divinis nominibus expositio,* ch. 2, lect. 4 (#181).

86 Cf. I *Sent.,* d. 12, q. 1, a. 2, ad 3; *In Ioan.* 15:26 (#2065).

of the personal relation according to origin, with the notion of "principle" and of "order" (expressing the origin), of such kind that the person of the Father never is posed without the relation of paternity which constitutes it, and cannot therefore be identified with the essence or with the divinity in a stage which would precede the deployment of the doctrine of relations.

There is thus no possibility, in Aquinas, of considering the essence in a manner of a fecund subject or of a "fount of being" from which would be drawn the persons, and therefore no derivation of the persons from the essence. The essence that is in question in the first section of the treatise on God is not a source of the plurality of persons. It is, from one end to the other of the treatise "the unique essence of three persons," numerically one, subsisting in each of the persons, never outside of the persons with whom it does not number.

Relation and Essence: A Unitarian Perspective?

The analysis of the relationship between essence and person poses in the last resort the difficult question of subsistence in God.[87] The terms of the debate are the following: Is subsistence the work of the essence or of the persons as such? If the persons hold their subsistence from the essence, is it not a matter of a return of the essence to the forefront? Would we not be faced with a "primacy" of the divine essence over the relation, since in this vision of things the essence grounds the subsistence, so that one affirms first the subsistence of the essence in order *then* to attribute it to the relations (to the persons) which receive it from the essence? Do we not find, then, in Thomas, despite a certain advance due to his theory of relation, a

---

[87] It suffices for our purpose to consider subsistence *(subsistentia)* as the mode of the substance existent by itself, without entering into the developments of the Thomist tradition on the distinction between existence and subsistence or on the terminal mode of the essence. "In so far as the substance exists by itself and not in another, one calls it 'subsistence *(subsistentia)*': because to subsist *(subsistere)* is said of what exists in itself and not in another thing" (*ST* I, q. 29, a. 2).

fundamentally "unitarian" perspective that makes the divine essence
the concept of reference in the doctrine on God the Trinity?[88]

The principles of the response of St. Thomas have already been
suggested above. In considering relations in creatures, where they are
accidents, one discovers a double aspect: (1) the being *(esse)* of the
relation, which it possesses, since it is an accident, by inherence in a
subject; (2) the essence or reason *(ratio)* of the relation, which is
proper to the relation, and which consists in the reference to another
(ad aliquid). The first aspect is grasped in the consideration of that in
which the relation exists, while the second aspect is grasped by the
reference to an exterior reality. In contrast to the approach nearly
universally adopted in the wake of nominalism, this analogy does
not consider the relation as a category thought *between* individuals,
but *in* individuals, "in the things." The transference of this category
into God leads to identifying the first aspect, the being of the relation, with the divine *esse*: that which is inherence of the accident, in
creatures becomes, in God, "the being of the divine essence" of such
kind that the relation exists or subsists as really identical to the
essence. Between essence and relation, on this point, there is no difference. As regards the second aspect, the proper *ratio* of relation, it
consists alone in the relationship to another thing, which does not
modify the subject but which is pure "ecstatic" reference to this other
reality (privilege of the relation): This is what permits an account of
a strict Trinitarian monotheism, since the constitution and the real
distinction of the persons by the relation affect in no way the unity

---

[88] G. Greshake, *Der dreieine Gott,* pp. 117–18. For a more complete overview of
the question, in an approach that extends the reflection of St. Thomas in a critical manner, cf. Klaus Obenauer, "Zur *subsistentia absoluta* in der Trinitätstheologie," *Theologie und Philosophie* 72 (1997): 188–215. This latter proposes to
grasp the divine essence *(das Wesen Gottes)* in a relational manner as the indivis-
ible reality of relations, consisting in this going forth [processus] of relations,
and being "absolute" in the measure in which this relative being, completed in
the personal relations, is in itself one. This proposition merits attention, but it
poses notably the question of the knowledge of the divine essence by natural
reason, as well as the question of the function of relation in God (realization of
the relational character of the essence?). We note that Thomas avoids all absorp-
tion of one notion by another since the essence does not constitute the relation,
and neither does the relation constitute the essence.

of the divine being.[89] It is on this basis that Thomas can show that the word "person," in God, signifies "the relation insofar as subsisting *(relatio ut subsistens)*," which comes back "to signifying the relation by manner of substance, that is to say of the hypostasis subsisting in the divine nature."[90]

The place of the essence in the subsistence of relations is found expressly formulated in the disputed questions *De potentia*:

> The relations in God, although they constitute the hypostases and thus make them subsist, do it however insofar as they are the divine essence; indeed, the relation insofar as it is relation does not have anything of what subsists or makes subsist: that belongs solely to the substance.
>
> The relation distinguishes the hypostases insofar as it is relation, but it constitutes the hypostasis insofar as it is the divine essence: it does the one and the other thing insofar as it is divine essence and relation.[91]

Following these texts, to which it is not difficult to attach the doctrine of the *Ipsum esse subsistens*, would the essence not play the decisive role in the subsistence of the divine person?

One path of understanding can consist in emphasizing that, for Thomas, "only the relation subsists," that subsistent relation being the only subject of attribution of acts in God (the acts are the work of supposits), the sole "subject-bearer of the essence" which has no reality outside of the persons.[92] But, if one wishes to withdraw from the substance or from the divine essence as such the dignity of subsistence, it remains in that case to explain the numerous texts of Thomas's corpus speaking of a subsistence of the essence or of the divine *esse*, or of an activity attributed to the essence.[93] Thus,

---

[89] Cf. *ST* I, q. 28, a. 2.

[90] *ST* I, q. 29, a. 4; *De potentia*, q. 9, a. 4.

[91] *De potentia*, q. 8, a. 3, ad 7 and ad 9; cf. ad 8.

[92] This thesis constitutes a leitmotiv of the work of H. C. Schmidbaur, *Personarum Trinitas*: see notably pp. 435–37, 445, 513–26.

[93] For example the creation, in I *Sent.*, d. 5, q. 1, a. 1. Thomas shows there that in contrast to the notional act, the creative act is attributed to a supposit which is not grasped on a different mode from the essence.

Thomas explains in the disputed questions *De potentia*: "In God, the personal properties only work to distinguish mutually the supposits from the divine nature, and they are not the principle of the subsistence of the divine essence, *because the essence is subsistent by itself;* it is, on the contrary, from the essence that the personal properties have subsistence."[94] As regards essential acts (to create, to govern, to understand, to will, etc.), one speaks more properly when one attributes them to a concrete essential name (for example, "God"), but the distinction is placed here on the level of the mode of signification and not of the reality signified: As regards the reality itself, in virtue of the identity between the *quod* and the *quo* in God, these essential acts return indeed to the divine essence, and Thomas does not deny that the latter could be signified—although in an improper manner—by the mode of a supposit.[95] When he treats of individuation, Thomas retains equally a double approach. On the one hand, the divine essence or nature exists singularly by itself and it is "individuated" by itself.[96] This is the reason for which a plurality of gods is presented as an impossibility: The divine essence plays here the role of a principle of individuation. In the distinction of three persons, on the other hand, the principle of individuation ("*quasi* principle of individuation") of persons can only be the personal property, and not the divine essence or nature.[97] In both cases, the principle of individuation is characterized by the fact of not existing in another (incommunicability): The divine essence is not possessed by another God, the personal property does not exist in another person. In conclusion, "For this reason, we say that there is only one God, since there is only one subsisting essence *(una essentia subsistens)*; and we say that there are many persons, in virtue

---

[94] *De potentia*, q. 9, a. 5, ad 13: "In divinis autem proprietates personales hoc solum habent quod supposita divinae naturae ab invicem distinguuntur, non autem sunt principium subsistendi divinae essentiae: ipsa enim divina essentia est secundum se subsistens; sed e converso proprietates personales habent quod subsistant ab essentia."

[95] Cf. *De potentia*, q. 8, a. 2, ad 7.

[96] *SCG* I, ch. 21 (#199): "Divina essentia est per se singulariter existens et in seipsa individuata;" ch. 42 (#346).

[97] *SCG* IV, ch. 14 (#3503); cf. ch. 10 (#3452).

of the distinction of subsisting relations *(propter distinctionem subsistentium relationum)*."[98]

It seems to us that in order to understand these texts without reducing their meaning, one ought to take into account two principles of reading. The first resides in the rule of *"redoublement"* set forth above and based on the distinction between "common" and "proper" in God the Trinity. The complexity of our knowledge of the mystery, faced with the impossibility of extracting the persons from the essence as if they were an emanation or an effusion of it, obliges us to approach subsistence by a double knowledge. The solution does not consequently consist in excluding the conception of subsistence from the essence, which conception the Thomist doctrine of pure Act cannot in fact renounce, but it is necessary rather to see *where the synthesis of the two approaches takes place.* Now it is very clearly in the teaching on the person—"what is most perfect *(perfectissimum)* in all nature"[99]—as subsisting relation, that this integration is effected.

It is necessary to note here a particular application that, under the aspect of our access to the knowledge of God, accounts for the fact that some non-Christians can conceive of God as a person who exists or subsists. Thomas gives here, as an example, the Jewish faith, but one can extend his explanation to other non-Christian religions as well as to philosophical reflection bordering on the idea of a personal God: "If, by our thought, one abstracts the personal properties, there still remains in our consideration the divine nature as a subsisting reality and as a person."[100] The reason advanced by Thomas is the real identity of *quo est* and of *quod est* in God: All that one attributes to God under an abstract mode (*quo*, for example the nature or the essence signified as a form), considered in itself, and even if one abstracts from the rest, ought necessarily to be thought as a subsist-

---

[98] *SCG* IV, ch. 14 (#3502). It is in order to account for this double approach that the Thomist tradition has developed the concept of "communicable subsistence" distinct from the "incommunicable subsistence" proper to the divine person.

[99] *ST* I, q. 29, a. 3.

[100] *ST* III, q. 3, a. 3, ad 1; cf. ad 2.

ing reality, because of the perfect simplicity of God. This thesis, which is not proper to Thomas (one finds it already in Albert and Bonaventure),[101] establishes clearly that the idea of a certain personality of God is accessible outside of Christian faith: In making precise our concepts, it constitutes an important foundation of interreligious dialogue. It is not a matter, however, of a consideration of the reality of God as the Christian faith teaches it, since in this case personality pertains exclusively to the Father, to the Son, and to the Holy Spirit, without the addition of a fourth term. Indeed, if one knows God "as he is *(sicuti est),*" Thomas specifies, it is impossible to proceed to the abstraction of one thing in order to maintain another thing, because all that is in God is one (divine simplicity); the abstraction of divine relations consequently cuts out the whole reality of God, because the essence is not a substrate other than the relation:[102] "nothing remains," as has been seen above. Thus, the particular case of the abstraction of Trinitarian relations leading to posing an "absolute" subsistence of the divine essence, in order to conceive of God as a person, hardly causes difficulties, since this abstraction explicitly separates Trinitarian faith and does not envisage the full reality of God. By isolating a concept, however, it reveals itself to be capable of conceiving the rational character of a non-Christian monotheism, safeguarding at the same time the prerogatives of faith which alone permits knowing the three persons in God. Thomas employs the same procedure of abstraction in order to deny that from the plenitude of God (goodness, love, beatitude) one could have deduced the plurality of persons:[103] Human reason can certainly arrive at the full goodness and beatitude of a unique God conceived as subsistent, but it cannot prove the divine tripersonality.

This point leads us to the second principle of reading. The opposition between essence and person, as the opposition between essence

---

[101] Cf. Albert the Great, I *Sent.,* d. 2, a. 12, ad 1; Bonaventure, III *Sent.,* d. 5, a. 1, q. 4.

[102] Cf. Thomas Aquinas, *ST* III, q. 3, a. 3, sol. and ad 3.

[103] St. Thomas Aquinas, I *Sent.,* d. 3, q. 1, a. 4, ad 3. The theological argumentation in this domain (the psychological analogy, for example) resides rather in certain "adaptations," and never in necessary reasons.

and subsisting relation, leads to an impasse, since it is not a matter of two great irreducibles, neither on the level of reality (there is only a distinction of reason between essence and person or relation), nor even on the level of concepts; because the notion of person, as we have said, assumes or integrates the reality of essence and because the notion of subsisting relation is unthinkable without the concept of essence. "The divine essence, although it is subsisting, cannot be separated from the relation that it is necessary to understand in God."[104] At stake is once again the numerical identity of the essence in each of the persons, following the *homoousion* of Nicea. In the subsisting relation, Thomas joins the two aspects, that of the *esse* and that of the *ratio*. When one speaks of subsisting relation, it is of the relation reuniting the two aspects that one treats. When Thomas isolates "the relation as relation," that is to say the relation according to its proper *ratio* which consists in the pure *ad aliquid*, he only describes a component, intended to manifest the distinction of persons which leaves intact the pure unity of the divine substance that this *ad aliquid* does not modify. And when he treats of the existence of relation in God, he specifies: "The *esse* of the relation does not depend on the substance *(nec esse relationis est esse dependens neque a substantia)*, nor on another exterior reality, since the being of the relation is the being of the essence."[105] Correlatively, there would be a profound misunderstanding in thinking that when one says "essence" in God, on the level of reality, one had spoken *another thing* than the relation.

The question, at bottom, is then this: What is a relation? If, following the path of a conceptualist nominalism, the relation is grasped as a category of understanding, a comparison or putting in relationship of two absolute realities of such kind that this relation

---

[104] *SCG* IV, 14 (#3502): "Essentia enim divina, etsi subsistens sit, non tamen potest separari a relatione quam oportet in Deo intelligi ex hoc quod Verbum conceptum divinae mentis est ab ipso Deo dicente. Nam et Verbum est divina essentia, ut ostensum est; et Deus dicens, a quo est Verbum, est etiam divina essentia; non alia et alia, sed eadem numero." The same thing holds for the spiration of Love.

[105] Ibid. (#3508). It is in creatures that there is a dependence between the 'to be' of the relation and the 'to be' of the substance bearing the accident. See Giovanni Ventimiglia, "Le relazioni divine secondo S. Tommaso d'Aquino, Riproposizione di un problema e prospettive di indagine," *Studi tomistici* 44 (1991): 166–82.

amounts to a concept or to the act by which the knowing subject refers this thing to that thing,[106] or if it is solely defined as a relationship existing *between* two realities but not *in* them, so that its being is posed necessarily against the being of realities referred to or outside of these realities, Trinitarian theology could only very laboriously try to reunite the being of the essence and that of the relation in a convincing way. The thought of Thomas would then become incomprehensible. But if the *esse* and the *ratio* of the relation are considered in the synthesis proposed by Thomas, one can in this case perfectly perceive that the constitution and distinction of divine persons comes back to the relation "in as much as it is divine essence and relation"[107] at the same time, although this implies no dependence of the relation with respect to the divine essence.

It is necessary here to recall the exegesis of Cajetan who—against the critique of Peter Auriol and with the purpose of avoiding the consequences of Scotist theology (which tends to pose the constitution of the divine person by an absolute property)[108]—reads in the *Summa theologiae* the affirmation of a constitution of the divine person by the relation as such. Cajetan interprets the texts by means of the following distinction: When one affirms that relation constitutes the divine person because it is identical to the essence *(quia est eadem essentiae)*, one indicates that relation holds this privilege from the essence as from its root *(radicaliter)*; when one affirms that relation constitutes the divine person inasmuch as it is the divine essence *(ut est essentia)*, one attributes formally *(formaliter)* the constitution of the divine person to the relation. Cajetan accounts for the theses of the *De potentia* by means of the first affirmation, although he

---

106 Cf. notably Rolf Schönberger, *Relation als Vergleich: Die Relationstheorie des Johannes Buridan im Kontext seines Denkens und der Scholastik* (Leiden: Brill, 1994) (a study of the doctrine of relation from Thomas Aquinas to Buridan).

107 *De potentia*, q. 8, a. 3, ad 9; cf. ad 7–8.

108 Duns Scotus, *Lectura in I Sent.*, d. 26, q. un. (Opera Omnia, vol. 17 [Vatican City: Ex typis Polyglottis Vaticanis, pp. 328–37]). Scotus, appealing to Bonaventure, holds as more probable the opinion according to which the person is not constituted by the relation but by an absolute reality of the kind that the divine persons are first thought of as absolutes and only secondly as the relations by which they are referred.

explains the thought of the *Summa theologiae,* where the presentation of relation is better unified, by means of the second. Whatever might be the difference posed between the *De potentia* and the *Summa* and the accuracy of the interpretation that Cajetan gives it, Cajetan notes quite rightly that Thomas has in view *divine* relation, and that it comes back to being able to speak of *divine relation* and *subsisting relation.* A relation in creatures, indeed, does not possess of itself that which constitutes a person: It is to the *divine* relation, from the fact of the exclusion of accidentality in God, that this belongs. In this way, if one thinks of the subsisting relation as a reality formally divine (in the "genre" of *divina*), it belongs to this relation insofar as it is a relation to constitute the person: The relation in this case constitutes the person in virtue of its very formality *(infra latitudinem relativam),* without thereby excluding the radical role of the essence. In other words, "the relation constitutes the person from this manner alone: by posing itself, because it is the person itself *(ponendo seipsam, quia est ipsa persona).*"[109]

These precisions certainly pretend to nothing more than to identify the order in the diverse aspects of our understanding of the mystery. Nevertheless they show that the divine relation, taken in a complete manner *(ratio* and *esse),* is not presented as an entity in concurrence with the essence, and that the *esse* that one should attribute to the essence does not diminish the privilege of the relation: The divine relation, taken in its formality and its integral reality, distinguishes the persons and constitutes them.

Conclusion

The relationship between the essence and the personal relation in God, according to Thomas Aquinas, is entirely bound up with the very structure of his treatise on God. This treatise is based on the path of our access to God and on a conceptual organization that

---

[109] Cajetan, *In Iam,* q. 40, a. 4 (Leonine edition, vol. 4, 419). Cf. P. Vanier, *Théologie trinitaire chez saint Thomas d'Aquin,* pp. 77–80; or, from the same author, "La relation trinitaire dans la Somme théologique de saint Thomas d'Aquin," *Sciences Ecclésiastiques* 1 (1948): 143–59, especially 156–59.

makes of the doctrine of persons, inasmuch as they are subsisting relations, the place of synthesis of all the preliminary elements. To place in concurrence essence and relation, as two great opposites or exterior one to the other, would amount to misunderstanding his synthesis of relation. The reading of the texts of Thomas consequently does not gain anything by posing the exclusive primacy of one notion or the other, as if the one should prevail to the detriment of the other. If the problem of essentialism and personalism should consist in a systematic opposition of these two notions, it is necessary to recognize that, in St. Thomas at least, this would be a matter of a false question where the terms are badly posed. The reading of the texts of Thomas articulating the perspective of *common* and of *proper* invites us rather to understand, through the process of *"redoublement"* of our discourse, the integration of the diverse elements in their summit, that is to say in the doctrine of subsisting relation which furnishes the key of the organization of the treatise of God: The constitution and the subsistence of persons come down to relation in its integral being, without negating the preliminary study of the essence and without refusing to the essence the fundamental role that our understanding of the mystery assigns it. The important accent placed by Thomas on the Trinitarian principle of the creation and on the personal dimension in the accomplishment of salvation, by means of notions keyed to his doctrine of divine persons, shows the fecundity of this teaching and its capacity to render account of the divine activity *ad extra*.

There is not, in Thomas, any attempt (or any possibility) of conceiving the person in God the Trinity as a divine Being personalized in a non-relational or pre-relational manner. The idea of a unique personality of God, which grounds the rational legitimacy of a monotheism outside of Christian faith (and which safeguards the gratuity of the revelation of the Trinity!), is not added to the divine tripersonality and offers only an incomplete knowledge which does not consider God as he is. The personal distinction in God is never posed as an emanation from the essence: Neither in the doctrine of processions, nor in the knowledge of the person of the Father, nor in the study of the distinct persons. This speculative argument, which grounds the distinction between the treatise on the essence and that on the plurality of the persons, retains the prerogatives of faith, since no knowledge of the essence or of the essential acts pertains to extracting a personal plurality in God. From this point of view, the replacement of a treatise on what concerns the essence by a treatise on the Father would constitute perhaps less an advance than a regression toward a pre-relational conception of the divine person. This is why, in the light of the thought of St. Thomas, the question of Trinitarian personalism invites an inquiry into the conception that one has of relation and the role that one recognizes for it in manifesting the intelligibility of the faith.

CHAPTER SIX

The Procession of the Holy Spirit *a Filio* According to St. Thomas Aquinas

P NEUMATOLOGY has for many years been prompting a vast body of research in all domains of theology.[1] This renewal is witnessed by an abundance of published papers, including those within the field of Thomist studies.[2] There are several reasons why this pneumatological debate cannot fail to take into account the question of the procession of the Holy Spirit *a Patre et a Filio*, as much because of the ecumenical issues involved as by reason of the fundamental tenets of Trinitarian theology which this debate brings to light.

We know that Thomas Aquinas, in common with all other theologians of the Western Church at that time, offers a Trinitarian doctrine which is quite resolute in its presentation of the doctrine of the procession of the Holy Spirit *a Patre et a Filio*. What is often far less appreciated is the considerable breadth of his schema in this domain. Several works have already brought to light certain aspects of Thomas's thinking on the subject, whether in terms of speculative theology,[3] in terms of his relationship with certain patristic

---

[1] Translation by Heather Buttery of "La procession du Saint-Esprit *a Filio* chez S. Thomas d'Aquin," *RT* 96 (1996): 531–74.

[2] See the list of 520 titles (up to 1993) assembled by Arnaldo Pedrini, *Bibliografia tomista sulla pneumatologia* (Vatican City: Editrice Vaticana, 1994).

[3] See the brief but remarkable article by Hyacinthe F. Dondaine, "La théologie latine de la procession du Saint-Esprit," in *Russie et Chrétienté* 3–4 (1950): 211–18 (devoted to St. Thomas and worthy of being added to Pedrini's list);

sources[4] or with Greek thinking,[5] or in terms of his relationship
with pneumatology in general.[6] A complete monograph on the subject is still, however, lacking. Without attempting a detailed exegesis
of all the relevant passages, this study seeks to present the main features of Thomas's "dossier" of the procession of the Spirit. This
means identifying the theological resources involved, placing them
within the overall context of pneumatology and examining the way
in which Thomas pursued his theological research in this field.

The Task of the Theologian and the
Doctrinal Issues Involved in the Procession
of the Spirit *a Patre* and *a Filio*

Thomas's view of the procession of the Holy Spirit *a Patre* and *a
Filio* is that of a truth of faith which does not require to be proven
in a philosophical sense but the intelligibility of which within the
mystery of the Trinity needs to be demonstrated. Even when he
establishes that, if we accept the doctrine of the Trinity *(supposita
Trinitata)*, the procession of the Spirit *a Filio* necessarily follows
(without which, as we shall see, the coherence of the faith and the
project of an *intellectus fidei* fall apart), Thomas's basic intention is

---

the points made are taken up by the author in *Saint Thomas d'Aquin, Somme
théologique, La Trinité*, vol. 2 (Paris: Editions de la Revue des Jeunes, 1950),
pp. 387–93.

[4] Jaroslav Pelikan, "The Doctrine of *Filioque* in Thomas Aquinas and its Patristic Antecedents, An Analysis of *Summa theologiae*, Part I, Question 36," in *St.
Thomas Aquinas 1274–1974: Commemorative Studies*, ed. Armand A. Maurer,
vol. 1 (Toronto: Pontifical Institute of Medieval Studies, 1974), pp. 315–36.

[5] Venance Grumel, "St. Thomas et la doctrine des Grecs sur la procession du
Saint-Esprit," *Échos d'Orient* 25 (1926): 257–80. This long-established study
remains one of the best works on the subject.

[6] Special mention should be made here of Yves Congar, *Je crois en l'Esprit-Saint*,
vol. 3, 2nd edition (Paris: Cerf, 1985), pp. 162–75 (with bibliographic details
on p. 162, note 1); Reinhard Simon, *Das Filioque bei Thomas von Aquin: Eine
Untersuchung zur dogmengeschichtlichen Stellung, theologischen Struktur und
ökumenischen Perspektive der thomanischen Gotteslehre* (Frankfurt a.M.: Peter
Lang, 1994). R. Simon's work seems too inclined to seek out aporia and insur-
mountable contradictions in Thomas's writing, prompted by highly debatable
interpretative readings. See my critical review: *RT* 94 (1994): 717–19.

to demonstrate the intelligibility of that which the Church confesses and which remains a mystery, inaccessible to the realms of unaided reason. On this basis, he makes use of several themes during his examination of the procession of the Spirit *a Filio* which plainly demonstrate the issues involved in the doctrine. Although he did not present them in a systematic manner, we can identify the following three strands which point to the importance of the themes.

1. *Defending the faith against heresy.* The defense of the faith against heresy brought about a clarification of all the doctrines of faith,[7] in Thomas's view. He repeats this when dealing with the details of Trinitarian doctrine: The Church Fathers provided a detailed clarification *(disserere)* of Trinitarian doctrine because they were compelled to do so by those who contradicted the true faith. This approach, characterized by an apologetic intent in the true sense of the term (1 Pt 3:15, "Always be ready to make your defense to anyone who demands from you an accounting for the hope that is in you [and for your faith]"[8]), is also enriched by a contemplative dimension, offering some degree of knowledge of things which we will only fully grasp in Heaven.[9] The discussion on the procession of the Spirit *a Filio* is conducted within this precise context.

But what are the errors which arise in connection with the procession of the Spirit *a Filio*? Firstly Arianism, as Thomas explains in his *Collationes* on the Credo: By confessing that the Holy Spirit proceeds from the Father and the Son, we

---

[7] Cf. CEG I, prol.

[8] Thomas generally quotes this passage mentioning *faith*, for example in the *Prooemium of De rationibus fidei* (Leonine edition, vol. 40B, 57) where he uses this biblical verse to define the task of the theologian. On this verse, see Joseph de Ghellinck, *Le mouvement théologique du XIIe siècle*, 2nd edition (Bruxelles/Paris: Edition Universelle/Desclée de Brouwer, 1948), pp. 279–84.

[9] *De potentia,* q. 9, a. 5: "Sed in patria intelligendum expectatur. . . . Sed tamen sancti patres propter instantiam eorum qui fidei contradicunt, coacti sunt et de hoc disserere." The text then goes on to refer directly to St. Hilary of Poitiers. The same explanation is given again, still with regard to the Trinity, in *De potentia,* q. 10, a. 2.

recognize that the Son is *the same substance* as the Father, and thereby acknowledge that the Son is not a creature.[10] This emphasis on the divinity of Christ seems to be bringing us back to the truth of the doctrinal history of the Western Church: The resurfacing of various forms of adoptionism, especially in Spain, had played a decisive role.[11] Thomas notes, moreover, that the first explicit denial of the procession of the Holy Spirit *a Filio* came from within the ranks of the Nestorians.[12] Here again, as we shall see later, it appears that the controversy between Theodoret of Cyrus and Cyril of Alexandria actually constitutes one of the first items of the historical dossier (despite the fact that, between the lines, the polemics engaged in by these two authors were neither "filioquist" nor "antifilioquist" in the later sense of the terms). Finally, in the field of speculative theology, Thomas was to show that affirmation of the procession of the Spirit *a Filio* would seem necessary in order to avoid Sabellianism, for in terms of Trinitarian doctrinal thinking in the Western Church, rejecting the *Filioque* amounted to an eradication of the personal distinction between the Son and the Holy Spirit. If the Holy Spirit does not proceed from the Son, there is no longer any means by which one may be distinguished from the other, and they would therefore have to be seen as one and the same person, which "destroys the Faith in the Trinity."[13] A concern to preserve the faith against the errors which the refusal of this article might imply—and we are talking here about the principal heresies affecting Trinitarian and Christological faith!—is a permanent feature of Thomas's writing.

---

[10] *In Symbolum apostolorum,* a. 8 (#962).

[11] See Jaroslav Pelikan, *La Tradition chrétienne,* vol. 2, *L'esprit du christianisme oriental (600–1700)* (Paris: PUF, 1994), p. 199. This is certainly not the only aspect, for Latin Church doctrine had, since Tertullian at least, used formulae implying somehow the *Filioque*; but the response to adoptionism certainly seems to have motivated or encouraged the confession of the *Filioque*.

[12] Cf. *ST* I, q. 36, a. 2, ad 3; see also *De potentia,* q. 10, a. 4, ad 24.

[13] *ST* I, q. 36, a. 2: "Cum tollat fidem Trinitatis." *SCG* IV, ch. 24 (#3616): "Quod est sabellianae impietatis."

2. *The dignity and the prerogatives of Christ.* This second theme is a continuation of the first, since it brings out the implications for Christology of all affirmations of faith. For Thomas, it is the acknowledged prerogatives of Christ himself which are under threat, to the extent that he sees a refusal to accept the procession of the Spirit *a Filio* as an attack upon the dignity of Christ *(eius dignitatem minuunt)* and as representing a danger of "dividing Christ" *(solvere Christum).*[14] This is because of the unity of the Father and the Son as the principle of spiration of the Holy Spirit: This unity requires that we attribute to the Son all that is found in the Father, excepting only the property of paternity which constitutes the first person. This theme of the dignity of Christ assumes a precise (Latin) understanding of the *homoousion* of Nicea and, in terms of its expository content, gives expression to one of the deeply held convictions which lead Thomas to devote such attention to this doctrine.

3. *The reality of salvation in Christ.* The procession of the Spirit *a Filio* not only involves reflection on relative opposition in the Trinity, but in Thomas's view also appears necessary in order to explain the truly Christological foundation of the grace given by the Holy Spirit. The soteriological issues implied, directly rooted in a Thomist reading of Scripture and too often neglected by studies undertaken, appear to be a constant presence in Thomas's thought. A few examples will allow us to assess the importance of the issues raised.

The filial adoption conferred by the Spirit is an assimilation into the Son of God because the Holy Spirit is the Spirit of *Christ* and because he configures us (Rom 8:29) to the Son whose nature he receives in proceeding from him.[15] Thomas is here incorporating the biblical and patristic themes of the unction by the Spirit as a seal *(sigillum)* and mark *(character)*

---

[14] CEG II, prol.; this expression is very forceful and recalls the Vulgate 1 Jn 4:3, "Omnis spiritus qui solvit Iesum, ex Deo non est."

[15] *SCG* IV, ch. 24 (#3606); *De potentia,* q. 10, a. 4; cf. *In Ioan.* 14:26 (#1957).

of the Son: "But nothing is configured to anything else except by its own mark. . . . And the Holy Spirit proceeds from the Son as his own mark."[16] The Spirit leads us to knowledge of the Truth which is the Son because he is the "Spirit of Truth" (Jn 14:17), in other words "because he proceeds from the Truth."[17] The Spirit *glorifies* the Son and announces that which belongs to the Son (Jn 16:15) because he proceeds from him, and it is for the same reason that he *manifests* the Son.[18] "The reason for the glorification [of the Son by the Spirit (Jn 16:14)], is that the Son is the principle of the Holy Spirit. All that proceeds from another manifests that from which it proceeds: The Son manifests the Father, because he proceeds from him. Therefore, since the Holy Spirit proceeds from the Son, it is his proper attribute to glorify him."[19] Then again, the Spirit is "breathed" by Christ into his Apostles (Jn 20:22) because he proceeds from the Son: For Thomas (following Augustine), this breath signifies that the Holy Spirit, given in truth, proceeds not only from the Father but also from the Son.[20] "For if the Spirit did not proceed from him, he would not have breathed him into his disciples after the resurrection."[21]

---

[16] *De potentia,* q. 10, a. 4: "Nihil autem configuratur alicui nisi per eius proprium characterem. . . . Spiritus autem sanctem est a Filio tanquam proprius character eius;" cf. CEG II, ch. 6–7.

[17] *In Ioan.* 14:17 (#1916): "Addit autem Veritatis, quia a Veritate procedit, et veritatem dicit. . . . Sed iste Spiritus ducit ad cognitionem veritatis, quia procedit a veritate, quae dicit supra eodem [v. 6]: *Ego sum via, et veritas, et vita.*"

[18] *In Ioan.* 16:15 (#2109–15).

[19] *In Ioan.* 16:14 (#2107): "Hic ponitur ratio clarificationis, quae est, quia Filius est principium Spiritus sancti. Omne enim quod est ab alio, manifestat id a quo est: Filius enim manifestat Patrem, quia est ab ipso. Quia ergo Spiritus sanctus est a Filio, proprium est ut clarificet eum." Cf. *De potentia,* q. 10, a. 4.

[20] *In Ioan.* 20:22 (#2538): "Flatus ille corporeus substantia Spiritus sancti non fuit, sed demonstratio per congruam significationem non tantum a Patre sed etiam a Filio procedere Spiritum sanctum." Cf. Augustine, *De Trinitate* IV, XX, 29 (quoted by St. Thomas in his *Catena in Ioan.* 20:22, p. 582).

[21] *Catena in Ioan.* 15:26 (p. 535): "Si enim ab eo non procederet, non post resurrectionem discipulis suis insufflasset" (Augustine, *Tract. In Ioan.* 99, 7; CCSL 36, 586).

Many more examples could be given, and we will examine later in greater detail the principal biblical themes called upon by Thomas. But these present examples are enough to enable us to understand that the Christological and soteriological impact of the procession of the Spirit *a Filio* lies at the heart of Thomas's reading of Scripture, and that this profoundly held conviction underlies his thinking. (We may remember that, in a very different historical and theological context, Karl Barth in the twentieth century was moved by a similar motive to make an extremely vigorous defense of the Latin doctrine concerning the procession of the Holy Spirit *a Filio*.)[22] This teaching may be summed up in the principle of the economic Trinity formulated by Albert the Great: "The Spirit who is sent brings back *(convertit)* to himself and to the Son, the Son brings back to himself and to the Father. . . . The person who proceeds from another person brings back to that other person, according to the order of nature, what he has received from that other person."[23] Thus the specific effect of the Son's mission from Thomas's viewpoint as well is to lead to the Father, "and in the same way, the specific mission of the Holy Spirit is to lead the faithful to the Son."[24] The structure of the temporal mission or procession reproduces and expresses the fundamental structure of the eternal procession. The grace of the Holy Spirit, drawn from Christ and drawing us toward and into the Son, is thus intrinsically linked to the eternal procession of the Spirit *a Patre et a Filio*.

---

[22] Karl Barth, *Dogmatique,* vol. I, 1/2 (Geneva: Labor et Fides, 1953), pp. 167–78; vol. I, 2/2 (Geneva, Labor et Fides, 1954), pp. 43–44.

[23] Albert, I *Sent.,* d. 31, a. 14, ad quaest. 2: "Spiritus missus convertit in se et in Filium, et Filius in se et in Patrem. . . . Persona enim quae est ab alia, refert in eam per naturae ordinem quod habet ab ea." Albert is fully aware of the relationship between this fundamental structure and the *Filioque* (ibid.: "et ideo constat errare Graecos").

[24] *Super Ioan.* 14:26 (#1958): "Nam, sicut effectus missionis Filii fuit ducere ad Patrem, ita effectus missionis Spiritus sancti est ducere fideles ad Filium." For further insight into this point, see Emile Bailleux, "Le Christ et son Esprit," *RT* 73 (1973): 373–400.

A Multisided Question within a Whole

In view of Thomas's vast teachings on the procession of the Spirit *a Filio*, care should be taken not to look at any particular article devoted to this problem in isolation, for the doctrine of the procession of the Holy Spirit *a Filio* becomes clear in the light of the writings on pneumatology as a whole, and also indicates various complementary approaches which should be taken into account.

The Basic Feature of Pneumatology

From the *Contra Gentiles* onward, Thomas develops his pneumatology around the theme of the love with which God loves himself: a loving momentum, affection, or impulse present in the divine will, presupposing the procession of the Word. This theological development is the result firstly of a systematic reading of Scripture concerning the work of the Holy Spirit, and Thomas compiles a large dossier on this subject which provides a foundation for and confirmation of the theological direction he is taking.[25] In terms of speculative theology, this development was made possible by the progress of his doctrine on the Word, and also through a deeper appreciation of the heritage of Augustine and of Aristotelian psychology. The doctrine of the procession of the Spirit *a Filio* does not always feature directly in this work, but was to benefit through the clarification offered by the analogy of the word and love (love follows knowledge, proceeding from the concept of the word).[26]

The Augustinian perspective of mutual love, which Thomas does not abandon but no longer retains as the first principle of his pneumatology, was in its turn to throw a particularly helpful light on the doctrine of the procession of the Holy Spirit *a Patre* and *a Filio* (Love of the Father and of the Son). It also clarifies the soteriological implications of this doctrine, for it is through the Spirit by whom the Father and the Son love each other that they also love all

---

[25] See ch. 3 above.

[26] See for example *SCG* IV, ch. 20 (#3558–59) and the implications in ch. 24 (#3617).

creatures, in the order of creation and in the order of grace.[27] Like Augustine, Thomas would moreover see the very name "Holy Spirit" as being indicative of the procession *a Patre* and *a Filio*, because of the *"communitas"* which the expression suggests.[28] In the continuation of the analytical study of the names "Holy Spirit" and "Love," the name of "Gift" *(donum)* was to reveal the same structure.[29] The fundamental structure of pneumatology, in terms of its internal coherence, therefore requires and presupposes the procession of the Spirit *a Filio*.

The Procession of the Holy Spirit a Patre per Filium *and the Other Formulae*

The Holy Spirit proceeds from the Father through the Son *(per Filium)*. Thomas continually attributes great importance to this traditional formula, in the commentary on the *Sentences* and elsewhere,[30] as is evident from the fact that he devotes an entire article to it in the *Summa theologiae*. From the commentary on the *Sentences* onward, the procession *per Filium* is clearly interpreted in the sense of the *ordo naturae*, that is to say of the order in the Trinity: *quia Filius est ex Patre et Spiritus sanctus simul a Patre et Filio*. In the commentary on the *Sentences*, perhaps influenced to a greater extent by his sources (especially Bonaventure), Thomas also emphasizes the concept of mediation *(mediatio)* or quasi-mediation.[31] This *mediatio* of the Son, expressed in the formula *per Filium*, should not be understood in the sense of power in respect of notional acts or in the sense of essence, but in the context of the supposita of the spiration. Such a "mediation" of the Son does not of course impugn the immediacy of the

---

[27] Cf. *ST* I, q. 37, a. 2.

[28] Cf. *ST* I, q. 36, a. 1: ". . . Ex ipsa communitate eius quod dicitur *Spiritus sanctus*. Ut enim Augustinus dicit, XV *De Trin.*, 'Quia Spiritus sanctus communis est ambobus, id vocatur ipse proprie quod ambo communiter'" (Augustine, *De Trinitate* XV, XIX, 37; cf. *De Trinitate* V, XI, 12).

[29] Because the "reason" for a gift follows on immediately from the "reason" of love (*ST* I, q. 38, a. 2; I *Sent.*, d. 18, q. un., a. 2).

[30] I *Sent.*, d. 12, q. un., a. 3 (chiefly ad 4); CEG II, ch. 8; *De potentia*, q. 10, a. 4; q. 10, a. 5, ad 14; *ST* I, q. 36, a. 3.

[31] I *Sent.*, d. 12, q. un., a. 3.

procession of the Holy Spirit *a Patre*.[32] What it does rather is give
clear expression, in terms of personal operation, to the *auctoritas*
belonging to the Father, that is the rightful place of the Father as
source or principle without principle in the Trinity. By employing
these concepts, Thomas is coming close to the eastern idea of the
monarchy of the Father, although evidently from a point of view
which remains that of the western Church. He is also careful to point
out that when we speak of the mediation of the Son or of the procession *per Filium*, we are not referring to an instrumental or ministerial
causality, nor of the property of a secondary cause, for there is no difference between the Father and the Son in terms of principle of operation *(principium operationis)*. The distinction articulated by these
formulae concerns the persons (the *operantes*): In receiving the power
of spiration from the Father, the Son is in a certain manner a *medium*
in the personal act of the Father *auctor*.[33] In addition, any idea of one
person taking priority over another is dispelled[34] (in contrast to
Bonaventure, Thomas also refuses to accept references to a "hierarchy" in the Trinity,[35] in any strict sense), as well as any idea of a
"greater" or a "lesser": The Holy Spirit does not proceed "to a greater
extent" nor "more fully" from the Father than from the Son.[36]
Thomas does, however, accept references to the Holy Spirit proceeding principally *(principaliter)* from the Father, following Albert who
was particularly given to using this Augustinian formula.[37] The pro-

---

[32] I *Sent.*, d. 12, q. un., a. 3, ad 2 and ad 4; *ST* I, q. 36, a. 3, ad 1 and ad 4.

[33] I *Sent.*, d. 12, q. un., a. 3, ad 4; *ST* I, q. 36, a. 3.

[34] I *Sent.*, d. 9, q. 2, a. 1; d. 12, q. un., a. 1. The Son, like the Father and the
Holy Spirit, is *simpliciter primum* (I *Sent.*, d. 9, q. 2, a. 1, contra). For Thomas,
there is nothing really *"prior"* in God: His view differs in this respect from
Bonaventure's, who accepts a certain degree of priority, notably through his
concept of *primitas* in the person of the Father. Bonaventure thus comes closer
to the Greek idea of the monarchy of the Father. (This does not however
encourage him to show any greater understanding as regards the rejection of
the *Filioque*, as his lively polemics demonstrate).

[35] Bonaventure, II *Sent.*, d. 9, *Praenotata;* Thomas, II *Sent.*, d. 9, q. un., a. 1, ad 6.

[36] Thomas, I *Sent.*, d. 12, q. un., a. 2.

[37] Cf. Albert, I *Sent.*, d. 12, a. 4 and 5. Albert also interprets this formula using
the auctoritas of the Father. For St. Thomas, see I *Sent.*, d. 12, exp. text.
Thomas's articles in this dist. 12 are very much in line with and consolidate the
explanations given by Albert. The expression *principaliter*, in this context,

cession *principaliter a Patre*, which recalls the theme of Father as *"archè"* in the Greek theological tradition, is also rigorously interpreted in the sense of the order of origin which it designates.

It is important that the full force of Thomas's insistence on the procession of the Spirit *a Patre per Filium* is understood. The themes of the order of origin and of the *auctoritas* of the Father, representing in their own way in a Latin context the *"taxis"* (order) and the "monarchy" of Cappadocian triadology, demonstrate that part of the Greek heritage which Thomas, particularly through Augustine, was able to incorporate into his Trinitarian theology. The expression *per Filium* thus constitutes an additional means of grasping the meaning of *ex Filio* or *a Filio*. Although, for Thomas, the affirmation of the procession *per Filium* necessarily implies that of the procession *a Filio*,[38] the two formulae are not interchangeable. One gives more emphasis to the order of and distinction between the persons, the other stresses their unity. The first ensures that this unity is not seen as being dissolved within an undifferentiated essence, and the second prevents the *per Filium* being understood in terms of an inferior or separate cause. As Venance Grumel noted, "the two need to be put together in order to arrive at an expression which fully conveys the dogma of the procession of the Holy Spirit."[39]

The Unity of the Principle and the Plurality of Persons

The Father and the Son are one single principle *(unum principium)* of the Holy Spirit.[40] It is important to make this clear, for it rules out any possibility of dual principles as well as any "subordinationism"

---

comes from Augustine, *De Trinitate* XV, XVII, 29, related by Peter Lombard, *Sententiae*, Book I, dist. 12, ch. 2.

[38] CEG II, ch. 8; *De potentia*, q. 10, a. 4; *ST* I, q. 36, a. 2. The reason for this is that any relationship of origin recognized between the Son and the Holy Spirit, and therefore also that expressed in the formula *per Filium*, implies the procession *a Filio*.

[39] V. Grumel, "Saint Thomas et la doctrine des Grecs," p. 275.

[40] I *Sent.*, d. 29, q. un., a. 3 and 4; *ST* I, q. 36, a. 4.

which would undermine the equality and the simplicity of the divine persons. However, for Thomas, there is perfect unity in the principle of spiration, by virtue of the unity of the power of spiration in the Father and in the Son (the shared notion of active spiration[41]). It must be emphasized that, for Thomas, the balance between the plurality of the persons who breathe the Spirit and the unity of the principle of the Spirit is ensured by the absolutely fundamental distinction between the person or suppositum on one hand and the power of notional acts on the other.

Thomas is here presenting a distinction to which too little attention is generally paid: The distinction between the "condition of the agent" *(conditio agentis)* and the "principle of the act" *(principium actionis)*.[42] In terms of the condition of the agent, the Father and the Son are indeed considered as two distinct persons to whom the act of spiration is attributed (acts are the work of "supposits"). This plurality of *supposita* is further explained by the theme of the mutual love of the Father and the Son.[43] In this context, the spiration of the Spirit "requires a prior distinction of 'supposits' (the Father and the Son): Coming in a certain manner from two supposita to the extent that they are distinct, since it is a personal act."[44] We should note that this theme is not an indication of any diffidence of the young theologian, but was indeed to feature in the mature teachings of the *Summa theologiae*: "But if we consider the 'supposits' of the spiration, then we may say that the Holy Spirit proceeds from the Father and the Son, as distinct;

---

[41] In the interests of precision, the term "notion" is preferred here to "property" since active spiration is not peculiar to a single person; the relevant property in the procession of the Spirit is actually that of *processio* or of "passive spiration," in other words the relation of origin of the Holy Spirit in regard to the Father and the Son, which constitutes the person of the Spirit; *ST* I, q. 32, a. 3.

[42] I *Sent.*, d. 11, q. un., a. 2. The *Summa theologiae* does not formulate this distinction in these terms, but the same thinking is evident in it.

[43] See I *Sent.*, d. 10, q. un., a. 5, ad 1.

[44] I *Sent.*, d. 29, q. un., a. 4, ad 2: "Quia spiratio praeexigit distinctionem in suppositis: unde est aliquo modo a pluribus suppositis inquantum distincta sunt, cum sit opus personalis."

for he proceeds from them as the unitive love of both."[45] But although the "condition of the agent" is characterized by the personal distinction of the Father and the Son, and understood in terms of the Augustinian theme of mutual love, the same may not be said for the "principle of the act." This principle of the act is the power in respect of notional acts, in this case the "power of spiration" common to the Father and the Son, which the Father communicates to the Son by the generation, and which is numerically one and the same in the two persons. It is this which justifies the affirmation of the unicity of the principle of spiration (the power designates the principle of action) and which makes legitimate the affirmation of one single "Spirator" (*unus Spirator*, Father and Son).[46]

The Procession and the Ekporeusis

The "procession" in God designates the immanent action by which one person takes his origin from another. Understood as an act or an operation perceived as being the foundation of the relationship,[47] the procession is the same reality as the subsistent relationship itself. To speak of the procession of the Spirit is thus nothing else than to speak of the *relation* by which the Spirit is constituted as a divine person within the Trinity. Thomas warns us of the dangers of an ill-considered use of metaphor, and particularly of the idea of a "local procession" (*ab uno in alium*, the movement of one term toward another),[48] which Latin theologians sometimes suspect of implying an affinity with the Greek (platonic?) conception of the divine procession and of having influenced the Greek rejection of the Latin doctrine.[49] A

---

[45] *ST* I, q. 36, a. 4, ad 1: "Si vero considerentur supposita spirationis, sic Spiritus sanctus procedit a Patre et Filio ut sunt plures: procedit enim ab eis ut amor unitivus duorum;" cf. ad 7.

[46] *ST* I, q. 36, a. 4, ad 7. In his commentary on the *Sentences* (I *Sent.*, d. 11, q. un., a. 4; d. 29, q. 1, a. 4, ad 2), Thomas uses the formula *duo spiratores*; the change in terminology is however connected with a deeper understanding of this term's mode of signification, rather than with doctrinal principles.

[47] Cf. *ST* I, q. 27, a. 1.

[48] I *Sent.*, d. 13, q. 1, a. 1.

[49] See for example Bonaventure, I *Sent.*, d. 11, a. un., q. 1, concl.

second problem which directly concerns this discussion arises with
the use of the term *processio* in the context of the origin of the Son
and of the Holy Spirit. Thomas makes use of it to designate the two
origins, taking care not to regard it as a generic concept coupled with
a specific concept, which would make it a universal and a particular
concept: He endows it with only one "common reason" (procession
of the Son and of the Holy Spirit) resulting from our consideration of
the two "determined reasons" (generation and spiration).[50] If we
name the origin of the Holy Spirit by the term "procession," Thomas
explains, it is because of the absence of a procession of a subsistent
being through the impulse of the will or of love in our world (in contrast with generation, for which we possess an appropriate word),
despite the fact that other reasons might conveniently be cited
(including the procession of the Spirit *a Filio*!).[51] In the theory of
notions, the term *processio* was to be used exclusively to name the
relation of spiration ("passive" spiration), that is the personal property
of the Holy Spirit.[52]

Latin theology possesses a rich vocabulary which Thomas
exploits to the full: The Spirit is "spirated" *(spirare)* and "originated"
(deoriginare) by the Father and the Son, he "emanates" *(emanare)* and
"flows forth" *(profluere)* from the Father and from the Son who are
described as "principle" *(principium)*, "author" *(auctor)*, and "source"
(fons) of the Spirit.[53] As regards the term "procession," there are
numerous instances of Thomas making every effort to legitimize its
use for the designation of the relation of the Holy Spirit regarding
the Son.[54] His chief reason, as he constantly explains, is connected
with the generality of this term: "The term 'procession,' out of all
the words concerning the origin, is the most common and the least

---

[50] Thomas, I *Sent.,* d. 13, q. 1, a. 3.

[51] I *Sent.,* d. 13, q. 1, a. 3, ad 2. Proceeding from the Son who proceeds from the
Father, the Holy Spirit "maxime accedit ad processionem." Cf. *ST* I, q. 27, a.
4; q. 28, a. 4: "Processio vero amoris non habet nomen proprium."

[52] See for example *ST* I, q. 28, a. 4; q. 32, a. 3.

[53] CEG II, ch. 15–25. All of this vocabulary is taken from texts examined here by
Thomas.

[54] CEG II, ch. 26–27; *SCG* IV, ch 24 (#3610); *De potentia,* q. 10, a. 4, ad 13; *ST*
I, q. 36, a. 2; *In Ioan.* 15:26 (#2064).

closely defined in terms of any given form of origin. Whenever anything [comes] in some way from another, we habitually say that it 'proceeds' from that other."[55] However, following the rules of theological grammar, it is perfectly appropriate to apply the most general and common terms to God, since they are less likely than other terms to carry particular connotations which are best avoided. For Thomas, steeped in the Latin tradition, the vocabulary of the *processio* (like that of *principium*)[56] seems the most suitable for signifying the relation of the Holy Spirit with regard to the Son.

The Angelic Doctor has not however grasped exactly why the "Greeks" can accept references to the Spirit flowing from the Son or "being poured out" by him *(profluit, procheitai)*, but cannot accept references in this context to "procession" (*procedere*, which is the translation of the verb *ekporeuetai* in John's gospel). In the eyes of the orthodox East, *ekporeusis* can only have the Father as principle. Modern studies agree about the need to emphasize this difference in Latin and Greek vocabulary, and about the resulting difficulties in mutual comprehension between East and West. This point is too well-known for us to linger over.[57]

Thomas proves himself to be less ignorant on this matter, however, than we often imagine. On one hand, he is perfectly aware of the distinction between the temporal gift of the Spirit and his eternal procession; he refers to it on numerous occasions (mission and procession), and he also provides references to eastern medieval texts which are perfectly clear on the subject (notably Theophylactus).[58] On the other hand, even if he does not understand the details of the distinction between the *procession* and the *ekporeusis*, he has nonetheless grasped the fundamental issue and raises it when he discusses the

---

[55] CEG II, ch 26: "Verbum enim 'processionis' inter omnia quae ad originem pertinent magis invenitur *esse* commune et minus modum originis determinare. Quicquid enim quocumque modo est ab aliquo, secundum consuetum modum loquendi ab ipso procedere dicimus."

[56] *De potentia*, q. 10, a. 1, ad 9: "Inter omnia ad originem spectantia magis convenit in divines hoc nomen principium." See also *ST* I, q. 33, a. 1.

[57] See V. Grumel, "Saint Thomas et la doctrine des Grecs;" Y. Congar, *Je crois en l'Esprit-Saint*, vol. 3, p. 170.

[58] *Catena in Ioan.* 15:26 (p. 535).

question of the preposition *ek (ex, ab)*. Observations on this point appear as early as the commentary on the *Sentences*: "Strictly speaking, we say that the Holy Spirit proceeds from the Father *(a Patre)*, chiefly because this preposition *'a,'* for the Greeks, designates the relation to the first origin *(prima origo)*: This is why the Greeks do not speak of the lake proceeding from the river *(lacus sit a rivo)* but from the source *(est a fonte)*; and this is also the reason why they refuse to concede that the Holy Spirit proceeds from the Son *(quod sit a Filio)* but rather from the Father *(a Patre)*. Nevertheless we should not say that he does not actually proceed also from the Son, who is, with the Father, one single principle of the Holy Spirit."[59] Thomas repeats the point in his commentary on St. John: "Certain Greeks say that we should not speak of the Holy Spirit proceeding from the Son *(procedere a Filio)*, for this preposition *'a,'* or *'ab,'* in their eyes designates the principle without principle *(principium non de principio)*, which only applies to the Father. But this is not a compelling reason."[60] This is certainly the most usual sense of the preposition *'ek,'* and we can see that Thomas is investing it with the meaning present in *ekporeusis* for the East (relation of origin as regards the "first Source" or the "Principle without principle"), but he has grasped the different or more precise sense which the Greeks attribute to the words. This observation confirms the close attention which Thomas constantly paid to problems of translation.[61] This should be remembered when reference is made in this context to misunderstandings on the level of vocabulary regarding the question of the procession of the Holy Spirit. *Thomas, however, does not contest*

---

[59] I *Sent.*, d. 12, q. 1, a. 2, ad 3.

[60] *In Ioan.* 15:26 (#2065): "Dicunt tamen aliqui Graecorum, quod non est dicendum Spiritum sanctum procedere *a Filio*, quia haec praepositio *a* vel *ab* apud eos designat principium non de principio, quod convenit soli Patri. Sed hoc non cogit: quia Filius cum Patre est unum principium Spiritus sancti." That which Thomas attributes here to the preposition alone corresponds fairly exactly to the signification of *ekporeusis* in the Greek sense.

[61] We may remember, for example, the Prologue to the *Contra errores Graecorum*. Trinitarian theology moreover provides one of the rare frameworks in which Thomas engages in discussions about translation, notably in connection with the terms *hypostasis, ousia, ousiosis,* etc; see for example *ST* I, q. 29, a. 2.

the Greek signification of a "first origin." He accepts this but, because of the unity of the spiratory principle, refuses to accept that this *relatio ad primam originem* can only be applied to the Father "for the Son is with the Father one single principle of the Holy Spirit." It is evident from this that in Thomas's judgment, the fundamental problem lies not within the field of vocabulary, where he knows there is a certain amount of discordant interpretation, but within the field of speculative theology, regarding the structure of Trinitarian doctrine.

The Biblical Dossier of the Procession of the Spirit *a Filio*

The main foundation of Thomas's belief is not rational theological argument; it is not the evidentes rationes, even though they constitute the right and proper tool for the theologian when he is applying himself to the work of demonstrating the intelligibility of the truths of the faith. "The Word of God, explained by the Church, is alone instantly homogeneous with the faith. This Word was also the foundation for belief among Christians in the West."[62] Thomas may turn his attention to scriptural foundations at different points in the various works where he deals with the procession of the Spirit *a Filio*, but there should be no mistake: In each case, in accordance with his unfailingly hermeneutic approach, it is Scripture which provides the primary source of theological work.[63] The range of scriptural themes should therefore be considered in the light of the methodological features of each work.

Scripture is thus given prominence in the chapters of the *Contra Gentiles* devoted to the procession of the Spirit *a Filio*, in line with the author's purpose and with the methodology of this work.[64] The same explanation lies behind the predominance of the Church Fathers in the *Contra errores Graecorum*, as well as the largely speculative emphasis of the *Disputed Questions de Potentia* and of the

---

[62] H.-F. Dondaine, "La théologie latine," p. 217.

[63] *ST* I, q. 1, a. 8, ad 2.

[64] *SCG* IV, ch. 24 (Scripture, Fathers/Councils, reason) and ch. 25 (Scripture, Fathers/Councils, reason).

Summa theologiae. But despite the various organizational structures, we are constantly confronted by the tripartite arrangement of Scripture, Fathers/Councils, and theological reason. This fact is worth mentioning, for only a few questions prompted Thomas to work his way through this three-stage process of argument, no doubt because of the "apologetic" approach motivating him here (the purpose is to show the *truth* of the faith). There is only one exception among the major works: the commentary on the *Sentences.* In this work undertaken when Thomas was a young man, and when his thinking on the procession of the Spirit *a Filio* was hugely influenced by Albert the Great, we cannot fail to be struck by the almost exclusively rational atmosphere dominating the question: Scripture takes up only a limited amount of space, and there is a relative paucity of patristic references.[65] This observation, taken in the context of the works as a whole, seems to be extremely revealing: Thomas's work consisted of a constant quest to enrich and deepen his understanding of pneumatology, involving speculative theology but primarily by means of biblical and patristic sources.

In order to illustrate the soteriological issues of the question, we referred earlier to several biblical passages which Thomas explores during his reflections on the procession of the Holy Spirit. Three principal themes emerge however, appearing first in the *Contra errores Graecorum* and the *Contra Gentiles*, by means of which Thomas structures his reading of Scripture: firstly, the property of the Spirit as Spirit *of the Son*; secondly, the mission *a Filio*; and thirdly, the *de meo accipiet* verse (Jn 16:14).[66]

---

[65] It can easily be shown that all the arguments in I *Sent.*, d. 11, q. un., a. 1 *(utrum Spiritus sanctus procedat a Patre et Filio)* are drawn from Albert, from Bonaventure, and from the *Summa fratris Alexandri*; the same observation applies to the *expositio textus* of this dist. 11, where we find a brief consideration of two biblical arguments: The Spirit is the Spirit of the Son, and he is sent by the Son.

[66] These three themes are evidently nothing new in the literature on the *Filioque*; we can be sure of this by looking at, for example, Bonaventure, I *Sent.*, d. 11, a. un., q. 1, contra 7–9. But their systematic development, as well as the progressive emphasis on the third theme, seems to be characteristic of Thomas. The themes are first presented in their fully developed form in CEG I, ch. 1–3.

The Spirit of the Son

The first biblical argument considers the relation of the Spirit to the Son designated in the expression "Spirit of the Son" *(Spiritus Filii).*[67] This theme, which Thomas generally places at the head of his expositions and judges to be "self-evident" on the basis of Scripture,[68] brings together several biblical expressions: "Spirit of Jesus" (Acts 16:7), "Spirit of Christ" (Rom 8:9), "Spirit of Truth" (Jn 15:26), "Spirit of Life" (Rom 8:2), and "Spirit of the Son of God" (Gal 4:6). Thomas works to show both that the Spirit of the Father is the Spirit of the Son, and that the relation indicated in this genitive is not limited to Jesus' humanity filled with grace (Lk 4:1), but also on another level concerns his divinity. This is where the soteriological argument comes in: The Spirit given by the Father makes us truly "sons of God" (adoptive filiation through grace) because, being the Spirit of the Son, he configures us to the "natural" Son by assimilation to him (Rom 8:29; the filiation through grace is a participation in the divine natural filiation of Christ). We become members "of Christ" because we receive the Spirit "of Christ" who unites us with the one from whom he proceeds.[69] For Thomas, this relation to the Son cannot be fully understood without the procession of the Spirit *a Filio* and necessarily requires affirmation of it, for—and this is a crucial point—any relation involving a real distinction between the divine persons must be understood in terms of some origin. But any relation of origin, however it is formulated, necessarily implies the procession *ab alio.* This structural form of interpretation of texts was to be applied in the examination of all the principal themes. We detect here a permanent characteristic of Thomas's biblical exegesis which, even at this initial level, brings in fundamental theological principles (distinction–origin–procession), to such an extent that we sometimes see no marked methodological difference between the theological

[67] CEG II, ch. 1; *SCG* IV, ch. 24 (#3606); *De potentia,* q. 10, a. 4; *In Rom.* 8:9 (#627); cf. *ST* I, q. 36, a. 2.
[68] *SCG* IV, ch. 24 (#3606).
[69] *In Rom.* 8:9 (#627).

syntheses and the scriptural commentaries concerning the biblical passages of this dossier.[70]

The Spirit Sent and Given by the Son

Thomas makes a clear distinction between the eternal procession and the temporal mission or procession. This does not prevent the temporal procession *a Filio* involving the eternal procession *a Filio* in the fullest sense, for it "includes" this eternal procession, adding to it the temporal effect of grace by virtue of which we say that the person is "sent" or "given."[71] Because of this, the personal relation of the principle engaged in the mission is absolutely identical to that of the eternal procession, even though the temporal relationship exists only in the mission. This is why Thomas, who demonstrates that he is in perfect agreement with the Greek theologians in making a rigorous distinction between the mission and the eternal procession,[72] can nonetheless make use of it in his argument in favor of the *Filioque*. He is also aware, from the period of the *Contra errores Graecorum* at least, that the concept of mission can be approached in different ways. For St. Augustine, the relationship with the created effect is sometimes more important than the order of eternal origin. Augustine attributes the mission solely to the person who proceeds (Son and Spirit), but considers it acceptable to say that the Son is sent by the Spirit or that the Spirit is sent by himself or by the Trinity as a whole.[73] For others, the divine person is sent only by the person from whom he proceeds eternally. Thomas accepts both conceptions, seeing them both to be true, depending upon whether it is the temporal effect or the eternal origin which is being considered (the two aspects of the mission), but he concentrates here on the second approach

---

[70] The most striking example is undoubtedly *In Ioan.* 15:26 (#2061–65), which presents a complete survey of the matter in a form comparable to that of a *Summa theologiae.*

[71] I *Sent.,* d. 14, q. 1, a. 2; *ST* I, q. 43, a. 2.

[72] Reference may be made for example to the passage by Theophylactus cited in the *Catena in Ioan.* 15:26 (p. 535).

[73] Augustine (*De Trinitate* II, V, 8–9) explains it through the inseparability of the action of divine persons in the world; the emphasis is thus less on the order of origin than on the created effect.

which provides him with a solid argument in support of his exposition of the procession of the Spirit.[74] From this point on, by taking up the argument outlined above (distinction, *auctoritas*, procession *ab alio*), he has no difficulty in demonstrating that the Holy Spirit sent by the Son exists and proceeds "infallibly" from him.

Thomas does not restrict himself to carrying out a dry analysis of the structure of the concept of temporal procession. He also engages in an exploration of sanctification, filiation, and all the works of the Spirit. Thomas explains in a general way in his commentary on St. John's Gospel that the Holy Spirit is said to be "sent" *(dicitur mitti)* by the Father and the Son so that his eternal procession *ab alio* may be made manifest, that is to say, *a Patre et Filio*.[75] This is also how Thomas understands Christ's gift of the Spirit to his disciples for the remission of sins *(demonstratio* of the procession *a Patre et a Filio*).[76] The same applies to the glorification of the Son by the Spirit (Jn 16:14; *ille me clarificabit*), since it is the work of the person who proceeds to reveal the person from whom he proceeds,[77] and so forth. This theme of the mission expresses the same fundamental structure of the economic Trinity mentioned earlier. We should read these passages in the light of those in which Thomas explains the patristic formula of the operation of the Son "through the Holy Spirit" *(Filius operatur per Spiritum sanctum)*, with reference to Rom 15:18–19, 1 Cor 2:10, and Heb 9:14.[78] Since the Holy Spirit cannot take the role of a principle of operation for the Son (for the Son does not proceed from the Spirit), and since we must rule out any ministerial or instrumental action of the Spirit (the error of the semi-Arians), the

---

[74] CEG I, ch. 14. Regarding the second conception, Thomas lists here Athanasius of Alexandria, Hilary of Poitiers, and Basil of Caesaria; *De potentia*, q. 10, a. 4, ad 14; *ST* I, q. 43, a. 8.

[75] *In Ioan.* 15:26 (#2061): "Dicitur autem mitti ut ostendatur processio ipsius ab alio. . . . Est etiam attendendum quod missio Spiritus sancti communiter est a Patre et Filio."

[76] *In Ioan.* 20:22 (#2538).

[77] *In Ioan.* 16:14 (#2107); see note 19 above.

[78] I *Sent.*, d. 12, q. un., a. 3, ad 4; CEG II, ch. 4; *De potentia*, q. 10, a. 4. Thomas's Eastern patristic references are here, as often elsewhere, of the Alexandrian School; we note in particular the ninth anathema of Cyril of Alexandria.

expression *per Spiritum* can only signify the power of operation which
the Holy Spirit receives from the Son through his procession. Using
another set of terms, we can say that the "economy" has its roots in
"theology," and reveals its very structure. This flotilla of scriptural texts,
anchored together by a theological reading, leaves Thomas with no
doubts: Sent by the Son, the Holy Spirit proceeds eternally from him.

"He Will Glorify Me, Because He Will Take of Mine and Declare It to You"

Starting with the *Contra errores Graecorum*, Thomas adds to the two
preceding themes his analysis of the verse of Jn 16:14, *Ille me clarificabit quia de meo accipiet et annuntiabit vobis.* The verse had not
been mentioned in the commentary on the *Sentences*, but henceforth plays an increasingly important role in Thomas's doctrine.[79]
In the *Summa theologiae*, he sums up its value as follows:

> Although we do not find it verbally expressed *(per verba)* in
> Holy Scripture that the Holy Spirit proceeds from the Son,
> still we do find it in the sense *(quantum ad sensum)* of
> Scripture, especially *(praecipue)* where the Son says, speak-
> ing of the Holy Spirit, "He will glorify Me, because He
> shall receive of Mine."[80]

The critical significance of placing this passage at this particular
point is confirmed by the absence of other scriptural texts of the
same kind in this article of the *Summa theologiae*, and this is therefore an indication that the interpretation given should be examined
with particular attention. As is often the case with Thomas, the
interpretation follows the grammatical construction of the sentence
very closely. *De meo*, on one hand, indicates the consubstantiality of
the Son and the Holy Spirit. This presents no difficulty: The Spirit
receives the entire substance of the Father and of the Son, that is the
divine essence in its entirety. In receiving that which belongs to the

[79] CEG II, ch. 3; *SCG* IV, ch. 24 (#3608); *ST* I, q. 36, a. 2, ad 1; *In Ioan.*
16:14–15 (#2107–15).

[80] *ST* I, q. 36, a. 2, ad 1. The translation "of mine," despite its lack of elegance,
must be preserved in order to follow the line of argument: *de meo—a Filio.*

Father and the Son, the Spirit does not however receive paternity and filiation, because they are incommunicable properties of the divine persons: He receives, however, that essence which is truly identical, in each person, with the personal property. Both the distinction of the persons by means of their properties, and their perfect consubstantiality, are therefore firmly upheld by this verse from St. John. However, in God, that which is communicated *(quod communicatur)* is truly identified with that by which it is communicated *(quo communicatur)*,[81] in such a way that the principle of communication and the "subject matter" of the communication are identical: It is the same essence or divine substance *which* is communicated or given to the Son and to the Holy Spirit, and *by which* the Father gives or communicates it. If therefore the divine essence is communicated to the Holy Spirit, this essence communicated *(de meo)* is really identical to the principle of the communication. However, the essence is common to the Father and to the Son, without exception ("All that the Father has is mine"). It follows then that if the Holy Spirit receives *from the Father* he receives also *from the Son.*

We must not be misled by the emphasis given here to essence: There is no question of reviving the argument of "essentialism," turning the essence into the agent of the notional act. What Thomas has in mind is the assimilation of the person proceeding into the person from whom he proceeds: an assimilation which is the foundation of their consubstantiality, without prejudice to their incommunicable properties, by virtue of the principle of the communication of the divine nature to the person. This is moreover one of the principal issues at stake in the essential *(in recto)* signification of the power in respect of notional acts.[82] If the Spirit were to receive "that which is of the Son" *(quod est Filii)* without receiving it *a Filio,* this would indicate that the Son would be excluded from the notional act of giving that which is "his *(de meo)*." According to the words of Christ in St. John's gospel, however, "All that the Father

---

81 This identity is developed at length in *De potentia*, q. 2, a. 1; see Gregory M. Reichberg, "La communication de la nature divine en Dieu selon Thomas d'Aquin," *RT* 93 (1993): 50–65.

82 *ST* I, q. 41, a. 5.

has is mine *(mea sunt)*. For this reason I said that he will take what is mine . . ." (Jn 16:15).[83] From Thomas's point of view, it would therefore be impossible to avoid implying a division of the divine essence or an attack on the perfect consubstantiality of the Father and of the Son. Finally, let us note that, in accordance with the text of St. John, this analysis has a bearing also upon the economic Trinity, since that which the Holy Spirit makes known to the disciples *(et annuntiabit vobis)* is precisely this "possession" of the Son which he receives through his eternal procession, thus allowing us to participate in the divine nature of the Savior.

The patristic sources of this interpretation are made clear in the Catena on St. John. They consist of Augustine in his *Homilies on John* and, further back still, Hilary of Poitiers and Didymus the Blind. Thomas actually includes a text by Hilary explaining that "the Lord has left us in no doubt as to whether we should think that the Paraclete Spirit is *ex Patre* or *ex Filio*." His exegesis, which contains the germ of that developed by Thomas, also shows that if the Holy Spirit receives everything *a Patre*, the clear implication is that he receives the same *a Filio*.[84] Didymus is cited in the Latin translation of Jerome, and provides Thomas with the following exegesis: The very substance of the Holy Spirit is none other than that which is given to him *a Filio*, such that what he receives from the Father is no different to what he receives from the Son.[85] These

---

[83] *In Ioan.* 16:14–15 (#2114–15).

[84] *Catena in Ioan.* 16:14–15 (p. 541): "Hilarius De Trin. Non ergo in incerto Dominus reliquit, utrum ex Patre an ex Filio Spiritus paraclitus esse putetur. . . . Cum enim ait omnia quaecumque habet Pater, sua esse, et idcirco dixisse, de suo accipiendum esse, docet etiam a Patre accipienda, a se tamen accipi, quia omnia quae Patris sunt, sua sunt." This extract deserves to be read in the context of the entire passage: Hilary, *De Trinitate* VIII, ch. 20 (CCSL 62A, 331–32).

[85] *Catena in Ioan.* 16:14–15 (p. 541): "Didymus. Siquidem et Filius eadem a Patre suscipere dicitur in quibus ipse subsistit: neque enim quid aliud est Filius, exceptis his quae ei dantur a Patre; neque alia est Spiritus sancti substantia praeter id quod datur a Filio. . . . Cave autem ne cum ista dicuntur, putes rem esse aliquam et possessionem quae a Patre habeatur, ac a Filio;" Didymus, *De Spiritu sancto* (Hieronymo interprete), ch. 37 (PL 23, 134–35). Cf. *SCG* IV, ch. 24 (#3609); *In Ioan.* 16:15 (#2114).

Patristic references were to reappear in various works, notably in the *Lectura in Ioannem*, and all the indications are that they convinced Thomas of the crucial importance, for the doctrine of the procession of the Spirit *a Patre* and *a Filio*, of this passage from the fourth gospel.

"Spiritus Veritatis Qui a Patre Procedit"

The absence of any mention of the Son in the text of Jn 15:26 ("the Spirit of truth who comes *from the Father*") of course presents a difficulty which Thomas does not fail to consider carefully. His exegesis, which shows no particular originality but exhibits a remarkable wealth of details, is in the vein of the Augustinian teaching so widespread among medieval theologians. The problem of the absence of any mention of one divine person, and the problem of "exclusive expressions" (a mention of one divine person without that of another) constitute typical questions for discussion in the scholastic tradition, and Thomas does little more than repeat the traditional responses.[86] The rule is as follows: The divine persons are always "jointly understood" in the mention of one of them, and all that is said of one divine person should be equally attributed to the other divine persons, except when it is a matter of incommunicable personal properties. The traditional examples given are notably Mt 11:27 ("no one knows the Son except the Father") and Jn 17:3 ("that they may know you, the only true God"). Thus, given that spiration of the Spirit belongs neither to the property of paternity nor of filiation, "When it is said in the Gospel that the Holy Spirit proceeds from the Father, we should understand that he proceeds also from the Son."[87] On the basis of the point made above, Thomas is able to add that, even if the biblical text were to consist of the expression "the Spirit of truth who comes from the Father *alone*," it would still not exclude the Son.[88] This rule of interpretation does not moreover concern only biblical hermeneutics.

---

[86] See for example I *Sent.*, d. 21, q. 1–2; *ST* I, q. 31, a. 3–4.

[87] CEG II, ch. 28; *SCG* IV, ch. 24 (#3621); *De potentia,* q. 10 a. 4, ad 12; *ST* I, q. 36, a. 2, ad 1; *In Ioan.* 17:3 (#2187); *In Gal.* 4:6 (#213); and so on.

[88] *ST* I, q. 36, a. 2, ad 1.

Although in a different context, the text of the Creed presents a similar case: We confess that the Father is almighty, creator of heaven and earth, but this does not mean that we exclude the Son and the Holy Spirit from the work of creation, since the power and act of creation are common to them all.[89] The same rule applies therefore to the mention of the Spirit "who proceeds from the Father" in the Symbol of Constantinople.

Thomas takes his exegesis further by adding that this "discretion" on the part of Christ is frequently found in the gospels, where Jesus "habitually refers everything back to the Father, from whom he receives everything he has."[90] This interpretation, which was common in the scholastic tradition,[91] was only repeating the explanations given by Augustine.[92] Thomas notes, however, with regard to Jn 15:26 that "the Lord did not altogether hide the fact that he is the principle of the Holy Spirit, since he calls him the *Spirit of Truth* following his own reference to himself as the *Truth* [Jn 14:16]."[93] This point, which theologians in the scholastic tradition inherited, notably, from Peter Lombard,[94] is a final confirmation of the interpretation of Jn 15:26, which in conclusion leaves Thomas without the slightest doubt. This all goes to explain Thomas's rather brusque description of the monopatristic argument derived from Jn 15:26 as being "completely frivolous."[95]

An examination of this biblical dossier provides ample evidence of Thomas's reasons for maintaining the orthodoxy of the Latin expression of the faith, in accordance with Scripture. The

---

[89] CEG II, ch. 28.

[90] *SCG* IV, ch. 24 (#3622), with an example taken from Jn 7:16, *mea doctrina non est mea.*

[91] See for example Bonaventure, I *Sent.,* d. 11, a. un., q. 1, ad 5.

[92] See for example the long quotation from Augustine in the *Catena in Ioan.* 15:26 (p. 535); Augustine, *Tract. In Ioan.* 99, 8 (CCSL 36, 587).

[93] *SCG* IV, ch. 24 (#3622); cf. *In Ioan.* 14:17 and 15:26 (#1916, 2062, and 2065).

[94] Peter Lombard, *Sententiae,* Book I, dist. 11, ch. 1–2 (vol. 1, pp. 115–16). Thomas also quotes the Venerable Bede on this point, in the *Catena in Ioan.* 14:17 (p. 521).

[95] *SCG* IV, ch. 24 (#3622).

common conclusion reached by pursuing each of the themes, their rigorous interpretation, and their foundation in patristic writing all combine to eliminate any possible hesitation, in Thomas's eyes. The procession of the Spirit *a Filio* is not present in the New Testament in the form of literal, explicit teaching but the meaning is clearly indicated. This is why, when he follows Dionysius in saying that "We should not speak of God in any way other than does Scripture,"[96] he can see nothing in this statement which contradicts the affirmation of the procession *a Filio*. This *sensus* of Scripture, as we have seen, is presented by means of a doctrinal reading which brings in the principles of speculative Trinitarian theology. This is perhaps where the principal difficulty for the modern reader of St. Thomas lies, for St. Thomas's literal reading of Scripture (one which allows theological argument) is a reading which is thoroughly centered on doctrine and speculative theology. This aspect also introduces a point of historical interest for, in essence, the Latin interpretation of all these themes and biblical passages had already prompted extremely detailed responses on the part of the Greeks, from Photius himself onward, to such an extent that the debate between the Greeks and the Latins might be said to have fully run its course in the very early days.[97] Was Thomas aware of this? If he said nothing more, he did at least raise the question in the *Disputed Questions on the Power of God.* Here, examining the argument drawn from the mission of the Holy Spirit and other biblical expressions, he asks in the form of an objection whether the *auctoritas* of Scripture is really sufficient grounds for the doctrine of the procession *a Filio.* An examination of the texts, however, together with various patristic references, leads him to the same conviction: The conclusion "infallibly" reached is that the Holy Spirit proceeds from the Son.[98]

---

[96] *SCG* IV, ch. 24 (#3621); *De potentia,* q. 10, a. 4, arg. 12; *ST* I, q. 36, a. 2, arg. 1.

[97] We cannot fail to note that the principal points made by the Latin argument had been discussed and rejected by Photius, *De Sancti Spiritus mystagogia,* n. 20–23, n. 29–30, n. 48–57 (PG 102, 298 ss, 310 ss, 327 ss).

[98] *De potentia,* q. 10, a. 4, arg. 14 ("Auctoritas quidem sacrae Scripturae ad hoc ostendendum nulla videtur *esse* sufficiens") and ad 14.

The Patristic Dossier of the Procession
of the Spirit *a Filio*

An examination of Thomas's patristic sources reveals a progression similar to that of his biblical documentation. Although considerably restricted in the commentary on the *Sentences*, presenting only a few texts taken from Thomas's predecessors, the patristic documentation on the procession of the Spirit first begins to flourish with the *Contra errores Graecorum*, then develops progressively with the *Contra Gentiles*, the *Catena aurea in Ioannem,* and the Disputed Questions *De potentia Dei.* The *Prima pars* of the *Summa theologiae* and the *Lectura* on the gospel of St. John only exploit the results of this body of research. This approach to documentation, and its importance in Thomas's work as we are currently beginning to appreciate, deserves our attention as much as does the content of the patristic texts.

The Greek and Latin Fathers

Which Fathers did Thomas consult? Firstly, in the commentary on the *Sentences*, three texts appear (each cited in the context of arguments against the procession *a Filio*). The first, from Dionysius the Pseudo-Areopagite *(De divinis nominibus)*, presents a Greek-inspired conception of the processions as "pullulation," an emanation of "flowers" or "lights," to which Thomas replies without difficulty (as did St. Albert) that these are metaphors, and theology does not use metaphors for the purposes of argument.[99] A second text, which Thomas was fond of citing throughout his teaching, would perhaps be only of passing interest to us were it not to include a theme which some Orthodox theologians today are seeking to reinstate as an issue for debate regarding the procession of the Spirit: The *resting* of the Spirit on the Son.[100] This concerns a passage taken from one of the

---

[99] I *Sent.,* d. 11, q. un., a. 1, arg. 1 and ad 1. Cf. Albert, I *Sent.,* d. 11, a. 6, arg. 2–3. The reference appears again in *De potentia,* q. 10, a. 4, arg. 1; a. 5, arg. 16.

[100] See for example Boris Bobrinskoy, "Le repos de l'Esprit sur le Fils chez les Cappadociens," in *La Pensée orthodoxe, Travaux de l'Institut de théologie orthodoxe Saint-Serge,* vol. 4 (Lausanne: l'Age d'homme, 1987), pp. 24–39; Boris Bobrinskoy, "Vers une vision commune du Mystère trinitaire," *La Documentation Catholique* 93/2 (1996): 89–90.

many apocryphal Acts of the Apostles, *The Martyrdom of the Holy Apostle Andrew*: Thomas notes that the Spirit remains or rests eternally in the Son *(permanens in Filio, manere in Filio, quiescere in Filio)*.[101] He welcomes this theme wholeheartedly, with its rich spiritual resonances, interpreting it by means of the doctrine of love (the love of the one who loves rests in the beloved), but sees no difficulty in connection with the procession *a Filio*: The Spirit proceeds from the Son and remains in him. Finally, a third text does present a serious difficulty: This concerns the well-known passage from the *De fide orthodoxa* of John Damascene affirming that "we call the Spirit 'the Spirit of the Son' *(Spiritus Filii)* but we do not say that he [proceeds] from the Son *(ex Filio)*."[102] It is all the more a thorny problem given the fact that Thomas generally gives a great deal of credit to John Damascene, both in terms of Trinitarian theology and Christology (John Damascene is the Eastern Father most often cited in the Treatise on the Trinity in the *Summa theologiae*). In his first work, Thomas explains that the passage does not formally deny that the Spirit proceeds from the Son. This *auctoritas* is none the less viewed with some suspicion. Following Bonaventure, Thomas (wrongly) points out that this comment by John Damascene should not be believed, for he had been writing this work at the very moment when the controversy between the Greeks and the Latins began.[103] Thomas's line of criticism was to develop in another direction, once he had access to other elements which we will discuss later.

The *Contra errores Graecorum* marks a first stage of progress by bringing in numerous texts which remain nonetheless of debatable

---

[101] I *Sent.*, d. 11, a. 1, arg. 2 and ad 2; *De potentia*, q. 10, a. 4, arg. 18; *ST* I, q. 36, a. 2, arg. 4 and ad 4. This passage has already been cited by Albert, I *Sent.*, d. 11, a. 6, arg. 7. The text may be seen in Greek and Latin in PG 2, 1217–18 or in *Acta Apostolorum Apocrypha*, vol. II/1, ed. Ricardus A. Lipsius and Maximilianus Bonnet (Darmstadt: Wissenschaftliche Buchgesellschaft, 1959), 2 (cf. p. XI–XIV). Thomas could have been aware of this same theme in John Damascene, *De fide orthodoxa* VIII, 12, Burgundio version, ed. Eligius M. Buytaert (New York: Franciscan Institute St. Bonaventure, 1955), pp. 38–39.

[102] John Damascene, *De fide orthodoxa* VIII, 18 (p. 47).

[103] I *Sent.*, d. 11, q. un., a. 1, ad 3; cf. Albert, I *Sent.*, d. 11, a. 6, arg. 6 and ad 6; Bonaventure, I *Sent.*, d. 11, a. un., q. 1, arg. 9 and ad 9.

value, judging from the selection which Thomas examines: Many of the passages are glosses and compilations carried out by the author of the *Libellus*, who sometimes allowed himself a degree of liberty. The Leonine editors themselves point to a large number of texts which are not to be found among the patristic works cited. We will see however that, amongst the authentic texts, there are several by Athanasius of Alexandria (the *Letters to Serapion* notably), by Cyril *(Thesaurus)*, Epiphanius of Salamis *(Ancoratus)*, and especially Basil of Caesarea *(Against Eunomius)*. These passages are not all of equal significance, but it is certain that Thomas finds himself particularly at home with the Alexandrines, whose thinking displays a definite affinity with Latin theology. Without wishing to exaggerate the implications of the texts written by Athanasius and Cyril, we can at least recognize that their thinking remains open to affirmation of the procession of the Spirit *a Filio*.[104] In his later works Thomas was to select only a few texts from this anthology, but we do find some extracts. One example is an Athanasian or pseudo-Athanasian passage describing the Holy Spirit as *Spiramen divinitatis* and providing Thomas with the opportunity to show that the vital operation is ordered by the intellect (analogy of the relationship of the spirit to the word). Another is an extract from Basil of Cesarea concerning the Spirit as "word of the Son," which Thomas explains by showing that the Spirit reveals the Son *(manifestativum Filii)*.[105]

Particularly worthy of note among these texts is an extract of the letter *Salvatore nostro* from Cyril of Alexandria to Nestorius. Thomas first quotes it in his *Contra errores Graecorum* in the translation given by the *Libellus de fide Trinitatis*,[106] then, in the *Contra Gentiles*, in the translation of the *Acts* of Ephesus found in the *Collectio Casinensis*:

---

[104] Bertrand de Margerie, "Vers une relecture du concile de Florence grâce à la reconsidération de l'Écriture et des Pères grecs et latins," *RT* 86 (1986): 31–81. Although the author makes no reference to St. Thomas in this article, he examines several texts highlighted by Thomas. See also Marie-Odile Boulnois, *Le paradoxe trinitaire chez Cyrille d'Alexandrie* (Paris: Institut d'Etudes Augustiniennes, 1994), pp. 492–529.

[105] CEG I, ch. 12; II, ch. 17; *De potentia*, q. 10, a. 4, arg. 4; a. 5, sol.

[106] CEG II, ch. 27.

"Spiritus Veritatis nominatur et est Spiritus Veritatis et profluit ab eo, sicut denique et ex Deo Patre."[107] The *Contra Gentiles* also marks the beginning of Thomas's efforts to emphasize the authority of this passage by pointing out that the letter *Salvatore nostro* was received by the Council of Chalcedon.[108] The principal references in the eastern patristic dossier are thus: Cyril of Alexandria, the pseudo-Athanasian Symbol[109] and the passage by Didymus the Blind, quoted at greater length in the *Catena in Ioannem*, and represented above in the form of an extract.[110] From a historical perspective, it is true to say that the groundwork for this dossier had already been prepared by Peter Lombard, who in turn had benefited from the dossier compiled by Abelard. If we wish to trace the historical influences back further, we will probably need to turn to Alcuin's *De processione Spiritus sancti*.[111]

It will be worth our while tracing the progression of Thomas's documentation on this Cyrillian *auctoritas*, for it provides a remarkable example of the meticulous approach adopted by Aquinas in his patristic research. In the *De potentia* he recalls the extract from Cyril's Letter to Nestorius, and then juxtaposes a letter from Theodoret of Cyrus to John of Antioch in which Theodoret reports a change of opinion on the part of Cyril regarding the procession of

---

[107] *SCG* IV, ch. 24 (#3609); cf. *Acta Conciliorum Œcumenicorum*, vol. I/3, ed. Eduardus Schwartz (Berlin/Leipzig: De Gruyter, 1929), 32 (abbreviated as *ACO*). We have seen earlier how Thomas justifies the transition from the verb *profluere* to *procedere*. See also *De potentia*, q. 10, a. 4, ad 13 and ad 24.

[108] Cf. *ACO* II/3 (Berlin/Leipzig: De Gruyter, 1936), p. 137. It is still debatable whether or not the letter *Salvatore nostro* was included in Cyril's Synodal Letter received by Chalcedon: see especially the comments made by the editors of the *Contra Gentiles*, vol. 3 (Marietti edition, 1961), pp. 433–34.

[109] *SCG* IV, ch. 24 (#3609): "Spiritus sanctus . . . a Filio . . . procedens." Thomas genuinely believed, as did all the Latin theologians of the time, that the Symbol *Quicumque* was by Athanasius. He takes up this major text again in *De potentia*, q. 10, a. 4, contra 1 and in *ST* I, q. 36, a. 2, contra.

[110] *SCG* IV, ch. 24 (#3609); *Catena in Ioan.* 16:13–15 (pp. 540–41, quoted in note 84 above); cf. *In Ioan.* 16:15 (#2114).

[111] Peter Lombard, *Sententiae*, Book I, d. 11, c. 2 (pp. 116–17); Abelard, *Theologia Scholarium*, II, pp. 157–59 (CCCM 13, 483–85); *Theologia christiana*, IV, 127–29 (CCCM 12, 328–29); Alcuin, *De processione Spiritus sancti* (PL 101, 70–73). For further details, see chapter 3 above.

the Spirit:[112] In a letter to John of Antioch, subsequent to his affirmation of the procession of the Spirit *a Filio*, Cyril allegedly rejected it. Thomas sought out this other letter and succeeds in producing the relevant extract, pointing out that Cyril does not, however, reject the procession *a Filio*. Theodoret has apparently reversed, in an Antiochian sense, the precise significance of this document from Cyril. The problem raised by this correspondence between Cyril and Theodoret (accusations levied by Theodoret, a change of tone on Cyril's part in an effort at reconciliation, and so on) was elucidated in 1979 by André de Halleux, who identified the precise documents involved in this controversy.[113] Based on these findings, the inescapable conclusion reached is not only that Thomas is not mistaken in noting that Theodoret has altered Cyril's line of thought, but also that Thomas's identification of the texts concerned is perfectly accurate! These passages are quoted again according to the translation in the *Collectio Casinensis*, and there is little doubt that this is further evidence of the work of historical documentation carried out by Thomas during his stay in Italy.[114] Without wishing to enter into unashamed eulogy, we should nonetheless be aware of the quality of Thomas's work which, in its time, was pioneering in outlook.

---

[112] *De potentia*, q. 10, a. 4, ad 24: "Theodoretus uero in quadam Epistola ad Iohannem Antiochenum sic dicit: 'Spiritus sanctus non ex Filio aut per Filium habens subsistenciam set procedens quidem a Patre, proprius uero Filii, eo quod et ei consubstancialis sit, nominatus'; hec autem uerba Theodoretus predictus imponit Cirillo tanquam ab eo sint dicta in Epistola quam ad Iohannem Antiochenum scripsit, licet in illa Epistola hoc non legatur, set dicitur ibi sic: 'Spiritus Dei Patris procedit quidem ex ipso, est autem et a Filio non alienus secundum unius essencie rationem.'" Since the text in current editions is particularly flawed, we have here presented the text prepared by Father René-Antoine Gauthier for the new critical edition and which he kindly provided.

[113] André de Halleux, "Cyrille, Théodoret et le *Filioque*," *Revue d'Histoire Ecclésiastique* 74 (1979): 597–625; repeated in Id., *Patrologie et œcuménisme*, pp. 367–95. A French translation of all the relevant texts is included, as well as a survey of the extent of previous research.

[114] The texts quoted in *De potentia*, q. 10, a. 4, ad 24, are: Theodoret of Cyrus, Letter *Deus qui sapienter* to John of Antioch (*ACO* I/4, 131–32); Cyril of Alexandria, *Letter Exultent caeli* to John of Antioch (*ACO* I/3, 191). Thomas includes the incident of the Nestorian Symbol condemned at Ephesus (*ST* I, q. 36, a. 2, ad 3).

Thomas therefore has no hesitation in attributing to Cyril, as to Didymus, the affirmation of the eternal procession of the Spirit *a Filio*.[115] Theodoret, on the other hand, was very poorly thought of by Latin authors in the Middle Ages, because of his "Nestorian" tendencies. We know that Hugh Etherianus had no qualms about describing Theoderet as "the inventor and diffuser of this negation [of the procession of the Holy Spirit *a Filio*]."[116] Thomas might also have known, through a Dominican who wrote on the subject at Constantinople in 1252, that Theoderet featured amongst the early writers cited by the Greeks in their refusal of the Latin doctrine.[117] He also dismisses Theoderet's teachings on the strength of the condemnation of his opinions *(dogmata Theodoreti),* together with those of Theodore of Mopsuestia, by the Second Council of Constantinople.[118] This dossier provides moreover an explanation of Thomas's dismissal of the text of John Damascene, mentioned above: According to Thomas, John Damascene is a follower of Theoderet of Cyrus in this, and his thinking should therefore be dismissed on this point.[119] Historical criticism does not really allow us to concur with Thomas's judgment, despite his efforts of

---

115 A. Halleux ("Cyrille, Théodoret et le *Filioque*") has shown that Cyril's conciliatory approach does not imply any basic change of mind or development in attitude. He points out, however, that Cyril is not "filioquist" nor Theoderet "anti-filioquist" in the later sense of the terms, and that the conflict was between two rival Christologies, Alexandrine and Antiochian. The fact remains that Cyril's thinking is not restricted simply to what is known as the "economy;" cf. B. de Margerie, "Vers une relecture," pp. 39–40.

116 Hugh Etherianus (PL 202, 236): "Theodoritus negationis hujus inventor et praeco." Albert the Great similarly saw in Theodoret's position on the procession of the Holy Spirit "the heresy of Nestorius and of Sabellius" (Albert, I *Sent.,* d. 11, a. 5, arg. 1).

117 Cf. Antoine Dondaine "*Contra Graecos,* Premiers écrits polémiques des dominicains d'Orient," *Archivum Fratrum Praedicatorum* 21 (1951): 320–456; cf. PG 140, 489.

118 *De potentia,* q. 10, a. 4, ad 24; *ST* I, q. 36, a. 2, ad 3 ("Theodoretus Nestorianus"). Cf. *ACO* IV/1, 219. We now realize, however, that Theodoret cannot be simply labelled as "Nestorian."

119 *De potentia,* q. 10, a. 4, ad 24: "Hanc autem Theodoreti sentenciam secutus est postmodum Damascenus, quamuis dogmata eiusdem Theodoreti sint in Quinta synodo condempnata; unde in hoc non est standum sentencie Damasceni." This judgment is repeated in *ST* I, q. 36, a. 2, ad 3.

documentation. Although it is true that John Damascene presents a series of texts which show similarities with Theodoret's thinking, it would be inappropriate to see in them a pure and simple ratification of Theodoret's pneumatology, just as it would be incorrect to see in them a rejection of Cyril's.[120]

At any rate, all of this justifies Thomas's conviction that the doctrine of the procession of the Spirit *a Filio* is not only found amongst the Latin Church Fathers: Its path may be traced amongst the Eastern Fathers themselves, and in consequence their authority may be established in this domain. Although Thomas had a good grasp of the line of thought offered by the Alexandrines, he cannot be said to have arrived at a deep understanding of those features of Trinitarian doctrine peculiar to the Cappadocians. The fundamental certainty remains, however: The faith expressed by the Greek and the Latin Church is identical, and there should be no confrontation on this point.[121]

As regards the Latin Fathers, Thomas has little difficulty in finding the expression of the procession of the Spirit *a Filio* in their writing. This applies particularly in the case of the Bishop of Hippo: "It is evident through Augustine, in a large number of *auctoritates*, and principally in his *De Trinitate* and in his *Homilies* on *John*, that the Holy Spirit is *a Filio*."[122] The explicit references to Augustinian texts are however less numerous than one might expect, no doubt because Thomas has neither any need to press the point nor any difficulty in integrating the Augustinian heritage into his own thinking. Alongside Augustine, we also find several references to Hilary of Poitiers, whom Thomas follows in his exegesis of Jn 16:14–15, and to whom he also refers in his analysis of the procession *per Filium*.[123]

---

[120] Research has confirmed this point. Furthermore, there are no polemics against the *Filioque* in the works of John Damascene. See José Grégoire, "La relation éternelle de l'Esprit au Fils d'après les écrits de Jean de Damas," *Revue d'Histoire Ecclésiastique* 64 (1969): 713–55.

[121] CEG II, ch. 1; II, ch. 28; II, ch. 31; SCG IV, ch. 24 (#3609).

[122] *SCG* IV, ch. 24 (#3611): "Manifestum est autem ex multis auctoritatibus Augustini, et praecipue in libro de Trinitate, et super Ioannem, quod Spiritus Sanctus sit a Filio." These are the two works chiefly cited by Thomas; see above footnotes 20, 21, 28, 37.

[123] *Catena in Ioan.* 16,14:15 (p. 541); see above footnote 84; *ST* I, q. 36, a. 3, contra.

The Councils and the Problem of the Addition to the Symbol

In his efforts to lend weight to the doctrine of the Roman Church, Thomas calls upon the councils of antiquity. This of course is nothing new: Latin theologians have fallen back on this conciliar tradition since Alcuin at least, who made precise references to it.[124] Thomas's principal concern is to demonstrate that the Western Church is expressing nothing other than the faith professed by the great councils of antiquity, that the *Filioque* is consonant *(consonum)* with the faith of the early councils and that it is upheld on the basis of the faith professed by these councils.[125] He does so by means of hermeneutics, "making explicit that which is implicit": this is what governs his approach to the problem of the addition to the Symbol and, in a general manner, his understanding of the development of all dogmatic formulation. The Latin Church made explicit that which the *Constantinopolitanum* contained implicitly. This interpretation, which Thomas derives notably from Albert the Great, who was aligning himself with Anselm of Canterbury, runs through all of his works.[126]

This hermeneutical principle is not presented as a premise without foundation, and Thomas takes care to include the textual confirmation found during his research. He recalls firstly the principle of the "adequacy of the *Nicaenum*," following a very long standing patristic tradition (before Constantinople I).[127] It is worth noting that for Thomas this principle is derived from primary sources. The

---

124 Alcuin, *De sancto Spiritu* (PL 101, 69–73): the first five Councils are reviewed.

125 *De potentia,* q. 10, a. 4, ad 13 (*ex determinatione principalium conciliorum habetur*).

126 I *Sent.,* d. 11, exp. text.; *SCG* IV, ch. 25 (#3624); *De potentia,* q. 10, a. 4, ad 13; *ST* I, q. 36, a. 2, ad 2. Albert, 1 *Sent.,* d. 11, a. 9. Anselm, *De processione Spiritus sancti,* ch. 13 (*L'Œuvre d'Anselme de Cantorbéry,* vol. 4, ed. Michel Corbin [Paris: Cerf, 1990], pp. 211–12 [288–91]). The same arguments are found here, notably the idea that not all tenets of belief are explicitly mentioned in the Symbol of Constantinople, since the descent of Christ into hell, for example, is not mentioned.

127 See André de Halleux, "Pour une profession commune de la foi selon l'esprit des Pères," in *Patrologie et œcuménisme,* pp. 3–24.

prohibition of any addition to the council, on pain of anathema, features in a long quotation he supplies from the *Acts* of Ephesus and
Chalcedon.[128] If the symbol of Constantinople may be said to complete that of Nicea, it does not follow that it consists of a foreign or
contradictory doctrine, of "another faith," but of a detailed explanation necessary to respond to the demands of the times. For Thomas,
the Council of Constantinople itself testifies to the legitimacy of a
clarification of the faith, providing thereby a context for the later
addition of the *Filioque*. In the service of the faith, "a later council
has the power to interpret *(potestas interpretandi)* the Symbol professed by an earlier council."[129] To support this claim, Thomas on
several occasions reproduces a long extract from the *Acts* of the
Council of Chalcedon explaining that the Fathers of Constantinople
did nothing but proclaim and "corroborate" the faith of Nicea concerning the Holy Spirit, in order to defend it against heretics.[130] This
passage from Chalcedon, as far as can be judged from research undertaken, is not frequently cited by Thomas's contemporaries (and is not
mentioned by Albert or Bonaventure when discussing the question),
and reveals once again the particular concern of Aquinas to provide
solid, positive documentation. It is by means of these same *Acts*, we
should remember, that Thomas underpinned the authority of Cyril
when he noted the reception at Chalcedon of his Synodal Letters,[131]
just as he turned to the *Acts* of Ephesus in the context of the controversy between Cyril and Theodoret.

Thomas's conciliar dossier does not, however, stop at this. Having confirmed the authority of Cyril through the *Acts* of Ephesus
and Chalcedon, he similarly confirms the authority of Augustine
and other Latin and Greek doctors (Athanasius, Hilary, Ambrose,
etc.) through an extract of the *Acts* of Constantinople II which

---

[128] *De potentia*, q. 10, a. 4, arg. 13. The principle alone, without any textual
quotes, is stated in *ST* I, q. 36, a. 2, arg. 2. Cf. *ACO* I/3, p. XVIIII; II/3, p.
138 (*Collectio Casinensis* version).

[129] *De potentia*, q. 10, a. 4, ad 13.

[130] The passage is quoted at length in *De potentia*, q. 10, a. 4, ad 13; more briefly
in *SCG* IV, ch. 25 (#3624); *ST* I, q. 36, a. 2, ad 2. Cf. *ACO* II/3, p. 137; G.
Geenen, "En marge du concile de Chalcédoine," 53–56.

[131] *SCG* IV, ch. 24 (#3609); *De potentia*, q. 10, a. 4, ad 13. Cf. *ACO* II/3, p. 137.

claims "to follow in all things the Holy Fathers and Doctors of the Church, Athanasius, Hilary, and so on," and "to receive all that they have demonstrated regarding the true faith and the condemnation of heretics."[132] Thomas of course sees in this declaration of reception, particularly that of Augustine, an implicit conciliar confirmation of the Latin doctrine. By applying it to the procession of the Spirit *a Filio* however, Thomas is pushing his interpretation further than the council intended. At any rate, we should bear in mind his intention never to leave an affirmation unsubstantiated, and to underline the common ground shared by the Fathers in matters of faith, as witnessed by the conciliar tradition of the Church.

The absence of the *Filioque* in the *Constantinopolitanum* does not therefore present any difficulty for Thomas in terms of doctrine: He decides to approach it in the same way as he approaches its absence in Jn 15:26.[133] The difficulty lies rather in the realm of the ecclesial authority deciding upon its insertion into the Symbol. Thomas has shown that explanatory clarification of the faith was practiced by the councils of antiquity themselves. In discussing later incidences of this conciliary practice, Thomas should be invoking the authority of the Roman Pontiff. It is at this point that Thomas reminds the reader that the ecumenical councils are "convoked and confirmed" by the Pope, and that further it is "to him that the council makes appeal," with the result that the Pope, even alone, has the competence and authority to allow such an insertion into the Credo.[134] In this context, the ecclesiological impact of the *Filioque* is of course evident, and the terms in which Thomas expresses it correspond perfectly to the position of the Pope within his ecclesiology. Without wishing to linger on this point, which has been

---

[132] *SCG* IV, ch. 24 (#3611); *De potentia*, q. 10, a. 4, ad 13. This text might have been suggested to him by Alcuin, *De processione Spiritus sancti*, ch. 1 (PL 101, 73), but Thomas quotes it as a primary source present in the Acts of the third session of Constantinople II (*ACO* IV/1, p. 37). For details of Thomas's documentation on this matter, see the conclusions reached by Martin Morard, "Une source de Saint Thomas d'Aquin: le deuxième concile de Constantinople," *RSPT* 81 (1997): 21–56.

[133] CEG II, ch. 28.

[134] *SCG* IV, ch. 25 (#3624); *De potentia*, q. 10, a. 4, ad 13; *ST* I, q. 36, a. 2, ad 2.

analyzed in detail in other works,[135] we should however note that in all the passages concerning the *Filioque*, it is only at the end of his expositions, in the form of an *ultima ratio*, that Thomas calls upon the prerogatives of the successor of Peter. To a greater extent perhaps than later theologians, who were able to consider the doctrine as being definitively accepted as dogma by the official declaration of the Council of Lyons,[136] Thomas applied himself to the task of demonstrating its worth through arguments based on Scripture, patristic writings, and speculative theology, as befits a theologian.

But what was the form of the magisterial intervention involved, in Thomas's view? He seems to have great difficulty in answering this, and brings in various elements to resolve the matter during the course of his works. In his commentary on the *Sentences*, Thomas mentions simply "the authority of the Roman Church to convoke a council which expressed that which was implicitly contained in the articles of faith." Following on from St. Albert, whose explanations he only repeats, Thomas adds rather peremptorily that such a decision was justified by "necessity" (that is, a danger to the faith) as demonstrated by the error of the Greeks.[137] But he cannot, and for good reason, identify the Roman synod from which it comes. The answer appears in a slightly more detailed form in the *De potentia*, where Thomas explains that the gathering of a universal council is not always necessary; an example given is the Council of Constantinople III (condemnation of Christological monothelitism), which was unable to reunite the entire body of bishops, but "those who assembled there resolved certain problems which had arisen concerning the faith, in accordance with the judgment of Pope Agatho."[138] No mention is made, on the other hand, in the *Contra errores Graecorum* or in the *Summa*

---

[135] See especially Serge-Thomas Bonino, "La place du pape dans l'Église selon saint Thomas d'Aquin," *RT* 86 (1986): 392–422.

[136] In the opinion of Hyacinthe Dondaine (*Thomas d'Aquin: La Trinité*, vol. 2, p. 387), this aspect has a bearing on the positions of Henry of Ghent and Duns Scotus, who were not to give the same weight to the doctrine of relative opposition.

[137] I *Sent.*, d. 11, exp. text.; Albert, I *Sent.*, d. 11, a. 9.

[138] *De potentia*, q. 10, a. 4, ad 13; the reference to Pope Agathon, included in the text of the council (cf. Denzinger-Schönmetzer, *Enchiridion Symbolorum*, #553),

contra Gentiles. It should be noted in this context that Thomas does not cite the Fourth Lateran Council, which taught that the Spirit proceeds equally from the Father and from the Son.[139]

It is not until the *Summa theologiae* that Thomas is a little more precise. On one hand, he points out that the councils of antiquity had no reason to proclaim the procession of the Spirit *a Filio*, since the opposing error had not yet appeared. On the other hand, he attributes the magisterial clarification of the *Filioque* and its addition to the Symbol to "a council assembled in the West" *(in quodam concilio in Occidentalibus partibus congretato)* under the authority of the Pope.[140] Which council might he have been thinking of? We might perhaps think of the Council of Aix-la-Chapelle in 809 which decreed that the *Filioque* is a doctrine of the Church and should be included in the Credo sung during Mass. But, although Pope Leo III agreed with the doctrine, we know that he flatly refused to modify or add anything to the Symbol.[141] Thomas's historical documentation is, in this case, lacking. But this passage provides us with a particularly interesting item. Thomas *no longer refers to the "error of the Greeks"* as the motive justifying a conciliar convocation or decision (this was the opinion of Albert, and of Thomas initially), but simply the "error of certain people" *(error quorundam)*. It could perhaps be connected with the Greeks, but it seems more probable that Thomas has detected the role being played by certain forms of Arianism, as he suggests in his homilies on the Credo.[142] This reference to a council in *occidentalibus partibus* is actually identical to the one found in the opuscule *Contra Graecos* by the Dominican writing in Constantinople in 1252. It is

---

is extended by means of a discussion of the role played by Leo the Great at Chalcedon.

139 *Enchiridion*, #800 and 805. Thomas was however very familiar with Lateran IV's condemnation of Albigensians and Cathars as well as its condemnation of Joachim of Fiore, that is to say with the decrees *Firmiter* and *Damnamus* for which he provided commentaries (*Expositio super Primam et Secundam Decretalem ad archidiaconum Tudertinum*, Leonine edition, vol. 40 E, 29–44).

140 *ST* I, q. 36, a. 2, ad 2.

141 See Y. Congar, *Je crois en l'Esprit Saint*, vol. 3, pp. 86–8.

142 *In Symbolum apostolorum*, a. 8 (#962); it should be noted that these homilies were written after the *Prima pars* of the *Summa theologiae*.

highly likely, as was shown by Father Antoine Dondaine, that there is a connection between Thomas's comment and the work of this other Dominican.[143] According to this text however, which is very similar to that by Thomas, the error being countered by the proclamation of the *Filioque* is *not* Eastern doctrine, but consists of a heresy which arose *in the West* and which was condemned by a Western council in the absence of members of the Eastern Church. But neither the polemicist in the Dominican priory in Constantinople, nor Thomas, gives us any more detail. It was not until the fourteenth century, by which time doubt had been cast upon the idea of a council having been assembled under the authority of the Pope in order to counteract the rejection of the procession *a Filio*, that critical research turned its attention toward the councils of Toledo.[144]

The "Evident Reasons"

Following the biblical foundations and the patristic references, the third approach to the question is composed of arguments of speculative theology. There are few theological questions which elicited from Thomas such a multiplicity of arguments expressed in such rich detail. It has to be acknowledged that, in the same way that he constantly extended his biblical and patristic documentation, Thomas progressively enriched his speculative thinking (up to *De potentia* at least). A detailed analysis would be required, resulting undoubtedly in a vast monograph, in order to demonstrate the worth of these "evident reasons"[145] and arrive at a precise evaluation of them. We

---

[143] A. Dondaine, *"Contra Graecos,"* 390–91: "Processu vero temporis, increscente in Occidentalibus partibus malitia quorumdam mente perversorum, dicentium Spiritum sanctum non procedere a Filio, pro eo quod in symbolo non reperiatur, congregati in unum episcopi illarum partium, de licentia et auctoritate summi pontificis, veritatem fidei quam tenemus in symbolo declarantes, cantari etiam hoc in ecclesia ab omnibus mandaverunt. Greci vero et ceteri Orientales vocati non sunt . . . ." Cf. PG 140, 502 C.

[144] According to A. Dondaine (*"Contra Graecos,"* p. 393), who has carried out a detailed examination of the history of this *Contra Graecos*, the path would seem to lead to Philip of Pera in 1359.

[145] *SCG* IV, ch. 24 (#3612): "evidentibus rationibus."

will limit ourselves here to identifying and briefly introducing the principal ones.

The Distinction by Relative Opposition
According to Origin[146]

Throughout Thomas's works, the principal argument lies in the principle of the distinction of divine persons by relative opposition. In the commentary on the *Sentences,* this is the only argument based on reason which Thomas produces in his summary of the accomplishments of Albert the Great.[147] In the later works, it is generally the first theme to be developed. The divine persons cannot be distinguished by an absolute reality (this would imply the existence of three gods): Only the relation or relative properties can account for this distinction which leaves intact the unity of the divine being. The starting point is thus found in the principle of distinction by relation, developed by the Cappadocians (especially St. Basil, in his *Against Eunomius*) and brought to the West by Augustine.[148] However, only relative opposition can adequately account for the distinction between the persons. Thomas here accepts the Anselmian principle unreservedly: In God, all is one where relative opposition does not prevent it.[149] The relations only distinguish or make up the persons to the extent that they involve a mutual "opposing" relationship. This is not, in Thomas's view, simply an opinion based on reasonably sound judgment: "The truth of the faith *(veritas fidei)* holds that the only distinction in

---

146 I *Sent.,* d. 11, q. un., a. 1; CEG II, ch. 29–30; SCG IV, ch. 24 (#3612); *De potentia,* q. 10, a. 4, and a. 5; *ST* I, q. 36, a. 2.

147 Thomas, I *Sent.,* d. 11, q. un., a. 1; Albert, I *Sent.,* d. 11, a. 6, contra 1–5.

148 See Irénée Chevalier, *Saint Augustin et la pensée grecque: Les relations trinitaires* (Fribourg: Librairie de l'Université, 1940).

149 Anselm, *De processione Spiritus sancti,* ch. 1: "Quatenus nec unitas amittat aliquando suum consequens, ubi non obviat aliqua relationis oppositio, nec relatio perdat quod suum est, nisi ubi obsistit unitas inseparabilis" (p. 229 of the edition cited above, note 126). We may note, however, that Thomas does not often quote this axiom of St. Anselm, but rather incorporates it into his own writing (see, for example, *ST* I, q. 28, a. 3). This passage from Anselm is not explicitly referred to in the discussion of Trinitarian theology in the *Summa theologiae.*

God is that of relative opposition."[150] Thomas holds firmly to this
principle, justifying it frequently by means of the following argument: The Father has two relations (one with the Son and the other
with the Spirit), but these two relations do not "divide" the Father
into two persons, precisely because these two relations (paternity
and active spiration) do not include any mutual opposition; the same
applies to the relations of filiation and active spiration in the Son.[151]
Thus, and for the same reason, if there were no relative opposition
between the Son and the Holy Spirit, they would be one and the
same person (Sabellian Monarchianism).[152] However, and this is
the last stage in the argument, the relation of opposition can only be
based upon the *origin*, the only "action" which justifies a real distinction of persons in God. Without this, we could certainly claim
to make a distinction between the Son and the Holy Spirit, but *we
could no longer provide a theological explanation for the distinction*.
The *intellectus fidei* would be destroyed at its foundations.

Following this line of reasoning, it is therefore necessary to pose
the procession of the Spirit *a Filio* in order to safeguard the personal
distinction of the Spirit and the Son. For those who are left in
doubt, Thomas reviews all the possible foundations for a real relation, following Aristotle: quantity (quality or substance do not constitute foundations as such except in terms of quantity), action or

---

[150] *Quodlibet* XII, q. 1, a. 1: "Dicendum quod ueritas fidei habet quod in diuinis
solum est distinctio que est secundum relationes oppositas" (Leonine edition,
vol. 25/2, 399).

[151] The same, equally, would apply to the relations of filiation and of procession if
the Spirit did not proceed from the Son: *SCG* IV, ch. 24 (#3613); *De potentia*,
q. 10, a. 5; *ST* I, q. 33, a. 4, ad 4; q. 36, a. 2.

[152] The impossibility of real distinction between the Son and the Holy Spirit if the
Holy Spirit does not proceed from the Son: A long article is devoted especially
to this problem in *De potentia*, q. 10, a. 5. This article (a. 5), located in current
editions at the end of the series of the Disputed Questions *De potentia*, is in
fact a separate question: rather than being a disputed question, it derives from
a request for expert opinion at the papal Curia, based in Orvieto, during
1264–65. This information was kindly supplied by Father R-A. Gauthier who
is preparing a critical edition. This explains in particular the repetitions and different aspects presented by this question in comparison with q. 10, a. 4. While
awaiting the appearance of the critical edition, however, we will continue to
refer to it in the conventional manner: q. 10, a. 5.

passion. He has no difficulty in showing that immanent action is the sole safeguard of the prerogatives of God: This action, however, as we have indicated, is in a strict sense the production of one person by another. A reading of the texts shows us that it is through the procession of the Spirit that Thomas developed his doctrine of relative opposition in its last details, with its examination of all forms of distinction, opposition, and real relation. Nothing is left out.[153] We will trace the main lines of the exposition: It is not in any sense a proof of the Trinity, for the argument presupposes faith in the Trinity; it is consistent with the declared aim of explaining the real distinction of the persons, as far as theological reason is able to do so; it involves an analysis which, by eliminating all other possible forms of distinction, results in the necessity *(supposita Trinitate)* to acknowledge relative opposition and therefore the procession of the Spirit *a Filio.*

The Difference According to the "First Source" of Distinction[154]

Despite the central position occupied by relative opposition, Thomas does not allow the entire weight of his rational argument to rest upon the precise exposition of this doctrine: The procession of the Holy Spirit *a Filio* "is also shown to be necessary for other reasons."[155] Most of these reasons are however linked more or less directly to relative opposition. One of the first is concerned with the differences *(differentia)* in the divine persons.[156] If we observe the differences in all things, explains Thomas, it is evident that they are consequent upon the first source *(prima radix)* of distinction, unless

---

[153] See in particular *SCG* IV, ch. 24 (#3612); *In Ioan.* 15:26 (#2063). The presence of a complete exposition on this subject within a scriptural commentary should be noted. The *Summa theologiae* first presents relative opposition in *ST* I, q. 28, a. 3.

[154] *De potentia,* q. 10, a. 4.

[155] *De potentia,* q. 10, a. 4: "Etiam ex aliis rationibus de necessitate probatur."

[156] Thomas is here using a term which he identifies elsewhere as being inappropriate to describe the divine persons. The *differentia* signifies the logical principle of distinction and puts the emphasis more specifically on the distinction of form (*ST* I, q. 31, a. 2, ad 2).

they are purely accidental differences which are of no interest to us here (because there are no accidents in God). The reason for this is that these differences are drawn from the essence of the beings or from their essential principles. In God, the "first source" of distinction between the Father and the Son is paternity and filiation, in other words the fact that one is the Father and the other the Son. However, the Father is Father only in his relation with the Son. If he were a *Father* of the Holy Spirit, there would be a confusion between the person of the Son and that of the Holy Spirit. The same applies to the Son, who is not the Son except in his relation with the Father. "Therefore, there cannot be any difference between the Father and the Son in the sense of the Father being the principle of the Holy Spirit and the Son not being so."[157]

This argument is based upon the following: Since the Father and the Son are distinguished by paternity and filiation, any suggestion that the Father might be the principle of the Spirit to the exclusion of the Son would be introducing between the Father and the Son a distinction which is alien to the first principle of distinction between them. In other words, it would add a heterogeneous element to that which distinguishes the Father from the Son and which constitutes them as persons. In a simplified form, Thomas was to recall elsewhere that there is no difference between the Father and the Son as regards divine essence, since the only distinction arises from their relative properties of paternity and of filiation. However, since being the principle of the Holy Spirit does not in a formal sense concern either the relation of filiation nor that of paternity (*esse principium Spiritus sancti est praeter rationem paternitatis et filationis*), the relation of principle with regard to the Holy Spirit must be common to the Father and to the Son.[158] The reader will have noticed that the idea of relative opposition, although not formulated in explicit terms, is not absent from this argument. We should note, moreover, that the theological thinking addresses the Father

---

[157] *De potentia*, q. 10, a. 4: "Non ergo potest esse differentia inter Patrem et Filium in hoc quod Pater sit principium Spiritus sancti, non autem Filius."
[158] *SCG* IV, ch. 24 (#3619).

and the Son first, and then the Spirit. This argument brings into play the coherent structure of Trinitarian thought (which, let us not forget, Thomas considers to be necessarily so). An additional perspective, bringing the argument to a positive conclusion, is supplied in the argument which follows.

Two Distinct Processions ab alio[159]

It has been established that the divine persons are distinguished by way of formal differences or differences per se, and not by way of accident. It should further be made clear that although the divine persons are distinct, they also possess a common aspect. However, in the case of realities possessing a distinct element on the one hand and a common element on the other, when it is a question of differences per se and not accidental differences, the principle of distinction (the *differentia*) is located in the order of the element common to both. This brings us back to the rule of homogeneity of the principle of distinction formulated earlier, but applied now in an affirmative way. For example, a horse and a man are distinguishable not only in terms of size and color (accidental differences), but in terms of their nature, that is first and foremost by the rationality and the absence of reason which characterize their essence. These two differences (rationality–irrationality), however, are of the same order or the same kind as the element common to both man and horse (animality), since rationality and irrationality are differences of animality (having one kind of soul or another). The same principle applies equally to Trinitarian theology. If we consider the Son and the Holy Spirit, we note that what they have in common is that they both receive their essence from another *(esse ab alio)*, for they both proceed from the Father. It is thus in this same order *(esse ab alio)* that the principle of distinction of the Son and the Holy Spirit must be located: The Son and the Holy Spirit must here be distinguished "by differences which divide per se the fact of being *ab alio*."[160] The

---

159 *SCG* IV, ch. 24 (#3614); *De potentia,* q. 10, a. 5. The argument is subject to the same necessity as the preceding argument.

160 *SCG* IV, ch. 24 (#3614): "Oportet quod hoc sit per differentias quae per se dividant hoc quod est ens ab alio."

only distinction possible is therefore one of origin, inasmuch as one (the Holy Spirit) proceeds from the other (the Son).

The strength of this argument obviously depends upon the validity of the principle of the homogeneity of the differences per se within the general theory of the distinction of the divine persons. This principle, without always being formulated in this manner, is found in the body of scholastic theology which Thomas fully accepts. He comes across it notably in Richard of St. Victor's Trinitarian theology: In the Trinity, one of the persons is innascible (without origin) and principle, the second is both the person who proceeds and the person who is the principle of another, and the third proceeds without being in turn the principle of another.[161] Any distinction in the Trinity can be traced back to the way in which the person receives the essence from another *(ab alio)*; because of this, the very distinction between the Son and the Holy Spirit lies in the reception of the essence *ab alio*: The Spirit is *a Filio*. We can see here a complementary approach to the theme of relative opposition, and will meet another version of this later in the context of order in the Trinity.

Insufficiency of the Distinction by Diverse Origins a Patre[162]

St. Thomas here confronts the "Greek" (Cappadocian) conception of triadology. However, his interpretation, and this is without doubt the limit of his accommodation of eastern thought, is governed by a typically "Latin" logic. It is worth making the effort to understand why Thomas's perception of the Greek doctrine cannot satisfy him. According to this doctrine, the distinction of the Son consists of his property of filiation, and the distinction of the Holy Spirit of his property of procession, so that these properties, which are rooted in the different origins *a Patre*, are considered sufficient to demonstrate

---

[161] This approach is found in various different forms throughout the *De Trinitate* of Richard of Saint Victor (Book V, ch. 3–14). Cf. St. Thomas, *De potentia,* q. 10, a. 5, arg. 1 and ad 1; CEG II, ch. 29; I *Sent.,* d. 10, q. un., a. 5.

[162] *SCG* IV, ch. 24 (#3615); *De potentia,* q. 10, a. 2; q. 10, a. 4; q. 10, a. 5, sol., arg. 1–6 and ad 1–6; *ST* I, q. 36, a. 2 (cf. ad 7); *In Ioan.* 15:26 (#2064).

the distinction between the Son and the Holy Spirit. In other words, it is the difference in the origin of which the Father is the principle (generation and procession) that makes the distinction between the Son and the Holy Spirit. For Thomas, this view is certainly correct, but does not go far enough: It should also be pointed out that this diversity of origin *a Patre* necessarily involves the positing of an order of origin between the Spirit who proceeds and the Son who is begotten: Otherwise, "[Filiation and procession] . . . would belong to one person."[163]

The argument is developed carefully, starting with the different aspects of origin. In creatures, Thomas explains, two origins cannot be distinguished except by means of three elements: Their principle, their *terminus*, or their subject. In God, however, such a diversity of subject must be ruled out, since this *subiectum* is linked to the matter, the principle of individuation in the reception of a specific form, while the divine persons are altogether immaterial. The same applies regarding the *terminus*, since the *terminus* of all eternal procession is the same divine essence received by the Son in the generation and by the Holy Spirit in the procession.[164] The distinction cannot therefore exist except in the *principle* of the procession. But if this principle were the Father alone in both cases, there would no longer be a means of explaining the real distinction between the Son and the Holy Spirit (for the two processions would thus be identical in all their aspects, making one single procession). It is therefore necessary that the generation or begetting of the Son is the *principle* of the procession of the Holy Spirit. Because of this, the diversity of origin *a Patre* includes and implies the affirmation of the procession of the Spirit *a Filio*. This

---

[163] *SCG* IV, ch. 24 (#3615).

[164] It is important to understand this idea of *terminus*: It is not a question of essence conceived purely in an abstract sense (we would not say that "essence is begotten") but of "essence possessed by the person": The essence received by the Son and the essence received by the Holy Spirit. The same essence is received by the Son and by the Holy Spirit. The point in question is therefore how the Son and the Holy Spirit, receiving and possessing the same essence, may be distinguished: Relative opposition must therefore apply. See I *Sent.*, d. 5, q. 3; *ST* I, q. 39, a. 5.

argument, as we can see, lays special emphasis on the principle of
distinction between the persons by relative opposition according
to origin.

Insufficiency of the Distinction by Mode of Origin Alone[165]

Continuing the preceding argument, this discourse examines the
possibility of a distinction between the persons by *mode* of origin
alone, that is, by the mode of intellect (or nature) for the Son and
by the mode of will or of love for the Holy Spirit. We have no
need to restate the central importance of both these modes in the
doctrine of St. Thomas: His whole Trinitarian theology depends
upon their validity.[166] Are they not in themselves sufficient to
provide an explanation of the distinction between the persons,
without any need to introduce the procession *a Filio*? The answer
to this, as we may well imagine, is in the negative, and the reasons
given are not lacking in substance. The intellect and the will (or
nature and the will), by which these modes of procession take
place, are essential attributes in God. But such divine attributes,
although possessing their own *ratio* which must indeed be accepted,
are not distinguishable except *secundum rationem*, that is through
a conceptual rather than a real distinction.[167] Therefore, if the
mode of origin were the only criterion, there would be no real distinction between the divine persons, and it would be impossible
to avoid the conclusions of Sabellianism: The Son and the Holy
Spirit would be really one and the same person. It is therefore necessary, in addition to the mode of procession, to bring in the relation of origin *ab alio*. This relation of origin is moreover rooted in
the very structure of the mode, as the following argument explains.

---

[165] *SCG* IV, ch. 24 (#3616); *De potentia*, q. 10, a. 2; q. 10, a. 5.

[166] A reading of *ST* I, q. 28 will demonstrate the truth of this point. With the
exception of the procession of the Son by mode of intellect in a precise sense,
which Thomas develops in his own line of argument, the general terms of this
doctrine were accepted by the great majority of scholastic theologians.

[167] I *Sent.*, d. 2, a. 3; *SCG* I, ch. 35–36; *ST* I, q. 13, a. 4.

Love Proceeds from the Word[168]

The elaboration of the "psychological" doctrine of the Trinity offers Thomas a solid framework in which to demonstrate the procession of the Spirit *a Filio*. Even though the consideration of modes alone is not sufficient, it does provide a structure which, when applied to the person who proceeds, demonstrates the relation of origin of the Spirit toward the Son. The reasoning here is crystal clear: The inclination of the will, which is a spiritual faculty, is directed toward the object presented by the intellect. There is therefore a relation of origin between love and the intellect: We love that which we know. This does not mean that the relation between intellect and love is "one-way," for love also exercises its influence on intellectual activity: But by its very structure, the activity of the will is rooted in the intellect. "We cannot love something unless we have first conceived it through the word of the heart."[169] A being must therefore be known by the intellect before any movement of love toward it may occur.[170] This relationship, which we may observe in human spiritual activity, is independent of any imperfection, which in God would have to be resolutely dismissed. Thomas points this out frequently using the Augustinian theme of the "perfect word," that is the word of spiritual activity brought to its full conclusion: Love.[171] The theme of the image of the Trinity in man draws its force directly from this Trinitarian model: Its spiritual implications are considerable.[172] Thomas's strength of conviction concerning the doctrine of

---

[168] *SCG* IV, ch. 24 (#3617); *De potentia*, q. 10, a. 5; *De rationibus fidei*, ch. 4; *CT* I, ch. 49; *ST* I, q. 36, a. 2; *In Ioan.* 14:17 (#1916).

[169] *SCG* IV, ch. 24 (#3617): "Nihil amare posssumus nisi verbo cordis illud concipiamus."

[170] This point is developed in a rigorous manner in several passages, notably *SCG* IV, ch. 19.

[171] I *Sent.*, d. 15, q. 4, a. 1, ad 3: "Et ideo ex tali notitia procedit amor." Cf. d. 10, q. un., a. 1, contra 2; d. 27, q. 2, a. 2, arg. 1; *ST* I, q. 43, a. 5, ad 2; Augustine, *De Trinitate* IX, X, 15. On this important theme, see Raimondo Spiazzi, "'Conoscenza con amore' in Sant'Agostino e in San Tommaso," *Doctor communis* 39 (1986): 315–28; Elsbeth Michel, *Nullus potest amare aliquid incognitum: Ein Beitrag zur Frage des Intellektualismus bei Thomas von Aquin* (Fribourg: Editions Universitaires, 1979).

[172] *ST* I, 45, a. 7; q. 93, a. 4–5.

the Word and of Love is such that he has no qualms about affirming, on the basis of his reading of St. John, that "if the procession of
the Word and of Love does not suffice for suggesting the personal
distinction, there could not be any personal distinction in God."[173]
It is then immediately clear that the Holy Spirit proceeds from the
Son: "Love proceeds from the Word."

This means of explanation is not fully exploited before Thomas's
mature works (from the *Contra Gentiles* onward) since it presupposes a detailed exposition of the doctrine of the Word, which in his
commentary on the *Sentences* still remained to be accomplished.
This first work certainly demonstrates the relation of origin between
Love and the Word, notably by means of the images of the Trinity
and of mutual love, but this is not fully exploited by Thomas in the
question of the procession of the Spirit *a Filio*.[174] In his major
works of synthesis *(Contra Gentiles, De potentia, Summa theologia)*,
this argument is never the most prominent: It is always preceded by
the theory of relative opposition (the major premise) and often by
yet other arguments. It is only in his less extensive works, aimed at
a wider public, that Thomas puts particular emphasis on the explanation using the theme of the Word and of Love. Thus, in the *Compendium theologiae* and in the opuscule *De rationibus fidei* which
follows, the theme of Love proceeding from the Word constitutes
the sole means of explaining the procession of the Holy Spirit *a
Filio*. The rationale at work must surely lie in the methodology of
these two works, in which Thomas is seeking a simplicity of exposition, as well as in the suggestive power of the analogy of the word
and of love. This argument relies however upon solid theological
work which provides, along with the doctrine of relative opposition,
the very structure of Trinitarian theology.

---

[173] *De potentia*, q. 9, a. 9, ad 7: "Si processio verbi et amoris non sufficit ad distinctionem personalem insinuandam, nulla poterit esse personalis distinctio in
divinis."

[174] I *Sent.*, d. 11, q. un., a. 1, contra 2 and 3. Its authoritative use in the context
of the *Filioque* was also to require a critical analysis of the idea of "gratuitous
love" and "mercenary love" developed by Richard of Saint Victor, as well as an
analysis of anthropomorphism generally in the attribution of love to God: see
De potentia, q. 10, a. 4, arg. 8–11 and ad 8–11.

Trinitarian Order[175]

A supplementary argument is provided through the consideration of order in the Trinity. This cannot be seen as a marginal consideration, for it has been a fundamental aspect of Trinitarian doctrine since antiquity. There is in the Trinity an "order of nature" *(ordo naturae)*, which does not signify any priority or posteriority of one person in respect to another, but only the relation of principle or of origin.[176] It is clear that Thomas is determined to rule out the idea of an "order of perfection," which would suggest an Arian approach to the mystery of God. The argument features prominently in all Thomas's major works (it is the third argument in the *Summa theologiae*, following that of relative opposition and of Love proceeding from the Word). To reject such order in the Trinity would be to introduce confusion and an incompatibility with faith in the Trinity and with divine perfection: All the theologians of Thomas's day (eastern as well as western, moreover) were in agreement on this point. Thomas elaborates in this context, no doubt to a greater extent than we would today, on the order to be observed in the world, in human activity, amongst the angels, and throughout the universe which is radiant with the beauty ordained by divine wisdom. The fact remains that the argument is not purely "aesthetic," but includes a metaphysical dimension closely linked to the doctrine of creation and to that of being: Any distinction or multiplicity implies an order such as this.[177] Faith, which rules out the possibility of the "confusion" of the divine persons, leads to acknowledge such an order in God by analogy. The doctrine of relative opposition according to origin comes in here, for Thomas cannot conceive of this order existing except by virtue of the origin *ab alio*; the other possibilities, touching upon composition and matter, must be ruled out. The procession of the Spirit *a Filio* alone can safeguard this order, without which there is no longer any way of avoiding the confusion of the Son and of the Holy Spirit.

---

[175] *SCG* IV, ch. 24 (#3618); *De potentia*, q. 10, a. 4 and 5; *ST* I, q. 36, a. 2.

[176] *ST* I, q. 42, a. 3.

[177] Andrew N. Woznicki, *Being and Order: The Metaphysics of Thomas Aquinas in Historical Perspective* (New York: Lang, 1990).

Linked to this argument is also the idea of the "immediate" relation of one person with another, which Thomas develops after Richard of St. Victor. If the Son and the Holy Spirit proceed from the Father alone, their mutual relationship must depend upon the "mediation" of the Father, and will not exist immediately.[178] We can evidently see here a very Latin idea, targeting the eastern under-standing of the monarchy of the Father. This argument rounds off that of the distinction by relative opposition according to origin, but draws upon it as well, since the order in God only exists because of this origin *ab alio*.

The Spirit Proceeds from the Father by Nature[179]

The divine processions are "natural" productions. By this term, Thomas does not in any sense intend to suggest a process of emana-tion in God along the lines of the Neoplatonic hypostases, but wants to demonstrate the essential difference between the Trinitar-ian processions and the production of creatures.[180] The first belong to divine nature, the second arise from free creative will. In the first *(per naturam)*, the divine nature is fully communicated, numerically and specifically identical, while the second *(per voluntatem)* offers only a limited participation in the divine being and divine perfec-tion. This reflection upon nature finds its roots in the oldest tradi-tion of Trinitarian thought, which Thomas develops here with reference to Hilary of Poitiers. In contrast to creatures, the Son and the Holy Spirit proceed from the Father by nature *(naturaliter)*, and because of this are perfectly equal to and like the Father.

On this basis, Thomas carries out a minute study of the idea of nature, in two separate but connected strands. On one hand, because of the identity of the *nature* of the Father and of the Son, the Holy Spirit cannot be produced "by nature" unless the Son is the principle together with the Father (it is thus also the case that the three persons are one single principle of the creature because of

---

178 *De potentia,* q. 10, a. 5. Cf. Richard of Saint Victor, *De Trinitate,* Book V, ch. 9. See also Albert the Great, I *Sent.,* d. 31, a. 14, ad quaest. 2.

179 *De potentia,* q. 10, a. 4 and a. 5.

180 I *Sent.,* d. 6, q. un., a. 2–3; *De potentia,* q. 10, a. 4.

their single creative will). This argument underlines the identity of the principle of production, and we can recognize the idea implicitly underlying this approach: That of the total unity of all things in God "except where relative opposition prevents it." On the other hand, Thomas points out the unity of the "terminus" of production: In contrast to creatures produced in a universe formed in multiplicity, that which proceeds *in* God is absolutely *one*. We find here the Platonic idea of the production of the One by the One, as well as the prerogatives of natural production *(natura semper ad unum se habet)*. Its application to the mystery of the Trinity reveals here once again a typically Latin approach: The only Son proceeds from the only Father; the Holy Spirit, perfectly One, must "necessarily" proceed from the Father and from the Son inasmuch as they are themselves One.

There are several variations on this argument, the principal being the one which takes up the idea of nature from the point of view of *the identity of the principle of communication and of that which is communicated*. We came across this argument earlier in the context of Jn 16:14–15, in which Thomas establishes the identical nature of the principle of communication *(quo)* and that which is communicated *(quod)* in the divine processions. It may be summed up as follows: The divine nature or essence common to the Father and the Son is communicated to the Holy Spirit. It is therefore by the Father and the Son that this essence is communicated to him. In other words, the identity of the principle of communication and of that which is communicated involves the unity of the Father and of the Son in the act of communication of the divine essence to the Holy Spirit.[181]

Since we have not yet, in the points covered so far, exhausted the dossier consisting of "evident reasons," we can judge just how far Thomas wanted to go in examining the relation of the Spirit to the Son, under all the aspects susceptible to speculative reflection. Detailed analysis is continued by means of other arguments which may be described as "minor" but to which Thomas has given a

---

[181] *In Ioan.* 16:15 (#2114–15); see above notes 79 and 81.

certain amount of attention. There is, for example, the argument
drawn from what is possible and what is necessary in God, which
reminds us that the property of filiation does not involve any
incompatibility with the notion of active spiration.[182] The essential points however have already been covered in the arguments
which we have looked at. Thomas also reviews most of the arguments raised against the procession of the Spirit *a Filio*. These provide him with the opportunity to show once again that the Latin
doctrine of the procession *a Filio* is not detrimental to other
aspects of the faith. Some of these responses are not without interest, for example when demonstrating the perfect simplicity of the
Holy Spirit (the Spirit proceeds from the Father and from the Son
but inasmuch as they are one) or the perfection of the Father (the
procession *a Filio* does not in any way detract from the *auctoritas*
of the Father),[183] or the balance which needs to be maintained
between the conception of the Son as principle of the Spirit on
one hand and the unique position of the Father as principle without principle on the other.[184]

   In reading the theological arguments highlighted by Thomas, we
cannot fail to be struck by the force of "necessity" which he explicitly
and constantly attributes to them. This necessity *(necesse est, de necessitate est, impossibile est, omnino esse non potest,* and so on) has an
explicit bearing upon almost all the arguments: relative opposition
according to origin, the lack of distinction between the Son and the
Spirit if the latter does not proceed from the Son, the procession *a
Filio* according to John 16:14–15, the distinction according to a dif-

---

[182] *SCG* IV, ch. 24 (#3620). The main idea is the following: All that which is not
against the nature of things is possible; being the principle of the Holy Spirit is
not against the notion of filiation; and since in God, being actually and being
possible (*esse* and *posse*) do not differ, we may conclude that the Son is the principle of the Spirit. The argument is not without weight, and the *Summa theologiae* was to take up the Aristotelian adage: "in divine things, the actual and
the possible do not differ," but this time in an argument against the *Filioque*
(*ST* I, q. 36, a. 2, arg. 7).

[183] See especially *SCG* IV, ch. 25 (#3625); *De potentia,* q. 10, a. 4, ad 15 and ad
19–20; a. 5, ad 9–10; *ST* I, q. 36, a. 2, ad 6.

[184] *De potentia,* q. 10, a. 4, ad 16: "Principium autem primum, ut ita dixerim, est
principium non de principio, quod est Pater."

ference in the origin *ab alio*, the insufficiency of the distinction by diverse origins *a Patre*, the procession of Love *a Verbo*, the argument drawn from the order in the Trinity, and so forth.[185] This meeting of the biblical, patristic, and speculative foundations of a doctrine held by faith indicates clearly why for Thomas the procession of the Spirit *a Filio* is "necessary for salvation *(de necessitate salutis)*."[186] The rational necessity which he underlines moreover gives eloquent expression to the fact that for Thomas, the procession of the Spirit *a Filio* is inherent in the very structure of Trinitarian doctrine to the extent that, if the fundamental principles are upheld (relative opposition according to origin and the doctrine of the Word and of Love principally), its authenticity is obvious on all counts. Leaving aside any notions of blatant polemics, or the extent of Thomas's understanding of the eastern tradition, we should be aware of the importance of the issue involved, whether in historical terms or in terms of speculative theology. Thomas is seeking to render account of faith in the Trinity within the context of a body of doctrine: Having examined all the aspects, he shows that this basic aim cannot be accomplished without the procession of the Spirit *a Filio*.

Attitudes Toward Medieval Eastern Orthodoxy

A reading of the issues relating to the procession of the Holy Spirit in Thomas's work reveals several pejorative expressions which impart a negative note to the "climate" of the discussion, and are often seen as obstacles by readers today: Their presence can appear irritating, and the reader can be tempted to pass over them in silence. Such remarks should however be given attention, placed within their historical context.

For Thomas, the Greeks who explicitly reject the procession of the Spirit *a Filio* are not only "in error" *(errare videntur, error)*, but an argument here is judged to be "ridiculous" *(ridiculosum)*,

---

[185] The numerous citations of this "necessity" may be seen in all the principal discussions of the procession *a Filio*.

[186] CEG II, ch. 31.

another there is "frivolous" *(frivolum)*, while a third is said to be
"easily resolved even by a novice theologian." In general, the objections formulated by the Greeks are treated very severely and considered "barely worthy of a response *(vix responsione sunt
digna)*."[187] Indeed, the theological standard of counterarguments
by the Greeks was not always very high.[188] The rejection of the
procession *a Filio* despite the concession offered by the expression
"profluere a Filio" is imputed to their ignorance *(ignorantia)* or
impudence *(protervia)*, or else to "another reason" of which
Thomas unfortunately tells us nothing (he seems to suggest that
arguments of a theological nature are not the only ones at issue).[189]
Faced with this problem, Thomas applies to the Greeks the judgment which Aristotle leveled at Anaxagoras: They are not aware of
the meaning of their own words *(propriam vocem ignorant)*. Or,
taking up the words of the First Letter to Timothy (1:7), he
describes them as "desiring to be teachers of the law, without
understanding either what they are saying or the things about
which they make assertions."[190] These are not the only signs of
impatience, and given Thomas's usual sobriety of language, their
impact upon the reader is all the more striking.[191]

These pejorative tones should however be seen in their historical context if they are to be given a fair hearing. They will be found
in the works of all of Thomas's contemporaries: Albert or Bonaventure, for example.[192] Unfortunately, this controversial tone had

---

[187] We find these expressions notably in *SCG* IV, ch. 24 (#3605, 3610, 3621, 3622, 3625).

[188] For example, it was argued that the Holy Spirit would be the grandson *(nepos)* of the Father; or that he would proceed from himself, and so on; *De potentia*, q. 10, a. 4, arg. 2–5.

[189] *ST* I, q. 36, a. 2, sol.; *De potentia*, q. 10, a. 5, sol. ("vel propter quamcumque aliam causam").

[190] *De potentia*, q. 10, a. 4, sol. For Anaxagore, see *In librum primum Aristotelis De generatione et corruptione*, Book I, lect. 1, ed. Raimondo Spiazzi (Turin: Mari-etti, 1952), p. 321 (#7): ". . . sicut ille qui ponit aliquid non conveniens suae positioni."

[191] There are, however, other examples of Thomas in polemical vein; see J.-P. Tor-rell, *Saint Thomas Aquinas*, vol. 1, *The Person and His Work*, pp. 90–95.

[192] Bonaventure, I *Sent.*, d. 11, q. un., a. 1; Albert, I *Sent.*, d. 11, a. 6.

been adopted since Photius, and the two parties were accustomed to addressing each other in the same terms of mutual reproach. If we wish to appreciate their significance, we should examine them once more in the light of Thomas's basic attitude toward the East and his pneumatology.

Firstly, and this should be emphasized, Thomas shows enormous interest in the Greek Fathers (he uses this term to refer to all the Fathers of the Eastern Church). We have seen that one of the principal characteristics of his patristic documentation is the research into Greek sources (as numerous, if not more so, than the Latin sources!). These bear a doctrinal content which he values very highly, not only from a point of view of apologetics, but also by virtue of their actual authority.[193] We cannot fail to notice that, amongst these Greek sources, Thomas has a particular affinity for the Alexandrines (Athanasius, Cyril, Didymus). His understanding of the Cappadocians, whose doctrine is extended and determined by Byzantine tradition, seems in contrast less penetrating, at least as far as the doctrine of the monarchy of the Father is concerned (despite the texts cited in the *Contra errores Graecorum*). Thomas is convinced that the *doctores Graecorum* are teaching the procession of the Holy Spirit *a Filio* in the same way, although using other words.[194]

We should also note Thomas's fundamentally positive attitude, in terms of the doctrine of faith, toward the Greeks of his day: "If we examine closely what the Greeks are saying, we will find that they differ from us more in the wording than in the sense *(magis differunt in verbis quam in sensu)*."[195] Such remarks are not isolated instances within medieval Latin theology (Thomas is probably echoing Peter Lombard), and we also find examples of this positive

---

[193] We are concerned here only with the procession of the Spirit *a Filio*, but other examples could be given. Thus, in the *Catena aurea*, there are far more Greek authors cited than Latin; cf. J. P. Torrell, *Saint Thomas Aquinas*, vol. 1, *The Person and His Work*, pp. 138–40.

[194] CEG II, ch. 28.

[195] *De potentia*, q. 10, a. 5. The context shows that he is referring to contemporary Greeks and not to Church Fathers. This observation introduces the long examination of the reasons why the Holy Spirit would not be distinguished from the Son if he did not proceed from him.

attitude amongst eastern theologians themselves.[196] Thomas thus acknowledges the existence of the same faith in the Eastern Church, but expressed in words which are different and which give rise to the controversy. As regards the procession of the Holy Spirit, he finds indications of this same sense of the faith in the fact that the Greeks recognize that the Holy Spirit is the *Spirit of the Son*, and in the fact that many of them accept the formula *the Holy Spirit proceeds from the Father through the Son*, "which they could not say if the procession of the Spirit were altogether separated from the Son; this shows that the Greeks also believe that the procession of the Holy Spirit possesses a certain relationship with the Son."[197]

This basic attitude explains why Thomas never accuses the Greeks outright of being "heretics." We might see this as being of cold comfort, but such reserve is more significant than might appear. In actual fact, there is no shortage of accusations of heresy launched at the Greeks by theologians, including even the greatest, of the thirteenth century. When addressing the procession of the Holy Spirit, Bonaventure for example does not hesitate to describe the Greeks as *haeretici*.[198] The Greeks certainly appear in Thomas's list of errors, side by side with the heretics whose doctrines he rejects,[199] but whenever he is dealing directly with the procession of the Holy

---

[196] Peter Lombard, *Sententiae,* Book I, dist. 11, ch. 2, p. 116: "Graeci in sensu nobiscum convenient etsi verbis differant. . . . In eandem nobiscum fidei sententiam convenire videntur, licet verbis dissentiant." Theophylactus, an author whom Thomas is fond of, demonstrates fundamentally the same attitude; yet further examples will be found in Yves Congar, "Quatre siècles de désunion et d'affrontement. Comment Grecs et Latins se sont appréciés réciproquement au point de vue ecclésiologique?" *Istina* 13 (1968): 131–52.

[197] *De potentia,* q. 10, a. 5: "Quod non posset dici, si processio Spiritus sancti omnino esset a Filio absoluta. Unde datur intelligi quod etiam ipsi Graeci processionem Spiritus sancti aliquem ordinem ad Filium habere intelligunt." Cf. *ST* I, q. 36, a. 2.

[198] Bonaventure, I *Sent.,* d. 11, a. un., q. 1, concl.: "Et ideo facti sunt haeretici, quia denegant fidei veritatem;" ad 9: "Et ideo tanquam haereticos et schismaticos eos damnat Romana Ecclesia." Albert the Great seems a little more measured in tone, but nonetheless states: "Error est dicere Spiritum Sanctum non procedere a Filio, et defendere haeresis est" (I *Sent.,* d. 11, a. 6). There is nothing of this sort in Thomas's corresponding article on the *Sentences.*

[199] Notably in the Prologues of the *Contra errores Graecorum* I and II.

Spirit he confines himself to describing their position as erroneous *(error, errare)*. The significance of these terms needs to be weighed carefully if Thomas is to be understood. The principal heresy pertaining to the question under discussion is Sabellianism (lack of a real distinction between the Son and the Holy Spirit), which is the logical outcome of the negation of the procession *a Filio*. Evidently, Thomas knows that the doctrine professed by the Greeks is not in any way Sabellian. The problem lies in the fact that, in his opinion—the strength of which we have witnessed in our survey of the biblical, patristic, and speculative dossier—the negation of the procession *a Filio*, if it is followed through to its logical conclusion, leads *necessarily* to Sabellianism: And it is *this* which is heretical *(hoc autem est haereticum)*.[200] As we have said, however, Thomas knows very well that the Greeks are not drawing any such conclusion. In the mind of a Latin theologian such as Thomas, the rejection of the procession of the Holy Spirit *a Patre* and *a Filio* on the part of Christians who firmly rule out any Sabellianism involves a sort of internal contradiction.[201] This is why the position of the Greeks seems to him utterly "incomprehensible." The pejorative comments which we mentioned earlier are giving voice precisely to this incomprehension. Thus, we can sum up Thomas's attitude in historical terms partly as one which was fundamentally positive in matters which touch upon faith (Greeks and Latins "differ more in the wording than in the sense"), and partly as one which associated the negation of the procession of the Spirit *a Filio* with an unfathomable incomprehensibility.

Our current knowledge of the pneumatology of the Fathers allows us a better understanding of the difficulties Thomas faced regarding the doctrine of the Eastern Church. We find ourselves in the midst of a tension between a doctrine which is at heart concerned with the relational constitution of the divine person (the Latin doctrine developed by Thomas) and a mode of thinking which conceives

---

[200] *ST* I, q. 36, a. 2.

[201] For further insight into the idea of implicit contradiction, see *De potentia*, q. 10, a. 5, ad 14.

of the person firstly in terms of the manner of possessing the divine essence (Cappadocian and Byzantine thought). A conflict such as this is hard to resolve. As Thomas reads the Greek Fathers he interprets their thinking in the light of his personalist doctrine of relation, and thus rather too readily harnesses the Eastern Fathers as a whole to the Latin expression of the faith. But he finds clear and authentic indications of consonant approaches in several Eastern Fathers (principally amongst the Alexandrines). His hermeneutic principles are still acknowledged as being well-founded, but theologians these days have good reason to show their awareness of more subtle distinctions in their historical interpretation of the doctrine of the Greek Fathers, which, together with that of the Latin Fathers before the schism, could provide the basis for theological agreement.[202] Thomas shows us, however, that the doctrine of the Roman Catholic Church cannot, without precipitating enormous harm, discard all that is involved in the affirmation of the procession *a Filio*. His theology appears particularly revealing in this regard, as much by virtue of his biblical and patristic hermeneutics as by virtue of the doctrinal grounds of the Latin tradition, which he was able to demonstrate in such extensive and penetrating detail.

Conclusion

A close study of Thomas's pneumatology clearly demonstrates that the procession of the Spirit *a Filio*, leaving aside the vocabulary problems of which he was aware, is intimately and inextricably linked with all the dominant influences of his Trinitarian doctrine: real distinction of the persons by relative opposition according to origin, the doctrine of the Word and of Love, and order in the Trinity. On this ground, it is the faith expressed at Nicea and Constantinople which is

---

[202] If agreement could be reached and the mutual respect of each doctrinal tradition ensured, the opportunity could also present itself to eliminate the mention of the *Filioque* in the Symbol of the Roman Catholic Church. This was the stand taken notably by André de Halleux and seconded, let us not forget, by Father Marie-Vincent Leroy; see *RT* 82 (1982): 106. The addition of the *Filioque* to the symbol should not however be confused with the doctrine itself.

at stake as far as Thomas is concerned, for the procession of the Spirit *a Patre et a Filio* seems to him indispensable to an explanation of the faith professed by the councils of antiquity. This idea of faith being at issue explains why he applies himself with such care to the scrutiny, in all its aspects, of this point of pneumatology.

From a historical viewpoint, the quality of patristic research undertaken by Thomas cannot fail to be appreciated, despite his limited comprehension of the Cappadocian and Byzantine tradition. We need only think of his documentation concerning the conciliar tradition of antiquity, or his research into the controversy engaged in by Cyril and Theodoret, for example, to be convinced of this. At an even deeper level, and in harmony with his gleanings from the patristic tradition, the procession of the Spirit *a Filio* is grounded in Thomas's reading of Scripture, which provides the basic foundation of this doctrine. This reading of Scripture involves a strictly theological interpretation which even at this stage brings in the principles of Trinitarian doctrine, and in which the issue at stake is none other than faith in the Trinity confronted by all forms of Arianism and Sabellianism. It also reveals the soteriorological implications, for the procession of the Spirit *a Filio* gives expression to the Christological reality of the life of grace. In reflecting with St. Thomas on the procession of the Holy Spirit, we are thus committing ourselves to an equally intensive exploration—within the bounds of a coherent synthesis—of biblical and patristic reflection, and of the most far-reaching elements of the structure of the Trinitarian doctrine which is driving him and defining his guiding principles.

CHAPTER SEVEN

Biblical Exegesis and the Speculative Doctrine of the Trinity in St. Thomas Aquinas's Commentary on St. John

T HE THEOLOGICAL exposition of the Gospel of St. John is certainly to be considered the most fully complete and most profound commentary that St. Thomas Aquinas has left us.[1] According to M.-D. Philippe, the commentary on St. John is "the theological work par excellence of St. Thomas": This commentary enables us to enter into the theological intelligence of St. Thomas, even better than does the *Summa theologiae* or the *Summa contra Gentiles*.[2] This special value of the *Lectura in Ioannem* is to be found notably in the importance of the speculative developments of the biblical exposition, which count among the characteristic features of this work. This general observation brings up a question: Is the biblical exegesis of St. Thomas in his commentary on St. John different than his speculative teaching in the *Summa theologiae*, and if so, what is the difference?

To try and give a partial response to this question, the present contribution proposes to consider the commentary's Trinitarian doctrine. Our approach does not examine the details of St. Thomas's teaching on particular points of Trinitarian doctrine, but it considers

---

[1] Translation by Matthew Levering.

[2] Marie-Dominique Philippe, "Preface" to *Thomas d'Aquin, Commentaire sur l'évangile de S. Jean*, vol. 1 (Paris: Cerf, 1998), pp. 10–11. Cf. J.-P. Torrell, *Saint Thomas Aquinas*, vol. 1: *The Person and His Work*, p. 200.

rather the body of the commentary's Trinitarian doctrine under the aspect of the whole and of its organic unity. The choice of Trinitarian theology is not without reasons: It concerns a cornerstone of the speculative theology of St. Thomas and, as such, gives a number of clues for measuring the connection between exegesis and speculative theology. Our comparative study will try to find the answers to three specific questions. (1) What is the Trinitarian doctrinal content of the commentary on St. John in relation to that of the *Summa theologiae*? (2) What is St. Thomas's exegetical and theological method in the Trinitarian teaching of the commentary on St. John? (3) What does the commentary on St. John bring to our understanding of the Trinitarian doctrine of St. Thomas?

The Trinitarian Doctrine of the Commentary of St. John and the *Summa theologiae*

To verify the extent of the Trinitarian themes treated in the commentary on St. John, the comparison with the treatise of the Trinity in the *Summa theologiae* (*Prima pars*, qq. 27–43) is very instructive. As a matter of fact, most of the themes expounded in the *Summa* are present in the commentary on St. John: They are not only mentioned indirectly, but they are expressly expounded or discussed by St. Thomas. The results of our comparison have been gathered together in the synoptic table which follows. This table however is not exhaustive, as one should still add numerous allusions and evocations which have not been given here. The passages indicated are sometimes comprised of a short insight on a theme, sometimes a more extensive account: The references are, for this reason, often of unequal value (the numbers in thick characters indicate the most important passages; the numbers in parentheses point to some themes mentioned by St. Thomas but which are not subject of discussion). This table therefore only gives an approximate material idea, but it allows one however to measure the amplitude of the Trinitarian doctrine of the commentary on St. John (passages of the commentary are indicated following the numeration used in the

Marietti edition and in the English translation by James A. Weisheipl and Fabian R. Larcher)[3] compared with that of the *Summa theologiae* (qq. 27–43):

Q. 27, a. 1: #**24–33, 41,** 56, 769, 2107, 2064, 2114, **2161,** 2172; a. 2: #**29, 31** (24–33), 41–42, 46, 218, 547, **750,** 768, 782, 977, 978, 1462, 1869, 2161, 2262; a. 3: #2064; a. 4: #545, 753, 2064; a. 5: –.

Q. 28, a. 1: #**2113;** a. 2: #**2113; a. 3**: #**2063, 2112–13;** a. 4: –.

Q. 29, a. 1: –; a. 2: –; a. 3: – (#28, 49); a. 4:–.

Q. 30, a. 1: – (#64, 2248); a. 2: –; a. 3: – (#1450–51, 1462, 2050, 2172); a. 4: –.

Q. 31, a. 1: – (#64, 1946); a. 2: #1451, 1911–12; a. 3: #2187; a. 4: #1154, 2172, **2187–88.**

Q. 32, a. 1: –; a. 2: –; a. 3: –; a. 4: –.

Q. 33, a. 1: #**36, 1183,** 1971, 2213; a. 2: #1278, 1922, 2195; a. 3: #36, 390, 741, 1060, 1278, 1922, 2195, 2520–21; a. 4: #747.

Q. 34, a. 1: #**24–33 [28–29],** 41, 46, 49, 50–51, 54, **55,** 56–59, 534, 540, 754, 780, 1874, 1878, 1893; a. 2: #**25,** 28–29, 33, 42, 754, 1720, 1726, 1869, 1951; a. 3: #7–8, **27, 32, 35,** 38, **68–78 [76–77], 79–88, 89–94, 118,** 133–34, 135, 136, 740, 761, 1183, 1450, 1553, 1695, **1723,** 1781, 1869, 1879, 2201.

Q. 35, a. 1: #1879 (#1712, 1878, 1951); a. 2: –.

Q. 36, a. 1: #452, **1916,** 1955, 2062, **2064;** a. 2: #543, 753, 1092, **1916,** 1956–1957, **2062–65, 2107–15,** 2538; a. 3: #2064 (#74–76); a. 4: #1183, 2065 (2115).

Q. 37, a. 1: #357, 545, 753, 1004, 2060, 2064, 2262; a. 2: #2214.

Q. 38, a. 1: –; a. 2: –.

Q. 39, a. 1: #2113, 2209; a. 2: – (#1450–51, 1794, 1929); a. 3: – (#187, 2188); a. 4: #**44,** 58, 59, 187, 1851; a. 5: #**44;** a. 6:

---

3 St. Thomas Aquinas, *Super Evangelium S. Ioannis lectura,* ed. Raffaele Cai (Turin/Rome: Marietti, 1952). *Commentary on the Gospel of John,* Part I, trans. James A. Weisheipl and Fabian R. Larcher (Albany, NY: Magi Books, 1980); Part II, trans. James A. Weisheipl and Fabian R. Larcher (Petersham, MA: St. Bede's Publications, 1999).

–; a. 7: –; a. 8: #1912, 1961, 2365 (#76, 77, 90, 207, 533, 1192, 1290, 1869).

Q. 40, a. 1: **#2113;** a. 2: **#2063, 2064, 2111–13;** a. 3: – (#2063); a. 4: –.

Q. 41, a. 1: –; a. 2: #545, 753, 2114, 2262; a. 3: #162, 202, 2108, **2115;** a. 4: – (#543); a. 5: –; a. 6: –.

Q. 42, a. 1: – (cf. a. 4); a. 2: #37–39, **41,** 62, 66–67, 70, 750, 783, 1059–60, 2161; a. 3: #**34,** 2064, **2107, 2112–13;** a. 4: #11, 59, 64, **741–47,** 769, 783, 1278, 1451, 1875, 1970–71, 2192, 2208; a. 5: #36, 49, 50, 54, **1466,** 1880–81, 1887, **1891,** 1926–29, 2161, 2172, 2214, 2239; a. 6: #62, 69, 71, 76, 452, 748, 749, **751–53,** 761, 786–87, 797, 817, 1304, 1450–51, 1743, 1775, 1999.

Q. 43, a. 1: #144, 769, 1794, 1944, 2061, 2088–90, 2161–62; a. 2: #1236, **2061, 2161–62,** 2204; a. 3: #176, 292, 541–44, 1853, 1915, 1920, 1930, 1943–47, 1958, 1961, 2061, 2246–47, 2248, 2269–70; a. 4: #176, 1192, 2248; a. 5: #292, 946, 1930, 1961, 2090; a. 6: – (cf. a. 3); a. 7: #1662, 2538–40; a. 8: #1794, 1911, 1956–57, 1958, 2059, 2061, 2248.

The Trinitarian Themes of the Commentary on St. John

The most important Trinitarian accounts in St. Thomas's commentary on John concern the five following fields: (1) the person of the Son and his generation (in particular the doctrine of the Word); (2) the person of the Spirit and his procession; (3) the person of the Father; (4) the equality of the persons; and (5) the mission of the persons (this corresponds to the teaching in the questions 33, 34, 36, 42, and 43 of the *Prima pars* of the *Summa theologiae*).

The most remarkable case is without a doubt the doctrine of the Word. If one excepts a few details, the whole doctrine of question 34 of the *Summa* is to be found in the commentary on St. John: The meaning of the word *verbum* explained on the basis of Aristotle's *Perihermeneias*, the relationship between the inner word and the exterior word, the mode of procession of the Word in God, the differences between the human and divine Word, the exclusively personal signification of the name *Verbum* in God, the relationship of the Word to the Father who says it (coeternity, consubstantiality, etc.), the distinction of the Word and of the Father, the relational character of the Word which constitutes the property of the Son, and so forth. The speculative account of the commentary on St. John is even more developed than that of the *Summa* on several points: One can observe this in the numerous explications which concern the creative action of the Word,[4] but also in the affirmation of the *necessity* of a word in all intellectual nature, and in the conception of the word as the relative object of intellection ("that in which the intellect knows [*in quo intellectus intelligit*]").[5] The doctrine of the Word, in the commentary on St. John, gives a characteristic example of a highly speculative point of view which is treated in such amplitude as to be comparable, even superior to, the *Summa theologiae*. It is also very near to the *Summa contra Gentiles* in which the exposition dedicated to the Word is structured by the *Prologue* of St. John (Book IV, ch. 11).[6]

The study of the person of the Father and of the Holy Spirit manifests equally the extent of the Trinitarian doctrine in the commentary on St. John: St. Thomas, in a way close to that of the *Summa theologiae*, expounds in what way the word "principium" applies to the Father, giving the precision that paternity constitutes the personal property of the Father. It gives details in several places of the analogic extension of the name "Father" which applies to the Trinitarian relation of the Father to the Son and then to the relationship which the Father has with the creatures, in the order of creation and in the order of grace. For that which concerns the Father, only the study of the innascibility seems to be less developed in the

---

[4] See the above table under the rubric: q. 34, a. 3.

[5] *In Ioan* 1·1 (#25). On these two points, see Yves Floucat, "L'intellection et son Verbe selon saint Thomas d'Aquin," *RT* 97 (1997): 650–54 and 684–91.

[6] See chapter 3 above: Approaches to a theological understanding of the mystery. St. Thomas's commentary on St. John does not cover the exclusion of the name "Verbum" to designate the Holy Spirit (*ST* I, q. 34, a. 2 ad 5): but this doctrinal point stays attached to biblical exegesis, as the commentary on the Epistle to the Hebrews explicitly witnesses (*In Heb.* 1:3, #34).

commentary on St. John in comparison to the *Summa theologiae*
(q. 33, a. 4). As to the Holy Spirit, the Johannine commentary presents also a teaching very similar to that of the q. 36 in the *Summa
theologiae*: Apart from the explanation of the proper name *"Spiritus
Sanctus,"* St. Thomas develops in a very broad way the doctrine of
the procession of the Holy Spirit *a Filio*, as well as that of the unity
of the Father and the Son as principle of the Spirit, treating the procession *per Filium* more briefly. The commentary on St. John (especially in the exegesis of John 14:15, John 15:26, and John 16:14–15)
presents a highly speculative technical doctrine, which brings to
light all the major themes of the doctrine of the *Summa*: the mode
of procession of the Son and the Spirit, the personal distinction by
relative opposition depending on the origin, the unity of the Father
and of the Son who are the one principle of the Spirit, the theme of
Love, Trinitarian order, the identity of the principle of communication and of the reality communicated. The biblical exegesis brings
St. Thomas to demonstrate that, *Trinitate posita*, it is necessary to
recognize that the Spirit proceeds from the Father and the Son.[7]
More developed in the commentary on St. John than in the *Summa
theologiae*, the doctrine of the *Filioque* also provides the place where
par excellence St. Thomas sets forth his doctrine on the various
types of distinction, in particular about the real relation depending
on the origin which alone distinguishes the persons in God. The exegesis of St. John gives the occasion for an exposition of the *Filioque*
which involves all essential elements of the doctrine of relation, as
one finds it in question 28 of the *Prima pars*. It is again in the exegesis of these pneumatological passages that St. Thomas expounds
several elements concerning the relationship of the persons to the
essence, or the relationship of the persons to properties and relations: the real identity of the person with the essence, the real identity of the relation with the essence, as well as the necessity to pose
the relation of origin (relative opposition) to be able to conceive the
distinct persons (cf. *Prima pars*, qq. 40 and 41). One can observe

---

[7] *In Ioan.* 15:26 (#2063; cf. #2064–65); *In Ioan.* 16:14–15 (#2110–15). On
these arguments, see above chapter 6.

here again the proximity of the commentary on St. John to the *Summa contra Gentiles*: In the *Summa contra Gentiles*, indeed, it is equally in the study of the procession of the Holy Spirit (Book IV, ch. 24–25) that St. Thomas placed his most complete exposition about the relations of origin in God.[8]

The equality of the divine persons and the mission of the persons constitute the two last particulary large Trinitarian themes developed by the commentary on St. John. If one excepts the general reflection on the notion of equality in God (I, q. 42, a. 1), the largest part of the doctrinal contents of question 42 of the *Prima pars* of the *Summa theologiae* is found in the commentary on St. John: the co-eternity of the Father and the Son, the Trinitarian order, the equal greatness of the Father and the Son, the mutual immanence of the Father and the Son, as well as the equality of power in the Father and the Son. The attention given to the equality of the persons corresponds to the general subject of the fourth Gospel, following St. Thomas: Whereas the other gospel writers are particulary attentive to what Christ accomplishes in his flesh, St. John "gazes on the very deity of our Lord Jesus Christ, by which he is equal to the Father."[9] Apart from the mutual immanence of the Father and of the Son, which reveals the divine unity of the persons, we must observe the numerous developments concerning the equality of power and of operation of the Father and the Son. St. Thomas gives us the reason: "For the clearest indication of the nature of a thing is taken from its works. Therefore, from the fact that he does the works of God it can be very clearly known and believed that Christ is God."[10] The attention given to the equality of the Father and the Son expressly aims at manifesting the divinity of Christ, which constitutes the trait proper to the fourth Gospel.

Lastly the long developments concerning the mission of the persons give place to complete expositions on the concepts of *"processio"*

---

[8] See in chapter 3: Approaches to a theological understanding of the mystery.

[9] *In Ioan.,* Prologue (#11).

[10] *In Ioan.* 10:38 (#1466).

and of *"missio,"* on the visible and invisible missions, and on the
indwelling of the persons by grace. It is in the context of missions, for
example, that St. Thomas explains in a broad way the notion of eternal procession *(exitus)*, which carries the double aspect of the identity
of nature (immanent action) and the personal distinction.[11] With the
exception of article 6 of question 43 of the *Prima pars*, where St.
Thomas establishes that the mission of the divine persons has place
in all those who live from grace, the biggest part of the doctrinal contents of question 43 is found in the commentary on St. John. One is
hardly surprised to note that this teaching is placed, in its essentials,
in the exegesis of the passages of St. John which concern the
announcement of the sending out of the Holy Spirit and the coming
of Christ to the faithful (chapters 15–17 of the fourth Gospel). It
must be added that, in the expositions of the Word and the Spirit, as
well as in the discussion of the missions, the commentary on St. John
includes most of the explanations concerning the procession in God
treated by the three first articles of question 27 of the *Prima pars*.

St. Thomas's commentary on St. John treats several other technical themes. We have already mentioned diverse doctrinal points
which touch on the relationship of persons, of relations, and of the
essence. It must be added that, in the context of anti-Arian criticism,
St. Thomas shows the necessity of the notional act of generation
(divine will is not the formal principle of the generation of the
Word) and the substantial principle of a notional act (the Son does
not proceed *de nihilo*, but he is engendered from the substance of the
Father). Treated in question 41 (a. 2 and 3) of the *Prima pars*, in the
section on notional acts, these problems are discussed by the commentary on St. John in the context of the generation of the Son and
the procession of the Holy Spirit. Here St. Thomas underlines, with
remarkable rigor, the identity of the principle of communication and
the reality communicated which is divine substance.[12] Lastly, several
problems of Trinitarian language hold St. Thomas's attention while
he comments on St. John. Whereas the *Summa theologiae* gathers

---

[11] *In Ioan.* 16:28 (#2161); cf. 15:26 (#2062).
[12] *In Ioan.* 16:15 (#2115).

these language problems in two defined sections (*Prima pars*, q. 31 and q. 39), the commentary on St. John explains them according to the texts of the fourth Gospel: the personal otherness meant by the word *"alius,"* the use of exclusive words qualifying essential or personal names (*"solus"*), the technical logic of *"suppositio"* in Trinitarian language, and the practice of Trinitarian appropriations. We are in the presence, in the middle of a biblical commentary, of a body of Trinitarian doctrine especially well developed.

Absent or Less Developed Trinitarian Themes

Before trying to evaluate the relationship of St. John's commentary and the *Summa theologiae*, it must noted that the commentary does not pay the same attention to all Trinitarian themes. The comparison with the *Summa theologiae* manifests that certain themes, to which St. Thomas gives over a question or an article in his systematic work, are not given the same place in the commentary on St. John. Among these less developed themes, one must first of all bring out the definition of the person, that is to say the signification of the word "persona" and the justification of the use of this term in Trinitarian theology. The commentary on St. John frequently employs the word "persona" or "hypostasis" to speak about the Father, Son, and Holy Spirit. St. Thomas explains that these two words both mean the same reality in God, and he specifies that the divine persons are distinct in virtue of their relations (or personal properties). But he does not explain the signification of the word "persona" and does not develop the speculative study of the concept of person in the context of Trinitarian faith. The statements about hypostatic union employ as frequently the words "person" or "hypostasis," but without precisely defining the concept of person.[13] The famous definition of person

---

13 The *Index thomisticus* allows one to discover 238 uses of the lemma "persona" in the commentary on St. John. For example: "persona Verbi seu suppositum" (#170); "hypostasis seu persona, quae est eadem utriusque naturae in Christo" (#175); "Trinitas personarum . . . tres personae" (#357); "si igitur Filius et Spiritus Sanctus sunt personae distinctae procedentes a Patre, oportet quod aliquibus proprietatibus oppositis distinguantur" (#2063); "cum personae divinae relationibus distinguantur" (#2113); and so on.

given by Boethius is absent from the commentary on St. John, as it
is absent from St. Thomas's commentary on St. Matthew and St.
Paul. In reality, despite the fact that St. Thomas does not use the
definition of the person made by Boethius, he employs a very precise concept when speaking of the divine Word as "something that
subsists in the divine nature *(aliquid subsistens in natura divina)*."[14]
St. Thomas's explanations focus on a distinct reality, in virtue of a
relation or a property, which subsists in the manner of a hypostasis
in the identity of the divine nature. If we take into account the affirmation of the distinction of hypostasis, which St. Thomas recalls in
the same place, one can ascertain that the expression *"aliquid subsistens in natura divina"* corresponds to the formal signification of the
word "person" in God, despite the fact that St. Thomas does not
specify it in his commentary.[15]

Thus, when he comments on the Gospel of St. John (as well as
on St. Matthew and the Epistles of St. Paul), St. Thomas uses a
very clear notion to set forth the hypostatic subsistence in God,
but without discussing the word "person" and its signification. This
silence is not exceptional: One can observe St. Thomas's similar
discretion concerning the word "person" in the Trinitarian treatise
in the *Summa contra Gentiles*.[16] It is not easy to evaluate the motives
of this discretion. Aquinas knows that the Bible does not apply the
word "persona" to the Three Divine: The Trinitarian concept of
"person" comes from the defense of faith by the Fathers in face of
heresies.[17] But the non-biblical origin of the concept of person
does not suffice to explain St. Thomas's reserve, for the commentary on St. John abundantly develops other doctrines issued from
patristic controversies (the doctrine of Trinitarian relations for example). At the risk of surprising, one must rather conclude that the
specific study of the word "person" (the study of the word, and not

---

[14] *In Ioan.* 1:1 (#28); cf. #49: "Verbum erat in principio, non ut accidens: sed
erat apud Deum, ut subsistens, et hypostasis divina."

[15] See for example *De potentia,* q. 9, a. 4: "persona vero divina, formali significa-
tione, significat distinctum subsistens in natura divina."

[16] See in chapter 3: "Problems of Trinitarian Theology."

[17] *ST* I, q. 29, a. 3, ad 1.

of the reality) does not constitute an indispensable element of a
doctrine on the Trinity by St. Thomas (biblical commentaries and
Summa contra Gentiles).

One can point out the absence of other important elements of St.
Thomas's speculative doctrine. Thus, whereas the exposition of the
Word is extremely well developed and complete, the parallel explications concerning the Holy Spirit as Love are quite thin. In his commentary on St. John, St. Thomas designates several times the Holy
Spirit as Love.[18] Aquinas specifies that the Holy Spirit proceeds as
Love by the mode of will,[19] and distinguishes essential Love from personal (or notional) Love in God.[20] St. Thomas excludes expressly that
the Son proceeds by mode of Love: Love is the reason of the procession of the Holy Spirit but not that of the Son who proceeds by mode
of nature or of intellect.[21] He also specifies that the Holy Spirit is the
mutual *"dilectio"* of the Father and the Son, their "mutual bond."[22]
The Father and the Son love each other though the Holy Spirit.[23] But
St. Thomas does not expound his doctrine of the presence of "God
loved in God who loves," that is to say the loving *"impressio"* or *"affectio"* that springs up in the will when it loves (which allows one to give
account, by analogy, of the personal name *Love* which we give to the
Holy Spirit): This doctrine, in the *Summa contra Gentiles* and in the
Summa theologiae (as well as in the *Disputed Questions De potentia* and
in the *Compendium theologiae*), has in the study of the Holy Spirit a
role comparable to the doctrine of the Word in the study on the
Son.[24] However, despite the fact that the doctrine of the Word is very
well developed in the commentary on St. John, the elaboration of the

---

[18] See for example *In Ioan.* 15:26 (#2060).
[19] *In Ioan.* 15:26 (#2064): "persona procedens per modum voluntatis ut amor."
The Son is designated as "persona procedens per modum naturae ut Filius"
(ibid.).
[20] *In Ioan.* 5:20 (#753) and 17.24 (#2262).
[21] *In Ioan.* 3:35 (#545), 5:20 (#753) and 15:26 (#2064).
[22] *In Ioan.* 3:35 (#545): "dilectio Patris ad Filium est Spiritus Sanctus;" cf. *Lectura in Ioan.* 6:70 (#1004): ". . . Spiritus Sancti, qui est amor Patris et Filii, et
nexus utriusque."
[23] *In Ioan.* 17:11 (#2214): "Pater et Filius diligunt se Spiritu Sancto."
[24] Cf. *ST* I, q. 37, a. 1. See chapters 3 and 4.

parallel doctrine of Love is very summary, or even absent: The commentary on St. John by St. Thomas designates several times the Holy Spirit as Love, without ever giving its speculative reason. This difference may be explained by the fact that the Prologue of the fourth Gospel expressly mentions the *Word* and thus gives the textual opening for an exposition on the Word, whereas it is not the same for Love. One can make the same observation about the commentary on St. Matthew and the commentary on St. Paul's Epistles. Despite the close links which attach the doctrine of the Word to that of Love in systematic works by St. Thomas, the commentary on St. John suggests that these two doctrines are not exactly on the same level. We can observe also that the personal name *"Donum,"* a proper name of the Holy Spirit to which the *Summa theologiae* gives up a whole question (I, q. 38), is not treated in the commentary on St. John: The theme of "Gift" is present, but St. Thomas does not explain the personal feature of this name.[25]

The absence of speculative developments on other Trinitarian themes is less surprising. Thus the commentary on St. John presents a very concise doctrine concerning the name "Image" to which the *Summa theologiae* gives a whole question (I, q. 35). St. Thomas does not give the elements which contribute to define the Image, and does not expose the reason of the personal signification of the word "Image." He explains however that the Son is the perfect Image of the Father, in a conformity of nature, because he is his Word: It is why the Son makes known the Father.[26] If the commentary on St. John is rather sober concerning this theme of the Image, it is without doubt because the fourth Gospel does not offer a textual occasion for such an exposition. Indeed, other biblical commentaries by St. Thomas offer complete expositions on the personal property of *"Imago,"* broader and more developed than question 35 of the *Prima pars*: This is the case, of course, of the

---

[25] The commentary on St. Matthew, as well as the commentaries on St. Paul, mention the theme of the Spirit as *Gift*, but do not offer any more speculative explanation about this proper name of the third person.

[26] *In Ioan.* 14:7 (#1878–1979); cf. 12:45 (#1712).

commentary on the Epistle to the Colossians.[27] The same observation can be applied to the position of natural reason facing the Trinitarian mystery. Whereas the *Summa theologiae* gives an article to this question (*ST* I, q. 32, a. 1), the commentary on St. John does not discuss the limits of the knowledge of the Trinity by natural reason, although St. Thomas does remind us of the prerogatives of faith. This theme, however, is not absent from the biblical commentaries of St. Thomas: One can find a brief statement in the commentary of the Epistle to the Romans.[28]

Lastly, one realizes without much surprise that several technical problems are absent from the commentary, or only evoked without being discussed. The commentary on St. John does not cover the questions which touch on the reasons for the number of processions, the number of persons and of real relations in God (I, q. 27, a. 5; q. 28, a. 4; q, 30, a. 1–4), neither on the Trinitarian notions (I, q. 32), nor on the conceptual priority of notional acts (I, q. 40, a. 4), nor on certain problems touching notional acts and the notional power in God (I, q. 41, a. 1, 4, 5 and 6). As well, the commentary on St. John does not discuss certain questions of language such as the signification of the word "Trinitas" (I, q. 31, a. 1), the attribution of essential terms to the persons, or the attribution of personal names to essential terms (I, q. 39, a. 3 and 6). Although St. Thomas does use Trinitarian appropriations when he comments on St. John, he does not give any speculative justification of the practice of appropriations (I, q. 39, a. 7 and 8); some elements are given in other biblical commentaries.[29] These academic problems are not the core of Trinitarian theology. They concern precisions about the conceptual technical tools which the theologian put to the service of the Trinitarian doctrine. The removal of these technical problems in the commentary on St. John is not surprising and does not

[27] See the commentary of St. Thomas on Col 1:15 (Marietti Edition, #31–37), but also his commentary on 1 Cor 11:7 (Marietti Edition, #604) and on 2 Cor 4:4 (Marietti Edition, #126).
[28] See the commentary of St. Thomas on Rom 1:20 (Marietti Edition, #122).
[29] See notably the commentary of St. Thomas on 2 Cor 13:13 (Marietti Edition, #544).

prejudice the richness of the Trinitarian teaching of the *Lectura* on
St. John.

Evaluation

As intermediary assessment, one can conclude that the Johannine
commentary by St. Thomas contains the essential of the Trinitarian
doctrine as taught in the *Summa theologiae*: The notion of procession, the modes of immanent procession of the Son and the Holy
Spirit (mode of intellect or of nature, and mode of love or of will),
personal subsistence, the doctrine of the Word, the origin of the
Spirit, the relative opposition and the distinction of persons by the
relations, the doctrine of real relation depending on the origin, the
personal properties, the relationship of the persons with the essence
and with the relations, the equality of the persons, the order of
nature *(ordo naturae)* in God, the relationship of the divine persons
to creatures, the mission of the persons as well as several problems
of Trinitarian language, are expounded in detail. The absence of a
study of the signification of the word "person" occurs elsewhere in
St. Thomas and reveals that St. Thomas is able to show the subsistence proper to the Father, to the Son, and to the Spirit in divine
nature, without specifying the meaning of the word that theological tradition has forged to describe this subsistence. The disparity
of the treatment of the personal names "Word" and "Love" shows
for its part that the doctrine of immanent procession is built principally on the study of emanation by intellectual mode, that is to
say, on the Christological doctrine of the Word. The doctrine of
the procession of the Spirit as Love, by mode of will, is much less
clear to our mind.[30]

 As regards the essential elements of Trinitarian theology, the
commentary on St. John shows in a brilliant way that St. Thomas
does not separate biblical Trinitarian theology and speculative Trinitarian theology: It is the same theology, that is to say the same
teaching of Holy Scripture reflected on and expounded, which one
can find in the biblical commentary and in the theological synthe-

---

[30] Cf. *In Ioan.* 15:16 (#2064).

sis of the *Summa*.[31] The doctrinal resources are similar. The principal difference is the order of exposition: Whereas the *Summa theologiae* follows the *ordo disciplinae* which allows one to grasp the speculative bases of Trinitarian theology in their coherence and internal organization,[32] the biblical commentary develops the doctrinal themes as they come up in the text, without loosing sight of the internal speculative arrangement of particular expositions, as we shall see later.

The comparison of the doctrinal content of the Johannine commentary with that of the *Summa theologiae* helps us to understand the very aim of Trinitarian theology. The main themes of the commentary are, as we noted above, the study of each divine person, the mutual relations of the persons and their action in the world. All the other themes are subordinated to the study of the persons and their agency. Such a priority of the divine persons is reinforced by the fact that, in the commentary, the discussion of processions and relations is directly integrated into the study of the persons. This observation confirms the "personalism" of Aquinas in the structure of the treatise on God in the *Summa theologiae*: Trinitarian theology aims to manifest the divine persons in their proper subsistence and in their mutual relations,[33] in order to clarify the economy of creation and salvation

---

[31] In his doctoral dissertation, Wilhelmus G. B. M. Valkenberg noted that "Aquinas's commentaries on the Gospels bear a greater resemblance to his sermons than to his other systematic theological works." (*Did Not Our Heart Burn? Place and Function of Holy Scripture in the Theology of St. Thomas Aquinas* [Utrecht: Thomas Instituut te Utrecht, 1990], p. 247). This does not seem to us to be verified in the commentary on St. John which, concerning Trinitarian theology, is very close to the *Summa theologiae* and even closer to the *Summa contra Gentiles*.

[32] The *Summa theologiae* presents firstly the notion of procession, then the relation, and then the concept of person (*ST* I, q. 27–29), because the theological intelligence of a divine person presupposes that of the relation (the person signifies the relation which subsists), which in turn presupposes the notion of procession (the procession is that which our spirit perceives as the foundation of the relation): that order of speculative exposition is not the one of the discovery of the mystery, but that of the expounding of concepts which allows one to grasp the Trinitarian faith. Cf. *ST* I, q. 27, prol.

[33] See in chapter 5: The essence and the persons in the structure of the treatise on God.

by the divine persons.[34] The Johannine commentary thereby invites us to rediscover the unity of the *Summa*'s Trinitarian treatise centered on the persons.

The More Developed Themes
in the Commentary on St. John

When comparing the commentary on St. John and the *Summa theologiae*, one can see that the commentary develops several themes that the *Summa* examines in the Trinitarian treatise without giving them a comparable amplitude. Without pretending to be complete, one can gather these themes of the commentary into three groups: (1) the unity of knowledge and will of the Father and the Son; (2) the action of the divine persons in the world; and (3) the soteriological dimension of Trinitarian thought.

1. *The first theme is the unity of knowledge and love of the Father and the Son.* The *Summa theologiae* is very clear on the essential unity of the three divine persons whose common attributes are studied in the section concerning the divine essence (I, qq. 2–26). As to the Trinitarian treatise, it indicates well the unity of knowledge and of love of the persons, but only briefly. The unity of science and will is included in the affirmation of the identity of the person and the essence (I, q. 39, a. 1), as in the affirmation of the mutual immanence of the persons (I, q. 42, a. 5), but without being explicitly developed. The unity of the knowledge of the Father and of the Son is more expressly mentioned in the answer to an objection concerning the Word (I, q. 34, a. 1, ad 3) and in the answer to an objection concerning the equality of the Father and the Son (I, q. 42, a. 6, ad 2); their unity of will and of love appears in the study of the property of the Holy Spirit (I, q. 37, a. 1–2). But the explanations of St. Thomas on the science and will of the Son are sober and are not the object of an ample exposition. It is different in the commentary on St. John. St. Thomas, following the biblical text, explains in many places that the Son

---

[34] *ST* I, q. 32, a. 1, ad 3.

knows the Father perfectly.[35] By his eternal generation, the Son receives from the Father divine science, identical to his nature. The Son understands the Father in a way which is proper to him, in mutual comprehension.[36] That is why the Son is the "doctrine of the Father."[37] In the same way, St. Thomas notes several times the unity of the will of the Father and of the Son,[38] by specifying that the Son accomplishes the will which he receives eternally from the Father.[39] This unity is twofold: It consists in the unity of nature, and in the unity of love.[40] In the wake of the knowledge and of the will, St. Thomas expounds the unity of action of the Father and the Son.[41]

In the *Summa theologiae*, several aspects of the unity of knowledge and of will of the Father and the Son have been placed under Christology *(Tertia pars)*, in the study of the science of Christ and his double will (divine and human). The commentary on St. John does not present such a distinction of Trinitarian doctrine and Christology, and thus it illumines the Trinitarian roots of Christological affirmations. At the same time, the commentary on St. John helps to better perceive the soteriological dimension of the Trinitarian unity. St. Thomas explains that the mutual knowledge of the Father and the Son is the basis for the illuminating and revealing work of the Word, and the source of the salvific activity of the Word: The Son knows the salvific will of the Father which he accomplishes,

---

[35] See, in the commentary on St. John, #216–19, 534, 754, 1037, 1062–65, 1228, 1286, 1414, 2017–18.

[36] *In Ioan.* 10:15 (#1414): "Cognoscere Patrem sicut cognitus est ab eo, est proprium solius Filii, quia solus Filius cognoscit Patrem comprehendendo, sicut Pater comprehendendo cognoscit Filium." The Son knows and sees the Father insofar as he proceeds as the personal Word of the Father's intellect (#534).

[37] *In Ioan.* 7:16 (#1037): "Cum doctrina uniuscuiusque nihil aliud sit quam verbum eius, doctrina Patris est ipse Filius "

[38] See, for example, #60 ("concordia voluntatis"), #798 ("eadem voluntas"), #1553.

[39] *In Ioan.* 5:30 (#798).

[40] *In Ioan.* 17:21 (#2240): "In Patre et Filio est duplex unitas, scilicet essentiae et amoris." Cf. 17:11 (#2214).

[41] See, in the commentary on St. John, #752, 761–63, 2246.

procuring for the faithful the security of faith.⁴² In a similar
way, St. Thomas notes the soteriological dimension of the unity
of the Father and of the Son. The double aspect of unity (unity
of nature and unity of love) flows from the Father and the Son
to mankind by similitude, that is to say by participation: The
human unity in the Church is a participation in the divine unity
of the Trinity.⁴³

2. *The commentary on St. John also develops, much more so than the*
Summa theologiae, *diverse themes which concern the actions of the
divine persons in the world.* These themes are not absent from the
Summa, where St. Thomas gathers them together in the study of
certain questions: the personal and the essential sense of the
name "Father" (I, q. 33, a. 3), the relationship to creatures carried by the name "Verbum" (I, q. 34, a. 3), the Holy Spirit as the
Love by which the Father and the Son love each other and love
us (I, q. 37, a. 2, ad 3), and the divine missions (I, q. 43). In all
these areas which touch the action of the three divine persons,
one must note the vast teaching of the commentary.

The action *ad extra* of the Word is the object of the most
numerous explanations of St. Thomas. Without coming back
here to the creative role of the Word in Jn 1:3, one must first
observe that the commentary gives great attention to the illuminating role of the Word and to the participation in the Word by
human knowledge. St. Thomas often explains that all natural
human knowledge is a participation in the Word,⁴⁴ and that the
knowledge of the mystery of God derives from the Word by
grace, in virtue of an illuminating action of the Word who communicates to man, by interior inspiration or revelation, a simili-

---

⁴² *In Ioan.* 10:15 (#1414); cf. In Ioan. 1:18 (#221) and 15:15 (#2017–18).

⁴³ *In Ioan.* 17:11 (#2214): "There is a twofold unity in God. There is a unity of
nature . . . and a unity of love in the Father and Son. . . . Both of these unities
are found in us, not in equal way, but with a certain likeness." Cf. 17:21
(#2239–41).

⁴⁴ *In Ioan.* 1:26 (#246): "He shines in everyone's understanding; because whatever light and whatever wisdom exists in men has come to them from participating in the Word." See the commentary, #95–103, 125, 129, 1869, 2267.

tude to himself.[45] "Because every imperfect thing derives from the perfect, all our knowledge is derived from the Word."[46] These explanations are founded on the doctrine of participation (exemplarity) and on the personal property of the Word: As the Word is in person the concept of the intellect of the Father, it comes to him to manifest the truth by communicating a part of his personal property in the Trinity. As the Son, in virtue of his property (he is the Word of the Father), expresses perfectly all the being of the Father and all the Father contains,[47] he is also in person the Truth which communicates and manifests the Father.[48] By the participation in the personal property of the Word who is the Son, St. Thomas explains, the faithful are deified and being made "connoisseurs of truth" and "sons of God" by participation.[49] This teaching is particularly useful to perceive the soteriological repercussions of the *Summa theologiae* on the Word.

As to the Holy Spirit, it is almost impossible to pick out exhaustively all the actions that St. Thomas mentions in the commentary on St. John. The Holy Spirit fills the earth, inspires and illuminates hearts, saves from slavery and from sin, gives freedom, procures the charity or the dilection whereby we love

---

[45] See, in the commentary, #95, 104–6, 125, 130, 136, 820, 1162, 1384, 1775, 1874, 1879, 2267. This kind of knowledge is the proper effect of the Word's mission: "Effectus missionis huiusmodi est ut faciat homines participes divinae sapientiae, et cognitores veritatis" (*In Ioan.* 14:26; #1958).

[46] *In Ioan.* 8:55 (#1284).

[47] *In Ioan.* 1:1 (#27): "Unicum Verbum divinum est expressivum totius quod in Deo est, non solum personarum, sed etiam creaturarum." "Verbum . . . totius *esse* Patris expressivum" (#29). Cf. *In Ioan.* 1:7 (#118): "Cum . . . omnes formae sint per Verbum, quod est ars plena rationum viventium, est ergo lumen, non solum in se, sed omnia manifestans. . . . Dei Verbum, quo Pater dicit se et omnem creaturam."

[48] *In Ioan.* 14:6 (#1869); cf. 16:25 (#2150). Inasmuch that the Word is the concept of the Father and the perfect expression of the whole being of the Father (who contains the creatures), the Word is personally the Truth, that is to say the Truth as it is expressed by the Father. But in the aspect where the truth is an attribute common to the three persons, St. Thomas explains that the truth derives of all the Trinity (#1156). It is precisely to join these two aspects (personal and essential aspect) that St. Thomas explains that the truth is appropriated to the Word.

[49] *In Ioan.* 1:14 (#187) and 14:26 (#1958).

God and our neighbor, drives to that which is just and right, gives life, procures grace and forgiveness of sins, gives the unction, instructs and teaches interiorly, lifts up to higher good and gives one the taste for divine things, makes one act according to the truth, sanctifies the Church and makes its unity, intercedes and makes one pray, sheds multiple gifts (joy, consolation, love, etc.) and charismata (tongues, prophecies, miracles, etc.), inspires the Scriptures and enables the faithful to live in conformity with the revelation, glorifies Christ, makes known the Father and the Son, says the truth and makes the truth known, renders the faithful capable to receive the doctrine of Christ, makes one invoke the name of Christ, configures the faithful to Christ and renders them sons of God, lives in the saints in whom he dwells intimately by grace, gives confidence and the power to witness and to announce Christ, makes one merit resurrection, gives the glory of eternal life, and so forth.[50] The exposition of the works of the Spirit is much more complete in the commentary on St. John than in the Trinitarian treatise of the *Summa theologiae.*[51]

In this vast fresco of the works of the Spirit, St. Thomas puts into play two major doctrinal principles. The first principle is the property of the Holy Spirit as Love: It is because he is personally Love that the Holy Spirit accomplishes the works of which love is the source.[52] The second systematic principle lies in the procession of the Holy Spirit *a Filio*: The Holy Spirit leads to the Son and makes manifest the Son, he deepens the teaching of the Son, because he proceeds from the Son.[53] We can grasp here the soteri-

---

[50] See, in the commentary, #452–56, 972, 973, 992, 1092–95, 1520, 1909–20, 1957–59, 2060–62, 2066–67, 2099–2107, 2321, 2541, 2605. Cf. Giuseppe Ferraro, *Lo Spirito e l'"ora" di Cristo: L'esegesi di San Tommaso d'Aquino sul quarto Vangelo* (Vatican City: Editrice Vaticana, 1996).

[51] So as to balance the comparison, one should, however, consider all the pneumatological teaching spread through diverse parts of the *Summa theologiae*. See specifically, for the *Prima secundae*, Albert Patfoort, "Morale et pneumatologie," in *Saint Thomas d'Aquin, Les clefs d'une théologie* (Paris: FAC Editions, 1983), pp. 71–102. The works of the Spirit are organized in a more complete systematic way in the *Summa contra Gentiles* (Book IV, ch. 20–22).

[52] See for example *In Ioan.* 14:17 (#1916); 15:26 (#2060).

[53] *In Ioan.* 14:17 (#1916).

ological stakes of the *Filioque.* "For since the Holy Spirit is from
the Truth, it is appropriate that the Spirit teach the truth, and
make those he teaches like the one who sent him."[54] "For everything which is from another manifests that from which it is."[55]
The commentary on St. John reveals with great amplitude the
soteriological repercussions of the doctrine of Love and of the *Filioque* and, by applying these doctrinal principles to the works of
the Spirit, it shows the breadth of the action of the Spirit about
whom a more formal account is given in the three questions of the
Summa (questions 36–38). One can make a similar observation
concerning the person of the Father, despite the fact that the teaching of St. Thomas on the action of the first person is more sober.
The Father acts in the world in conformity with his property as
principle of the Son and the Holy Spirit: The Father acts in a *personal* way, a way that is *proper* to him (not only by appropriation)
as such that he is Father: The Father acts *through his Son.*[56] The
Father creates, accomplishes everything through his Word and his
Spirit, gives his Son and glorifies him, attracts mankind to the Son,
adopts them by sending his Son and the Holy Spirit, lives in the
saints with the Son and the Holy Spirit, and so forth.[57]

St. Thomas formulates on this basis an organizing doctrinal
principle which takes into account the Trinitarian economy in a
synthetic way: "Just as the effect of the mission of the Son was to
lead us to the Father, so the effect of the mission of the Holy
Spirit is to lead the faithful to the Son."[58] This rule is inspired by
the teaching of some Fathers of the Church (we could cite here
St. Irenaeus of Lyons or St. Basil of Caesarea), but St. Thomas
takes it more directly from St. Albert the Great who formulates it
in similar terms: "The Spirit who is sent brings back *(convertit)*

---

[54] *In Ioan.* 16:13 (#2102).
[55] *In Ioan.* 16:14 (#2107).
[56] *In Ioan.* 1:3 (#76). The commentary here gives all its vigor to the briefer
explanation of the *Summa* (*ST* I, q. 39, a. 8).
[57] See notably, in the commentary, #76, 176, 935–37, 997, 1192, 1648, 2189–92,
2248.
[58] *In Ioan.* 14:26 (#1958).

to himself and to the Son, the Son brings back to himself and to
the Father. . . . The person who proceeds from another person
brings back to that other person, according to the order of
nature, what he has from that other person."[59] This fundamental
structure of Trinitarian economy rests on the doctrine of the
Trinitarian order in God. The same structure of order of origin
was already at work in the explanations on the glorification of the
Father and the Son: "Now we see the reason why the Holy Spirit
will glorify Christ: it is because the Son is the principle of the
Holy Spirit. For every thing which is from another manifests that
from which it is. Thus the Son manifests the Father because he is
from the Father. And so because the Holy Spirit is from the Son,
to glorify the Son is proper *(proprium)* to the Spirit."[60] "The
Holy Spirit leads to the knowledge of truth, because he proceeds
from the Truth."[61]

One can perceive very well that the doctrine of Trinitarian
economy ("economic Trinity") in St. Thomas is not limited to a
mere description of the works of the Trinity as told by the Scriptures. The doctrine of Trinitarian economy appears when the biblical data are explained in the light of a speculative principle
which allows St. Thomas to organize the biblical texts and to
show their profound reason. St. Thomas formulates himself this
philosophical and theological rule: "What acts in virtue of
another tends in its effect to reveal that other: for the action of a
principle which proceeds from another principle manifests this
principle."[62] This rule brings together the metaphysics of participation and the metaphysics of order. It is included in the doctrine

---

[59] Albert the Great, I *Sent.,* d. 31, a. 14, ad quaest. 2: "Spiritus missus convertit
in se et in Filium, et Filius in se et in Patrem. . . . Persona enim quae est ab alia,
refert in eam per naturae ordinem quod habet ab ea." Albert is fully aware of
the rapport of this fundamental structure with the *Filioque* (ibid.: "et ideo constat errare Graecos").

[60] *In Ioan.* 16:14 (#2107). Cf. *In Ioan.* 1:32 (#268): "As the Son, existing by the
Father, manifests the Father, so the Holy Spirit, existing by the Son, manifests
the Son."

[61] *In Ioan.* 14:17 (#1916).

[62] *In Ioan.* 17:1 (#2185).

of *"reductio,"* dear to St. Bonaventure who found in it the heart of his doctrine of the return to God, and that St. Thomas applies often in Trinitarian theology.[63] According to that metaphysical rule, the reality which proceeds from a principle returns or leads to this principle, in virtue of the *order* which it has with this principle. We could mention many examples. Thus, when he explain that Christ is the source of all things *(principium)*, St. Thomas puts into action the similar rule of *"maxime tale."* The creative causality of the Son is manifested by the rule of the causality of the *primum*: That which sovereignly possesses a perfection is the cause of that which has this perfection in a secondary way (by participation). "Our Lord says that he is the source or beginning with regards to all creatures; for whatever is such by essence is the source and the cause of all those things which are by participation."[64] The doctrine of Trinitarian economy rests on metaphysical principles which St. Thomas applies to the teaching of the Bible so as to make manifest its signification and profound truth.

Theological literature today more often distinguishes the doctrine of the "immanent Trinity," resulting from the speculative effort inaugurated by the Fathers of the Church, and the doctrine of the "economic Trinity." Very often, the doctrine of the economic Trinity is identified with biblical teaching, whereas the study of the immanent Trinity is viewed as constructed by later dogmatic or systematic reflections on the eternal being of the Trinity. The reading of St. Thomas does not lead us to reject the distinction between the immanent and economic Trinity (Thomas speaks of the Trinity "in itself" and of the Trinity in its relationship to creatures or in its work), but it invites us rather to question the identification of biblical teaching as a doctrine of

---

[63] See G. Emery, *La Trinité créatrice,* pp. 221–27.

[64] *In Ioan* 8·25 (#1183). This principle is often applied to the Son or to the Trinity in the commentary of St. Thomas on the *Sentences*: "Sicut trames a fluvio derivatur, ita processus temporalis creaturarum ab aeterno processu personarum . . . semper enim id quod est primum est causa eorum quae sunt post" (I *Sent.*, prol.). Cf. G. Emery, *La Trinité créatrice,* pp. 273–85. The same principle is found in the *quarta via* of our natural knowledge of God's existence (*ST* I, q. 2, a. 3).

the "economic Trinity."[65] Indeed the commentary on St. John demonstrates that there is only a veritable teaching on the economic Trinity when we can clarify and organize, through speculative thought, the agency of the divine persons taught by Scripture. For Aquinas, the simple identification of biblical teaching with the economic Trinity is an error. The Trinitarian doctrine of economy (doctrine of the action of the Father by the Son and by the Spirit), according to the commentary on St. John, rests on the doctrine of the Trinity in itself, as taught by the Scriptures, which is necessary to understand the biblical text in depth. The doctrine of the economic Trinity is no less speculative than that of the immanent Trinity. The revelation of the Trinity by its works is admittedly first in the order of our discovery of the mystery. But the *doctrine* of the economic Trinity is not only the starting point of a theological reflection: It is rather the last fruit of a reflection founded in the speculative reading of the documents of revelation, when doctrinal speculative principles are applied to the agency of the persons as taught by Scriptures.

According to our reading of the commentary of St. John by Aquinas, Trinitarian theology consists of three steps: (1) the discovery of the mystery of the Trinity, by faith, through the action of the Trinity as taught by Scriptures; (2) a speculative reflection on the being and properties of the divine persons (doctrine of the "immanent Trinity"); and (3) a speculative reflection on the creative and salvific action of the persons in the world (doctrine of the "economic Trinity") in the light of the properties and relations of the persons. In other words, the doctrine of the economic Trinity (third step) is achieved when a speculative reflection on the divine persons (second step) is applied to the agency of the persons discovered in the reading of Scripture (first step). In this way, Trinitarian theology moves from Scripture to Scripture.

---

[65] See on this matter the interesting remarks made by David Coffey, *Deus Trinitas: The Doctrine of the Triune God* (Oxford/New York: Oxford University Press, 1999), pp. 9–45.

3. *The commentary on St. John also shows how we come to the knowledge of the eternal Trinity by considering its works in the world.* On the basis of the preceding explanations, so as to make manifest the divinity of the Son and the Spirit, St. Thomas brings into play the "soteriological argument," dear to St. Athanasius of Alexandria and other Greek Fathers. The best example concerns the Holy Spirit: "He from whom men are spiritually reborn is God; but men are reborn through the Holy Spirit, as it is stated here; therefore, the Holy Spirit is God."[66] St. Thomas presents this reflection as an argument *(ratio)* which theological reasoning forms from John 3:5: "Unless one is born again of water and the Holy Spirit, he cannot enter the kingdom of God." The same argument is applied to the divinity of the Son:

> It is clear that a person by participating in the Word of God becomes "god" by participation. But a thing does not become this or that by participation unless it participates in what is this or that by its essence. . . . Therefore, one does not become "god" by participation unless he participates in what is God by essence. Therefore, the Word of God, that is the Son, by participation in whom we become "gods," is God by essence.[67]

In the *Summa theologiae*, St. Thomas explains the secondary reality (our salvation) from the primary reality (the divinity of the Father and the Son): The Son deifies, the Spirit vivifies, because the Son and the Spirit are God; this is the order of the doctrinal statement which the *Summa theologiae* follows. But here, in the commentary on St. John, St. Thomas follows the inverse order: He establishes the primary reality (the divinity of the persons) from the secondary reality (our salvation). Using St. Hilary's argument, but also that of St. John Chrysostom and St. Augustine (as the *Catena aurea* shows on these passages), Aquinas

---

[66] *In Ioan.* 3:5 (#444).
[67] *In Ioan.* 10:35 (#1460); 17:3 (#2187): "Because the Son exercises the true activities of divinity, it is clear that the Son is true God."

starts from the experience of salvation through faith, that is to say, the true and real re-creation and divinization of the believer, so as to establish the divinity of the persons: Only the true God can divinize and re-create. We find here the way of Trinitarian theology, which starts from the action of the persons so as to show, by reasoning, a truth concerning the eternal Trinity in itself (the "immanent Trinity"). These explanations are of great value for rediscovering, behind the *ordo disciplinae* of the *Summa*, the patristic roots of Aquinas's Trinitarian theology and its foundations in the economy of salvation.

The reflection on power and operation gathers together, on a more general level, the principles of this soteriological way of thought. In virtue of the mode of human knowledge, St. Thomas explains, "It is natural for man to learn of the power and natures of things from their actions, and therefore our Lord fittingly says that the sort of person he is can be learned through the works he does."[68] For that reason, the works of Christ bear witness to him. In chapter 5, this witness concerns the judgment and, in particular, the life-giving power of the Son. St. Thomas explains, "Here we should point out that in the Old Testament the power is particularly emphasized by the fact that God is the author of life."[69] As the Son has the power to give life, the power of God himself, he is therefore himself true God. In neighboring passages, St. Thomas notes that "the clearest indication of the nature of a thing is taken from its works," "different actions indicate different natures."[70] Applied to Christ, this principle leads to the following conclusion: "Therefore, from the fact that he does the works of God, it can be clearly known and believed that Christ is God."[71] St. Thomas's argument associates most often operation and nature, but it also applies to the relationship of *power* and of nature. Thus, as "All things were made through him," we know that the Word possesses the

---

[68] *In Ioan.* 5:36 (#817).
[69] *In Ioan.* 5:21 (#761).
[70] *In Ioan.* 10:38 (#1466) and 14:16 (#1912).
[71] *In Ioan.* 10:38 (#1466); cf. 17:3 (#2187).

divine omnipotence. St. Thomas conceives power as the principle of action, and he specifies that "to be the principle of all things that are made is proper to the great omnipotent God. . . . Thus the Word, through whom all things were made, is God, great and co-equal to the Father."[72] Here again, Aquinas's arguments come from his anti-Arian and anti-Eunomian patristic sources: notably St. Hilary and St. John Chrysostom.[73]

Furthermore, St. Thomas integrates this teaching on power and operation in his doctrine of relative personal properties. The Son receives from his Father the power and the operation: "The Son, just as he does not have his being *(esse)* except from the Father, so he cannot do anything *(posse facere aliquid)* except from the Father. For in natural things, a thing receives its power to act from the very thing from which it receives its being." When John 5:19 says that the Son cannot do anything of himself, "no inequality is implied, because this refers to a relation."[74] Therefore it is the doctrine of relation which allows one to grasp the power of the Son under its two aspects, namely its equality with the power of the Father, and its reception *a Patre* by eternal generation. The exposition concerning the "other Paraclete" in John 14:16 gives place to more ample precisions. The Son and the Holy Spirit are both called "Paraclete," but they do not exercise their action of Paraclete in the same way. As diversity of action is the sign of a diversity of nature, does it not signify that the nature of the Spirit is different to that of the Son? St. Thomas answers this question by introducing the property of the persons: The Son and the Holy Spirit exercise the same action, but each one acts in his own distinct mode.

> The Holy Spirit is called a consoler because *(inquantum)* he is formally Love. But the Son is called a consoler because *(inquantum)* he is the Word. . . . Thus the word

---

[72] *In Ioan.* 1:3 (#69).

[73] On the patristic argument about divine power, see M. R. Barnes, *The Power of God*.

[74] *In Ioan.* 5:19 (#749).

"another" does not indicate a different nature in the Son
and in the Holy Spirit. Rather, it indicates the different
way *(modus)* each is an advocate and a consoler.[75]

The divine persons therefore exercise the same action of consolation, but in a distinct mode, namely in the mode of their personal properties (Word and Love). We find again here, precisely,
the heart of the teaching of St. Thomas on Trinitarian action: The
three persons act inseparably in the same action, in virtue of their
common nature and of their mutual relations, but each person acts
in a distinct mode following the personal property. When commenting on St. John, St. Thomas integrates patristic exegesis on
nature and power, and clarifies this teaching by his own reflection
on relations and properties in the Trinity.

This way of Trinitarian thought is confirmed by several
explanations of the commentary concerning the divine missions.
Indeed, St. Thomas explains, "The mission indicates the origin."[76] Aquinas goes back on this subject to the teaching of St.
Augustine by explaining: "[The Holy Spirit] is said to be sent
(mitti) to indicate his procession from another, for the fact that
he sanctifies the rational creature by indwelling he has from that
other, from whom he has it that he is *(a quo habet ut sit)*."[77] The
mission (temporal procession) of the Son and of the Spirit is thus
the way to the knowledge of eternal procession.[78] The commentary on St. John, by giving details of the action of the divine persons in the world, allows us to grasp better the economic
foundation of Trinitarian theology.

Exegetical Method and Speculative Theology

To evaluate the contribution that the commentary brings to the
Trinitarian doctrine of St. Thomas, it is necessary to specify St.

---

[75] *In Ioan.* 14:16 (#1912).

[76] *In Ioan.* 5:23 (#769).

[77] *In Ioan.* 15:26 (#2061). Cf. St. Augustine, *De Trinitate* IV, XX, 28.

[78] See also *In Ioan.* 3:12 (#464): "If you do not believe in a spiritual generation
occuring in time, how will you believe in the eternal generation of the Son?"

Thomas's method. For our subject, three principal aspects merit to be retained: the forms of speculative exposition, the place given to the Fathers of the Church, as well as the role of errors and heresies to make manifest the truth.

The Forms of Speculative Exegesis

The speculative Trinitarian expositions of the commentary on St. John, putting on one side a few rare exceptions, do not concern the spiritual or mystical sense of Scripture,[79] but they concern the literal exegesis of the text, as it is exclusively on this literal sense that theological arguments are properly founded, following the hermeneutics of St. Thomas.[80] The lecture of St. Thomas spreads over the three levels or stages of literal exposition formulated by Hugh of Saint-Victor: The *littera* in the strict sense (textual analysis, grammatical and linguistic, a brief explanation of the words according to their content and their immediate sequence), the *sensus* (analysis of the signification of each element), and then the *sententia* (the true understanding of the text which extricates the profound theological and philosophical content of a text).[81] This *sententia*, that is to say, the development of theological and philosophical themes which make up the doctrine provided by the finished exposition, takes on two principal forms in the Trinitarian exegesis of the commentary on St. John.

1. Following a first form, the speculative doctrine intervenes in the continuous explanation of the commented pericope, where a strict exegesis of the words allows St. Thomas to

---

[79] When St. Thomas introduces a mystical or spiritual sense, it usually is on Christological themes (mysteries lived out by Christ in his flesh), but also eschatological or moral. The Trinitarian themes are not absent but are much more rare in the context of spiritual exegesis; see for example the mystical Trinitarian sense of the "three measures" in John 2:6 (#357), or the "causa mystica et allegorica" in the exegesis of John 9:6–7 (#1311).

[80] Cf. *ST* I, q. 1, a. 10.

[81] See Gilbert Dahan, *L'exégèse chrétienne de la Bible en Occident médiéval, XIIe-XIVe siècle* (Paris: Cerf, 1999), pp. 239–97; Marie-Dominique Chenu, *Introduction à l'étude de saint Thomas d'Aquin*, pp. 70–71, and 214. Cf. Hugh of Saint-Victor, *Didascalicon* VI, 8: "Expositio tria continet: litteram, sensum, sententiam" (ed. Charles H. Buttimer [Washington, DC: The Catholic University of America Press, 1939], p. 125).

extract the immediate sense so as to come to the doctrine contained in the text. This method often includes several intermediate approaches, among which we can count the following: (a) preliminary precisions concerning the biblical vocabulary, which can include a definition of words;[82] (b) a research for the reasons why the Gospel writer (or the person speaking, Christ for example) brings such a precision by using such words;[83] (c) preliminary or complementary doctrinal precisions;[84] and, (d) indication and refutation of the errors and heresies which a good exegesis must avoid.[85] Going against a too widely spread prejudice, one must insist on this point: The speculative reflection of an exegete does not necessarily take the form of a scholastic question. We can easily see it in, for example, the exegesis of the word *"Verbum"* in John 1:1 (#25–29): The complete speculative exposition of St. Thomas details the sense of the words and brings doctrinal precisions in the form of a continuous explanation where the academic sort of *quaestio* does not appear.

2. Following a second form, the speculative doctrine is the object of *quaestiones, obiectiones,* or *dubitationes* brought out

---

[82] See, for example, the commentary on John 1:1, #25 (definition of the name "Word"), #34 (precisions on the word "principium"), #44 (signification of the word *"Deus"*), #45 (signification of the preposition *"apud"*); on John 1:3, #46 (signification of the preposition *"per"*), and so on.

[83] See, for example, the commentary on John 1:1, #59 (the reason why the word *"Deus"* in John 1:1c does not carry an article), or John 5:19, #750 (the reason why the Gospel talks of the communication of wisdom to the Son by generation). The motive of such a word is often given in reference to errors which the evangelical text removes, as one can see for example in the exegesis of John 1:1–2 (#60–66), then in John 1:3 (#69), and so on.

[84] See, for example, the commentary on John 5:20, #753 (preliminary precision on the role of fatherly dilection in the generation of the Son, then on the distinction between the essential sense and notional sense of "love" in God), on John 16:14, #2107 (analogical sense of the word *"recipere"* applied to the creatures and to God), on John 16:15, #2114 (on the relationship between the agent and the formal principle of action), and so on.

[85] See, for example, the commentary on John 1:1 (#58–59), on John 1:1–2 (#60–66), on John 1:3 (#69–70 and 73–75). We shall come back later to the place of errors and heresies.

in the text, and which forms a specific unity. The vocabulary is, then, that of the scholastic question, comprising the terms of the question and the master's own answer.[86] One must note however that these *quaestiones* do not always concern speculative doctrinal points developed in the manner of the *Summa theologiae*. Very often these questions are rather of a strictly exegetical order, or discuss diverse patristic interpretations of a verse of St. John.[87]

3. In other more developed passages, the speculative exegesis of St. Thomas associates these two forms and takes on a complex figure which combines the continuous exposition (form 1) and the questions (form 2), so as to come to a synthetic conclusion which summarizes the doctrine taught, as one can observe, in particular, in the first verses of the Prologue and in the interpretation of the passages about the origin of the Holy Spirit.

Thus, the exegesis of the first words of the Prologue *("In principio erat Verbum")* details the analysis of each term. For the first word *(Verbum)*, the exposition of St. Thomas has the following structure: (1) philosophical and theological explanation of the word *Verbum*;

---

[86] See, for example, the commentary on John 1:1 concerning the Word (#41: *"potest aliquis quaerere," "ad quod dicendum est;"* #46–50: *"sunt quatuor obiectiones"*); on John 3:34 concerning the gift of the Holy Spirit (#542: *"responsio"*); on John 16:15 concerning the relation in God (#2113: *"sed quaeritur utrum," "dicendum"*), and so on. The question can be presented as a *dubitatio* (see, for example, the commentary on John 16:13, #2103–4, concerning the Holy Spirit) or as a notice (*"sed nota," "notandum"*: see, for example, the commentary on John 16:14, #2108 and 2112).

[87] There is a good example in the four *quaestiones* which St. Thomas asks about John 1:1 (#30–33), concerning the reason of the words chosen by St. John according to John Chrysostom, Augustine, and Origen. See also the commentary on John 1:1, #54 (the order of the words in the statement "Et Deus erat Verbum," according to Origen) and #55–56 (patristic discussion on two objections); on John 5:19 (#745–51: the action of the Son and his relationship to the Father, following Augustine, Hilary, and Chrysostom); and so on. In other passages, St. Thomas speaks of *"quaestio litteralis"* to designate a question searching for the reason of a word in the Gospel (see, for example, the commentary on John 1:42, #306, or on John 3:22, #498, etc.).

(2) application of the results of this analysis and determination of the sense of the word *Verbum* in the Prologue; (3) precisions on the differences of the human word and of the divine Word; (4) theological conclusion on the exclusively personal sense of the name *Verbum* in God and on the properties of the divine Word (the divine Word is the perfect expression of the Father, coeternal and consubstantial with the Father). At this stage St. Thomas has shown the profound meaning of *Verbum* in the first verse of the Gospel, but he continues his exegesis: (5) discussion of four *quaestiones* which are raised by the name "Word." These four questions come from the patristic documentation of St. Thomas (St. John Chrysostom, St. Augustine, and Origen).

The exegesis of the following word *("principium")* proceeds in a similar way: (1) philosophical and theological exposition of the sense of the word *principium*; (2) application of this sense in the Prologue of St. John, with indication of three possible interpretations (all originally patristic); (3) doctrinal conclusion on the properties of the divine Word manifested in the exegesis of *"principium"* (causality, consubstantiality, and co-eternity of the Word and the Father). As to the interpretation of the third word *("erat")*, it comprises: (1) the exposition of the signification of the past imperfect; (2) a precision taken from the *Glossa*; (3) a theological question *("sed potest aliquis quaerere")* on the eternity of the generation in God; and, (4) a conclusion on the names which express the personal property of the Son.

The exegesis of John 16:14–15, which gives place to a remarkable speculative exposition on the procession of the Holy Spirit *a Filio*, reveals a similar complex structure (#2105–14): (1) a first explanation of the biblical text concerning the glorification of the Son by the Holy Spirit; (2) a theological explanation of the reasons of the Son's glorification by the Spirit; (3) a theological precision on the way that the Holy Spirit "receives" from the Son; (4) a theological precision on the consubstantiality signified by the Latin preposition *"de"*; (5) a theological precision on the way that a divine person possesses *(habet)* something; (6) objection and answer concerning the personal property of paternity; (7) a complementary precision on the order *("ordo")* of the persons in God; (8) a speculative question on the relation in God; and, (9) a conclusion on the procession of the Holy Spirit *a Filio*, with an argument founded on the concept of procession and on the essence in God.

These examples manifest that by associating all the resources of theological reading, St. Thomas integrates exegesis and speculative reflection in a complex unity. It is not sufficient to say that St. Thomas goes from biblical exegesis to theology, because speculative reflection intervenes to offer the profound sense of the text which the exegesis is looking for. Questions and theological precisions are neither juxtaposed nor superimposed on biblical exegesis, but they are integrated into biblical exegesis, in such a way so as to be fully part of the exegesis practiced by St. Thomas. The arguments brought out by the reading of the biblical text aim at making clear the profound doctrine taught by the Gospel in its literal content.[88] The theologian exercises his speculative reflection in the very act of the literal interpreting of the Gospel. This exegetical practice is founded on the understanding of the nature of *sacra doctrina*: we shall come to that later.

Patristic Exegesis

The Trinitarian doctrine of St. Thomas's commentary on St. John carries no explicit reference to scholastic authors from the twelfth and thirteenth centuries. This is a remarkable difference of method between the commentary on the fourth Gospel and the Trinitarian doctrine of the *Summa theologiae*. The Trinitarian treatise of the *Summa theologiae* (I, q. 27–43) names Peter Lombard, Gilbertus of Poitiers, Richard of Saint-Victor, Joachim of Fiore, Praepositinus of Cremona, as well as older medieval authors (Boethius). The commentary on St. John does not mention any of these theologians. It is not easy to evaluate the reasons for their absence from the commentary. St. Thomas's reserve may stem from the dignity of Holy Scripture and from the sort of scriptural exposition: The biblical

---

[88] In his general survey on exegesis in medieval universities, G. Dahan distinguishes on one side the *expositio*, and on the other the *quaestiones* (Gilbert Dahan, *L'exégèse chrétienne de la Bible*, p. 112). The commentary by St. Thomas on St. John does not separate these two elements.

exposition mainly brings to light the Fathers of the Church *(doctores)* who constitute a "proper" authority of sacred doctrine (sacred Scripture), which is not the case for the other authors.[89] St. Thomas's silence on these mediaeval theologians make Aristotle's presence all the more remarkable: Aristotle is mentioned nearly fifteen times in the commentary on St. John, and intervenes from the exegesis of the first verse in the exposition of the name *"Verbum."*[90] The same reference to Aristotle's *Perihermeneias* appears, in an identical context, in the *Summa theologiae* (I, q. 34, a. 1): This parallel underlines the close relationship of the commentary on St. John and the *Summa theologiae.* The references to Aristotle are not however without criticism for, as one knows, the commentary on St. John makes up part of the works in which St. Thomas qualifies as error the teachings of Aristotle on the eternity of the world.[91]

The only Christian authors to whom Aquinas refers in the exegesis of Trinitarian passages are the Fathers of the Church. St. Augustine, St. John Chrysostom, Origen, and St. Hilary occupy the first place.[92] But St. Thomas also refers to St. Basil of Caesarea, Didymus the Blind, St. Ambrose, Pseudo-Dionysius, St. John Damascene, St. Gregory the Great, as well as Bede and Alcuin.[93] The Fathers occupy a very considerable place in the Trinitarian exegesis of St. Thomas, from the very first verses. Thus, for example, the interpretation of

---

[89] Cf. *ST* I, q. 1, a. 8.

[90] *In Ioan.* 1:1 (#25: two occurrences). The philosophers are present from the Prologue by St. Thomas, who mentions the *"antiqui philosophi"* when explaining our ways to the knowledge of God (#3).

[91] *In Ioan.* 1:1–2 (#65).

[92] The Fathers the most quoted in the commentary on St. John are St. Augustine (426 times) and St. John Chrysostom (259 times), many more than Origen (91 times), St. Gregory the Great (54 times), and St. Hilary of Poitiers (46 times). For a more complete comparative table, see Leo J. Elders, "Santo Tomás de Aquino y los Padres de la Iglesia," *Doctor Communis* 48 (1993): 55–80 (table on p. 66).

[93] Bede and Alcuin are considered as *"doctores"* as the Fathers: they are often quoted by St. Thomas in his *Catena* on the Gospels. The *Catena* does not mention St. Anselm, whose opinion concerning the "cogitatio" is corrected by St. Thomas in his commentary on John 1:1 (#26): his criticism of St. Anselm, in the context of the Word, is identical in the *Summa theologiae* (*ST* I, q. 34, a. 1, ad 2).

"In principio" consists mainly of the exegesis of Origen, Chrysostom, Basil, and Hilary.[94] The four *quaestiones* raised by *"Verbum erat apud Deum"* are asked and answered with Basil, Hilary, Chrysostom, Alcuin, Bede, and Origen.[95] The utility of the phrase *"per eum omnia facta sunt"* goes back to the explanations of Chrysostom and of Hilary, and the theological sense of this expression is developed with reference to Augustine, Origen, Chrysostom, and Hilary.[96] One could easily add numerous examples. Often St. Thomas multiplies the patristic exegeses which offer diverse and complementary interpretations of the text.[97] Sometimes, the exposition of a verse by St. Thomas is limited to an introduction and presentation of patristic exegesis: This is the case, among many examples, in John 13:20 on the faithful receiving the Father, or in John 17:22 on the gift of glory to the Son by the Father.[98] In some other places, the reference to the Fathers is used to introduce St. Thomas's own exposition.[99] The Fathers are again often invoked on the occasion of a *quaestio* or of a complementary precision, as one can see several times in the exegesis of John 1:1–3.[100] The commentary of St. Thomas benefits greatly from his *Catena aurea* on St. John, from which he integrates a considerable number of patristic sources.

This massive material presence of the Fathers constitutes a characteristic of the Trinitarian doctrine of the commentary on St. John when compared to Aquinas's systematic works *(Summa theologiae,* Commentary on the *Sentences, De potentia).* Let us take an example among many other Trinitarian themes: the equality of power of the Father and of the Son. In the *Summa theologiae,* the article given over to this problem (I, q. 42, a. 6) mentions several texts from St. John in the objections (John 5:19, John 5:20, John 5:30, John 14:31) and

[94] *In Ioan.* 1:1 (#35–37).
[95] *In Ioan.* 1:1 (#47–52).
[96] *In Ioan.* 1:3 (#84–88).
[97] See, for example, *In Ioan.* 1:1 (#35–37); *In Ioan.* 1:3 (#84–88); and so on.
[98] *In Ioan.* 13:20 (#1793); *In Ioan.* 17:22–23 (#2245–49): Augustine and Chrysostom.
[99] See, for example, *In Ioan.* 16:15 (#2114) on the relation of the Holy Spirit to the Son: Hilary and Didymus.
[100] See also, for example, *In Ioan.* 14:9 (#1886–90).

in the argument *sed contra* (John 5:19). The main response of St.
Thomas does not indicate any patristic authority, despite there being
a reference to Augustine's *Contra Maximinum* in the third objection
as well as a reference to Hilary's *De Trinitate* (Book IX) in the
response to the first objection. The commentary on St. John is much
more instructive about St. Thomas's patristic sources. The commentary on John 5:19 ("The Son cannot do anything of himself, but
only what he sees his Father doing") presents in a very complete way
an anti-Arian exegesis from the *De Trinitate* (Book VII) by St. Hilary
who, by associating power and nature, shows that the Son receives
power from the Father as he receives from him his nature, being, and
operation, without any inequality.[101] The commentary also recalls
the exegesis of St. Augustine who takes in the interpretations of St.
Hilary and St. John Chrysostom.[102] The commentary allows one
then to discover that, in the *Summa theologiae*, St. Thomas's response
to the objections taken from John 5:20 and John 5:30 comes principally from St. Augustine (in his *Homilies on John* notably): When it
is said that the Son has received a commandment from the Father, or
that the Son receives knowledge from the Father to whom he listens,
it concerns Christ in his human nature, or it concerns the eternal
generation by which the Father communicates science and divine
will to the Son.[103] As to the relations or the personal properties
which cannot be communicated (the Son receives the essence from
the Father but not the personal property of paternity), the commentary shows that the answer given by the *Summa* is taken from the
Treatise on the Holy Spirit by Didymus.[104]

In this way, one can see that the *Summa* organizes and summarizes the patristic teaching of the *Catena aurea* which the commentary on St. John (posterior in time) presents in greater detail. The

---

[101] *In Ioan.* 5:19 (#749); cf. *Catena in Ioan.* 5:19 (pp. 401–3). This enlightens the
response of *ST* I, q. 42, a. 6, ad 1.

[102] *In Ioan.* 5:19 (#747 and 751).

[103] *In Ioan.* 5:20 (#754) and In Ioan. 5:30 (#795); cf. *Catena in Ioan.* 5:20 and
5:30 (pp. 402–3 and 407–8). This enlightens the response of *ST* I, q. 42, a. 6,
ad 2.

[104] *In Ioan.* 16:15 (#2111, cf. #2114); cf. *Catena in Ioan.* 16:15 (*ed. cit.,* p. 541).
This enlightens the response of *ST* I, q. 42, a. 6, ad 3.

commentary allows one to measure the deep patristic roots of the *Summa's* doctrine on the subject of the equality of power of the Father and the Son. One could multiply similar examples: The exegesis of the commentary is guided by the inheritance of the Fathers, and aids us to rediscover the patristic foundation, both Latin and Greek, of the Trinitarian theology of the *Summa*.

Trinitarian Heresies

Trinitarian errors deserve a special place in this patristic file. The attention paid to heresies is far from being secondary or marginal: The commentary on St. John mentions and discusses nearly fifty times the errors of Arius and the Arians, and sixteen times the error of Sabellius and the Sabellians. In Trinitarian matters, it indicates too the error of Eunomius of Cyzicus, of Macedonius and the Macedonians, as well as the error of Photinus of Sirmium and of Paul of Samosata.[105]

The list of errors with which Arius is reproached is complex and detailed: the negation of the eternity of the Son (very often repeated), that is to say the rejection of the co-eternity of the Father and the Son; the affirmation of the superiority of the Father *(maior)* and the inferiority of the Son *(minor)*; the negation of the equality of the Father and the Son, the negation of their consubstantiality; the negation of their identity of nature and unity of essence; the affirmation of the diversity of the Father and the Son; the negation of the all powerfulness of the Son; the negation of the equality of power of the Father and the Son; the negation of the true divinity of the Son; the negation of the incomprehensibility of the Son; the conception of the Son as "God by participation" or as creature.[106] Against the Arians *(ariani)* St. Thomas criticizes the

---

[105] One can count in the commentary respectively 32 explicit mentions of Arius, 17 of the *Ariani*, 14 of Sabellius, and 2 of the *Sabelliani*, 1 mention of Macedonius and 1 mention of the *Macedoniani*, 1 mention of Eunomius, as well as 4 mentions of Photinus, and 3 mentions of Paul of Samosata.

[106] For the details of Arius's errors in the commentary on St. John, see #61, 62, 64, 69, 126, 262, 477, 769, 935, 978, 1355, 1451, 1696, 1794, 1879, 1888, 1895, 1970, 2181, 2183, 2240, 2248, 2520. St. Thomas also refutes the Christological error of Arius on the human soul of Christ (negation of a human soul in Christ, because the divine Word takes the place of a soul in Christ): #167, 168, 1654.

affirmation of the superiority of the Father and the inferiority of
the Son, the negation of the eternity of the Son and of the equality
of the Father and the Son, the affirmation of the essential diversity
of the Father and the Son, the conception of the Son as creature, as
well as the generation of the Son by will rather than by nature.[107]

St. Thomas distinguishes very well the error of Arius and the
error of Eunomius of Cyzicus, the latter having radicalized Arianism
by teaching the total dissimilarity of the Father and the Son.[108] The
precision of these historical details of the Trinitarian doctrine makes
the commentary on St. John "our most fruitful source for St.
Thomas's account for Arianism."[109] The important discussion of
Arianism in the commentary of St. John is materially linked to the
place of the Fathers of the Church: The commentary conveys the
anti-Arian (and anti-subordinationist) purpose of patristic exegesis
from the fourth century. For this reason, the commentary aids us to
discover the sources of Aquinas on Arianism. These sources are
taken mostly from St. Hilary, but also from St. John Chrysostom
and St. Augustine.[110]

Concerning semi-Arianism, St. Thomas mentions the error of
Macedonius and the Macedonians. He notes correctly that the
Macedonians undermined the divinity of the Holy Spirit under the
aspect of the *power* of the Spirit, as they conceived the Spirit as an
instrument or "minister" of the Father and the Son.[111] There again
the commentary and the *Catena* allow us to identify St. Thomas's
sources, namely St. John Chrysostom and Theophylactus, who are
among the principal authors of Aquinas's Eastern documentation.

The precisions concerning Sabellius and Sabellianism are a little
less detailed. According to St. Thomas, Sabellius denied the personal
distinction and the personal plurality in the Trinity, by affirming
that the Father and the Son are the same person and are only distin-

---

[107] See, in the commentary on St. John, #41, 61, 198, 545, 742, 745, 783, 1278,
1290, 1451, 1456, 1704, 1929, 1999, 2187.
[108] *In Ioan.* 1:1 (#64).
[109] P. Worrall, "St. Thomas and Arianism," p. 211.
[110] Ibid.
[111] See, in the commentary, #452 and 2089.

guished by their name: Sabellius confused the persons by attributing the incarnation to the Father.[112] In the wake of Sabellius, the Sabellians taught the personal identity of the Father and the Son, holding that the Son is inengendered.[113] The commentary on St. John and the *Catena* on the fourth Gospel allow us to identify fairly easily St. Thomas's sources concerning Sabellianism: St. Augustine, St. Hilary, and St. John Chrysostom principally.

St. Thomas also reproaches Photinus of Sirmium for having taught that Christ is a mere man whose existence started in the womb of the Virgin Mary and who merited divinity (this does away with faith in the Trinity).[114] Among his sources on Photinus, one discovers Augustine and Chrysostom. But a more detailed study has allowed us to show that St. Thomas's principal source on Photinus is a work of Vigilius of Thapsus transmitted under the name of St. Athanasius.[115] It is from these sources that St. Thomas must have associated a little too closely Photinus with Paul of Samosata, neglecting Photinus's Sabellianism, and his links to Marcellus of Ancyra. St. Thomas reproaches Origen for having taught that the Son is inferior to the Father, in the way of an instrument of the Father who is not God by essence but only by participation. Origen's exegesis concerning the absence of an article for the word "God" in John 1:1c *("Et Deus erat Verbum")* is ruled out by going back to St. John Chrysostom.[116] Still concerning the Word, St. Thomas dismisses the Gnostic error of Valentinus for whom the Word is the cause of the creating act of the Father (it is because of the Word that the Father created the world): St. Thomas owes the knowledge of this thesis and its refutation to having read Origen.[117]

---

[112] See, in the commentary, #64, 769, 783, 1154, 1237, 1451, 1696, 1887, 1895, 1911, 2181, 2248.

[113] On the *"sabelliani,"* see in the commentary #749 and 1037.

[114] See, in the commentary, #64, 126, 783, 786, 935.

[115] G. Emery, "Le photinisme," pp. 371–98.

[116] See the commentary on John 1:1–3 (#58 and 75) and on John 1:9 (#126), as well as the *Catena aurea* on John 1:1–3 (p. 329). On this subordinationism in Origen, see *Super Boetium de Trinitate*, q. 3, a. 4.

[117] *In Ioan.* 1:3 (#73); cf. *Catena in Ioan.* 1:3 (p. 331).

The exclusion of heresies is present, in a significant way, in all the principal Trinitarian sections of the commentary of St. Thomas: in the exegesis of the Prologue on the Word, in the teachings on the gift of the Spirit in chapter 3, in the exposition on the action of Christ in chapter 5 and in chapter 10, in the exposition of the speech after the Last Supper in chapters 14 through 17 (the immanence of the Son and the Father, the promise of the Paraclete, the work of the Spirit, the glorification of the Father and of the Son). St. Thomas indicates sometimes, depending on his patristic sources, that a heretical doctrine comes from the wrong interpretation of such and such a verse,[118] or that the heretics tried to found or confirm their heresy on this or that particular verse of St. John.[119] He refutes Arianism and Sabellianism by using the exegesis of one of the Fathers of the Church, or refers to several patristic authorities which dismiss the heretical interpretation,[120] indicating sometimes that the letter of the Gospel excludes such an interpretation.[121]

Sometimes the heretical opinion is the object of a particular question *(quaestio, obiectio)* raised by the biblical text,[122] but most often the mention of heretical exegesis appears in the course of a continuous exposition. St. Thomas rules out the heretical interpretation by showing the reasons of the error and by giving a correct

---

[118] See, for example, *In Ioan.* 1:1 (#58 and 60); *In Ioan.* 1:3 (#80: "Three heresies came from this," cf. #83); *In Ioan.* 1:15 (#198: "It is from this text that the Arians took occasion for their error"); *In Ioan.* 8:19 (#1161); *In Ioan.* 12:38 (#1696: "From this word Sabellius took occasion for his error").

[119] See, for example, *In Ioan.* 5:19 (#745: "The Arians use what Christ said here, 'the Son cannot do anything of himself,' to support their error that the Son is less than the Father"); *In Ioan.* 14:9 (#1887: "Sabellius made this statement the basis of his error"); *In Ioan.* 14:10 (#1895: "Two heresies were based on the above texts"); *In Ioan.* 17:21 (#2240: "Arius uses this passage to argue that. . . ."); *In Ioan.* 20:17 (#2520: "Arius based his error on these words").

[120] See, for example, the commentary on John 5:19 (#747–51), where St. Thomas refutes the Arian interpretation of this verse using the exegesis of St. Hilary, St. Augustine, and St. John Chrysostom.

[121] *In Ioan.* 5:18 (#742): "Sed per ea quae dicta sunt in ipso textu, aliter etiam manifestum est;" cf. *In Ioan.* 14:9 (#1888) and 14:28 (#1970).

[122] See, for example, *In Ioan.* 1:1 (#46–48: "duplex obiectio fit ab haereticis," "secunda quaestio;" #55).

exposition of the Gospel with the Fathers: It is by showing the truth of the Gospel that one excludes errors. In any case, the exclusion of errors is closely linked to the exposition of the truth of the Gospel, to such a degree that the manifestation of the truth and the rejection of errors are indissociable. One finds a good example at the end of the commentary on John 1:1–2, where St. Thomas presents a long list of errors excluded by the two first verses of the Gospel and concludes: "If one considers these four propositions well, he will find that they clearly destroy all the errors of the heretics and of the philosophers."[123] As well, St. Thomas explains many times that it is *to exclude an error* that the Gospel text uses such a word or gives such an explanation: "To exclude this, the Evangelist says . . . ," "To exclude this the Evangelist added . . . ," "To avoid such an understanding, the Evangelist John added . . . ," "So you do not understand this teaching in that way, the Evangelist says. . . ."[124] The exclusion of heresies does not only concern the subject of the theologian, but it concerns already the subject of Scripture itself.

The place given to heresies in the commentary of St. Thomas has two principal motives. In the first place, the refutal of heresies is linked to patristic exegesis: By resuming the exegesis of the Fathers, St. Thomas takes on their concern to eliminate heretical interpretations of the Scriptures. Furthermore, St. Thomas knows that heresies were the historical motive for the development of the Trinitarian dogma.[125] But in second place, one must observe a deeper motive: to make manifest the truth and to exclude errors are the two faces of one and the same subject. This is the goal of Christian wisdom, the task of the wise person that St. Thomas expresses and systematically puts to work in the *Summa contra Gentiles*: To announce and make manifest the contemplated truth, and to discard errors which contradict this

---

[123] *In Ioan.* 1:1–2 (#64, cf. #65–66); see also, for example, the commentary on John 5:26: "Destruuntur autem per haec verba tres errores, secundum Hilarium" (#783).

[124] See, for example, the commentary on John 1:1–2 (#60, 61, 62); on John 1:3 (#84); on John 1:14 (#174); on John 5:19 (#749); on John 5:23 (#769), and so on.

[125] See notably *De potentia*, q. 9, a. 5.

truth.[126] We find here, again, one of the aspects of the astonishing likenesses between the *Lectura* on St. John and the *Summa contra Gentiles*. It is by showing the truth that one excludes errors, and the truth is not fully made clear unless one is able to show the falseness of the errors that oppose it. One must remark on this subject that, except for the "error" of the Greeks on the procession of the Holy Spirit,[127] St. Thomas does not mention contemporary medieval errors on Trinitarian faith (neither errors of theologians nor errors of medieval religious groups). He only argues against the errors of antiquity. The reason for this choice is probably of a speculative order: If one considers the intelligence of faith, the error allows one to better grasp the truth to which it is opposed, in the measure that, by contrast, it lights up the truth. From then on, as R.-A. Gauthier has so well explained, "an error is not all the more interesting because it is more widespread, but it is all the more interesting when it opposes a deeper truth."[128] The interest for the heresies is not therefore only historical, nor is it only motivated by patristic documentation, but it is properly systematic with a speculative aim.

In the Prologue of his commentary on St. John, St. Thomas presents this Gospel as the fruit of the Apostle's contemplation: The portrait of St. John is that of a contemplative par excellence, whose contemplation was "high, full and perfect." It is about the contemplation of God, more precisely the "contemplation of the nature of the divine Word and of his essence" and of "the power of the Word as it extends to all things," that is to say of the "very deity of our Lord Jesus Christ, by which he is equal to the Father."[129] According to St. Thomas, "John represents those who are devoted to the contemplation of truth."[130] We must remember here that, for

[126] *SCG* I, ch. 1 (#7) and Book IV, ch. 1 (#3348). See especially R.-A. Gauthier, *Saint Thomas d'Aquin, Somme contre les Gentils*, pp. 143–63. One can see the same attention given to errors in other works of St. Thomas, in his *De articulis fidei* for example: see G. Emery, *Saint Thomas d'Aquin, Les raisons de la foi*, pp. 200–8.

[127] *In Ioan.* 15:26 (#2063–65).

[128] R.-A. Gauthier, *Saint Thomas d'Aquin, Somme contre les Gentils*, p. 142.

[129] *In Ioan.*, Prologue (#1–11).

[130] *In Ioan.* 20:8 (#2487).

St. Thomas, the words "contemplative" and "speculative" are practically equivalent and designate the same reality (*speculativus* is employed in the treatises inspired by Aristotle whereas St. Thomas uses the word *contemplativus* in the treatises which have Christian sources).[131] Theological science is speculative because its end is the contemplation of the truth.[132] The fourth Gospel appears thus to be a privileged source of speculation. The attention given to Trinitarian heresies, in the context of this speculative exegesis, is therefore not surprising. It shows that the aim of the exposition of the fourth Gospel is identical to the subject of theological wisdom formulated in the *Summa contra Gentiles*: to make manifest the contemplated truth and get rid of the errors which oppose this truth.[133]

We find here again, exactly, the aim or the goal of Scripture (or *sacra doctrina*), such as St. Thomas explains it from the start of his *Scriptum super Sententiis*: "We make our way to three things in Sacred Scripture *(in sacra Scriptura)*, namely: to the destruction of errors . . . ; it also proceeds to the instruction of moral actions . . . ; third, it proceeds to the contemplation of truth in questions of Sacred Scripture."[134] In the *Summa theologiae*, St. Thomas shows that *sacra doctrina* is principally speculative, and states also the equivalence of *sacra doctrina* and *sacra scriptura* when he explains that "Sacred Scripture disputes with one who denies its principles."[135] For St. Thomas, the expressions *"sacra doctrina," "theologia"* and *"sacra scriptura"* are employed as synonyms and designate the whole of divine teaching founded on the revelation.[136] The aims of theological reflection are those of Holy Scripture, as St. Albert the Great already explained on the subject of the modes of exposition of Holy Scripture *(de modis exponendi sacram Scripturam)*: Holy Scripture carries

---

131 Servais Pinckaers, "Recherche de la signification véritable du terme 'spéculatif,'" *Nouvelle Revue Théologique* 81 (1959): 673–95.

132 I *Sent.,* prol., q. 1, a. 3, qla 1; cf. *ST* I, q. 1, a. 4.

133 This subject is not foreign to the *Summa theologiae*, whose Trinitarian treatise begins precisely by indicating the reasons for the Arian and Sabellian errors, and the ways to avoid such errors (*ST* I, q. 27, a. 1).

134 I *Sent.,* prol., q. 1, a. 5.

135 *ST* I, q. 1, a. 8.

136 Henry Donneaud, "Insaisissable sacra doctrina ?" *RT* 98 (1998): 179–224.

a double aim *(duplex finis)*, that is to say the exhortation in the holy doctrine and the refutation of those who wish to contradict it.[137] In this way, exegesis and theological reflection dismiss errors as the Scripture discards errors. Biblical exegesis is speculative as Holy Scripture is speculative; it leads one to the contemplation of truth, because such is the aim of Scripture itself.

Conclusion: The Contribution of the Commentary on St. John

Our study of the commentary on St. John by St. Thomas has not examined in detail the particular Trinitarian themes: It has been limited to considering the body of the Trinitarian doctrine, taken as a whole and with its inner coherence, by comparing it to the *Summa theologiae*. This general approach offers the following results which can help to renew our reading of St. Thomas's Trinitarian theology.

1. The comparison with the Trinitarian treatise of the *Summa theologiae* shows the amplitude of the Trinitarian doctrine in the biblical commentary. The speculative doctrine of the Trinity, even in its technical elements, is very broad in the exposition of the Gospel. All the principal doctrinal themes are present in the commentary on the fourth Gospel. Let us remember them: the notion of procession, the immanent procession of the Son by mode of intellect or of nature, the eternal procession of the Holy Spirit, the personal subsistence in God, the doctrine of the Word, the origin of the Spirit, the property of the Father, the unity of the Father and the Son as principle of the Holy Spirit, relative opposition and the distinction of the persons by the relations, the doctrine of the real relation according to the origin, the personal properties, the order of nature in God, the necessity of notional acts, the relationship between the divine persons and creatures, the mission of the persons, as well as several problems about Trinitarian language. The most developed themes concern the

---

[137] Albert the Great, I *Sent.*, d. 1, a. 5.

three divine persons and their properties (with an accent on the doctrine of the Word, and on the procession of the Holy Spirit *a Patre et a Filio*), as well as the equality of the persons, their mutual relationships, the mission of the persons, and their action in the world. The commentary invites us to reread the Trinitarian treatise of the *Summa* in the light of these principal themes which occupy the first place in the theologian's subject.

2. The commentary on St. John allows us to identify the biblical context of several doctrinal themes. These biblical places are obvious for the doctrine of the Word, the procession of the Spirit, or the unity and immanence of the persons, as Aquinas's teaching on these themes, even in the *Summa theologiae*, is directly attached to the Gospel text. But the commentary also reveals other biblical places: Thus, for example, it is in the study of the procession of the Holy Spirit that the commentary on St. John gives the most complete exposition on relative opposition. The statement on the personal subsistence in God is found principally in the study on the Word. Likewise, the study of the notion of procession is particularly developed in the exposition on the divine missions. The *Summa theologiae* treats the procession, the relation, and the properties in special questions, at the risk of suggesting a certain isolation of these themes if one omits to consider their place in the structure of the Trinitarian treatise. The commentary on St. John, very close to the *Summa contra Gentiles* in this aspect, shows on its side that these doctrinal themes are attached to the study of the persons and their agency, and invites a rereading of the Trinitarian treatise of the *Summa* centered on the persons.

3. The commentary on St. John reveals a more special attention given to certain themes, which the *Summa theologiae* also treats but without giving them such amplitude: the knowledge and mutual love of the divine persons, the action of the divine persons in the world, and the knowledge of the eternal Trinity through the actions of these persons. The commentary on St.

John develops the soteriological repercussions of the Trinitarian doctrine: The property of the Word and the mutual knowledge of the Father and the Son are the source of the illuminating and revealing role of the Son, the Trinitarian unity is the source of human and ecclesial unity, and so forth. By explaining the agency of the Son and of the Holy Spirit in the light of their personal property, St. Thomas shows that the speculative doctrine of the Word and Love does not constitute a formal "psychological" reflection detached from the history of salvation. The speculative study of the Word and Love has not only for its aim the manifestation of the distinction of the persons in the unity of divine essence, but also allows one to account for the work of the divine persons in the world, and to organize the biblical teachings on the acts of the persons.

4. By exposing the actions of the divine persons in the world, St. Thomas does not content himself with the enumeration of the works of the Father, the Son, and the Spirit, but he organizes and explains these works in a doctrine on Trinitarian activity *ad extra* ("economic Trinity") by means of speculative principles—namely, the relative properties of the persons, but also the Trinitarian order, and the metaphysics of action and participation. The commentary on St. John invites one to criticize the thesis, widespread today, which identifies purely and simply biblical teaching as a doctrine of the "economic Trinity," whereas the doctrine of the "immanent Trinity" would be the result of a second and posterior reflection. In St. Thomas, the teaching on the economic Trinity is as speculative as the teaching on the immanent Trinity. The doctrine of the "economic Trinity" appears to be rather the fruit of a reflection which, benefiting from the study of the Trinity in itself, explains the Trinitarian economy in the light of the eternal being of the Trinity. The doctrine of Trinitarian economy is not first: It constitutes rather the last stage of Trinitarian theology.[138] The

---

[138] For this reason, the *Summa theologiae* treats the mission of the persons at the end of the Trinitarian treatise, in the last question (*ST* I, q. 43): The study of the works of the person benefits from all the preliminary reflection.

commentary on St. John suggests that one should perceive the development of Trinitarian theology in the following way: (1) Revelation of the Trinity through its actions in the world (economy of salvation) according to the witness of Holy Scriptures; (2) speculative reflection on the persons in their distinction and their unity; (3) speculative reflection on the agency of the persons in the world. Trinitarian theology starts from the agency of the divine persons in the world and comes back to this agency, in the same way that it starts from Scripture to return to Scripture.

5. The commentary on St. John manifests the deeply patristic roots of the Trinitarian doctrine of St. Thomas. Without having been able to give in detail here the extraordinary amplitude of this patristic inheritance, we have given some examples. The comparison shows that certain articles from the *Summa theologiae*, when reread in the light of the commentary on St. John, are taken directly from patristic exegesis (even when, in the *Summa*, St. Thomas omits explicit references to the Fathers of the Church). The exegesis of the Trinitarian passages of the Gospel benefits massively from the work of the *Catena aurea*: It is led principally by the reading of the Fathers of the Church. The Trinitarian exegesis of St. Thomas is clearly presented as a resumption of the patristic exegesis, prolonged in a personal way.

6. The Trinitarian exposition on St. John gives great attention to errors and heresies. The commentary furnishes one of our principal sources for appreciating, in a detailed way, the place of Trinitarian heresies in St. Thomas's thought. These heresies, present in all the important sections on the Trinity, all come from antiquity and manifest the patristic roots of St. Thomas's exegesis. The interest in Trinitarian heresies is not only of a documentary order. It belongs first of all to the subject of Scripture itself, which teaches the truth and excludes errors. It is inscribed, in St. Thomas, in the speculative enterprise of the manifestation of truth. St. Thomas is interested in heresies because the exposition of Scripture aims at manifesting the catholic faith, and

because the manifestation of truth is intrinsically linked to the exclusion of errors. Commenting on St. John, St. Thomas seeks to accomplish the task of Christian wisdom which consists in exposing the truth that one has meditated upon and in excluding errors. This subject is not foreign to the *Summa theologiae*, but it is more like the Trinitarian treatise of the *Summa contra Gentiles*.

7. The commentary on St. John can help one to perceive the unity of the *sacra doctrina* in St. Thomas better. The subject he pursues in exposing the Scriptures is identical to the aim of the Scriptures themselves and to that of Christian theology: To teach the revealed truth and to banish errors, to perceive that which we hope to contemplate one day in full light. The speculative reflection comes in then, in the commentary on St. John as well as in the *Summa theologiae*, to manifest (that is to say, *make more manifest for our spirit*) the truth taught by the revelation. The most speculative reflection on personal properties and Trinitarian relations is not superimposed on biblical teaching, but is included in biblical exegesis, because it has as its aim to extract the profound sense of the text by the means of intellectual resources, in faith.

8. One must conclude that the principal difference of the Trinitarian doctrine of the commentary and that of the *Summa theologiae* does not reside in the themes treated nor in the aim which consists in exposing the truth, neither in the conceptual tools, but simply in the organization of the matter. Whereas the *Summa theologiae* presents the Trinitarian doctrine according to the *ordo disciplinae* which manifests the internal arrangement and coherence (the order of exposition where the different aspects and concepts of the Trinitarian doctrine are connected according to their mutual implications), the commentary on St. John presents the same teaching following to the letter the biblical text. One can see it easily in the examination of the soteriological foundations of the knowledge of the eternal Trinity (soteriological argument, reflection on power and operation, manifestation of a person by

the person who proceeds from him). The commentary on St. John reveals the way to elaborate a Trinitarian doctrine, which the *Summa* on its side organizes in a systematic way.

It is perhaps in this last point that we find the principal contribution of the commentary of St. Thomas on St. John. In the nineteenth and twentieth centuries, neo-scholastic Trinitarian theology gave itself the task of explaining dogmatic formulas recalling that the dogma constitutes the norm of the reading of Scripture. The development of exegesis and historical sciences, as well as the influence of contemporary philosophical currents, have led many to argue against the pertinence and value of classical Trinitarian dogmatics. If we want to follow St. Thomas today, our first task is to show the deep biblical and patristic foundations of his Trinitarian doctrine. The movement has been, in a way, inversed. The commentary of St. Thomas Aquinas on St. John allows us to return along the path by showing how the speculative doctrine of St. Thomas is inscribed in the reading of Scripture. This speculative doctrine of the Trinity is one with the reading of the biblical text and, put to the service of the intelligence of Scripture, it does not look for anything else than the manifestation of the deep sense of the Gospel.

Bibliography

Primary

Abelard, Peter. *Opera Theologica.* Vols. 2–3. Edited by Eligius M. Buytaert and Constant J. Mews. Corpus Christianorum, Continuatio Mediaevalis. Vols. 12–13. Turnhout: Brepols, 1969 and 1987.

Acta Apostolorum Apocrypha. Edited by Ricardus A. Lipsius and Maximilianus Bonnet. Vol. II/1. Darmstadt: Wissenschaftliche Buchgesellschaft, 1959.

Acta Conciliorum Œcumenicorum. Vol. I/3. Edited by Eduardus Schwartz. Berlin/Leipzig: De Gruyter, 1929. Vol. II/3. Edited by Eduardus Schwartz. Berlin/Leipzig: De Gruyter, 1936. Vol. IV/1. Edited by Johannes Straub. Berlin: De Gruyter, 1971.

Albert the Great. *Opera Omnia.* Vols. 25–26: *Commentarium in I Sententiarum.* Edited by Auguste Borgnet. Paris: Louis Vivès, 1893.

———. *Opera Omnia.* Vol. 34: *Summa de creaturis.* Edited by Auguste Borgnet. Paris: Louis Vivès, 1895.

———. *De resurrectione.* In: *Opera Omnia.* Vol. 26. Edited by Wilhelm Kübel. Münster: Aschendorff, 1958, pp. 237–354.

———. *Opera Omnia.* Vol. 37/1–2: *Super Dionysium De divinis nominibus et Super Dionysii mysticam theologiam et epistulas.* Edited by Paulus Simon. Münster: Aschendorff, 1972.

———. *Opera Omnia.* Vol. 34/1: *Summa theologiae sive De mirabili scientia Dei Libri I Pars I.* Edited by Wilhelm Kübel. Münster: Aschendorff, 1978.

———. *Opera Omnia.* Vol. 36: *Super Dionysium De caelesti hierarchia.* Edited by Paulus Simon and Wilhelm Kübel. Münster: Aschendorff, 1993.

Alcuin. *Libellus de processione Spiritus Sancti.* Edited by Jacques-Paul Migne. In *Patrologia Latina.* Vol. 101. Paris/Turnhout: Brepols, 1976, pp. 63–82.

Alexander of Hales. *Summa Theologica seu Summa fratris Alexandri.* Vol. 1. Quarrachi: Editiones Collegii S. Bonaventurae, 1924.

———. *Glossa in quatuor Libros Sententiarum Petri Lombardi.* Vol. 1: *In Librum primum.* Quaracchi: Editiones Collegii S. Bonaventurae, 1951.

Ambrose of Milan. *De Spiritu Sancto libri tres.* Edited by Jacques-Paul Migne. In *Patrologia Latina.* Vol. 16. Paris/Turnhout: Brepols, 1966, pp. 703–816.

Anselm of Canterbury. *Opera Omnia.* 2 vols. Edited by Franciscus S. Schmitt. Stuttgart: F. Frommann, 1968.

———. *L'oeuvre de S. Anselme de Cantorbéry.* Vols. 1–4. Edited by Michel Corbin. Paris: Cerf, 1986–90.

———. *The Major Works.* Edited by Brian Davies and Gillian R. Evans. Oxford/New York: Oxford University Press, 1998.

Aquinas, Thomas. *Opera omnia iussu Leonis XIII P.M. edita.* Tomus 4–12: *Summa theologiae.* Rome: Ex typographia polyglotta S.C. de Propaganda Fide, 1888–1906.

———. *Opera omnia iussu Leonis XIII P.M. edita.* Tomus 13–15: *Summa contra Gentiles.* Rome: Typis Riccardi Garroni, 1918–30.

———. *Scriptum super Libros Sententiarum.* Vols. 1–2. Edited by Pierre Mandonnet. Paris: Lethielleux, 1929. Vols. 3–4. Edited by Maria F. Moos. Paris: Lethielleux, 1933 and 1947.

———. *In librum Beati Dionysii de divinis nominibus expositio.* Edited by Ceslas Pera. Turin/Rome: Marietti, 1950.

———. *Super Evangelium S. Matthaei lectura.* Edited by Raffaele Cai. Turin/Rome: Marietti, 1951.

———. *Super Evangelium S. Ioannis lectura.* Edited by Raffaele Cai. Turin/Rome: Marietti, 1952.

———. *In librum primum Aristotelis De generatione et corruptione.* Edited by Raimondo Spiazzi. Turin/Rome: Marietti, 1952.

———. *Catena aurea in quatuor Evangelia.* Edited by Angelico Guarienti. 2 vols. Turin/Rome: Marietti, 1953.

———. *Super Epistolas S. Pauli lectura.* Edited by Raffaele Cai. Editio VIII. 2 vols. Turin/Rome: Marietti, 1953.

———. *In symbolorum Apostolorum expositio.* In *Opuscula Theologica.* Vol. 2. Edited by Raimondo Spiazzi. Turin/Rome: Marietti, 1954, pp. 193–217.

————. *Liber de Veritate Catholicae Fidei contra errores Infidelium qui dicitur Summa contra Gentiles.* Edited by Petrus Marc, Ceslas Pera et al. 3 vols. Turin/Paris: Marietti/Lethielleux, 1961–67.

————. *Quaestiones disputatae de potentia.* In *Quaestiones disputatae.* Vol. 2. Edited by Pio Bazzi et al. Turin/Rome: Marietti, 1965: 7–276.

————. *Opera omnia iussu Leonis XIII P.M. edita.* Tomus 40 A: *Contra errores Graecorum.* Edited by Hyacinthe F. Dondaine. Rome: Ad Sanctae Sabinae, 1967.

————. *Opera omnia iussu Leonis XIII P.M. edita.* Tomus 40 B: *De rationibus fidei.* Edited by Hyacinthe F. Dondaine. Rome: Ad Sanctae Sabinae, 1968.

————. *Opera omnia iussu Leonis XIII P.M. edita.* Tomus 40 E: *Super Decretalem.* Edited by Hyacinthe F. Dondaine. Rome: Ad Sanctae Sabinae, 1968.

————. *Opera omnia iussu Leonis XIII P.M. edita.* Tomus 22 (3 vols): *Quaestiones disputatae de veritate.* Rome: Editori di San Tommaso, 1975–76.

————. *De articulis fidei et Ecclesiae sacramentis.* In *Opera omnia iussu Leonis XIII P.M. edita.* Tomus 42. Edited by Hyacinthe F. Dondaine. Rome: Editori di San Tommaso, 1979, pp. 245–57.

————. *Compendium Theologiae.* In *Opera omnia iussu Leonis XIII P.M. edita.* Tomus 42. Edited by Gilles de Grandpré. Rome: Editori di San Tommaso, 1979, pp. 83–205.

————. *Responsio ad magistrum Ioannem de Vercellis de 108 articulis.* In *Opera omnia iussu Leonis XIII P.M. edita.* Tomus 42. Edited by Hyacinthe F. Dondaine. Rome: Editori di San Tommaso, 1979: 277–94.

————. *Summa theologiae.* Cinisello Balsamo (Milano): Edizioni Paoline, 1988.

————. *Opera omnia iussu Leonis XIII P.M. edita.* Tomus 50: *Super Boetium de Trinitate.* Edited by Pierre-M. J. Gils. Rome/Paris: Commissio Leonina/Cerf, 1992, pp. 75–171.

————. *Opera omnia iussu Leonis XIII P.M. edita.* Tomus 25 (2 vols.): *Quaestiones de Quolibet.* Edited by René-Antoine Gauthier. Rome/Paris: Commissio Leonina/Cerf, 1996.

————. *Thomas d'Aquin, Commentaire sur l'évangile de S. Jean.* Vol. 1: *Le Prologue, La vie apostolique du Christ.* Préface par Marie-Dominique Philippe, Traduction et notes sous sa direction. Paris: Cerf, 1998.

————. *Commentary on the Gospel of John.* Part I. Translated by James A. Weisheipl and Fabian R. Larcher. Magi Books: Albany, NY, 1980. Part II. Translated by James A. Weisheipl and Fabian R. Larcher. Petersham, MA: St. Bede's Publications, 1999.

————. *Traités: Les raisons de la foi, Les articles de la foi et les sacrements de l'Eglise.* Introduction, traduction du Latin et annotation par Gilles Emery. Paris: Cerf, 1999.

Aristotle. *Ethica Nichomachea.* Edited by William D. Ross. Oxford: Oxford University Press, 1931.

————. *Physica.* Edited by William D. Ross. Oxford: Oxford University Press, 1936 ; repr. 1992.

————. *Metaphysica.* Edited by Werner Jaeger. Oxford: Oxford University Press, 1957.

Augustine. *De Genesi ad litteram libri duodecim.* Edited by Joseph Zycha. Corpus Scriptorum Ecclesiasticorum Latinorum. Vol. 28/1. Prague/Vienna: Bibliotheca Academiae litterarum Caesareae Vindobonensis, 1894.

————. *In Iohannis Evangelium Tractatus CXXIV.* Edited by Radbodus Willems. Corpus Christianorum, Series Latina. Vol. 36. Turnhout: Brepols, 1936.

————. *De vera religione.* Edited by Joseph Martin. Corpus Christianorum, Series Latina. Vol. 32. Turnhout: Brepols, 1962, pp. 187–260.

————. *De Trinitate libri XV.* 2 vols. Edited by W. J. Mountain. Corpus Christianorum, Series Latina. Vols 50–50A. Turnhout: Brepols, 1968.

————. *De diversis quaestionibus octoginta tribus.* Edited by Almut Mutzenbecher. Corpus Christianorum, Series Latina. Vol. 44A. Turnhout: Brepols, 1975.

Basil of Caesarea. *Saint Basile, Lettres.* Edited by Yves Courtonne. Vol. 2. Paris: Belles Lettres, 1961.

————. *Against Eunomius.* 2 vols. Edited by Bernard Sesboüé. Sources chrétiennes 299 and 305. Paris: Cerf, 1982–83.

Boethius. *The Theological Tractates.* Translated by Hugh F. Stewart and E. K. Rand. Cambridge, MA: Harvard University Press, 1973.

Bonaventure. *Opera Omnia.* Vol. 1: *Commentarium in Primum Librum Sententiarum.* Quaracchi: Editiones Coleggi S. Bonaventurae, 1882.

————. *Opera Omnia.* Vol. 2: *Commentarium in Secundum Librum Sententiarum.* Quaracchi: Editiones Colleggi S. Bonaventurae, 1885.

————. *Opera Omnia.* Vol. 3: *Commentarium in Tertium Librum Sententiarum.* Quaracchi: Editiones Collegii S. Bonaventurae, 1887.

————. *Opera Omnia*. Vol. 5: *Opuscula Varia Theologica*. Quaracchi: Editiones Collegii S. Bonaventurae, 1892.

Damascene, John. *De fide orthodoxa*. Versions of Burgundio and Cerbanus. Edited by Eligius M. Buytaert. New York: Franciscan Institute St. Bonaventure, 1955.

Decrees of the Ecumenical Councils. Vol. 1. Edited by Norman P. Tanner. Washington, DC: Georgetown University Press, 1990.

Dionysius (Pseudo-Dionysius). *Dionysiaca*. Edited by Philippe Chevallier. Vol. 1. Paris/Bruges: Desclée de Brouwer, 1937.

Duns Scotus (John Duns Scotus). *Opera Omnia*. Vol. 17: *Lectura in Librum primum Sententiarum a distinctione octava ad quadragesimam quintam*. Vatican City: Typis polyglottis Vaticanis, 1966.

Enchiridion symbolorum definitionum et declarationum de rebus fidei et morum. Edited by Henricus Denzinger and Adolfus Schönmetzer. Editio XXXVI emendata. Freiburg im Breisgau: Herder, 1971.

Gilbert of Poitiers (Gilbertus Porreta). *The Commentaries on Boethius by Gilbert of Poitiers*. Edited by Nikolaus M. Häring. Toronto: Pontifical Institute of Medieval Studies, 1966.

Henry of Ghent. *Opera Omnia*. Vol. 10: *Quodlibet VI*. Edited by Gordon A. Wilson. Louvain/Leiden: Leuven University Press/Brill, 1987.

Hilary of Poitiers. *Liber De synodis*. Edited by Jacques-Paul Migne. In *Patrologia Latina*. Vol. 10. Paris: Excudebat Vrayet, 1845, pp. 479–546.

————. *De Trinitate*. Edited by P. Smulders. Corpus Christianorum, Series Latina. Vols. 62–62A. Turnhout: Brepols, 1979–84.

Hugh of Saint-Victor. *Didascalicon*. Edited by Charles H. Buttimer. Washington, DC: The Catholic University of America Press, 1939.

Joachim of Fiore. *De vita Sancti Benedicti et de officio divino secundum eius doctrinam*. Edited by Cipriano Baraut. In *Analecta Sacra Tarraconensia*. Vol. 24. Barcelona: Biblioteca Balmes, 1951, pp. 33–122.

Lombard, Peter. *In Psalmos davidicos commentarii*. Edited by Jacques-Paul Migne. In *Patrologia Latina*. Vol. 101. Paris/Turhnout: Brepols, 1968, pp. 55–1296.

————. *Sententiae in IV Libris distinctae*. Edited by Ignatius Brady. Vol. I/1 and I/2. Grottaferrata/Rome: Editiones Collegii S. Bonaventurae ad Claras Aquas, 1971.

Marius Victorinus. *Traités théologiques sur la Trinité*. Edited by Paul Henry. Sources chrétiennes. Vol. 68. Paris: Cerf, 1960.

Moneta Cremonensis. *Adversus Catharos et Valdenses libri quinque.* Edited by Thomas Augustinus Ricchinius. Rome: Ex typographia Palladis, 1743 (Repr. Ridgewood, Greg Riss, 1966).

Photius. *Liber de Sacra Sanctissimi Spiritus doctrina seu De Sancti Spiritus mystagogia.* Edited by Jacques-Paul Migne. In *Patrologia Graeca.* Vol. 102. Paris/Turnhout: Brepols, 1993: 279–400.

Proclus. *Elementatio theologica translata a Guillelmo de Morbecca.* Edited by Helmut Boese. Leuven: University Press, 1987.

Rainierius Sacconi. *Summa de Catharis.* Edited by Francis Sanjek. *Archivum Fratrum Praedicatorum* 44 (1974): 31–60.

Richard of Saint Victor. *De Trinitate.* Edited by Gaston Salet. Paris: Cerf, 1999.

Roscellinus of Compiègne. *Epistola XV ad Petrum Abaelardum.* In *Patrologia Latina,* vol. 178. Edited by Jacques-Paul Migne. Paris/Turnhout: Brepols, 1979, pp. 357–72.

Tertullian. *Adversus Praxean.* In *Opera.* Vol. 2: *Opera montanistica.* Edited by A. Gerlo. Corpus Christianorum, Series Latina. Vol. 2. Turnhout: Brepols, 1954, pp. 1159–205.

Vigilius of Thapsus. *Contra arianos, sabellianos et photinianos dialogus.* Edited by Jacques-Paul Migne. In *Patrologia Latina.* Vol. 62. Paris/Turnhout: Brepols, s.d., pp. 179–238.

William of Auxerre, *Summa aurea.* Vol. 1: *Liber primus.* Vol. 2: *Liber secundus, tomus I.* Edited by Jean Ribaillier. Paris/Grottaferrata: Vrin/Editiones Collegii S. Bonaventurae, 1980 and 1982.

Secondary

Aertsen, Jan et al. *Vruchtbaar Woord: Wijsgerige beschouwingen bij een theologische tekst van Thomas van Aquino (Summa contra Gentiles boek IV, hoofdstuk 11.)* Leuven: Leuven University Press, 1990.

Backes, Ignaz. *Die Christologie des hl. Thomas von Aquin und die griechischen Kirchenväter.* Paderborn: Schoeningh, 1931.

Bailleux, Emile. "Le personnalisme de saint Thomas en théologie trinitaire." *Revue Thomiste* 61 (1961): 25–42.

———. "Le Christ et son Esprit." *Revue Thomiste* 73 (1973): 373–400.

———. *Le don de Dieu: Essai de théologie personnaliste.* 2 vols. Lille, 1958.

Balthasar, Hans Urs von. "Création et Trinité." *Communio* 13 (1988): 9–17.

Barnes, Michel R. "De Régnon Reconsidered" *Augustinian Studies* 26 (1995): 51–79.

————. *The Power of God: Dunamis in Gregory of Nyssa's Trinitarian Theology.* Washington, DC: The Catholic University of America Press, 2001.

Barth, Karl. *Dogmatique.* Vol. I, 1/2. Geneva: Labor et Fides, 1953.

Bobrinskoy, Boris. "Le repos de l'Esprit sur le Fils chez les Cappadociens." In *La Pensée orthodoxe, Travaux de l'Institut de théologie orthodoxe Saint-Serge.* Vol. 4. Lausanne: l'Age d'homme, 1987, pp. 24–39.

————. "Vers une vision commune du Mystère trinitaire." *La Documentation Catholique* 93/2 (1996): 89–90.

Bonanni, Sergio Paolo. *Parlare della Trinità: Lettura della Theologia Scholarium di Abelardo.* Rome: Edited by Pontifica Università Gregoriana, 1996.

Bonino, Serge-Thomas. "La place du pape dans l'Église selon saint Thomas d'Aquin." *Revue Thomiste* 86 (1986): 392–422.

————. "Les 'voiles sacrés': à propos d'une citation de Denys." *Studi Tomistici* 45 (1992): 158–71.

Bouillard, Henri. *Vérité du christianisme.* Paris: Desclée de Brouwer, 1989.

Boulnois, Marie-Odile. *Le paradoxe trinitaire chez Cyrille d'Alexandrie.* Paris: Institut d'Etudes Augustiniennes, 1994.

Bourassa, François. *Questions de théologie trinitaire.* Rome: Gregorian University Press, 1970.

————. "Note sur le traité de la Trinité de la Somme théologique de saint Thomas." *Science et Esprit* 27 (1975): 187–207.

————. "Sur la propriété de l'Esprit-Saint. Questions disputées." *Science et Esprit* 28 (1976): 243–65 and 29 (1977): 23–43.

Breuning, Wilhelm. "La Trinité." In *Bilan de la théologie du XXe siècle.* Edited by Robert Vander Gucht and Herbert Vorgrimler. Vol. 2. Tournai-Paris: Casterman, 1970, pp. 252–67.

Butterworth, Edward J. *The Doctrine of the Trinity in Saint Thomas Aquinas and Saint Bonaventure.* Diss. Fordham University. New York: UMI, 1985.

Cacciapuoti, Pierluigi. *"Deus existentia amoris": Teologia della carità e teologia della Trinità negli scritti di Riccardo di San Vittore.* Paris/Turnhout: Brepols, 1998.

Chacon, Alfonso C. "El tratado sobre la gracia en la *Summa contra Gentiles.*" *Scripta theologica* 16 (1984): 113–46.

Châtillon, Jean. "*Unitas, aequalitas, concordia vel connexio.* Recherches sur les Origines de la Théorie Thomiste des Appropriations *(Sum. Theol.,* I, q. 39, art. 7–8)." In *St. Thomas Aquinas 1274–1974: Commemorative Studies.* Edited by Armand A. Maurer. Vol. 1. Toronto: Pontifical Institute of Medieval Studies, 1974, pp. 337–79.

Chenu, Marie-Dominique. *Introduction à l'étude de saint Thomas d'Aquin.* Montréal/Paris: Institut d'Etudes médiévales/Vrin, 1984.

Chevalier, Irénée. *Saint Augustin et la pensée grecque: Les relations trinitaires.* Fribourg: Librairie de l'Université, 1940.

Coffey, David. *Deus Trinitas: The Doctrine of the Triune God.* Oxford/New York: Oxford University Press, 1999.

Colish, Marcia L. "Gilbert, The Early Porretans, and Peter Lombard: Semantics and Theology." In *Gilbert de Poitiers et ses contemporains aux origines de la "Logica modernorum."* Edited by Jean Jolivet and Alain de Libera. Naples: Bibliopolis, 1987, pp. 229–50.

Congar, Yves. "Quatre siècles de désunion et d'affrontement. Comment Grecs et Latins se sont appréciés réciproquement au point de vue ecclésiologique?" *Istina* 13 (1968): 131–52.

———. *Je crois en l'Esprit-Saint.* Vol. 3: *Le Fleuve de Vie coule en Orient et en Occident.* 2nd edition. Paris: Cerf, 1985.

Corbin, Michel. *La Trinité ou l'Excès de Dieu.* Paris: Cerf, 1997.

Couesnongle, Vincent de. "La causalité du maximum." *RSPT* 38 (1954): 433–44 and 658–80.

Courth, Franz. *Trinität in der Scholastik.* Freiburg im Breisgau: Herder, 1985.

Cunningham, Francis L. B. *The Indwelling of the Trinity: A Historico-Doctrinal Study of the Theory of St. Thomas Aquinas.* Dubuque, IA: The Priory Press, 1955.

Dahan, Gilbert. *L'exégèse chrétienne de la Bible en Occident médiéval, XIIe–XIVe siècle.* Paris: Cerf, 1999.

Den Bok, Nico. *Communicating the Most High: A Systematic Study of Person and Trinity in the Theology of Richard of St. Victor.* Paris/Turnhout: Brepols, 1996.

Di Napoli, Giovanni. "Gioachino da Fiore e Pietro Lombardo." *Rivista di Filosofia Neo-scolastica* 71 (1979): 621–85.

Dondaine, Antoine. "*Contra Graecos.* Premiers écrits polémiques des Dominicains d'Orient." *Archivum Fratrum Praedicatorum* 21 (1951): 320–446.

Dondaine, Hyacinthe F. "La théologie latine de la procession du Saint-Esprit." *Russie et Chrétienté* 3–4 (1950): 211–18.

———. *Saint Thomas d'Aquin, Somme théologique, La Trinité.* 2 Vols. Paris: Editions de la Revue des Jeunes, 1950, repr. Cerf, 1997.

Donneaud, Henry. "Insaisissable sacra doctrina?" *Revue Thomiste* 98 (1998): 179–224.

Elders, Leo J. "Santo Tomás de Aquino y los Padres de la Iglesia." *Doctor Communis* 48 (1993): 55–80.

Emery, Gilles. "Le Père et l'oeuvre trinitaire de création selon le Commentaire des *Sentences* de S. Thomas d'Aquin." In *Ordo sapientiae et amoris: Hommage au Professeur Jean-Pierre Torrell OP à l'occasion de son 65e anniversaire.* Edited by Carlos-Josaphat Pinto de Oliveira. Fribourg: Editions universitaires, 1993, pp. 85–117.

———. "Le photinisme et ses précurseurs chez saint Thomas: Cérinthe, les ébionites, Paul de Samosate et Photin." *Revue Thomiste* 95 (1995): 371–98.

———. "Trinité et création. Le principe trinitaire de la création dans les commentaires d'Albert le Grand, de Bonaventure et de Thomas d'Aquin sur les *Sentences.*" *Revue des Sciences Philosophiques et Théologiques* 79 (1995): 405–30.

———. *La Trinité créatrice: Trinité et Création dans les commentaires aux Sentences de Thomas d'Aquin et de ses précurseurs Albert le Grand et Bonaventure.* Paris: Vrin, 1995.

———. "La procession du Saint-Esprit *a Filio* chez S. Thomas d'Aquin." *Revue Thomiste* 96 (1996): 531–74.

———. "Le traité de saint Thomas sur la Trinité dans la *Somme contre les Gentils.*" *Revue Thomiste* 96 (1996): 5–40.

———. "Essentialisme ou personnalisme dans le traité de Dieu chez saint Thomas d'Aquin?" *Revue Thomiste* 98 (1998): 5–38.

———. "Dieu, la foi et la théologie chez Durand de Saint-Pourçain." *Revue Thomiste* 99 (1999): 659–99.

———. "La relation dans la théologie de saint Albert le Grand." In *Albertus Magnus, Zum Gedenken nach 800 Jahren: Neue Zugänge, Aspekte und Perspektiven.* Edited by Walter Senner. Berlin: Akademie Verlag, 2001, pp. 455–65.

———. "Trinité et unité de Dieu dans la scolastique. XIIe–XIVe siècle." In *Le christianisme est-il un monothéisme? Actes du 3e cycle de théologie systématique des Facultés de théologie de Suisse romande.* Edited by Pierre Gisel and Gilles Emery. Geneva: Labor et Fides, 2001, pp. 195–220.

Evans, Gillian R. *Concordance to the Works of St. Anselm.* 4 vols. New York: Kraus International Publications,1984.

Ferraro. Giuseppe. *Lo Spirito e l'"ora" di Cristo: L'esegesi di San Tommaso d'Aquino sul quarto Vangelo.* Vatican City: Editrice Vaticana, 1996.

Fidalgo Herranz, José A. "La SS. Trinidad en la *Suma contra los Gentiles:* fuentes bíblicas." In *Excerpta e dissertationibus in sacra theologia.* Vol. 8. Pamplona: Ediciones Universidad de Navarra, 1986, pp. 329–402.

Floucat, Yves. "L'intellection et son verbe selon saint Thomas d'Aquin." *Revue Thomiste* 97 (1997): 443–84 and 640–93.

———. *L'intime fécondité de l'intelligence: Le verbe mental selon saint Thomas d'Aquin.* Paris: Téqui, 2001.

Gauthier, René-Antoine. "Introduction historique." In *Thomas d'Aquin, Contra Gentiles.* Vol. 1. Paris: Lethielleux, 1961, pp. 7–123.

———. *Saint Thomas d'Aquin, Somme contre les Gentils, Introduction.* Paris: Editions universitaires, 1993.

Geenen, Godefridus. "En marge du concile de Chalcédoine, Les textes du quatrième concile dans les œuvres de saint Thomas." *Angelicum* 29 (1952): 43–59.

Geiger, Louis-Bertrand. "Les rédactions successives de *Contra Gentiles* I,53 d'après l'autographe." In *Saint Thomas d'Aquin aujourd'hui, Recherches de philosophie 6.* Paris/Bruges: Desclée de Brouwer, 1963, pp. 221–40.

Gelabert, Martin. "La creación a la luz del misterio trinitario." *Escritos del Vedat* 22 (1992): 7–45.

Gerken, Alexander. *La théologie du Verbe: La relation entre l'incarnation et la création selon S. Bonaventure.* Paris: Editions Franciscaines, 1970.

Ghellinck, Joseph de. *Le mouvement théologique du XIIe siècle.* 2nd edition. Bruxelles/Paris: Edition Universelle/Desclée de Brouwer, 1948.

González, Olegario. *Misterio Trinitario y existencia humana: Estudio histórico teológico en torno a San Buenaventura.* Madrid: Rialp, 1966.

Grégoire, José. "La relation éternelle de l'Esprit au Fils d'après les écrits de Jean de Damas." *Revue d'Histoire Ecclésiastique* 64 (1969): 713–55.

Greshake, Gisbert. *Der Dreieine Gott: Eine trinitarische Theologie.* Freiburg im Breisgau: Herder, 1997.

Grumel, Venance. "St. Thomas et la doctrine des Grecs sur la procession du Saint-Esprit." *Échos d'Orient* 25 (1926): 257–80.

Gunten, François von. "Gibt es eine zweite Redaktion des Sentenzenkommentars des hl. Thomas von Aquin?" *Freiburger Zeitschrift für Philosophie und Theologie* 3 (1956): 137–68.

————. "*In principio erat Verbum.* Une évolution de saint Thomas en théologie trinitaire." In *Ordo sapientiae et amoris: Hommage au Professeur Jean-Pierre Torrell OP à l'occasion de son 65e anniversaire.* Edited by Carlos-Josaphat Pinto de Oliveira. Fribourg: Éditions universitaires, 1993: 119–41.

Halleux, André de. *Patrologie et œcuménisme: Recueil d'études.* Leuven: University Press/Peeters, 1990.

Hayen, André. "Le concile de Reims et l'erreur théologique de Gilbert de la Porrée." *Archives d'Histoire Doctrinale et Littéraire du Moyen Âge* 10–11 (1936): 29–102.

Hofmeier, Johann. *Die Trinitätslehre des Hugo von St. Viktor.* Munich: Max Hueber Verlag, 1963.

Hunt, Anne. *What Are They Saying About the Trinity?* New York: Paulist Press, 1998.

Izquierdo, César. "La teología del Verbo en la *Summa contra Gentiles.*" *Scripta theologica* 14 (1982): 551–80.

Jolivet, Jean. *La théologie d'Abélard.* Paris: Cerf, 1997.

Jorissen, Hans. "Zur Struktur des Traktates 'De Deo' in der *Summa theologiae* des Thomas von Aquin." In *Im Gespräch mit dem dreieinigen Gott: Elemente einer trinitarischen Theologie.* Edited by Michael Böhnke and Hanspeter Heinz. Düsseldorf: Patmos, 1985, pp. 231–57.

Kasper, Walter. *The God of Jesus Christ.* Translated by Matthew J. O'Connell. New York: Crossroad, 1986.

Kenny, Joseph. "Saint Thomas Aquinas: Reasons for the Faith Against Muslim Objections (and one objection of the Greeks and Armenians) to the Cantor of Antioch." *Islamochristiana* 22 (1996): 31–52.

Lafont, Ghislain. *Peut-on connaître Dieu en Jésus-Christ?* Paris: Cerf, 1969.

Levering, Matthew. *Scripture and Metaphysics: Aquinas and the Renewal of Trinitarian Theology.* Oxford: Blackwell, forthcoming.

Libera, Alain de. "L'Un ou la Trinité? Sur un aspect trop connu de la théologie eckhartienne." *Revue des Sciences Religieuses* 70 (1996): 31–47.

————. *La querelle des universaux de Platon à la fin du Moyen Âge.* Paris: Seuil, 1996.

Lottin, Odon. "Problèmes concernant la 'Summa de creaturis' et le Commentaire des Sentences de saint Albert le Grand." *Recherches de Théologie Ancienne et Médiévale* 17 (1950): 319–28.

Malet, André. "La synthèse de la personne et de la nature dans la théologie trinitaire de saint Thomas." *Revue Thomiste* 54 (1954): 483–522 and 55 (1955): 43–84.

———. *Personne et amour dans la théologie trinitaire de saint Thomas d'Aquin.* Paris: Vrin, 1956.

Marengo, Gildfredo. *Trinità e creazione: Indagine sulla teologia di Tommaso d'Aquino.* Rome: Città Nuova, 1990.

———. "Il principio trinitario della creazione nella teologia di Tommaso d'Aquino." *Studi Tomistici* 44 (1991): 183–88.

Margerie, Bertrand de. "Vers une relecture du concile de Florence grâce à la reconsidération de l'Écriture et des Pères grecs et latins." *Revue Thomiste* 86 (1986): 31–81.

Marinelli, Francesco. *Personalismo trinitario nella storia della salvezza: Rapporti tra la SS.ma Trinità e le opere ad extra nello Scriptum super Sententiis di San Tommaso.* Rome/Paris: Pontificia Università Lateranense/Vrin, 1969.

Mathieu, Luc. *La Trinité créatrice d'après S. Bonaventure.* Paris: Editions Franciscaines, 1992.

Mehlmann, Axel. *De unitate trinitatis: Forschungen und Dokumente zur Trinitätstheologie Joachims von Fiore im Zusammenhang mit senem verschollenen Traktat gegen Petrus Lombardus.* Freiburg im Breisgau, 1991.

Mews, Constant J. "The Lists of Heresies Imputed to Peter Abelard." *Revue Bénédictine* 95 (1985): 73–110.

Michel, Elsbeth. *Nullus potest amare aliquid incognitum: Ein Beitrag zur Frage des Intellektualismus bei Thomas von Aquin.* Fribourg: Editions Universitaires, 1979.

Montagnes, Bernard. *La doctrine de l'analogie de l'être d'après saint Thomas d'Aquin.* Louvain/Paris: Publications Universitaires de Louvain/Béatrice-Nauwelaerts, 1963.

Morard, Martin. "Une source de Saint Thomas d'Aquin: le deuxième concile de Constantinople." *Revue des Sciences Philosophiques et Théologiques* 81 (1997): 21–56.

Mühlen, Heribert. "Person und Appropriation. Zum Verständnis des Axioms: *In Deo omnia sunt unum, ubi non obviat relationis oppositio.*" *Münchener theologische Zeitschrift* 16 (1965): 37–57.

Müller, Wolfgang. *Die Theologie des Dritten: Entwurf einer sozialen Trinitätslehre.* St. Ottilien: EOS Verlag, 1996.

Obenauer, Klaus. *Summa Actualitas: Zum Verhältnis von Einheit und Verschiedenheit in der Dreieinigkeitslehre des heiligen Bonaventura.* Frankfurt am Main: Lang, 1996.

———. "Zur *subsistentia absoluta* in der Trinitätstheologie." *Theologie und Philosophie* 72 (1997): 188–215.

Paissac, Hyacinthe. *Théologie du Verbe, Saint Augustin et Saint Thomas.* Paris: Cerf, 1951.

Patfoort, Albert. *Saint Thomas d'Aquin: Les clefs d'une théologie.* Paris: FAC Editions, 1983.

———. "*Cognitio ista est quasi experimentalis* (I *Sent.*, d. 14, q. 2, a. 2, ad 3)." *Angelicum* 63 (1986): 3–13.

———. "Missions divines et expérience des Personnes divines selon saint Thomas." *Angelicum* 63 (1986): 545–59.

Pedrini, Arnaldo. *Bibliografia tomista sulla pneumatologia.* Vatican City: Editrice Vaticana, 1994.

Pelikan, Jaroslav. "The Doctrine of *Filioque* in Thomas Aquinas and its Patristic Antecedents, An Analysis of *Summa theologiae*, Part I, Question 36." In *St. Thomas Aquinas 1274–1974: Commemorative Studies.* Edited by Armand A. Maurer. Vol. 1. Toronto: Pontifical Institute of Medieval Studies, 1974, pp. 315–36.

———. *La Tradition chrétienne.* Vol. 2: *L'esprit du christianisme oriental (600–1700).* Paris: PUF, 1994.

Perino, Renato. *La dottrina di S. Anselmo nel quadro nel suo metodo teologico e del suo concetto di Dio.* Rome: Herder, 1952.

Pinckaers, Servais. "Recherche de la signifiation véritable du terme *spéculatif*." *Nouvelle Revue Théologique* 81 (1959): 673–95.

Prades, Javier. *"Deus specialiter est in sanctis per gratiam": El misterio de la inhabitación de la Trinidad en los escritos de santo Tomás.* Rome: Gregorian University Press, 1993.

Rahner, Karl. *The Trinity.* Translated by Joseph Donceel. New York: Herder and Herder, 1970.

———. "Remarks on the Dogmatic Treatise 'De Trinitate.' " In *Theological Investigations.* Translated by Kevin Smyth. Vol. 4. New York. Crossroad, 1982, pp. 79–102.

———. "Theos in the New Testament." In *Theological Investigations.* Translated by C. Ernst. Vol. 1. New York: Crossroad, 1982, pp. 79–148.

Régnon, Théodore de. *Études de théologie positive sur la sainte Trinité.* 4 Vols. Paris: Victor Retaux, 1892–98.

Reichberg, Gregory M. "La communication de la nature divine en Dieu selon Thomas d'Aquin." *Revue Thomiste* 93 (1993): 50–65.

Richard, Robert L. *The Problem of an Apologetical Perspective in the Trinitarian Theology of St. Thomas Aquinas.* Rome: Gregorian University Press, 1963.

Robb, Fiona. "A Late Thirteenth Century Attack on the Fourth Lateran Council: The *Liber contra Lombardum* and Contemporary Debates on the Trinity." *Recherches de Théologie Ancienne et Médiévale* 62 (1995): 110–44.

Rottenwöhrer, Gerhard. *Der Katharismus.* Vol. I/1. Bad Honnef: Bock und Herchen, 1982.

Roy, Olivier du. *L'intelligence de la foi en la Trinité selon saint Augustin: Genèse de sa théologie trinitaire jusqu'en 391.* Paris: Etudes Augustiniennes, 1966.

Ruello, Francis. *Les "Noms Divins" et leurs "raisons" selon saint Albert le Grand commentateur du "De divinis nominibus."* Paris: Vrin, 1963.

———. "Saint Thomas et Pierre Lombard. Les relations trinitaires et la structure du commentaire des Sentences de saint Thomas d'Aquin." *Studi Tomistici* 1 (1974): 176–209.

Salvati, Giuseppe M. "Dimensione trinitaria della creazione." In *La creazione, Dio, il cosmo, l'uomo.* Edited by R. Gerardi. Roma: Studium, 1990, pp. 65–93.

Scheffczyk, Leo. "Die Trinitätslehre des Thomas von Aquin im Spiegel gegenwärtiger Kritik." *Studi Tomistici* 59 (1995): 163–90.

Schlapkohl, Corinna. *Persona est naturae rationabilis individua substantia: Boethius und die Debatte über den Personbegriff.* Marburg: N. G. Elwert Verlag, 1999.

Schmaus, Michael. *Der Liber propugnatorius des Thomas Anglicus und die Lehrunterschiede zwischen Thomas von Aquin und Duns Scotus.* Vol II/1: *Die trinitarischen Lehrdifferenzen: Systematische Darstellung und historische Würdigung.* Münster: Aschendorff, 1930.

———. "Die Spannung von Metaphysik und Heilsgeschichte in der Trinitätslehre Augustins." In *Studia patristica.* Vol. 6. Edited by Frank L. Cross. Berlin: Akademie Verlag, 1962, pp. 503–18.

Schmidbaur, Hans Christian. *Personarum Trinitas: Die trinitarische Gotteslehre des heiligen Thomas von Aquin.* St. Ottilien: EOS Verlag, 1995.

Schmidt, Martin A. *Gottheit und Trinität nach dem Kommentar des Gilbert Porreta zu Boethius De Trinitate.* Basel: Verlag für Recht und Gesellschaft, 1956.

Schmitz-Valckenberg, Georg. *Grundlehren katharischer Sekten des 13. Jahrhunderts: Eine theologische Untersuchung mit besonderer Berückstchtigung von 'Adversus Catharos et Valdenses' des Moneta von Cremona.* Munich: Schöningh, 1971.

Schönberger, Rolf. *Relation als Vergleich: Die Relationstheorie des Johannes Buridan im Kontext seines Denkens und der Scholastik.* Leiden: Brill, 1994.

Schoot, Henk. "Theologisch miniatuur: de proloog op het Scriptum." *Werkgroep Thomas van Aquino, Jaarboek* 5 (1985): 73–84.

Serverat, Vincent. "L'irrisio fidei. Encore sur Raymond Lulle et Thomas d'Aquin." *Revue Thomiste* 90 (1990): 436–48.

Sesboüé, Bernard. *Saint Basile et la Trinité.* Paris: Desclée, 1998.

Simon, Reinhard. *Das Filioque bei Thomas von Aquin: Eine Untersuchung zur dogmengeschichtlichen Stellung, theologischen Struktur und ökumenischen Perspektive der thomanischen Gotteslehre.* Frankfurt a.M.: Peter Lang, 1994.

Simonin, Henri D. "Autour de la solution thomiste du problème de l'amour." *Archives d'Histoire Doctrinale et Littéraire du Moyen Âge* 6 (1931): 174–274.

Spiazzi, Raimondo. "'Conoscenza con amore' in Sant'Agostino e in San Tommaso." *Doctor communis* 39 (1986): 315–28.

Stickelbroeck, Michael. *Mysterium Venerandum: Der trinitarische Gedanke im Werk des Bernhard von Clairvaux.* Münster: Aschendorff, 1994.

Sträter, Carl. "Le point de départ du traité thomiste de la Trinité." *Sciences Ecclésiastiques* 12 (1962): 71–87.

Studer, Basil. *Mysterium caritatis.* Roma: Pontificio Ateneo S. Anselmo, 1999.

Terracciano, Antonio. "Dibattito sulla Trinità e orientamenti teologici nel XII secolo." *Asprenas* 34 (1987): 284–303.

Torrell, Jean-Pierre. "Le savoir théologique chez saint Thomas." *Revue Thomiste* 96 (1996): 355–96.

———. *Saint Thomas Aquinas.* Vol. 1: *The Person and His Work.* Washington, DC: The Catholic University of America Press, 1996.

———. "Philosophie et théologie d'après le Prologue de Thomas d'Aquin au *Super Boetium de Trinitate.* Essai d'une lecture théologique." *Documenti e Studi sulla tradizione filosofica medievale* 10 (1999): 299–353.

Valkenberg, Wilhelmus G. B. M. *Did Not Our Heart Burn? Place and Function of Holy Scripture in the Theology of St. Thomas Aquinas.* Utrecht: Thomas Instituut te Utrecht, 1990.

Vanier, Paul. La relation trinitaire dans la Somme théologique de saint Thomas d'Aquin." *Sciences Ecclésiastiques* 1 (1948): 143–59.

————. *Théologie trinitaire chez saint Thomas d'Aquin: Evolution du concept d'action notionnelle.* Montréal/Paris: Institut d'Etudes médiévales/Vrin, 1953.

Ventimiglia, Giovanni. "Le relazioni divine secondo S. Tommaso d'Aquino, Riproposizione di un problema e prospettive di indagine." *Studi Tomistici* 44 (1991): 166–82.

————. *Differenza e contraddizione.* Milan: Vita e Pensiero, 1997.

Vignaux, Paul. "Nécessité des raisons dans le Monologion." *Revue des Sciences Philosophiques et Théologiques* 64 (1980): 3–25.

Villalmonte, Alejandro de. "El Padre plenitud fontal de la Deidad." In *S. Bonaventura 1274–1974, Volumen commemorativum.* Vol. 4. Grottaferrata: Editiones Collegii S. Bonaventurae, 1974, pp. 221–42.

Wawrykow, Joseph. "The *Summa Contra Gentiles* Reconsidered: on the Contribution of the De Trinitate of Hilary of Poitiers." *The Thomist* 58 (1994): 617–34.

Weisheipl, James A. "The Life and Works of St. Albert the Great." In *Albertus Magnus and the Sciences: Commemorative Essays 1980.* Edited by James A. Weisheipl. Toronto: Pontifical Institute of Mediaeval Studies, 1980, pp. 13–51.

————. *Thomas d'Aquino and Albert His Teacher.* Toronto: Pontifical Institute of Mediaeval Studies, 1980.

————. *Friar Thomas d'Aquino: His Life, Thought, and Works.* Washington, DC: The Catholic University of America Press, 1983.

Wetter, Friedrich. *Die Trinitätslehre des Johannes Duns Scotus.* Münster: Aschendorff, 1967.

Williams, Michael E. *The Teaching of Gilbert Porreta on the Trinity as Found in his Commentaries on Boethius.* Rome: Edited by Pontificia Università Gregoriana, 1951.

Worrall, Peter. "St. Thomas and Arianism." *Recherches de Théologie Ancienne et Médiévale* 23 (1956): 208–59 and 24 (1957): 45–100.

Woznicki, Andrew N. *Being and Order: The Metaphysics of Thomas Aquinas in Historical Perspective.* New York: Lang, 1990.

Index